James Phelan

History of Tennessee

The Making of a State

James Phelan

History of Tennessee
The Making of a State

ISBN/EAN: 9783743404342

Manufactured in Europe, USA, Canada, Australia, Japa

Cover: Foto ©ninafisch / pixelio.de

Manufactured and distributed by brebook publishing software (www.brebook.com)

James Phelan

History of Tennessee

THE MAKING OF A STATE

BY

JAMES PHELAN

BOSTON AND NEW YORK
HOUGHTON, MIFFLIN AND COMPANY
The Riverside Press, Cambridge
1888

DEDICATED TO H. M. DOAK,

OF NASHVILLE, TENNESSEE.

DEAR MR. DOAK, — Your great-grandfather, Samuel Doak, built upon Tennessee soil the first school-house erected in the Mississippi Valley. His influence has, in a measure, left an impress upon the entire social fabric of this State. You yourself are a native born Tennessean. You have been in turn a brave soldier and a worthy citizen. As a journalist, as editor-in-chief of the Nashville American in Middle Tennessee and the Memphis Avalanche in West Tennessee, you have liberalized the minds of the people of our State, and elevated the tone of public discussion. You have filled many positions, and all with efficiency, honor, and dignity. Your friends see in you a noble type of the true Tennessean. You have taken deep interest in the preparation of this work. You are one of my dearest friends. We have been associates in business. It has seemed to me, in view of these things, to be both natural and appropriate that I should dedicate to yourself this, the first attempt to write a History of Tennessee covering a later period than the earliest settlement of the State. Please accept this dedication as a tribute of respect and a pledge of friendship.

JAMES PHELAN.

CONTENTS.

	PAGE
INTRODUCTION	1

CHAPTER

I.	THE FIRST APPROACH OF POPULATION	5
II.	THE FOUNDING OF THE HOUSEHOLD	20
III.	THE WATAUGA ASSOCIATION FORMED	32
IV.	THE REVOLUTION AND INDIAN WARS	38
V.	ANNEXED TO NORTH CAROLINA, AND LIMITS DEFINED	46
VI.	NEW COUNTIES FORMED	52
VII.	KING'S MOUNTAIN	57
VIII.	SEVIER'S INDIAN WARS	63
IX.	CEDED BY NORTH CAROLINA	67
X.	STATE OF FRANKLIN FORMED	76
XI.	STATE OF FRANKLIN	81
XII.	END OF THE STATE OF FRANKLIN	93
XIII.	FIRST SETTLEMENTS ON THE CUMBERLAND	105
XIV.	JAMES ROBERTSON	118
XV.	DAVIDSON COUNTY	130
XVI.	TROUBLE WITH THE INDIANS	139
XVII.	TERRITORY AND NICKOJACK EXPEDITION	146
XVIII.	SPANISH INTRIGUES	163
XIX.	MANNERS, CUSTOMS, AND MODE OF LIFE	169
XX.	ADMISSION TO THE UNION	186
XXI.	TENNESSEE INSTITUTES	190
XXII.	LOCAL SELF-GOVERNMENT	203
XXIII.	RELIGION IN TENNESSEE	215
XXIV.	SCHOOLS	233
XXV.	SEVIER TO CARROLL	241
XXVI.	BANKS OF TENNESSEE	258

XXVII. INTERNAL IMPROVEMENTS	276
XXVIII. CARROLL, HOUSTON, AND CONSTITUTIONAL CONVENTION	296
XXIX. WEST TENNESSEE	303
XXX. MEMPHIS	312
XXXI. SOUTH MEMPHIS AND FORT PICKERING	339
XXXII. JOHN A. MURRELL AND THE REIGN OF DISORDER	346
XXXIII. RISE OF THE WHIG PARTY	357
XXXIV. POLK AND CANNON	376
XXXV. THE FIRST WHIG VICTORY	383
XXXVI. POLK AND JONES IN 1841	393
XXXVII. POLK AND JONES IN 1843	406
XXXVIII. THE GREAT WHIG CONVENTION OF 1844	413
XXXIX. THE DOWNFALL OF THE WHIGS AND SECESSION	424
LIST OF AUTHORITIES	446
INDEX	463

INTRODUCTION.

ALTHOUGH the annals of Tennessee are not filled with accounts of the revolutions which have changed the complexion of the world, yet her history, in addition to the interest which it possesses for her children as giving an account of the achievements of their ancestors, has one claim upon the attention of the thoughtful student of history which is peculiarly her own. In it can be studied, as under a glass and in an hour, the process of development which in other States is either imperfectly displayed or is spread over a long stretch of time, the periods of which are indistinctly understood, or marred by extraneous and disturbing causes. In the Thirteen Colonies the chief causes of disturbances were the cupidity of colonial proprietors and the despotism of rulers. In the younger States, excepting Kentucky, and perhaps Vermont, the line of advancement began at or after a point where the full development of American principles had been attained. In Tennessee we have within the limits of a century a picture of national life as complete as that of England through its two thousand years, or that of Rome from the kings to the emperors. We can study the process by which wildernesses were turned into gardens, and observe the stages of development from primitive rudeness to civilization and refinement, — from disorganization to organization; from the absence of all law, through all the grades of a complete system of laws imperfectly obeyed, to a time when a community of nearly two millions of people live together in the bonds of a sober, industrious, and law-abiding citizenship. In a study of her annals we shall find that her instruments were often uncouth, that her progress was often slow, that many blunders were committed, and that there was much violence and frequent shedding of blood for evil and disgraceful causes; but those of us who are proud of our native State shall also be rewarded by finding at times, and often in most unexpected places, exhibitions of those qualities which constitute what is most noble and admirable in the human character.

The history of a State, judged by the political discussions between aspirants for state offices, is merely a resulting incident of the history of the United States. There have been in the history of Tennessee questions of local policy important enough to cause division among the voters of the State. But, apart from the state debt, the time and attention accorded the discussion of this class of questions has been altogether insignificant in comparison with the overwhelming importance attached to questions of national politics. The reason of this is neither hard to find nor of remote origin. The ultimate decision of all local questions is in the immediate power of the State. Any mistake can easily be rectified, and results can be promptly changed. But the case was and is different in national affairs. Here the State is but one of many factors, and any decision involving its welfare is more permanent in its nature and less liable to be changed, should a change be desirable. This is the main reason. In addition to this, there is more fascination in the discussion of a question which occupies the minds and hearts of forty millions of people than in the discussion of a question which merely involves one and one's neighbor. This being the case, a state history cannot entirely ignore national politics. But the opposite extreme is more vicious still. The real history of a state, especially Tennessee, is to be found within its own limits. Each State having an organized government, an advanced state of society, a general diffusion of knowledge, and a measurable quantity of commercial prosperity, has necessarily had stages of development, or, in other words, a history. There was a time when those who inhabited the geographical division now called Tennessee dwelt in log-cabins, and ate from wooden plates with iron knives and horn spoons. They attended the worship of God either in the open air or in a large barn. They wore cotton cloth spun by the women of the family and woven at home, or brought from beyond seas to Charleston in ships, and from Charleston across the mountains on pack-horses. The men as a rule wore caps made of the skins of the raccoon, generally with the tail hanging down behind. The head-dress of the women was a kind of bonnet made of calico sewed on strips of whalebone or white pine, which stuck forward six or eight inches beyond the face. All articles of feminine adornment were of the simplest materials. The men used muskets which a Kaffir of the present day would not think fit for decent savages. Coffee, sugar, and tea, the staples of the housewife of this date, were considered precious and costly luxuries. Everything was rude and primitive. Let a stranger compare this picture of ninety years ago with what he will see in walking through Main Street in Memphis on a bright spring morning, and, remembering the words of the Psalmist on the shortness of human life, let him reflect that there are men in the State enjoying a green old age who were then living and breathing human beings. Even the least reflective mind, remembering these things, will picture to itself the contrast, and will realize that the interval between then and now has been rife with changes, and that the present is in some way, and under the influence of some law of development, the logical sequence of that past. This law of development, its processes and its results, form the real history of Tennessee. It is the story of this history which I have attempted to narrate without going unduly into detail, and not passing over wholly in silence the individuals who have been the factors of this law, or the occasional adventures which surround them with the golden light of a mediæval romance. This story, if accurately and impartially told, the author imagines may not be altogether without interest; showing to the outside world the justice of this State's claim to a place of honor among the commonwealths of the Union, and recalling to the minds of her children the fact that their forefathers were men of brave hearts, of pure ambition, and of great achievements, worthy to be ranked among the noblest of those who, by undaunted courage, calm foresight, and liberal statesmanship, founded in the midst of danger, solitude, and even desolation, the empire which is now greater than all the rest. National politics in such a narrative play a subordinate though important part. It gives a certain tinge to the history of a State, a certain mixture of light and shade, which must be taken into reckoning. But national history is treated of only where it directly affects or is directly affected by the State. Even slavery, which indeed profoundly influenced the social life of this as well as all other Southern and Southwestern States, was always a national and never a state issue.

HISTORY OF TENNESSEE.

CHAPTER I.

THE FIRST APPROACH OF POPULATION.

THE history of Tennessee as a distinctive individuality begins with the erection in 1769 of William Bean's cabin, near the junction of the Watauga and Boone's Creek, in East Tennessee, or, as it was then, in the western part of North Carolina. In this cabin, the most important and the best known if not the first of those which were built, we find the germ of a future political organism. From now on, there is a new and an independent growth. Before this, though there are mentions of matters which took place upon the soil of what subsequently became Tennessee, there was nothing coherent or consistent within to meet the activity of the organized and restless world without. The fort which La Salle, returning from the voyage which he vainly hoped would add new lustre to the crown of the Grand Monarch, built on the Chickasaw Bluffs and to which he gave the name of Prud'homme,[1] was, apart from the association of ideas, of no more importance in the history of Tennessee than the death of an Indian chief, or the significance of the mysterious symbols on a piece of wampum. Even the trading post which he attempted to establish there, and the treaties of commerce

---

[1] Ramsey (p. 39) says that this fort was built on the first Chickasaw Bluff. It was the fourth.

which he entered into with the resident Chickasaws dwindle into insignificance when viewed in the light of subsequent failure which left no trace behind. Of the same nature is the fact that a few years earlier a Canadian missionary named Marquette, with several companions, descended the Mississippi River "to plant the banner of France side by side with that of Spain on the Gulf of Mexico;" and that Marquette's journal describes several bank elevations which correspond very nearly with what is now known as the Chickasaw Bluffs, and an island, the description of which leaves no doubt of its identity with President's Island, of infamous notoriety in the annals of local criminal jurisprudence.

But adventurers like La Salle and Marquette merely saw the western borders of the State. Tennessee was distant from the coast line from which its future population was to come. Hence, like all interior regions, it was exempt from the visits of European adventurers and the white race, until the increase of population, by confining the more restless spirits of the original colonies, caused them to overflow the boundaries of social limitations and the barriers of daily life to seek new homes in the wilderness. The interval from the grant of Queen Elizabeth to Raleigh until the erection of William Bean's cabin was the period of preparation for this overflow. Before taking up the history of Tennessee it will be profitable to review, however succinctly, the events which fill the period from 1584 to 1769, or such part of them as throw light upon the subsequent development of the then unformed State.

There is a tradition, founded upon ingenious supposition and a certain superficial resemblance of topographical features, that De Soto, on that wonderful march of conquest and discovery which is at once the brightest and the saddest page in the history of American colonization, entered the eastern part of the then undistinguished district which now bears the name of Tennessee, and, turning westward across the continent, continued his progress until it finally brought him to the banks of the Mississippi. It is even conjectured that the village near which he encamped, to which the Indians gave the name Chisca in honor of their chief, and which stood on a high embankment, occupied the site of the present city of Memphis, which is known in the familiar language of the present day as the City of the Bluffs. This may be true. But it is a matter of speculation. We know indeed that De Soto crossed a tedious range of mountains, that he came into a region of country rich in harvests and thickly settled, full of valleys, brooks, rivers, and forests, and that after many days' marching, during which he passed through the provinces of some tribes of Indians who are known to have inhabited parts of this State, he came to the banks of the Mississippi River. Several laborious attempts have been made to establish the exact line of this march by the aid of topographical maps of the present day and contemporaneous accounts of De Soto's adventurous course, but without satisfactory result. It is not impossible that the great Spanish captain, who had seen so many of the wonders of the young world, may have trod upon the soil of Tennessee. Imagination must do the rest. Queen Elizabeth, whose generosity towards Raleigh was not less tempered with prudence than her generosity towards the Bishop of Ely, gave him by royal patent the right to discover, view, and take possession of such remote heathen and barbarous lands not possessed or inhabited by Christian people as to him should seem good. In pursuance of this gracious allowance, Raleigh at his own expense made three several attempts to colonize what is now Virginia and North Carolina, but failed signally in all. A later attempt under James having been more successful, the attention of the Londoners — for London furnished the motive-power of colonization — was called to the southern coast line, and resulted in a rapid influx of emigrants to the new settlements. The grant of 1630 to Sir Robert Heath having been forfeited, another charter was granted to another company. Charles II., in 1663, careless of the condition of the colonies, ignorant of their growing wealth, and eager to repay substantial services rendered him during the dark days of his exile and the doubtful days of the Restoration without sacrificing the means of royal dissipation, granted to Clarendon, General Monk, Lord Ashley, and others, all of the New World that lay between the thirty-first and thirty-sixth parallels of latitude, and subsequently increased his profuse munificence by so extending the grant as to include all between 36° 30' and 29°. The northern line of Tennessee ran substantially with the 36° 30' parallel. The proprietors, conforming to the spirit of the grant and actuated no doubt by the clear and luminous intellect of the statesman-like historian who was one of them, as well as by the vacillating and brilliant Shaftesbury, applied to Locke, who with Spinoza was to revolutionize the intellectual methods of Europe, to frame a form of government for the new colony. In compliance with this request, Locke devised a scheme which was hailed by the intellects of Oxford and the coffee-houses as the "Grand Model" of what a government should be, but which, for practical purposes, was not much superior to that in which, the law-making power being vested in barbers, official rank and social grades were dependent upon the growth of the beard and the color of the hair. The Grand Model still remains as an enduring monument of the kinship of human wisdom and human folly. The infant colony never fully adopted it, and the attempts of various successive governors to introduce it were the cause of almost uninterrupted internal dissensions for twenty years. Finally, during one of the domestic revolutions which, though as a rule bloodless, were violent enough to delight a Jacobin, it was completely subverted and then abrogated. In 1719 the government passed from the hands of the proprietors into those of the king, and South Carolina and North Carolina, being separated about this time, both became independent royal colonies.

The relations existing between the colonies and the Indians were on the whole variable, and liable to quick and violent changes. At times the colonies would unite with one tribe to chastise or exterminate another. A combination of this kind between the Cherokees and the colonies against the Tuscaroras was the cause of the migration of the latter to the northern lakes. A few years later we find the Cherokees themselves at the head of a conspiracy of all the adjacent tribes, having for its object the complete annihilation of the colonists. During this time were sown the seeds of hatred which subsequently produced many a harvest of rapine and butchery. Nor were the Indians the most dangerous or the most malignant foes of the colonies. While the English were spreading into the interior, and securing themselves as they went by the building of villages and forts and the extension of agriculture, the Spaniards had been gaining firm foothold in Florida, and the French in the Mississippi Valley. It was the bitter complaint of the colonists to the mother country during the Cherokee-Catawba conspiracy, that St. Augustine was used by the Spaniards as a point for the distribution of guns and ammunition to the hostile tribes. England did nothing to stop the outrage. A hundred years later, the Spaniards adopted the same method of harassing the United States during the War of 1812. It was a Tennessean who put a stop to it. He caught two of them and shot them.[1] The French especially, after having planted themselves upon the banks of the northern lakes, had succeeded in founding a new empire at the mouth of the Mississippi, and, borne along by the inspiration of conquest caught from the victorious arms of Luxembourg and

[1] Arbuthnot and Ambrister claimed to be British subjects, but were in Spanish service.

Turenne at home, were already dreaming of uniting the North and the South in one grand Western dominion, confining the English and the Spanish to the narrow strip of land actually occupied by them at that time. Their plan was boldly conceived, but the history of the Western hemisphere has been an exemplification of the difference between conquest and colonization. The idea of La Salle, Talon, and Montcalm was to take the Mississippi River, which was even then a theme of wonder and admiration, as a centre, and, gradually subduing the adjacent territory, to extend the French sway across to the Pacific Ocean. The first necessity of this plan was of course the downfall of the English. The general outline of the method to be adopted for the carrying out of this scheme was to establish trading posts along the banks of the Mississippi and its tributaries, to make treaties of friendship with the natives where possible, to exterminate or overawe them where treaties could not be brought about, and to instigate their allies to continual warfare against the English. In pursuance of this plan forts were erected at the mouth of the Kentucky, on the Ohio, at the mouth of the Wabash, at the meeting of the Ohio and the Mississippi, on the Chickasaw Bluffs, near the mouth of the Arkansas, and on the Cumberland. There were probably as many more at other points, with these as centres. The instruments for the accomplishment of their object were bribery, artifice, cunning, and cruelty. The colonies, fearful of the encroachments of their old and dreaded enemy, adopted the policy of their antagonists, and the friendship of half-naked savages, who danced war dances and painted their bodies to frighten their enemies, became an object of eager rivalry between the two most powerful and enlightened races on the globe. The English secured the Creeks and Cherokees, — the French, the Choctaws and minor tribes. The Chickasaws, who inhabited the region of Memphis and North Mississippi, remained neutral. The contest went in favor of the English from the first. They not only made treaties of peace with them, but took advantage of the Indians' fear of their villages being attacked by the French, during their absence on the war-path, to erect forts among them, and create permanent settlements to hold them to their professed allegiance to King George, the Great Father. The French under Bienville, finding the neutrality of the Chickasaws as great an obstacle in their way as active hostilities would have been, made an expedition against them, but were repulsed. A repetition of the attack shortly afterwards under the same commander, who made the Memphis Bluffs — called Fort Assumption — his camping point and basis of supplies, ended literally in smoke, for, according to Bancroft, " in the March of next year a small detachment proceeded towards the Chickasaw country; they were met by messengers who supplicated for peace, and Bienville gladly accepted the calumet."

During this time the English were gradually extending their forts toward the Catawba region and the beautiful valley of the Appalachian range. Fort Dobbs, situated probably in Rowan County, North Carolina, was built in 1756. In 1758 Colonel Bird built a fort opposite Long Island, on the banks of the Holston. Fort Prince George was built about the same time on the Keowee, a tributary of the Savannah. These brought the tide of emigration to the base of the hills which skirt the eastern extremity of Tennessee; and Fort Loudon, which was built on the Little Tennessee, near the mouth of the Tellico, by Andrew Lewis at the instigation of Lord Loudon, governor of Virginia, brought it across the mountains and fairly into the boundaries of the State. Fort Loudon was garrisoned by royal troops, and the Cherokees, regarding it as a protection against the vengeance of the French, offered donations of land to artisans as an inducement to come there. The warfare between the English and the French which raged in all parts of the world was too far from the region of East Tennessee to affect it otherwise than indirectly. In addition to this, in all parts of the world, the armies of England, under the administration of the Great Commoner, were uniformly victorious. The power of the French was broken in both hemispheres. They were confined in America to their Canadian possessions in the north and to the delta region of the Mississippi in the south. With the capture of Fort Du Quesne the French disappeared as an important factor in the difficulties which beset Virginia and the Carolinas, but left as a discordant legacy a feeling of bitter hostility between the Indians and the colonies, which filled the annals of that time with sickening and uninteresting details of vengeance, rapine, and butchery.

The immediate cause of the outbreak of hostilities was the killing of several of the friendly Cherokees who had assisted in the reduction of Fort Du Quesne. Having lost their horses, the Indians supplied their loss from a herd which they found running at large in some part of Virginia. The exasperated Virginians, regarding them as horse thieves, captured and put several of them to death. The Cherokees retaliated, and in a few weeks the horrors of an Indian war had broken loose. Fort Loudon, which was manned by twelve cannon, was captured, and, in defiance of the terms of capitulation, those in it were massacred.[1] Fort Prince George was besieged, and was saved only by an accident. All the whites who at the beginning were unable to reach some adjacent fort or station were massacred. Troops were sent from the north and from the seacoast. The Cherokees were eventually defeated at Etchoe by Colonel Grant, a British officer.

It appears to have been the history of those times that each successful Indian war brought the victors — the whites were always successful — an accession of population as well as of dignity and honor. The peace which followed

[1] For an interesting account of this event by I. Christe, an eye-witness, see *Nashville Politician*, 15th September, 1847.

Grant's victory attracted the attention of the New World, from St. Augustine to Salem, to the new settlements, and crowds of emigrants came pouring in from Europe and the older colonies. In a few years they were scattered up and down the banks of the rivers, and through the valleys of all the western part of North Carolina and Virginia. But as yet no permanent foothold had been gained in Tennessee since the destruction of Fort Loudon. An active trade was carried on between the white man and the Indian, but no plow had entered the soil. Forts were built as they were demanded by the necessities of military or civil life. Fort Loudon and other forts on Tennessee soil were of the former class. Fort Prince George was demanded by both, and from the battle of Etchoe in 1761 until 1769 the region around it became gradually covered with cow-pens, or, as the Texans of the present day say, " ranches "— little fields of corn and the cabins of settlers. The greater part of the most desirable land had been taken possession of. It was no longer easy to get on a horse, ride a few miles, and select a site for a cabin in the midst of grass, meadow, water, game, and fertile soil. The country was not yet thickly enough settled to repay the tillage of any but the most exuberant fields. Each settler who arrived at Fort Prince George, with his little store of household goods on one or two pack-horses, was advised to go farther west. After a few days' rest, he went, leaving the next comer to follow and go farther than himself, lapping one over another. Hence, after the victory of Grant over the Cherokees, the wave of emigration, which the destruction of Fort Loudon had caused to recede, may be said to have risen up the sides of the Alleghanies.

Occasionally a party of hunters passed over in search of game and adventure. As early as 1748 a party of Virginians, with Dr. Thomas Walker at their head, had penetrated the distant wilds, and given the name of Cumberland to the mountains, the river, and the gap which still bear it, in honor of the royal duke of England.[1] About 1761 a party of nineteen penetrated to the present Carter's Valley, and left in the geography of Tennessee the name of Wallen's Creek and Wallen's Ridge, in honor of their leader and as souvenirs of the expedition. Daniel Boone, whose solitary figure and long unerring rifle are forever identified with the early history of the Southwest as the type of all the finer qualities in the pioneer character, was also among those who first at this time ventured into the wilds of the unexplored West. The Wallen party returned several years in succession in pursuit of game, each year venturing farther into the interior. In 1764 Daniel Boone and Sam Callaway made an attempt to explore the country, and gather some details of its topography for practical purposes. Two years later Colonel James Smith explored the region beyond the Holston and south of Kentucky, and his account of its richness and beauty gave increased impetus to the flow of emigration.

Nor were the Indians insensible to the danger which now threatened them. No particular tribe could establish a clear title to the valleys of the Cumberland and the Holston, and the vast tracts between the Ohio and the Tennessee. The treaty of Paris in 1763, which the servility of a minister had negotiated for the stupidity of a master, but which, as the legacy of Pitt's powerful and omniscient management, brought rich gains to the territory of England, gave the sovereignty of the region east of the Mississippi to George III. The Indians had never been acknowledged as independent sovereigns by any European power, and no mention was made in the treaty of those

[1] This is variously attributed to the Wood and to the Wallen party and to Governor Spotswood, who crossed the Appalachian range about thirty years earlier, and whose attendants, having found a horse path, Cumberland Gap, were called Knights of the Horseshoe.

tribes who claimed to be independent of all European control, some of whom had been allies of France. The apprehension of the Indians being excited by the frequent incursions of the whites, a proclamation of King George, in 1763, prohibited the granting of lands to any one in the region west of the mountains, or beyond the sources of those streams which emptied into the Atlantic, and no private person was to presume to purchase from the Indians themselves. The proclamation contained these significant words: "If the Indians should be inclined to dispose of their lands, the same shall be purchased only for us in our name, at some general meeting or assembly of the Indians to be held for that purpose, by the governor or commander-in-chief of our colony respectively." Traders were required to obtain licenses from their respective governors.

In 1766 the cession which was foreshadowed in the proclamation was obtained. The Iroquois, whose possession embraced the region of country around Lake Erie and Lake Ontario and the waters of the St. Lawrence, and who composed the Five Nations, appear to have made some claim to the section of country between the Ohio and the Tennessee. This title, however, was purely one of conquest and of the vaguest description. Their union and their superior organization, which attracted the attention of the earliest French writers, gave them a terrible advantage in the endless warfare that raged among the original tribes, and enabled them literally to sweep unobstructed through vast regions of country with the same ease that a European army finds in attacking the Bedouins of the desert. It was for a time a repetition of the history of Wessex. But moving armed bodies across a country, and dispersing an occasional horde of assailants, is by no means a conquest of the country. They had no doubt destroyed or expelled many smaller tribes who inhabited that country, as the Cherokees had destroyed and expelled the Uchees. The country itself had never been subdued, and the original inhabitants returned after each raid, as untrammeled as before, acknowledging no master and paying no tribute.

Certainly that part which is now Tennessee was never under their domination. The region of the Holston and the Cumberland and the Tennessee was regarded by the Cherokees, the Creeks, the Miamis, the Choctaws, and the Chickasaws as a kind of common hunting and fighting ground. It was inhabited by none of them, because none of them could hold it. That the Iroquois laid claim to it by conquest alone is evinced by the words of their envoys, who according to Ramsey are reputed to have said, "All the world knows that we conquered all the nations residing there and that land; if the Virginians ever get a good right to it, it must be by us." The deposition of George Croghan, a deputy superintendent of the Indians who had lived among them for thirty years, was taken 1781, in order to fix the limits of certain Indian claims. In this he said, "The Six Nations claim by right of conquest all the lands on the southeast side of the river called Stony River."[1] This is clear proof of how flimsy was the title upon which the Iroquois rested their claim. It was merely a piece of gasconade on the part of the Six Nations, which was taken advantage of by the colonists to excuse the occupation which would have been effected without the permission of their grantors, had permission been denied.

On the 5th of November, 1768,[2] the Six Nations, in convention assembled, passed to the king of England their title to the tract of land beyond the Blue Ridge Mountains and down to the Tennessee. This embraced the best and the fairest portion of this State. It gave a pretext to the colonists, but it utterly failed to quiet the title in so far as the claim of those in interest was concerned. The ratification of the few Cherokees who hap-

---

[1] The Great Miami.
[2] Haywood says 1776, but erroneously.

pened to be present when the cession was made, and who very prudently acknowledged, though as indirectly as possible, the right of the Six Nations to the country in question, was never regarded by the tribe itself as of the least validity. An attempt was made in 1768, during the pendency of the negotiations between the English and the Six Nations, to extinguish the claims of the Cherokees themselves by purchase. By a treaty which was concluded with them at Hard Labor, in South Carolina, in 1768, it was agreed that the boundary line of Virginia on the southwest should be a line " extending from the point where the northern line of North Carolina intersects the Cherokee hunting grounds, or about thirty-six miles east of Long Island, in the Holston River, and thence extending in a direct course, north by east, to Chiswell's mine, on the east bank of the Kenawha River, and thence down that stream to its junction with the Ohio." A dividing line was run, but failed to take in all settlements which had actually been made, and a new treaty was entered into in order to accomplish that purpose.

This was the beginning of a mournful repetition which still continues at the end of what has aptly been termed "a century of dishonor." Provincial governments had been issuing land grants and land warrants for military services against the French and their Indian allies, and their owners were in no mood to be bound by the restrictions even of a proclamation from beyond the sea. Where a trader had the opportunity of buying a tract of five thousand acres of the richest land in the richest part of the globe for a pair of blankets and a rifle, it required something more than an edict which he knew to be without power of enforcement to interrupt the bargain.

Having fixed the limits of encroachment, and seeing them daily disregarded, the Indians became jealous, full of revengeful fear, and bitterly exasperated. Each additional encroachment they regarded as an injury, each hunting party as an insult. From the Miami to the Tennessee, they were aroused to a sense of the danger which was impending. As usual, the red man was brought face to face with the white man, each filled with relentless determination, and each recognizing in the other the impossible element of coexistence. As usual, the former, after a brave and despairing contest and superhuman desperation, yielded stubbornly but surely to the fate which to him meant passing away from the face of the earth. Even then the leading minds among the tribes, those who saw beyond the chasing of the deer and the trapping of the beaver, and whose mental vision was not circumscribed by the orgies of the war dance and the preparations for the war path, realized the mournful destiny of oppression and dishonor and eventual annihilation which the future concealed from less penetrating sight. Oconostota was one of this class. He was brave, with all the impulse and daring of his race, and as noble as the unlearned ideas of his people would permit in a heart which found its ideal in the panther and the leopard, — fearless, bloodthirsty, and relentless, stealthy of foot, quick of stroke, and sharp of fang. At the treaty of the Sycamore Shoals, where Daniel Boone, Colonel Richard Henderson, and others had collected the Indians to buy from them the tract between the Kentucky and the Cumberland rivers, Oconostota predicted the fate of his tribe in a speech which, to Bushy Head and his people of to-day, must be like the remembered words of the prophet to the children of Israel during the days of their bondage. In words full of the imaginative glow and the pathetic eloquence of Indian oratory, he drew a picture of the gradual encroachments of the white people, impelled by an insatiable thirst for land, and the gradual yielding of those who had once possessed all the country of America as a great, free, and powerful people. "This is but the beginning," he said. " Whole nations have passed away, and there remains not a stone to mark the place where rest the bones of our ancestors. They have melted like the snow before the rays of the sun, and their names are unrecorded, save in the deeds and the charters of those who have brought destruction upon them. The invader has crossed the great sea in ships; he has not been stayed by broad rivers, and now he has penetrated the wilderness and overcome the ruggedness of the mountains. Neither will he stop here. He will force the Indian steadily before him across the Mississippi ever towards the west, to find a shelter and a refuge in the seclusion of solitude. But even here he will come at last; and there being no place remaining where the Indian may dwell in the habitations of his people, he will proclaim the extinction of the race, till the red man be no longer a roamer of the forests and a pursuer of wild game." But the best words and the best actions of the fated race have never availed against that irresistible and unpitying personification which is called the spirit of civilization. Oconostota himself signed the treaty against which he made his eloquent protest.

CHAPTER II.

THE FOUNDING OF THE HOUSEHOLD.

In 1769 the waves poured over the mountains which had so long stemmed their tide, and carried with them the germs of a new dynasty of people among the republics of the earth. In 1769 we meet with William Bean's cabin and the beginnings of the Watauga Association. The first small beginnings of the Watauga settlement were made at a time peculiarly fortunate. The Indian warfare, which made Tennessee as dark and bloody a ground as Kentucky itself, had exterminated nearly all of the Indian race in the neighborhood of the Watauga. The Shawnees existed only in small, wandering detachments, and were, for the most part, hidden away in the lofty recesses of the Cumberland mountains. The Creeks of the Cumberland region had been massacred, almost to a man, by the Cherokees. These, emboldened by continued success, had made an incursion into the country of the Chickasaws and had been repulsed with terrible slaughter. The Chickasaws, indeed, were kindly disposed, but were too far away either to injure or assist the infant settlement. For the time being, and until the Cherokees had recuperated sufficiently to make war upon the new race, the chief danger arose from bands of roving Indians. The great thoroughfare of Indian travel was along the range and through the valleys of the Cumberland and the Appalachian mountains. The stream of emigration having once begun, it kept on with the force of the incoming tide, each wave rising higher, rushing farther, and spreading broader than the one preceding it. A party of explorers in 1769 noticed, on their return along the banks of the Holston, that there was a cabin on every desirable site they passed, where only six weeks previous no sign of human habitation had been visible. Captain William Bean, from Pittsylvania County in Virginia, advanced farther into the wilderness than any one who had preceded him, and his son Russell was the first white child born in Tennessee. Each month, each week, brought new settlers. They spread daily down the Watauga, up the north fork of the Holston, down the Holston through the valley between the Watauga, and the north fork — from valley to valley, from creek to creek. More than a century has passed since the first ten families of whom Haywood tells came from the neighborhood of the present site of Raleigh to begin life anew on the banks of the Watauga, but the figures of the old emigrants are still as distinct and as clear-cut to us as to the sentinel who paced in front of the bastions of Fort Prince George, watching their anxious faces and listening to their eager cries as they rode slowly up on their way-worn horses to make inquiries about the unknown country they were seeking. They were not heroes or heroines to themselves, neither had they any idea of founding a great empire. They recognized in themselves merely commonplace people, actuated by commonplace motives. They thought to improve their condition, and they were willing to run what risks might come to them from the casualties of tomahawk and rifle, for the sake of the experiment. But to us, who see them through a lapse of time which in our history wraps them in the mists of a hoary antiquity, they are a picturesque group filled with great motives and suggestive of great ideas. Those earlier days are far away. Our Anglo-Saxon progenitors who lived upon the sandy marshes of the Baltic do not appear so distant. Almost every book of those days tells us of what they did, how they did it, and how they dressed, — in short, how they acted their part. We can see them all, from the solitary hunter who follows on foot the blazed path to the group whose number makes a cavalcade. As a rule they come in groups for mutual protection, and perhaps, also, despite their fearless indifference, for mutual encouragement. The household goods are borne on the backs of horses, called pack-horses, and consist, as a rule, of a few cooking utensils, a wooden trencher for kneading dough, several small packages containing salt and some seed corn, a flask or two of medicine, wearing apparel, a wife, and generally a baby at the breast. If of a luxurious turn of mind, — fortune and the last crop of tobacco permitting, — a little sugar and coffee, or perhaps, indeed, unexcised tea, were added, or a flitch of bacon, as a relief from "dry jerk" or deer's meat, smoked or sun-dried; sometimes even a peck or two of meal or flour, especially if the master and head man was fortunate enough to have an extra pack-horse. Their daughters walk beside the mother on the horse, and the sons are with the father a few paces in front. Each of them has a rifle on his shoulder, or dropped forward in the bend of the arm. The rifle, however, is but an unsatisfactory weapon in close quarters. The long-barreled horse-pistol is regarded as a child's weapon, capable at most of disposing of one Indian when the question is of dozens. The foe for whom all these preparations are made has himself supplied the requisite armor. The belt around the waist holds on one side a tomahawk, on the other a scalping-knife. The head is covered with a fur cap; if inclined to be a little affected, the tail of the animal furnishing the cap is allowed to remain and hangs down behind, reminding one strongly of the costume of the gentleman whose morning walk was described by the two poets of the Lake. The body is covered with a hunting shirt, which allows all manner of variations in the matter of fringe and savage embroidery. It is loose and rather bagging, allowing free use of the arms. The legs are incased in buckskin "leggins" up to the thigh, where they are met by the breech-cloth. This is a kind of cloth which is passed between the legs, and the ends of which are passed under the girdle before and behind, and allowed to hang down. Some of the old writers say this idea was gotten from the Indians. Others say the suggestion came from the baby on the arm of the mother who rides the horse. The feet again pay tribute to Indian ingenuity, for they are incased in moccasins, each made of a single piece of dressed buckskin, as if it had been laid upon the ground with the foot placed upon it, and then drawn up around the leg, being cut and sewed so as to make it fit both foot and leg. Thus accoutred, the wearer is ready to encounter any reasonable vicissitudes of weather and all the vicissitudes of a frontier life. If a cow and a few pigs are added to his outfit, the future founder of the commonwealth regards his lot as one peculiarly fortunate.

Having arrived at his place of destination, the newcomer selects a site for his cabin, according to the relation he occupies towards those in whom the title vests. Frequently, but also erroneously, he imagines himself on Virginia soil. In this case he is entitled to buy for a song six hundred, afterwards a thousand, acres of land, and one hundred each for his wife and children, provided he lives on the land. If not in Virginia, he is on Indian soil, and he thinks he can both take and keep. North Carolina has no interest in the matter, and is, at all events, too indifferent ever to raise the question.

Having, therefore, selected his location, he and his family set to work to do what is to be done, quickly and with good-will. He is in the midst of a wilderness so deep and so vast that the echoes from the strokes of his axe sound as if they came from the bowels of the mountains that rise up in blue perspective to the east and the north. Before him runs the Watauga, a bright little stream that melts away into the gloom of the surrounding forest. He is far away from any source of assistance, except perhaps, some one no stronger than himself; and for all that the skies are so blue, and the woods are so green, and the splendor of the sun so gorgeous on cloud and on hilltop, the ruthless foe whom he is wronging may be lurking just beyond his ken in the shadow of the oak, or hidden in the tangles of the vine. At any moment he may hear a sound like the screaming of a panther, then the hoot of an owl in daytime, and then a wild burst of human sound that is terrible even to those who, in the security of the frontier forts of to-day, pay to hear it as a tickling of their curiosity. If his cabin is not built, if he has not the security of his palisades, his venture is for nothing. His spirit is likely to rise into the hidden eternities from the smoke of a fire-heap and without a scalp. The children — as a rule there are children — are set to clearing away the wild brush in a glade as nearly open as can be found, and piling it up in heaps where it can be burnt. The father, and the sons if old enough to work, cut down trees, so as to serve the double purpose of clearing the land and building the cabin. If there is not force sufficient to build one of hewn logs, it is built of long poles on which the bark is allowed to remain, the roof being covered with grass and bark and brush and the like. If possible, a cabin of hewn logs is preferred. Trees from eight to sixteen inches in diameter are cut down so as to present on two sides as much flat surface as is consistent with the maximum strength and power of resistance. Having been cut into logs from ten to sixteen feet long, and so notched at the end as to fit into each other, they are built into the cabin, apertures being left for doors, windows, and chimney. The largest oak to be found — if cypress, ash, or pine cannot be had — is laboriously and slowly split with mauls and wedges into shingles an indefinite number of feet long. These are called clapboards.

Next comes the labor of the floor. Logs are split in two parts, and the flat part of each half is hewn as smooth as possible. These are allowed to rest on the ground, making the celebrated puncheon floor. Frequently the floor is mother earth, with perhaps a covering of pine-tree needles or oak leaves. The floor having been laid, the sides of the cabin are built up the requisite height. The roof is either level, or one side is lower than the other, or it is gabled by erecting ridge-poles running the length of the cabin. The clapboards are laid on in rows, each one being held in place by weights. The chimney, which is built outside the house, is of rock, if it is to be obtained. If not, the lower part is of heavy logs cut the proper length and thickly plastered on the inside with a mixture of clay, in which hay or hog bristles or the hair from tanned deerskins has been put to temper it. From a point sufficiently high to be beyond the flames, the chimney is made of small billets of oak with alternate layers of mud, hence called "dirt and stick" chimneys. The chimney grows smaller as it goes higher. This done, the cracks between the logs of the cabin are filled with pieces and blocks of wood, and these in turn are covered over with the plaster both inside and out until the walls are thoroughly weather and bullet proof. The door is of oaken clapboards pinned to crosspieces, as also the window. The fireplace is of rock and pebbles or plastered and burnt clay. A tongue having been fastened in the chimney for pot-hooks and kettle, the cabin is ready for use.

The furniture is not less primitive than the cabin. It consists of a bedstead, a washstand, a few three-legged stools, a table perhaps, a water bucket, a gourd dipper, and pegs about the walls for hanging clothes, rifles, game, and the like. Partitions are made by suspending deer and bear skins, if the number and the size of the family require it. If the roof is gabled, an attic is often added by covering the top of the cabin with clapboards. The chief covering for the family in cold weather is rarely a blanket, often the skins of deer and bear and occasionally buffalo, tanned so as to be soft and supple. The mattresses are generally of the same material. The fare consists of game, which is abundant and delicate. Bread is made of corn, beaten as fine as possible in an improvised mortar, or ground in a hand mill, if one has been bought. When traveling parched corn supplies the place of bread. Frequently bread was not to be had, and instances are still remembered of hunters and settlers who for months went without eating anything but meat.

If corn could be obtained, — and after the first crop, the lack of it was rarely felt again, unless through the inroads of the Indians, or the accidents of nature, — it was made into dough on a "trencher," and either baked in the ashes and called "ash-cake," or baked before the fire and called "Johnny-cake"— a corruption of "Journey-cake," from the ease with which it could be made. The corn itself could also be made into mush, and where the cow had prospered, mush and milk was the favorite diet, for supper, especially. A delicious syrup was frequently gotten from the maple. Butter was supplied by the fat of bear's meat or the gravy of the goose, and there are still living old hunters who declare that the finest Jersey butter of Columbia does not equal in savor the "goose-fat" of the olden days. Coffee was made from parched rye and dried beans; tea was supplied by the sassafras-tree. Cisterns and wells were unknown. The water supply from mountain brooks and valley streams was sufficient for all uses. The location was chosen with reference to the convenience of running water, for the builder always had before his mind the possibility of a siege, when it might be with danger of life or limb that water must be obtained. This very reason, however, soon caused the boring of wells within the palisade or picket fence, with which the settler, in imitation of his forefathers, who lived upon the banks of the Weser, surrounded his cabin and frequently his garden. This latter, called "truck-patch," was laid off for cultivation as near the cabin as practicable. Generally there was a vacant space behind the cabin, over which a shed was built to ward off the rain and the rays of the sun when the housewife was ironing. The washing was done at the spring except in times of danger, and the clothes were thrown across the fence pickets to dry. The "truck-patch" and the "out-houses" were behind the washing shed. All trees within gunshot of the cabin, large enough to conceal the body of an Indian, were carefully cut down. A shed was built in one corner of the yard for the horses and the pigs, which were allowed to run at large during times of peace, to grow fat upon the mast which was either plentiful or scant or just middling. They were trained to return to the cabin at eventide and seek shelter from wolves and the depredations of the bears. It was even said that hogs became so astute as to appreciate when Indians were in the woods, and old settlers were fond of relating how the return in midday of some unusually precocious pet sow was a warning, never disregarded and never falsified, of the neighborhood of the dreaded "redskins."

After the inner economy of his household had been organized, the pioneer turned his attention to that task, the most important of all, which has secured his ascendency in the land of his adoption in every part of the globe. The method of clearing when carried on by a small family was a tedious process. It must not be supposed, however, that clearing land meant stripping it of all growth. It meant getting it in such a condition that the necessary requirements of husbandry could be fulfilled. The first step taken was to deaden the large trees, generally in the autumn or winter before the sap had begun to rise. This was done by cutting with the axe a belt or girdle around the tree so as to break through the bark. This caused the tree to wither and decay. Those which were too large to haul away were burned by having small "kindling wood" heaped about them. They burned sometimes for weeks without interruption. Fire was one of the greatest instruments for clearing, and frequently, when a long drought had rendered the forests combustible, they were fired to facilitate the clearing of the land upon which they stood. Many statutes were passed against this practice, and heavy penalties were prescribed for it. In some localities more thickly settled than others, neighbors rendered each other mutual assistance. In this case, the trunks of very large trees were cut down, "chopped" into logs, rolled together, and set on fire. Hence the phrase, "log-rolling" in the vocabulary of our political commonplaces. After the trees were disposed of, the undergrowth was cut down, carried together in heaps, and burnt. The land was immediately put under cultivation to destroy the underbrush, which would otherwise come up and redouble the labor of clearing. The crop the first year was poor, though, where the land was fertile, interspersed with "patches of likely growth." The next year the decay of roots had probably progressed far enough to allow the land to be ordinarily well plowed. When this was done, the work of clearing was practically accomplished. Time and an occasional storm and a few strokes of the axe, aided by a little fire, did the rest. The pioneer was now a settler, and had perfected the organization of the elemental germ of the state.

His nearest neighbor was probably five to ten miles away. In the fall, after his crop had been gathered, they occasionally met on bear and deer and wild turkey hunts. The community of danger and of interest drew them together. As we recall the times in which they lived, we can see them stride across the stage with their long rifles, loose hunting-shirts, moccasined feet, and fur caps, in stalwart pursuit of the game which abounds in the forests, casting cautious, but not fearful glances to either side as they move through the overhanging trees. Or perhaps we see a canoe glide swiftly down one of the numerous creeks that empty into the Holston, above whose sides emerge two broad shoulders, which bend backwards and forwards in swift alternation as the boat swirls onward.

But as yet, although we see the type, and although we can live as one of the class, no individual figure has come within the range of our vision. Even the oft-mentioned William Bean is scarcely more than a shadow — *umbra nominis*. We find his name among the Council of Thirteen of the Watauga Association (spelt Been), and he appears occasionally during the Indians wars, but this is all. Even the sad fate of his wife throws no light upon him. At times, a presence becomes manifest, but only for a second, and then it is quickly swallowed up in the gloom of the surrounding indistinctness. Daniel Boone appears in the background, and we watch him for a second as he cuts a few misspelled words upon the trunk of a tree commemorative of a bear just killed, which perhaps had given unusually much to do; or we follow him as he arrives at Bean's cabin near a creek which bears his name, and spends a night with that adventurous pioneer. But straightway he is gone, to subdue the beautiful region which surrounds the fairest town of the commonwealth he founded, and only returns to listen to the eloquent protest of Oconostota, and to help Colonel Henderson juggle the Indians out of all that region which lies between the Ohio, the Tennessee, and the Cumberland, "including all its waters to the Ohio River." There is nothing individually heroic in the spectacle — it is the group which gives breadth and color and intensity.

The reports brought back to the older settlements in Virginia, North Carolina, and South Carolina created an eager desire to enter into a land so beautiful, so fertile, and so easily obtained. Emigrants even came from the banks of the Susquehanna, and from the thriving towns of the north, to take possession of a country which more than fulfilled the promises of the Lord to his chosen people. Hunting and exploring parties, which had first attracted attention to the new country, continued to pass and repass the gradual growth of cabins in the east, on their way to and from the interior. In June, 1769, a party penetrated beyond the valleys at the foot of the Stone and Bald mountains into the Cumberland region of Middle Tennessee. A month previous, Daniel Boone and two others, one of whom was killed, had passed through East Tennessee into Kentucky. In June, 1770, Colonel James Knox, at the head of a small party called the "Long Hunters," from the length of their absence, explored the region of country around the junction of the Cumberland and the Ohio, and the lower bend of the Cumberland. From now on, these parties come and go in rapid sequence. Parties of surveyors and their guards, sent out from Virginia to locate warrants and royal grants in Kentucky, made the Watauga settlement a place of rest and refreshment, some of them even remaining permanently. Disturbances in both North and South Carolina, resulting from the oppressive measures which followed resistance to the Stamp Act and other illegal modes of taxation, increased the number of emigrants.

In 1770 James Robertson came from North Carolina, and in him we find for the first time a figure of Tennessee history standing before us in the life. His is one of the great names and one of the heroic figures in the annals of the State. He returned, after having raised one harvest, but came back the year following as a permanent settler upon the banks of the Watauga. About the same time a party of new-comers settled in Carter's Valley, in the neighborhood of where Rogersville now is, being the advance guard of the column which was gradually overrunning the country from Wolfs Hill near the present site of Abingdon towards the southwest. Two of them opened a store in the valley. A year later a man named Jacob Brown settled with several families on the Nollichucky, and also opened a store to barter ammunition, whiskey, trinkets, and the like with the Indians for land. This was the last formed of the three original settlements from which all future development radiates. Though weak at first, consisting of a few cabins, the accession of inhabitants gradually gave strength, and we find among those whom the treachery of Lord Dunmore had hoped to sacrifice at the battle of Kanawha, in 1774, a company of fifty Tennesseans, commanded by Evan Shelby. The political agitation in North Carolina having assumed formidable proportions, Governor Tryon attempted to repress the Regulators, as they termed themselves, and at the battle of the Alamance killed over two hundred of them. This caused such an influx of new-comers to the young settlement that it enabled them to put themselves upon a firmer basis. Wherever several cabins were built together in a cluster they were called stations, and in each station was a fort, generally formed by running palisades from one cabin to the other. The earliest forts were the Watauga Fort and Fort Gillespie, for the protection respectively of the Watauga and the Nollichucky or Brown settlement, and one in Carter's Valley.

CHAPTER III.

THE WATAUGA ASSOCIATION FORMED.

Thus far had the settlements progressed, when a trouble arose as regards the State to which they owed allegiance. Those who had settled north of the Holston had preëmpted their lands under the laws of Virginia. But Colonel Anthony Bledsoe, a surveyor and Indian fighter of the old times, discovered that the extension of the line beyond the Steep Rock, the Virginia and North Carolina boundary line, would leave the Carter's Valley as well as the Nollichucky and Watauga settlements in North Carolina. When this became patent, those who had purchased land from Carter and Parker, and others who had originally purchased from the Indians, attempted to remedy the defect in their title by refusing to hold under them, and claiming their lands as original settlers. It was only after many acts of legislation that the confusion of titles was eventually reformed.

But a still more serious trouble than this was impending over the infant communities. About 1769 Colonel Donelson had made a treaty with the Indians by which Virginia bought what was called the western frontiers. By this treaty it was supposed that the Watauga region went to that colony. Believing themselves in Virginia, the Watauga people supposed themselves governed by Virginia laws, and looked to that State or Colony for protection against Indian aggressions and the raids of horse-thieves. There was no desire to acknowledge the sovereignty of a State from whose oppression the majority of them had just fled. In addition to this, North Carolina itself took no steps looking to the exercise of any authority over the settlements, many of which had been made in violation of the provisions of the treaty with the Cherokees at Lochaber in 1770. It had everything to lose, and nothing to gain, by recognizing them as being on North Carolina territory, which recognition would carry with it the obligation of protecting them against the inroads of the Indians.

The Watauga people, therefore, owing no allegiance to Virginia, and being unable to render any to North Carolina, were for the moment elevated in the annals of America to the dignity of a new and independent colony. That they were worthy cannot be doubted by any one who observes the ease, assurance, and moderate self-restraint with which they began to select from the old storehouse of English law and precedent such material as was necessary for the primitive structure they desired to raise. Regarding themselves as beyond the pale of North Carolina law, and following the precedents of two thousand years, they organized a government which, like all governments formed by the Anglo-Saxon race or those inheriting their traditions, was adapted to the actual needs of those for whom it was framed, without theories, without abstractions, without generalizations, without any provision for any future contingency not clearly imminent. An association was formed and articles of association entered into. These indeed have been lost, yet material enough has come down to us to enable us to reconstruct, with some degree of assurance, the first scheme of government ever devised for the inhabitants of Tennessee soil. It was simple but efficient.

Having assembled in general convention, like the inhabitants of the old New England towns, a committee of thirteen was elected as a kind of general body for legislative purposes. The executive and judicial power was lodged in five commissioners elected by the thirteen from their own body. The five commissioners elected one of their number chairman, who was *ex officio* chairman of the committee of thirteen. A clerk was elected by the committee. Among the most important legislative functions performed by this body was the establishment of instruments for the recording of deeds and wills. The laws of Virginia were adopted as far as applicable. There was a sheriff and an attorney. The sessions of the court were held at stated periods. The committee appear to have been conscious of their anomalous position, and carefully refrained from taking any steps that could embroil them with the legislatures of the older colonies. When dealing with people who were non-residents of their district, they took care to avoid any necessity for the exercise of physical force by requiring them to give bond, so as to proceed against their property, instead of their persons, if the contingency arose. The suits of plaintiffs refusing to give bond were dismissed. It is not possible to establish the date of the formation of the association, but it was most probably in 1772. The names of the committee-men at the time of the petition to North Carolina were John Carter, Charles Robertson, James Robertson, Zach Isbell, John Sevier, James Smith, Jacob Brown, William Bean, John Jones, George Russell, Jacob Womack, and Robert Lucas. William Tatham was clerk *pro tem.* The name of the regular clerk is unknown. Felix Walker, subsequently a member of Congress from North Carolina, Thomas Gomley, William Tatham, and even John Sevier were at various times incumbents of the clerkship.

At first only the two original settlements lived under the articles. In 1775 the Brown or Nollichucky settlement, being composed for the most part of Tories, was compelled by the Watauga people and a band of Virginians from Wolfs Hill, who had heard of their lukewarmness towards the Revolutionary cause, to take the oath of "fidelity to the common cause," and from that time on

THE WATAUGA ASSOCIATION FORMED. 35

became identified with those who had framed the articles of association. Until 1776, the date of the petition to North Carolina for annexation, the history of the three settlements generally known in Tennessee history by the collective term of Watauga Association is in the main the history of the increase of population, the building of cabins, and the tilling of the soil. But few events of importance beyond this occurred, and we have only the bold outlines which are dimly visible like the highest peaks of a mountain range on a misty day.

In 1772 a line was run between Virginia and the Cherokee hunting-grounds. This followed the 36° 30' line of parallel, and hence left the members of the association on Cherokee soil. Alarmed by finding that the title to the lands they had entered in the belief they were entering Virginia lands were still in the Indians, and not looking to North Carolina to take any decisive steps in their favor as against the latter, the members of the association, through James Robertson and John Boone, obtained a ten years' lease from the aboriginal owners of the land upon which they had settled. An incident which occurred at the making of this lease is worthy of mention as an illustration both of the times and the men. After the lease had been made, it was celebrated by gymnastic festivities and races, in which both the whites and the Indians took part. Late in the evening a crowd of ruffians from Wolfs Hill, Virginia, wantonly slew one of the latter. The Indians immediately withdrew with dark faces and clouded brows, and those who knew the temper of their blood were in no doubt of a prompt retaliation. Anticipating a general war, and appreciating the dangers to the settlements which would result, involving perhaps their complete destruction, James Robertson made a long journey to the Indian nation, met their chief warriors in council, pacified their anger, and propitiated them by denouncing the perpetrators of the outrage as hostile to the whites. This mark of condescension had its effect, and the danger was for the time averted.

On the 17th of March, 1772, Colonel Richard Henderson, Colonel Nathaniel Hart, and Daniel Boone succeeded in getting a general council of the Indians together at Sycamore Shoals on the Watauga, and purchased from them a tract of country already alluded to, between the Kentucky and the Cumberland rivers. This was the celebrated Transylvania purchase. It suggested to the Watauga people the feasibility of perfecting their own precarious tenure. In spite of their friendly relations with the Indians, the settlers, who, like true Englishry, as Mr. Freeman calls them, had a strong desire to have the occupation of the lands they held sanctioned by acquiring an outstanding adverse title, which they held in no esteem whatsoever so long as it was adverse, were uneasy about the possible results which might follow the termination of their lease. Among the causes of apprehension was the fact that many men of distinction, among them several lawyers, were buying the reversion from the Indians. Two days after the Transylvania treaty, the Watauga people took advantage of the opportunity, and it may be added the treacherous generosity of the Indians, to purchase from them the fee of the land which they themselves held as lessees. The Indians made a deed to Charles Robertson, who afterwards made individual deeds to the occupants, who still further perfected their title by patenting the same in the Watauga land office, of which James Smith was clerk. Carter and Parker, of the Carter's Valley settlement, whose store had been robbed and destroyed by the Indians, received from them in payment of their losses an increase of territory extending from Cloud Creek to Chimney Top Mountain, paying in addition to the estimated worth of the store and its contents a nominal consideration, which was advanced by Robert Lucas. Jacob Brown increased his purchase by buying from them a tract of land beginning at the Chimney Top, and running to Camp Creek, and thence to Brown's line, which was subsequently made the dividing line between the Indians and the settlers. The consideration which he paid for a body of land equal to one half of Hawkins County of the present day was ten shillings.

CHAPTER IV.

THE REVOLUTION AND INDIAN WARS.

On September 5, 1775, the Continental Congress met in Philadelphia. On the 19th of April, 1776, the battle of Lexington was fought, and immediately the colonists found themselves on the threshold of a war with more dangerous and powerful antagonists than a few hundred Indian braves. On the 10th of May, George Washington was elected commander-in-chief of the American forces, and the war of independence was fairly begun. The part which North Carolina took in the preliminary stages of the Revolutionary war was at once bold and uncompromising. As early as the 25th of August, 1774, a provincial congress assembled at Newbern, in defiance of a proclamation of the royal governor, who bitterly denounced their proceedings as derogatory to the authority of the king. They promulgated the doctrine which was then regarded as radical and revolutionary, but which is now one of the rudiments of nineteenth century politics, that no person should be taxed without his consent, and declared illegal and oppressive the taxes on tea and other articles, which the English Parliament had levied. Members were elected to represent North Carolina in a general congress, to be held in Philadelphia in September. One of the delegates was William Hooper, of Orange County, who was among the first, if not the first, of those who declared for total separation of the colonies from England, at a time when only a redress of grievances was generally contemplated. The colonial assembly met at Newbern, now called New Berne, and despite the governor's indignant remonstrance passed resolutions approving the measures of the Philadelphia Congress. A few days later the flight of Governor Martin left the government in the hands of the people. This is the governor who pronounced the treaties between the Indians and Henderson and the Watauga people violations of the law, and null. On the 20th of May, 1775, the people of Mecklenburgh passed the celebrated Mecklenburgh resolutions, which laid the foundation of the Declaration of Independence of the year following in form, in substance, and almost in phrase.[1] Among the names signed to these resolutions was that of Thomas Polk. But while these preparations were being made for the impending contest in the mother State, the little settlements beyond the utmost range of the mountains that fringed her western borders were founding a new commonwealth, and growing steadily in strength and in self-confidence. The area of cleared land grew larger from day to day. The road from Wolfs Hill, and the road which led by Fort Prince George, were crowded by incoming emigrants. The woods echoed with the sound of human voices. The prattle of children was daily heard in regions which, till then, were familiar with no other sounds than the pattering of a falling acorn, the bark of a squirrel, the hoot of an owl, or the scream of a panther. Each band of new-comers brought a cow, or a horse, or a few pigs, or barnyard fowls as the means of comfort, and as the nucleus of future wealth. The growth of population rivaled the wonders of Cadmus. Despite the ravages of wild beasts, and the deadly diseases which followed the breaking of the surface of new soil, and the assassinations committed by roving bands of Indians, and accidents by field and flood, increasing numbers literally sprang from the soil. Cabins came up like fungi, and the thirst for land and wandering out which has made the history of

---

[1] See List of Authorities.

the Anglo-Saxon race the history of colonization gave a steady, unwavering impulse to the inflow. We have no statistics, but the probable population of the three settlements in 1776 was about six hundred.[1] Some time in 1775 or 1776, the citizens of the infant settlements which had been formed and others which were being formed gave to the district of country in which they lived the name of Washington District, in honor of the commander-in-chief of the American armies. During the excitement of the colonial difficulties the District of Washington had taken a lively interest in the impending conflict, and "in open committee acknowledged themselves indebted to the united colonies their full proportion of the continental expenses." Their position was one peculiarly exposed to all the worst influences that exist in an unsettled state of society, especially when a weaker and less compact territory offers a place of refuge to the criminals of one larger and more powerful. Fugitives from justice in Virginia and North Carolina fled to the District of Washington, and relying on the lack of judicial organization and the fear felt by those in power of trespassing on the authority of the larger colonies, they escaped, if not detection, at least arrest. The articles of association made no provision for the punishment of those who denied their validity. As a result murderers, forgers, horse-thieves, and all classes of criminals fairly infested the new settlements. The doors of the settlers, who were proverbially hospitable, were always open to those who craved a meal and a pallet. Often the host would awake in the morning to find not merely his guest but his horse gone, and with it perhaps all the powder and lead to be found in the cabin. One is compelled to admire the self-restraint the old settlers evince in their declaration that "murderers, horse-thieves, and robbers have escaped us for want of proper authority."

[1] This estimate is based upon a careful comparison of the names of those who composed Shelby's company at Kanawha and the names signed to a petition for annexation in 1776.

The history of that period gives no finer example of the natural aptitude of those who inherit English traditions for self-government, and the least imaginative mind, following the gradual stages of the evolution of old Anglo-Saxon ideas of government, can easily hear on the banks of the Watauga and among the hills of the Cumberland echoes of the voices which were raised at Runnymede. In addition to these troubles, their frontier position and the neighborhood of the Cherokees exposed the people of the district to the double danger of British and Indian hostilities. Their loyalty to the cause, however, was never shaken, though often severely tested. On one occasion they compelled all the Tories in the district to take the oath of allegiance to the Continental Congress. Many of them had fled there hoping to find a place of refuge from the oppressive measures of the colonies, which required of them a test oath of loyalty. But the war for independence cannot be said ever to have actually found a battle-field on Tennessee soil. Its effects could be seen and felt, and frequently the war itself swept along its confines. But the actual suffering which came to those who then inhabited the District of Washington was either the result of their own seeking, as in the battle of King's Mountain, or it came from the policy of the British agents who incited the Indians to make war upon the adherents of the American cause. The intrigues of a Scotchman named Alexander Cameron were peculiarly fruitful of disastrous results. In 1776 the inhabitants of the district were suddenly warned of an impending outbreak on the part of the Indians. It appears that Cameron, under the direction of John Stuart, the British superintendent of Indian affairs in the south, assembled the chiefs of the Cherokees, and bribed them with arms, ammunition, and promises of plunder, to make war on the colonies. The plan was to attack the District of Washington, destroy the inhabitants to a man, and then invade Virginia and the

Carolinas. A friendly Indian squaw first gave warning to the settlements, and enabled them to put themselves in a posture of defense. An open communication from Henry Stuart, a brother of John Stuart, at that time a resident agent among the Cherokees, to the Tories of the district confirmed the news and increased the alacrity of the people. This communication and the apprehension of the dangers it threatened to those who refused to return to their allegiance to King George were followed by the reports of traveling traders, which the settlers, knowing the ways of those who travel and trade, required them to swear to in due form of law. The plan of attack suggested a more than Indian mind. Seven hundred warriors were to make the attack in two divisions of equal strength and each division was to attack one of the two important forts, which were the Watauga fort and Fort Heaton. The Watauga committee took prompt and energetic measures to meet the threatened invasion. Runners were sent through the settlement to give notice to all who were isolated to abandon their houses and repair to the protection of the forts. The forts themselves were strengthened and provisioned. Those too weak to hold, among them Fort Lee,[1] were dismantled and destroyed.

[1] There is some confusion in reference to these forts and their names. Ramsey makes Fort Gillespie and Fort Lee distinct. In a letter written 6th April, 1793, and published in the *Knoxville Gazette*, we find the following statement: "Others fortified themselves at Amos Heaton's, now Sullivan's Old Court House, and those in Watauga and Nollichucky posted about thirty volunteers under Captain (now General) James Robertson, just above the mouth of Big Limestone, where Mr. Gillespie lives. Shortly after this party took post and before they had completed their fort (called Fort Lee) four traders escaped." The people then fled again, leaving about fifteen volunteers behind, who, being joined by about the same number in their rear, "were thus compelled to fortify near the Sycamore Shoals on Watauga, on much weaker ground than they had vacated." It is evident that Fort Lee was abandoned after Sevier wrote the letter dated at that fort.

Officers were elected, and companies were organized. Petitions for aid were sent to Virginia. The destiny of the settlements was at stake. The Virginians had seen with pleasure a bulwark gradually rising between themselves and the ferocity and cruelty of Indian warfare. This bulwark was now to be put to the test; its fate might involve their own and aid was promptly furnished. Five companies were raised in the border counties, and marched to Fort Heaton. Having arrived there, a council of war was held, and Captain William Cocke, at whose suggestion the fort had been built, urged immediate action. His suggestion was acted upon, and it was decided to march out at once and meet the Indians, signs of whose near approach had been discovered and reported by the scouts. An advance guard was thrown forward, which came in contact with a scouting party of Indians and drove them back. Some hours later the main body of the Indians came up, and Thompson, the officer in command, gave the order to engage them. The battle which ensued, though of short duration, is remarkable as being among the first attempts ever made by the Indians to adopt the civilized plan of fighting a battle. They made a direct attack, charging over open ground, and their chief, Dragging Canoe, a savage Napoleon, attempted to break through the centre of Thompson's command and then crush his flanks in detail. The Indians, however, have never had the ability, which comes only from organized training, of standing direct fire, and on this occasion they fled after a few volleys, leaving dead on the field about twenty-six men, including Dragging Canoe himself. During the fight occurred one of those sanguinary hand-to-hand conflicts, the accounts of which fill the annals of that time, and which is here given entire, as an example of all the rest. It is copied from Ramsey, who appears to have had it from Moore himself. "Moore had shot the chief, wounding him in the knee, but not so badly as to prevent him from standing. Moore advanced towards him, and the Indian threw his tomahawk but missed him. Moore sprang at him with his large butcher knife drawn, which the Indian caught by the blade, and attempted to wrest from the hand of his antagonist. Holding on with desperate tenacity to the knife, both clinched with their left hands. A scuffle ensued in which the Indian was thrown to the ground, his right hand being nearly dissevered and bleeding profusely. Moore, still holding the handle of his knife in the right hand, succeeded with the other to disengage his own tomahawk from his belt, and ended the strife by sinking it in the skull of the Indian." Among those who took part in this battle, called the battle of Island Flats, was Isaac Shelby, who was present as a private and volunteer. The other division of Indians was under a crafty chief named Old Abraham. He was to attack Fort Lee, but the Nollichucky inhabitants, fearing their fortifications were not sufficient, had broken them up and retreated to Watauga, leaving crops and stock open to the attack of their enemies. The garrison was only forty men strong, but they were under the command of an officer not less resolute, not less fertile in resources, not less cool in the presence of danger, than the Englishman who, three years later, gained immortality and an English peerage by the defense of Gibraltar against equally overwhelming odds. The achievements of one were viewed with wondering admiration by the civilization of the world. The achievements of the other, though not less worthy of all honor and renown, were performed under the shadows of a primitive forest in a frontier fort, against unrecorded savages. James Robertson deserves for his memorable defense of the Watauga fort a place not less illustrious in the annals of Tennessee than that accorded to Lord Heathfield in the annals of England. More than three hundred Indians were held at bay by less than forty men capable of active service, and despite stratagems, and all the arts and cunning of an Indian warfare, midnight attacks, and daily onslaughts, were eventually compelled to raise the siege and retire. This defense of the Watauga fort is deserving of special mention in the history of Tennessee as the first display on Tennessee soil, and for the people of Tennessee, of that martial prowess to which a Tennessean may call attention with justifiable pride, and of which he may say without any feeling of provincial exaggeration or gasconade that it has, as a whole, never been surpassed by anything recorded in the histories of the world's warfares.

Although defeated in their attacks on the infant settlements, the Indians renewed the war in another quarter and invaded Virginia. Angered by what was regarded as a flagrant outrage, it was determined to strike terror to the hearts of the Cherokees by invading their country with an overwhelming force. Their estimated population was two thousand. North Carolina and Virginia both sent bodies of troops, and these in conjunction with the settlers formed what in those days was regarded as a large force. The country of the Cherokees was laid waste, and they were compelled to sue for peace. The proper blow had been struck at the proper time. The implacable Indians were taught that the boasted sanctity of their strongholds could be violated with impunity. Town after town, the most secluded, the most distant, the most thoroughly guarded, was taken and razed to the ground. But little mercy was shown and but few prisoners taken. The Indians were glad to make treaties of peace and cessions of territory. The boundary line agreed upon between the Cherokees and North Carolina was so run as to leave the District of Washington in possession of the latter.

The law of development that the end of each successive Indian war brought an addition of population was again exemplified after the Cherokee war. The troops from the colonies were charmed with the natural advantages of the country they had seen in passing through the Watauga country, and their accounts, doubtless highly colored, painted an Eldorado, which drew to the new settlement a rapid influx of adventurous pioneers.

CHAPTER V.

ANNEXED TO NORTH CAROLINA, AND LIMITS DEFINED.

THE Watauga people had hopes, when the articles of association were adopted, of being able eventually to form an independent government, governed as the older colonies were governed, by royal governors. When the disagreements between the colonies and the mother country arose, they modified their views to the new order of things, and regarded themselves as a distinct though as yet inchoate state. But their weakness, and the dangers which resulted from Indians and horse-thieves, bands of desperadoes who sold stolen horses to the Indians, rendered the protection of some more powerful state necessary for their welfare. They had not the material to construct the machinery of government, nor the strength to set it in motion. They petitioned North Carolina for annexation in 1776. Their petition was granted. It was signed by the committee of thirteen, and many others. The provincial congress of North Carolina met at Halifax in November, 1776, and Charles Robertson, John Carter, John Haile,[1] and John Sevier were delegates from Washington District, Watauga settlement. Five in all were elected, but only four took their seats. At this session a bill of rights and a state constitution, one modeled upon an English statute declaratory of the common law, the other upon the common law itself, were formally adopted. It is significant that in the declaration of rights is the following clause: " It [the boundary line of the State] shall not be so

[1] Haywood says Hill.

construed as to prevent the establishment of one or more governments westward of this State by consent of the legislature."

After the annexation of the Washington District the old form of government was allowed to stand until the spring of 1777. An act was then passed establishing courts of pleas and quarter sessions, and also a bill for the appointment of justices of the peace, and sheriffs for the several courts in the District of Washington. In November of this year, 1777, the District of Washington became Washington County. It was made a part of the Salisbury judicial district, and the act establishing it is noteworthy as being the first determinate expression of the geographical outlines of Tennessee.

From 1777 until the disturbances of eight years later, the history of Tennessee was a part of the history of North Carolina. The policy of the mother State, for such it had now become, was to open the new territory to settlement, and to encourage emigration. In several counties offices "for the entry of lands acquired by treaty or conquest" were established, and a land office was opened in Washington County. The land system of Tennessee is founded upon that of North Carolina, and the general outlines are the same in both States. The earlier laws of Tennessee modified the North Carolina system, and the later laws have modified the earlier.

The system of Carolina was in many respects the result of a peculiar combination of the rigidity of English and the laxity of American ideas of landed proprietorship. In many points the grants of land in North Carolina, beginning with the charter of Charles II., to the colonial proprietors give the student of history numerous examples of the continuity of popular institutions, and serve as chains of tradition to link the present and the past. With the change of those details which need to be changed for the sake of the larger example, the conquest and settlement of England by the Saxons is the conquest and settlement of Virginia and the Carolinas by the English. A comparative study, however, of the two stages of history, though interesting and rich in material, lies beyond the measure of proportion of such a work as this. Still, a proper comprehension of the earlier system of North Carolina, with its paraphernalia of grants, charters, deeds, entries, certificates, bounties, entry-takers, land-agents, and charts, is not without value for an intelligent investigation into the gradual growth of Tennessee from a state of barbarity to a state of civilization, to enable the mind to bridge the interval from the time when the country was inhabited by a few tribes of Indians with small tent-spread villages scattered here and there along the banks of the rivers and on the plateaus of steep mountains, from which scarcely a film of vapor ascended, to the time when its surface is covered by the houses, towns and cities, roads and railroads, and its skies are darkened by the smoke that arises from the industries of nearly two millions of people. When the government of North Carolina passed out of the hands of the proprietors, and their title was extinguished, this extinction carried with it all that region of country west of the Appalachian Mountains, which as yet lay beyond the *Ultima Thule* of colonial geography, known only by the vague tissue of surmises which had grown like cobwebs around the old and half-forgotten traditions of De Soto's ill-starred expedition. Occasionally a trader would pass over the range. Frequently he disappeared never to return. If he did return, he brought with him pictures of a primeval Eldorado which caused a stir of excitement for the moment, and were then quickly forgotten in the struggles of colonial life. The accounts of Marquette, Hennepin, Allouez, Membré, and Anastaste Douay detracted nothing from the prevailing ignorance. The North Carolinians regarded the western country very much as one of the less active litigants in Jarndyce against Jarndyce might have regarded the estate in question, having in it indeterminate possibilities, but too remote to form any basis of immediate action. The extinction of the English title gave this title to North Carolina, but until her own children had in a manner rushed into it, and suddenly founded a new commonwealth, and then applied for a recognition of their importance and the work they had performed, the parent State made no movement implying a knowledge or desire of proprietorship. After the annexation an entry-taker's office was opened in the recently erected Washington County, and Tennessee was thrown open to the land system of North Carolina. But however simple the system, the early history of this State is filled with accounts of the troubles and conflicts which arose in reference to lands and claims of preëmption and doubtful grants. The frequent changes of government, together with the lack of interest in the frontier settlements, occasioned a state of confusion which required act after act for its disentanglement. Those who had settled beyond the Steep Rock and entered their lands under the laws of Virginia had incessant conflicts with those who, when the running of the line threw them into North Carolina, made haste to enter the lands under the laws of that State. Sometimes five or six claimants would appear for the same land, — one claiming under grant from the lords proprietors, one under executor's sale, one under an unrecorded grant from Lord Granville's office, one who wished to enter the lands under the laws of North Carolina, and one in possession. The various treaties with the Indians and the little regard paid them by the settlers added to the causes of confusion. In 1778 an act was passed declaring null and void all entries made on the hunting-grounds of the Indians. Grants of land were the means adopted for rewarding the soldiers who had fought the war for independence, there being no money having a marketable value in the treasury. In 1780 an act laid off a certain tract of land for bounty purposes, but when in 1782 the grants were made, it was found that "sundry families had before the passing of the said act settled on the said tract of country," and it became necessary to allow them to "retain their entries to the usual limit of 640 acres."

There were several causes which tended to produce this confusion, but the main cause of all was the ignorance that existed in the minds of those who were the centres of government as to the limits of their territory. They appear to have known the grant of Charles II. by reputation alone, and it is doubtful if any members of the earlier government, except Lord Granville, attempted to fix in his own mind the limits of the land which was subject to the laws of North Carolina. In the act of 1777, which formed Washington County, the boundaries are specified as running to the Mississippi River.

No clearer proof of dense ignorance could be adduced than this act. John Sevier had virtually forced the annexation upon North Carolina, and the legislature, their minds filled with the great struggle which was going on, passed this as they would have passed any act to satisfy the importunities of a bold, persistent, and active advocate, who asked no money, and promised them soldiers. The grant of Charles II., which was the only claim of North Carolina upon the country in question, extended to the Pacific coast-line.[1] Their title to the land west of the Mississippi was as good as their title to the land east of it.

It is a remarkable fact that Sevier alone of all the men of his times inhabiting what subsequently became Tennessee had a definite idea of what should be the logical limits of the future State. These limits were not recognized in

---

[1] The words of the grant are: "West in a direct line as far as the South Seas."

the statutes of North Carolina, except the one drawn most probably by Sevier and in the cession to the United States. The act of cession cedes a certain district in direct terms, and by implication allows the United States to follow their pleasure in reference to the rest. When the constitution was framed, the limits of the State were fixed according to the ideas of Sevier of twenty years before. It is necessary to bear in mind the confusion of boundary lines resulting from the encroachments of the settlers upon the Indians, and the recognition of the rights of the latter by the home government, in order to have a clear view of the gradual formation and making of the State. The general groundwork was the same in all cases. Indian lands were taken possession of and improved. The Indians entered into hostilities, and were eventually defeated and compelled to sue for peace. Treaties were made and increased territory given the whites, and new boundary lines established which were soon again overstepped. Act after act was passed to legalize usurpations, and all the worst features of civilization were brought into play to win a field for the foundation of a government, the formation of which called forth all that is noble and admirable in the character of man.

CHAPTER VI.

NEW COUNTIES FORMED.

AFTER the formation of the county of Washington immediate steps were taken to attract emigration, and a land office was opened. Another aid to emigration was the improvement of the road into Washington County from North Carolina. Commissioners were appointed to survey and lay off a road from Washington County Court House into Burke County, and the new road, allowing the passage of vehicles, materially increased the inflowing stream of population. But if the frontier position of the settlements brought them increase of population, it also brought the elements of lawless violence, which were expelled from more settled communities. In 1778 bands of Tories, who were said to have combined with the robbers that infested the country, inflicted heavy losses on the settlers by continuous thieving and highway robbery, sometimes accompanied by personal violence, and even murder. Finding the agents of the law inadequate to their protection, the militia having been disbanded, the old Watauga pioneers, whose self-reliance had been in no wise weakened by the lapse of time and the successive prosecution of Indian wars, again devised means to restore order to the troubled settlements, and selected from among themselves committees, to whom they gave power to adopt any measures they saw fit, to put a stop to the evil. The evil was great, the remedy was adequate. Two companies, thirty each, were organized and set immediately to work. All suspicious persons were arrested. The mere fact of arrest was a proof of guilt, which was all but conclusive. The prisoner who "failed to give a good account of himself," or to give security for his appearance before the committee, was summarily dealt with, shot, hanged, whipped, branded, or drowned, according to circumstances. A heavy fine was the lightest punishment inflicted. A few purchased freedom with infamy, and as the price of liberty betrayed the names of their associates. The punishments were severe, and ruthlessly inflicted. The forger was branded, the murderer was whipped, the horse thief was hanged. It is needless to say that in a short time law and order, according to the Watauga idea of what constituted law and order, were restored. True to tradition, the vigilance committee was dissolved, or dissolved itself, as soon as its work had been performed.

The main strength of the Tories and robbers (the terms were almost synonymous in the backwoods) being broken, the individual offenders were left to the regular tribunals of the country, who it is to be feared exercised power that would have made Lord Strafford himself stand aghast. One indictment, the caption of which has been preserved, is against the defendant, "in toryism." The judgment of the court was that the culprit be kept prisoner until the termination of the war then raging, and that one half of his goods, which must be valued by a jury at the next court, "be kept by the sheriff for the use of the State, the rest to go to the family of the offender." Ramsey, with unconscious irony, says, "the court thus exhibited a marked instance of judgment and mercy in the same order, combining patriotism with justice and humanity." On another occasion a certain J. H., "for his ill practices in harboring and abetting disorderly persons who are prejudicial and inimical to the common cause of liberty, and frequently disturbing our tranquillity in general," is by the court "duly considering the allegations alleged and objected against the said J. H. imprisoned for the term of one year." This action was taken on motion of E. Dunlap, state attorney. The most remarkable exercise of power by this remarkable court is the order granted upon motion of this same E. Dunlap that the property of one H. be retained in the hands of some debtor because "there is sufficient reason to believe that the said H.'s estate will be confiscated to the use of the State for his misdemeanors, etc." The humorous records of the judiciary show nothing equal to this. The settlers had scarcely restored order before they were again called on to invade the territory of their implacable foes. The Chickamaugas, a tribe of the Cherokees of peculiar ferocity and daring, who had formed a settlement on the Tennessee about fifty miles below the creek which bears their name, were notorious above all the aboriginal inhabitants of Tennessee soil for their fierceness, their treachery, their love of danger, their daring exploits, and their implacable hatred of the paleface. In the general councils of the nation they were the first to call for revenge, and the last to consent to the treaties by which the white race attempted to put some moral facing upon their spoliation of the red. They eagerly accepted the gifts which tickled their fancy with the tinsel of color, or alleviated the squalid discomfort of their miserable wigwams. But gratitude was an emotion which had never stirred the heart of a Chickamauga brave. In bands of two and three they would lurk on the outskirts of the white settlements, and frequently one of them under the guise of a desire to trade, would gain admittance to the cabins of the settlers. He used the opportunities which hospitality had offered to observe the easiest ingress, and would return the night following with his associates, to burn the cabin, scalp its inmates, plunder its contents, and escape into the pathless wilds of of the Cumberland Hills before pursuit could be organized. At times they came in larger bands and wrought greater destruction. They dwelt upon the banks of the river above the rapids, where the current had cut numerous gorges through the mountains. The vulture's nest was not regarded as half so secluded, as half so hedged in with security by the safeguards which steep ascents and narrow paths and cavernous *cul-de-sacs* had thrown around them. Their incursions were quiet, stealthy, and terrible, their retreat was the flight of the fox to his hole.

In 1779 Virginia and North Carolina determined to destroy their settlements. The leader chosen was Evan Shelby, who had served under Braddock at Fort Du Quesne, and who with fifty Tennesseans had withstood the impetuous assaults with which the fearless chief of the Indians, Cornstalk, had vainly attempted to break the line of the Virginians at Point Pleasant during the Kanawha campaign. Shelby lacked the brilliant rapidity of action which made the name of Sevier an evil omen to the Cherokees, but he was peculiarly fitted to the task assigned him. He was eminently cautious, and he understood the habits of the Indians, as the trapper understands the habits of the beaver. He was given about two thousand men, part of whom had originally been designed for the western service under John Montgomery, who was marching to join Colonel Clark in his expedition against Vincennes and Detroit. Haywood gives to Isaac Shelby, the son of Evan, the credit of furnishing the army transportation and supplies. Shelby descended the river in canoes and pirogues from the mouth of Big Creek, and came upon the enemy with the swiftness and silence learned from the Indians themselves. He took them completely by surprise. They were unable to offer resistance. They fled to the woods without striking a blow. Shelby destroyed their towns and their crops and carried off everything of value which could be carried off, including large supplies which the British had collected at that point for distribution among their allies. Shelby was promoted to a generalship in the Virginia military service.

In the same year a new county was taken from Washington, and named in honor of General Sullivan. Among the first commissioned justices of the peace was Isaac Shelby, who was also appointed colonel of the county militia. In this year also was laid out the first town of the State. Jonesboro, named after William Jones, a North Carolina statesman, was made the county seat of Washington County, and John Wood, Jesse Walton, George Russell, James Stewart, and Benjamin Clark were appointed commissioners to make a plat of the ground, erect public buildings, and to sell lots. The unchinked and clapboarded cabin which had served as the temple of justice for the old Watauga people was ordered to be torn down and in its place it was suggested should be built a court-house of hewn logs, and with shingled roof. In 1783 a new county was formed from Washington County and named Greene, in honor of General Greene, and two years later Greeneville, the county seat, was laid off. This, however, was after the termination of the war.

CHAPTER VII.

KING'S MOUNTAIN.

The part played by the inhabitants of Tennessee in the war for independence was active, and in one instance decisive. Their operations were chiefly of a desultory, guerrilla kind, under the leadership of Sevier, who had been commissioned colonel-commandant of Washington County, and Shelby, who held the same position in the newly formed county of Sullivan.

Their distant and inaccessible position among the fastnesses of the mountains and hidden away among the valleys of the Holston was eminently favorable for a sudden attack, a quick blow, and a hasty retreat. In 1780 Governor Rutherford of South Carolina issued a requisition on Washington and Sullivan counties for one hundred men each. Two companies were promptly raised, but too late to render any assistance to Charleston, for whose defense they had been required. Shortly after, however, twice the number called for joined McDowell, who was trying to stem the advance of Cornwallis through South Carolina. McDowell was one of the first of the guerrilla captains who so often have redeemed the bitterness of defeat by expeditions of personal daring, and substituted quickness of movement, dauntless courage, and unexpected attack for the more ponderous operations of regular warfare. He had under him Clark, Williams, Sevier, and Shelby, all of whom were brave to recklessness, as fertile in resources as Sumter, and as stealthy as the swamp-fox. McDowell, after the formation of his troops, detached Clark, Sevier, and Shelby to attack and disperse a force of Tories who, under Patrick Moore, had intrenched themselves in a fort on the Pacolet. Within less than twenty-four hours, although Moore was twenty miles distant, they had performed their mission and returned. Shelby and Clark not long after this had a brush with Ferguson himself, the gallant, fearless, and unfortunate hero of King's Mountain, and withdrew with small loss before a force four times their strength under a leader who combined the noblest qualities of Cornwallis and Tarleton both as soldier and commander. During the latter part of the year, Shelby, Clark, and Williams were sent to scatter a party of Tories on the Enoree. They pushed forward rapidly from McDowell's encampment on Broad River, made a wide détour around Ferguson's camp, who lay between McDowell and the Tories with a large force with which he had vainly been attempting to bring McDowell to a decisive battle, and riding hard all night, arrived about daybreak within a short distance of the enemy's camp. The Tories fled without offering resistance, and the Americans were pressing them hotly, when a farmer informed their leader that a large body of regular troops was near with reinforcements for the enemy. Retreat was impossible. The men were tired, the horses were jaded. Breastworks were hastily improvised. Preparations were made for a desperate resistance. In a short time Colonel Innes of the British army arrived with six hundred regulars and a rabble of Tories. He immediately attacked and put to flight a small detachment of troops, which had been thrown forward to try to prevent his crossing the Enoree. The Americans held their position and drove back the assailants time after time. They were just begining to yield before the stubborn onslaughts of the British, when Innes was dangerously wounded. His fall was the signal for retreat to the Tories, and their flight demoralized the regular troops.

The Americans saw their opportunity and seized it. They won a decided victory, and captured two hundred of Innes' men. The Tories all escaped.

The victors, flushed with success and eager for new exploits, were on the point of making an incursion towards the sea-coast, for the double purpose of harrying the Tories and avoiding Ferguson, when they received the news of the defeat of General Gates at Camden, and the probable downfall of the American cause. Advance was impossible, and Ferguson's neighborhood rendered retreat hazardous and difficult. Their fears of danger from this source were not without foundation. Ferguson sent a detachment after them, well accoutred, and mounted on fresh horses. The Americans were incumbered with two hundred prisoners. A forced march alone held out prospects of escape to the captors. The prisoners were distributed among the men, one prisoner to three horsemen, who carried him in rotation. In this way they marched two days and one night without intermission, and thus eluded pursuit and reached the mountains in safety, where they were joined by McDowell himself. The defeat of Gates and the misfortune of Sumter cast a cloud of apprehension over the spirits of the partisan leaders, and McDowell's command was dissolved, he and his men crossing the mountains with the mountaineers.

The next movement of the Watauga people was made under Sevier and Shelby. They raised a body of five hundred troops with the hope of surprising and overpowering Ferguson, who was making threatening demonstrations against the settlements of the border. They induced Colonel William Campbell of Virginia to join them. Campbell had under him a body of four hundred men, and Sevier and Shelby, to gain his hearty coöperation, elected him commander of the united forces. Under his leadership, and after having received reinforcements sufficient to give them about fifteen hundred men, they performed one of the most brilliant feats of the war. Ferguson was at Gilbert-town when he heard of the impending onslaught of the enraged mountaineers. He had threatened to burn their houses and destroy their settlements unless they returned to their allegiance, and had advanced as far as Gilbert-town in the apparent execution of his threats. Campbell's command consisted of four hundred Virginians which he had raised, about five hundred men under Sevier and Shelby, about four hundred under Colonel Cleveland, of Wilkes County, N. C., and nearly four hundred under James Williams from South Carolina. Ferguson was almost entirely dependent upon Tory troops. Appreciating the danger of an encounter between a body of men smarting under defeat and notorious for their bravery and a body of men notorious for their lack of it, Ferguson manœuvred to gain time for reinforcements to arrive from Cornwallis, to whom he wrote praying for assistance. He retreated from Gilbert-town to the Cowpens, crossing the main Broad River and again at Dear's Ferry, and pushed forward to King's Mountain, hoping to unite with Cornwallis. Campbell pursued him without intermission, stopping but once for refreshments, in the face of a driving rain that drenched his men to the skin. Ferguson had selected his position with admirable foresight. It was a comparatively isolated point, whose crest could not be approached from any side without encountering the direct fire of those on top. One who had been in the wars of Napoleon praised the skill of the officer who selected a place for which nature had provided such strategic advantages. Ferguson himself gave it the name of King's Mountain in honor of his sovereign, and declared that all the "rebels out of hell" could not drive him from it. Campbell's plan of attack was to surround Ferguson on all sides and prevent him from concentrating an army. The two regiments of Shelby and Campbell himself were sent directly up the sides of the mountain to divert the enemy, while Sevier and the rest surrounded them. Ferguson, finding himself in the midst of a baptism of fire, unable to keep his men steady, realized the hopelessness of resistance. But his courage was as desperate as his generalship was skillful. Time after time he rallied his men. The well-practiced aim of the American marksmen mowed them down. He charged with the bayonet, but his men refused to follow. He ordered them to mount and rode himself along the line, but they fell as fast as they mounted, and the survivors finally refused to move. Ferguson had only been wounded in the hand. He carried a silver whistle as a signal of encouragement to his soldiers. Resistance became hopeless. De Peyster, his second in command, prayed him to surrender, but he refused. A white flag was raised and he pulled it down. A second time it was lifted and he cut it down. De Peyster again entreated him to surrender, but he declared he would never surrender to "a damned set of banditti." The Americans soon noticed that the whistle was the centre of the most active resistance, and in a few minutes afterwards it was silenced forever. Ferguson was killed and De Peyster almost immediately surrendered. All the British were captured, about eight hundred in all, and fifteen hundred stands of arms. The wagons and supplies were burnt, and fearing Cornwallis, who was in Mecklenburgh County near the Catawba, the mountaineers made a forced march and escaped to the mountains. They had, however, struck a decisive blow, and the battle of King's Mountain has always figured in American history as the turning-point of the war for independence. It came after the disasters of Charleston and Savannah and Camden, and was the cause that the advocates of American freedom did not despair of the republic. It threw Cornwallis back upon his base of supplies in South Carolina, and it forced the evacuation of North Carolina. Time was gained for hope, for thought, for reorganization, for renewed resistance. The battle of King's Mountain connects the history of Tennessee with Bunker Hill and the ancient history of the United States. A sword and a pair of pistols were by the General Assembly of North Carolina voted to Sevier and Shelby for their part in this memorable affair. A more substantial recognition of their services was the resolution passed by the General Assembly in February, 1781, calling on them by name to urge those who had formerly served under them again to take up arms for their native State and the common cause. But the latter were unable to heed the call. They were in the midst of a war with the Indians, and could not leave their homes. Subsequently General Greene entered into correspondence with Sevier with a view to securing the Watauga soldiers for his army. Eventually Sevier raised two hundred men and joined Marion. Later still, Shelby and the Sullivan County men joined their old friends under the Swamp Fox, and both took part in the closing scenes of the great war.[1]

[1] Ramsey's indignation is excited by a sneer of Sims, that Shelby and his men left Marion before the object of the war was attained. This was scarcely a matter of reproach in view of the fact that the war was generally regarded as practically at an end, that Shelby's men had only been enlisted for sixty days, that they had already overstayed their time by several weeks, and that the Indians were threatening their homes with destruction. In addition to this, a large number of them actually did stay.

CHAPTER VIII.

SEVIER'S INDIAN WARS.

AFTER the battle of King's Mountain in 1780, Sevier, whose ever watchful eye was never allowed to wander from the settlements of which he may have been considered in lawyer's phrase the *guardian ad litem*, sent forward a messenger to ascertain the condition of those at home and the attitude of the Indians. He was informed that a large body of them were preparing to invade the settlements. He at once marched hurriedly home, made preparations for organizing a large force, and taking with him a company of a hundred men, pushed forward the day after his return to meet the main body of the invaders. He came upon them at Boyd's Creek and routed them. The promptness of the act saved the settlement from an Indian warfare and made their country the field of battle. He formed a camp on French Broad and waited for reinforcements. He crossed the Little Tennessee, and burned every town between the Hiwassee and the Tennessee rivers, including Chilhowee. At Tellico a treaty of peace was made as to the adjacent villages; but Sevier had passed through all the phases of Indian warfare, and he understood all the intricacies of Indian subtilty and Indian cunning. From Tellico he pushed forward to the village of Hiwassee and found it deserted. He destroyed it. He pushed forward to the Look-Out towns, the scattered villages where dwelt the bulk of the Chickamaugas, and destroyed them. He also destroyed all crops and supplies and drove off or killed all living animals. From the

Chickamauga towns he continued his march southward towards the mouth of the Coosa and to the flats of pine and cypress that are found upon its lower banks. He found it a country of surpassing beauty and filled with clusters of wigwams, known to the earlier chroniclers as towns. They had not expected to be approached by the whites. Sevier had a large force under him. Perhaps years might elapse before the opportunity would be so favorable for striking a blow — one which would crush and annihilate. He laid his hand heavily upon them. It was a barbarous mode of warfare. This he knew. No one, indeed, was more generous and kind-hearted than he. In many respects he is one of the heroes of our history, a veritable Knight Templar. But this was not a contest of knight errantry. It was the grim struggle for existence. The fittest alone could survive. If his mode of warfare was barbarous, he was waging war against barbarians, brave, cruel, relentless, and treacherous, without any of the things which civilization gave except its engines of destruction. Sevier was not the man to trifle with his task. Indian incursions could only be stopped by exterminating the Indians. Hence he tried to exterminate them. General Sheridan in the valley of Virginia was not more thorough. Every grain of corn was destroyed. Everything which could be used was burned, broken, or carried away. Every wigwam received the torch. Every boat was sunk. Nothing was spared except a few helpless human lives. A British agent was shot and his body left unburied. But few prisoners were taken; enough to exchange, but no more. The Indians soon made peace. Sevier, however, knew that the end would never be until the Indians were no more, and he established and garrisoned stations or forts along the frontier.

The year following, depredations were committed upon the settlements by bands of Indians from a region where Sevier had not before penetrated. He immediately collected a force to invade their country again. He penetrated to the head-waters of the Little Tennessee and surprised and captured a town called Tuckasejah. He slew fifty Indian braves and captured a large number of women and children. Following his invariable rule of warfare, he destroyed all their corn and burnt all their villages. The settlement of the country was progressing with steady regularity. When Sevier returned from his campaign of 1780 against the Indians, he found along the banks of the French Broad numbers of new cabins and tracts of freshly cleared lands. The limits of the three original settlements were being broadened. The lines of division established by treaty for Indian lands were being overstepped, and each encroachment excited the same feelings of revenge and hatred which had already made red the annals of American colonization. The frontier settlements had no desire to put a stop to them. The State was unable to do so. North Carolina was forced by the logic of circumstances to adopt the same line of policy towards the Indians which the United States have since adopted. Individual settlers were allowed to encroach until they became too powerful to remove, and gifts and treaties were then resorted to in order to remove the Indians. In 1782, Governor Martin, in a letter to Colonel Sevier, says: "I am distressed with the repeated complaints of the Indians respecting the daily intrusions of our people on their lands beyond the French Broad River. The Indian goods are not yet arrived from Philadelphia, through the inclemency of the late season; as soon as they will be in the State, I shall send them to the Great Island and hold a treaty with the Cherokees." This was in 1782, in the spring. In the autumn of the same year, the Indians still complained to Governor Martin that the people from Nollichucky were daily pushing them out fo their lands, and that they had built houses within one day's walk of their towns. They said with pathetic directness and simplicity, "We don't want to quarrel with our elder brother; we therefore hope our elder brother will not take our lands from us that our father gave us because he is stronger than we are. We are the first people that ever lived on this land; it is ours, and why will our elder brother take it from us?" They complained that those who encroached had not been removed, and they pray that Colonel Sevier, "who is a good man," be sent to have them all removed. But those who encroached were not removed, the goods were not sent, and in the same month Sevier retaliated for some minor aggression of a few straggling Chickamaugas by again invading the Cherokee country with rifle and flame.

But not all recorded events of those times were of such evil complexion. The better instincts which nature has implanted in every human bosom occasionally asserted themselves, and in the general gloom we occasionally catch glimpses of things that are gentler and more humane. On one occasion the supply of corn in the Nollichucky settlement gave out. Two adventurous oarsmen went down in canoes for the purpose of bartering supplies and trinkets for maize. They reached a village called Coiatee in safety and went ashore. They were stopped by some Indians, who received them with evident surprise and suspicion, still further increased by finding rifles hidden under some clothing in the boat. It is probable that Jeremiah Jack and William Rankin would never have related the adventure but for the interposition of Nancy Ward, the same who had saved the settlement on a previous occasion. She succeeded in placating the Indians, who, with the impulse of children, went to the opposite extreme, loaded the canoe with corn, and sent them rejoicing to their friends.

CHAPTER IX.

CEDED BY NORTH CAROLINA.

ABOUT this time the District of Salisbury was divided by the General Assembly, and Washington and Sullivan, with several other counties, were made a new district by the name of Morgan District. A court of oyer and terminer and general gaol delivery was directed to sit at Jonesboro for Washington and Sullivan counties. John Sevier was clerk. The General Assembly of North Carolina in 1783 gave a renewed impulse to emigration by reopening the land office which had been closed in 1781. In 1784 the settlement had been extended to Long Creek. The court of quarter sessions of Washington County in this year gave permission to erect a mill on that stream. In the same year we meet with cabins along the banks of the Little and Big Pigeon, and a few settlers had even ventured as far as Boyd's Creek. The class of emigrants now coming in was better provided with the initial material for wealth and prosperity. The new road into Burke County allowed the passage of wagons. Men of greater family and of larger means could settle in the new country. Houses were built at greater distances from the forts, which till then had been the centres of population as well as religion and learning. An "old field school" appeared here and there, and occasionally the traveler, as he passed a log cabin, could see a row of tawny heads and hear the cosmopolitan *hic-hæc-hoc* which betokened the first glimmer of mental activity in a community where "book larnin" was ranked infinitely below wood-craft, and where an accurate aim with the rifle was more ardently appreciated than a thorough knowledge of classical antiquities. The friction which comes from the rubbing together in daily contact of many minds and characters was beginning to furbish the people. The feeling of dependence in local affairs which precedes the desire of independence in the larger section was strong. It was gradually embracing settlement after settlement, creeping from fort to fort, from valley to valley. There was a recognized diversity of interests existing between the young and unnamed settlements and the older community of North Carolina. People began to recall the time when the Watauga Association was a kind of sovereignty, and when its members dreamed of having its head appointed by the King himself. The consciousness which in the individual is called the beginning of manhood, but which in a people is called rebellion or independence according to the point of view of the historian, was gradually stealing out from Jonesboro through the valleys and along the hills among all the people. They began to recognize that North Carolina did nothing for them but dispose of their lands for its debts. All the rest was accomplished through agents and with material furnished by the settlers. But as yet this feeling was dormant. It was soon aroused into life and activity.

It has already been pointed out that the Watauga settlement occupied a peculiar position in the colonial history of this country, and that like Connecticut it grew into a determinate form of government free from extraneous control or influence. But Connecticut had succeeded by the wise policy of its controlling forces in becoming an independent unit. The Watauga settlement, unable to cope with the hostile forces around it, had been compelled voluntarily to surrender its autonomy in order to find protection in union with a larger and a stronger organization. But the surrender, although voluntary, failed to accomplish the effect it was designed to accomplish. The old

Watauga people, remembering the achievements of Sevier and Shelby and the glory of King's Mountain, and recognizing no adequate return, felt sore and belittled. They were keenly alive to any lack of appreciation, and North Carolina was too strongly immersed in troubles of its own to have much thought of a handful of men beyond the mountains.

In the April session of 1784, the General Assembly of North Carolina, in accordance with the recommendation of Congress itself as well as with the dictates of a far-seeing and enlightened statesmanship, imitated the example of Virginia and New York, and ceded to the United States all the territory which is now the State of Tennessee. This of course included all the settlements. The condition of the cession was its acceptance by Congress within two years. Until Congress should have accepted the ceded territory, the jurisdiction of North Carolina over it was to remain in every respect the same as heretofore. The Hillsboro land office was closed. North Carolina was in reality weary of the empty honor of having as a part of herself a territory which paid no taxes, which made constant requisition for supplies, which demanded almost a standing army for its protection, and which expected to be reimbursed for the expenses incurred in defending itself. The relations were not unlike those which now exist between England and Canada.

When the question of cession was first broached, it was accepted by the four representatives of the western counties at Hillsboro, as well as by those who proposed it as the natural and legitimate solution of a complex problem. No one apparently dreamed of opposition on the part of the settlers themselves, and the news of the passage was first brought to the settlement by the representatives who had voted for it. There is no reason to think that the Watauga people had any objection to the cession. On the contrary, they desired a dissolution of the irksome bonds which bound them to North Carolina, and were ripe for dissolution. The objection was against the manner of cession and its conditions. Those most interested were not consulted, though this might have been pardoned in view of the fact that their representatives were present and consenting. But the main cause of complaint was that North Carolina had left them without any form of government for two years. Some pretended to believe that no provision had been made for asserting the sovereignty of the State during the interval. But all knew that whatever may have been the provisions of the bill, the reality was a worse state of things than had existed before.

A storm of indignation swept through the entire settlement. The Watauga pride had been cut to the quick. North Carolina was bitterly reviled, and the most extravagant denunciations of her ingratitude and tyranny were heard. No terms of reproach were too severe, no threats were regarded as foreshadowing steps towards an impossible revenge. Even the most unprejudiced, even those who regarded the popular indignation as in a measure a ridiculous ebullition of local vanity, were alarmed by the impending contingency of two years of lawlessness and disorder. The impression was general and well founded that North Carolina would trouble herself but little about the administration in a section which was soon to pass from her control. The most pressing evil was the lack of a proper judiciary or of an available militia organization. The Superior Court alone had jurisdiction of felonies, and no judge for the western district had ever been appointed. Only a brigadier-general could call out the entire militia of a district, and there was at that time no brigadier-general. An Indian war was always an impending contingency. There was no adequate military organization, no method of compulsory enlistment, no means of collecting taxes. It was confidently expected, and with reason, that the country would again be the resort of the thriftless and the lawless — the vagabond and the assassin. The people regarded themselves without government, and, true to the traditions of their race, they sought the solution of the difficulty in their own resources. As naturally as they spoke the language of England, they turned to the laws of England.

It is one of the noteworthy facts in the history of institutions that the possessors of English tradition always begin with the first primal germ of local self-government at hand, be it court leet, court of quarter sessions, township, county, school district, or military company, and build upward. The Watauga people had nothing so convenient as the militia companies, and they began with them as representing a more minutely varied constituency than the county court. Each company elected two representatives, and the representatives so elected in each county formed themselves into a committee, and the three committees of Washington, Sullivan, and Greene counties met as a kind of impromptu or temporary legislature, and decided to call a general convention to be elected by the people of the different counties. This convention met on the 23d of August, 1784, at Jonesboro. John Sevier was elected president, and Landon Carter, secretary. John Sevier is the most prominent name in Tennessee history, and within these limits and upon this field he is the most brilliant military and civil figure this State has ever produced. Jackson attained a larger fame upon a broader field of action, and perhaps his mental scope may appear to fill a wider horizon to those who think his statesmanship equal to his generalship. But the results he accomplished affected the history of Tennessee only in so far as it formed a part of the United States. Sevier, however, was purely a Tennessean. He fought for Tennessee, he defined its boundaries, he watched over and guarded it in its beginning, he helped form it, and he exercised a decisive influence upon its development. It is safe to say that without Sevier the history of Tennessee would in many important respects not be what it now is.

He came of a Huguenot family named Xavier, though his immediate ancestors were from England, and the infusion of French blood gave him all the vivacity, impetuosity, ardent sympathies, and suave bearing which are popularly supposed to be characteristic of that nation. In personal appearance he was rather tall, erect, and even when young inclined to robustness. He had the quick flash of eye and the hasty temper of the impetuous character. He excelled in the manly accomplishments of the age and surroundings in which he lived. As a horseman he had no equal, and he was fond of showing his craft to the best advantage by riding an animal of temper and mettle. In the art of Indian warfare he had no equal, and he never met a reverse. Mad Anthony Wayne was not a greater terror to the Indians of the Miami than was Sevier to the Indians of the Cumberland and the Tennessee. His rule of tactics was extreme caution in the absence or concealment of the enemy, reckless impetuosity in their presence. Governor Blount on one occasion declared that "his name carried more terror to the Cherokees than an additional regiment would have done." To his men he evinced that suave cordiality and well-judged familiarity characteristic of all the great captains of the world. His enthusiasm, his personal daring, his resolute quickness, his knightly disposition, made him the idol of his soldiers and his neighbors. His tenderness to his wife and his generosity to his children were proverbial. His house was always open, and nearly all of his expeditions against the Indians were partly at his own expense or the expense of the family. He was popularly known as "Nollichucky Jack," and the grim mountaineers worshiped him with an extravagance of adoration. They loved him with a warm, almost intense, personal regard which had grown from the time when with Robertson he successfully defended the Watauga fort against the largest band of Indians that had ever invaded the settlement, to the time when he had crushed them at Boyd's Creek. Sevier was not skilled in the learning of books, but of the life around him he was a thorough master. He could read the woods and the rivers, and the minds and the thoughts of men, and he knew how to use his knowledge. This was sufficient. But it must not be thought that he lacked the rudiments of education. He could write well and forcibly, and though a "spelling bee" of the present day might have put him to the blush, he could spell as well as the average. His chief claim to a higher order of ability is justified by his clear vision of the present needs of his people, and of the future requirements of the State whose greatness he foresaw. He was one of the Committee of Five in the Watauga Association. He saw the necessity of a union between Watauga and North Carolina until the former had sufficient strength to maintain itself against outward encroachments. He wrote the petition for annexation, and he secured its adoption by the Congress of North Carolina. He saw the necessity of keeping the British troops from the young settlements. If Ferguson had once passed the Appalachian chain he would have been met with fire and sword. His very mode of warfare made manifest his statesmanship. Of all the men of his time, he alone foresaw and had a determinate idea of the limits of the future State. He foresaw and denounced the ruinous restrictions with which Jay's proposition in reference to the navigation of the Mississippi would cripple the commerce of the Mississippi valley and of the young State about to be formed between North Carolina and the Great River. He recognized what should be the logical enlargement of the three original settlements. He realized the necessity of a sure and compact growth, and he advocated only such purchases from the

Indians as could be secured by settlement when purchased. He was frequently termed by the Indians "Treaty Maker," and he figured in every treaty of importance which was made until the appearance of Andrew Jackson upon the stage of state history.

It is partly due to the latter that Sevier has been overclouded. Jackson appeared when Sevier had practically accomplished the work, and he reaped the reward. Jackson was a bitter man in his temper, relentless and unforgiving. Sevier was a school-boy in disposition, oscillating between the tear forgot as soon as shed and the sunshine of the breast.[1] He could harbor no malice. He was quick and self-assertive in defense. Jackson was quick and self-assertive in attack. The former was a leader in battle, the foremost of his soldiers. The latter was a leader in war, and his soldiers to him were implements of war, to attack here, to retreat there, to storm a strong hold, to carry a height, to hold a fort. Sevier was a great fighter, Jackson was a great general. The writer has given more space to the character of Sevier than he perhaps would otherwise have been able to do in a work of this size because of the undeserved neglect into which he has fallen in popular esteem. Jackson is a popular figure both in history and among the people. Sevier is almost entirely unknown to the great mass of the people of the State, whose reading goes no farther than the magazine and the newspaper. But among historians the reverse holds good. Parton has all but ruined Jackson's reputation among the thoughtful. Sumner sinks him almost to the level of a "guerrilla chief" and a cross-road politician. But Sevier has been treated with remarkable indulgence by historians and writers. Haywood, Wheeler, Flint, Ramsey, Monette, and others all recognize different points in his character, his mind, and his career to praise and exalt. To say that he was in his sphere a

[1] Gray.

statesman of the first order of ability, and that as a warrior he was excelled by none who engaged in the same mode of warfare, and that he never lost a battle, claims for him a high place among the great men of the world. Only he acted on a small stage. There can be no doubt that he is the greatest figure in Tennessee history, and there is as little doubt that outside the mountains and valleys of East Tennessee he is, from a popular standpoint, as little known as if he had been one of the shepherd kings of Egypt.

When the convention at Jonesboro elected him leader of the movement to form a new State, they did so with a full recognition of his character. He was known as one who stormed his way through the world, and when he accepted the leadership, those who knew his fiery resolution realized the crisis which had called him to the front. The deputies felt with general satisfaction that the impending responsibility had been shifted upon shoulders amply able to bear it. An intimation of his ability to act well the part assigned him was the conservative reluctance which he evinced to proceed to extreme measures. He favored the end aimed at most heartily, but he reprobated too great haste. After North Carolina removed the most crying of the grievances complained of by the western people, and after it became apparent that provision had been made for maintaining at least the semblance of sovereignty until Congress accepted the cession, Sevier advised a cessation of the movement. When his advice was disregarded, he threw all hesitation aside, and, like the Southern Unionist at the South when the war began, entered into the contest with earnest zeal.

CHAPTER X.

STATE OF FRANKLIN FORMED.

THE data upon which rests our knowledge of the history of the State of Franklin are so meagre that it is impossible to follow accurately the progress of events. It is supposed that the convention which met at Jonesboro adopted the resolution to form a "separate and distinct State, independent of the State of North Carolina, at this time."[1] William Cocke was appointed on a committee, either at this or a subsequent meeting, to prepare a plan of association. The one reported was simple and directly suited to the exigencies of the case. Provision was made for the calling of a future convention in which representation was to be according to companies. It was further resolved that clerks having the bonds of public officers should hold the same until some mode should be prescribed for having their accounts fairly and properly liquidated with North Carolina. Those holding public moneys were required to render due account of them. The first symptom of internal dissension became manifest in the action of Samuel Doak and Richard White, who entered their protest against both these resolutions because, in their opinion, contrary to law.

The plan of holding a convention to form a constitu-

---

[1] A discrepancy between the names of the members who were elected to the first Jonesboro convention and those who voted for this resolution seems to indicate that this action may have been taken at a subsequent convention. The proceedings were found in manuscript among the papers of Rev. Samuel Houston, but bear no date.

tion and provide a name for the new State was then adopted, and Jonesboro appointed as the place of meeting. Each county was to send five delegates. The meeting adjourned, having fairly inaugurated the contest with North Carolina, which still claimed jurisdiction until the expiration of the two years, and whose pride was aroused by the proceedings of the Watauga people. But in the mean while opposition began to develop itself. John Tipton grew lukewarm. Some were opposed to any steps being taken at all, and a great many were opposed to any movement in the direction of separation until all reasonable means had been exhausted in an attempt to accomplish the separation from the parent State in the more legitimate channels of peaceful agitation. The natural reverence for established institutions, the fear of violent or radical change, anticipations of unforeseen evils, personal reasons of self-interest dependent upon the existing order of things, a lack of local sensitiveness, all tended to create a party more or less opposed to the movement just inaugurated. Their opposition was still further increased by the action of the legislature of North Carolina, which repealed the act of cession, formed the western counties, including Davidson, into a judicial district by the name of Washington District, and appointed an assistant judge and an attorney-general for the Superior Court to be held at Jonesboro. The militia of Washington District was formed into a brigade, and John Sevier was appointed brigadier-general.

For a time it was supposed that this would terminate the agitation in favor of a new State. Even John Sevier thought this was the end. In a letter to Kennedy of Greene County, he says: " I conclude this step will satisfy the people with the old State, and we shall pursue no further measures as to a new State." But the revolution could not be turned backwards. There had been too much neglect on the part of the mother, or, as many now said, the step-mother State. Many of the reasons which justified the secession of America from England justified the secession of the western counties from North Carolina. One chief cause of indignation was the fact of being ceded to the confederacy. It must not be forgotten that the United States of America were then a collection of independent States, not unlike the principalities which professed a nominal allegiance to the descendants of Frederick Barbarossa, bound together only by treaties which could not be enforced. The general government possessed none of the attributes of administrative strength. The public debt at the close of the war amounted to $42,000,000, and Congress was unable to pay even the interest upon it. Over $300,000,000 in bills of credit had been issued during the first few years of the war, and in 1780 they had ceased to circulate. It was considered a double disgrace to be the slave of an imbecile.

When the new convention met John Sevier was elected president, and F. A. Ramsey, the father of the historian, was elected secretary. A plan of government was drawn up and adopted and ordered to be submitted to the action of a convention chosen by the people, which was to assemble in the latter part of the year at Greeneville. In the mean time, however, it was deemed expedient to make provision for a temporary form of government, and delegates to the legislature of the new and as yet unnamed State were ordered to be elected according to the laws of North Carolina. This legislature met in the early part of 1785, and was the first legislative body that ever assembled in this State. The name of the speaker of the Senate was Landon Carter, and of the clerk, Thomas Talbot. The speaker of the House of Commons, so called, was William Cage, and of the clerk, Thomas Chapman. John Sevier was elected governor. David Campbell was elected judge of the Superior Court. The state officers were secretary of state, treasurer, surveyor-general, attorney-general, and brigadier-general of militia. The governor was given a kind of cabinet, called Council of State. County courts were established in both old and new counties. Greene County was divided into three, and two new counties, Caswell and Sevier, erected. A new county, Spencer, was also taken from Sullivan and Greene, and Wayne from Washington. Justices of the peace were appointed. Taxes and poll taxes were levied, and were allowed to be paid in the products of the country at a fixed valuation. Raccoon and fox skins were valued at one shilling and six pence. Clean beaver skins, six shillings. Bacon well cured, six pence per pound. Good country-made butter, one shilling per pound. Good distilled rye whiskey, two shillings six pence per gallon. The salaries of the officers were to be paid in kind or in money of the State of Franklin. Over twenty articles were enumerated and valued, and were such as would pass from hand to hand almost as readily as currency. Acts were passed for the promotion of learning in the county of Washington, to establish a militia, to procure a great seal for the State, to direct the method of electing members of the General Assembly, to ascertain the value of gold and silver, foreign coin, and the paper currency in circulation in North Carolina, and to declare the same a lawful tender in the State of Franklin, to ascertain the salaries of the public officers, to ascertain the power and authorities of the judges of the different courts and the like.

Governor Sevier, wishing to have his hands free for the contest which he saw impending, at once assembled the Cherokees in order to make treaties with them by which their depredations might be obviated, at least until the difficulty with North Carolina had been definitely settled. He met them at the mouth of Dumplin Creek, on the north bank of the French Broad. The Indians ceded all the lands south of the Holston and the French Broad to the dividing ridge between Little River and the Tennessee, and Sevier promised to prevent any further encroachments upon them. He made a speech deprecating and deploring the animosities existing between the white and the red man. In addition to this, nearly all who had held county offices under North Carolina were continued in the enjoyment of their honors.

CHAPTER XI.

STATE OF FRANKLIN.

WHEN the news of the separation reached North Carolina, Governor Martin sent Major Samuel Henderson as a kind of confidential agent to the new State to learn the true extent of the disaffection. But before Henderson's return, Governor Martin received an official declaration of independence signed by the Governor and General Assembly of the new State. Martin, in reply, issued a manifesto to the inhabitants of Franklin, in which he calmly and dispassionately reviews and refutes the various causes of discontent which had been advanced to justify separation. One of the most decisive had been the failure of the government to send goods promised the Indians in payment of their lands, in consequence of which failure the latter had committed serious depredations. The goods in question had merely been delayed by the act of cession, and would be delivered in due time. The hostilities of the Indians were attributed to provocations given by the settlers, notably the murder of one of their chiefs by Hubbard. The manifesto closed with a threat: "North Carolina's resources are not yet so exhausted or her spirits damped but she may take satisfaction for this great injury received, regain her government over the revolted territory, or render it not worth possessing." The name of the chief to whose murder Governor Martin alluded in his manifesto was Untoola or Gun Rod. To the whites he was known as Butler. The circumstances attending his death have been preserved, and give us a vivid picture of one phase of the life of those days.

There lived in Watauga a man by the name of James Hubbard, a wild, vindictive character, whose parents had been murdered by the Indians whilst he was a boy, and the passion of whose life was an unending and deadly revenge. He was just such a character as we are familiar with in the highly-wrought sketches of Mr. Sylvanus Cobb and the "New York Weekly." Hubbard possessed, in an eminent degree, the coolness, courage, and wily cunning of the white man turned savage. He could practice and had practiced for years, and successfully, the strategies of single-handed warfare, and excelled the boldest and shrewdest of the race he hated. The Indians knew him and feared him more than any man of his time, not excepting, perhaps, Simon Kenton and Daniel Boone. In an encounter with Butler, Hubbard had disarmed him, and harboring, perhaps, an unusually bitter hatred, had taken his weapon from him and sent him back to his people. This was a disgrace so degrading, so humiliatingly low, that a white man cannot adequately grasp its extent. The death of him who had caused the disgrace could alone wash it even partially out. During a cessation of hostilities between the Cherokees of the upper towns and the settlers, corn became scarce. The influx of emigrants had been too rapid. Several parties visited the Indian towns to obtain a supply, — among the rest, Hubbard and a companion. Hubbard selected the village of which Butler had been chief, hoping perhaps to gloat over him in his degradation. Butler heard of his approach and quietly slipped away from Citico with a friend. He met Hubbard and his companion leading their horses, which were heavily laden with articles to be bartered for corn. Butler and his companion were on horseback, the former armed with a double-barreled rifle. As soon as Hubbard saw the two approaching, he put his associate on his guard. As Butler rode up he demanded, with an air of insult, the object of the visit to his people's country. Hubbard, appreciating the need of the settlers for corn, and desiring to avoid anything which would bring on a renewal of hostilities, answered civilly that he had come to buy corn, and showed an empty sack. He at the same time drew forth a bottle of whiskey, and invited Butler and his friend to take a drink. Butler made no reply, but gazed at his enemy with burning eyes. No other word was uttered. In showing the bag and taking out the bottle, Hubbard had leaned his rifle against a small tree near him, hoping to propitiate Butler by this act of confidence. The latter now attempted to ride up to Hubbard, evidently with the design of getting between him and his gun. Hubbard quietly laid his hand upon the muzzle of his rifle. He turned calmly towards Butler as if to invite his attack by his own composure. There was an air of lofty assurance and of self-confidence in his manner which reminded the savage of the former contest. Blind with rage, he aimed a blow at his enemy, who adroitly avoided it. Butler then raised his gun and fired. Hubbard caught the sight and the line of the bullet and bent his head to one side. The bullet cut a scar in his temple. Butler had immediately wheeled his horse, and was eighty yards distant when Hubbard pulled his trigger. Butler fell from his horse wounded but not dead. His companion escaped. Hubbard, who was brave but not generous, raised his foe and leaned him against a tree. Having failed to extract any information from Butler, and irritated by his taunts, he cleft his skull with his rifle barrel. The Indians retaliated, and to this, rather than the stoppage of the goods, Governor Martin attributed the Indian hostilities.

The temperate tone of Governor Martin's manifesto gained new adherents for the cause of North Carolina, but the general sentiment of the people still turned towards independence as the least of several evils. All admitted that permanent connection with North Carolina was out of the question. If ceded by North Carolina the public lands would go to enrich the federal treasury. If admitted as an independent State or Colony with the rest, these would accrue to its own benefit. This reason outweighed all others for the time, and the large majority of the people remained firm in their position, despite Governor Martin's manifesto. Having assumed this attitude, they felt in some degree irritated by the threats he had uttered. Sevier's reply to Martin's manifesto was addressed to Governor Caswell, his successor. It was decisive, direct, and uncompromising. Without indulging in the rhetorical generalities which distinguish most official documents of that day, he stated forcibly and clearly the views of the question which obtained in Franklin, and answered categorically the arguments in Martin's manifesto.

Governor Caswell's reply [1] was well calculated to allay irritation by waiving any further discussion of the question until the meeting of the North Carolina Assembly. As regards the distribution of goods intended for the Indians, Governor Caswell expressed his readiness to distribute them in case the militia under Sevier's command be placed under his control. Sevier in his reply ignored this proposition, but informed the governor of North Carolina that the legislature of the State of Franklin had appointed a commissioner to wait upon the North Carolina Assembly. The people of the new State had not ceased their preparations, and by the time the assembly of North Carolina met, had strengthened and rendered more compact their internal organization. An attempt was made at this time by the inhabitants of Virginia along the Washington District border, to secede from Virginia and unite with the new State, but it was frustrated by the prompt action of Patrick Henry, who was then governor.

In the mean time an active discussion was carried on in the young State, relative to the proposed form of constitution. A committee appointed at the last convention had

[1] Caswell succeeded Martin.

drawn up a constitution, which was, no doubt, intended to inaugurate a radical departure in American constitutional history. But when made public, it met with universal objection. It is too long to be given in full, and occupies too small a position in the history of institutions to deserve more than a cursory review. It was a visionary scheme, without coherence, and possible only in the minds of those who had an imperfect understanding of the science of government. It is sufficient to say that there was to be but one legislative body, and that only land-owners were eligible. Lawyers, ministers of the gospel, and doctors were ineligible. The name of the State was Frankland. A university was to be erected, endowed with lands, and a tax laid on every pound of indigo carried out of the State, every barrel of flour, and every hogshead of tobacco. These were the chief innovations and caused its defeat. The very name of Frankland sounded odd and strange. Why so many checks and counter-checks, it was asked? Why should there be no senate? Why should doctors be excluded from the legislature? Lawyers are supposed to be the best judges of law, why should they be excluded from law-making? These and countless other objections caused the overwhelming rejection of the new constitution, and when the convention assembled at Greeneville, in November, 1785, it was at once voted down. Sevier proposed the constitution of North Carolina, under which the State was being organized, and it was adopted with a few slight changes. The name of Franklin was retained in honor of Dr. Benjamin Franklin. The next step taken was to appoint William Cocke, afterwards senator from Tennessee, and one of the most eloquent orators of the Southwest, to present the constitution to Congress with a memorial requesting to be admitted as a State. However, Congress ignored both the message and the messenger. Shortly after the adoption of the constitution for the new State, the North Carolina Assembly met at Newbern and passed an act of oblivion in favor of those who would return to their allegiance, and invited the revolted counties to send representatives to the General Assembly of the parent State. The moderate tone of this act tended greatly to allay irritation, and increased the favorable impression made by Governor Martin's manifesto and Governor Caswell's letter. The reaction had set in, and reasons, which in the first moment of excitement had been regarded as of no importance, were now brought forward as new, unimpeachable by fair-minded logic, and conclusive upon all but fools and office-holders. In Washington County a senator and two representatives to the North Carolina General Assembly were elected on the third Friday of August, 1786. The names of those voting were enrolled, and from now on, says Haywood, opposition to the new State "put on a more solemn and determined aspect than it ever had done before." John Tipton was elected senator, and James Stuart and Richard White were elected to the House of Commons.

Tipton, even before his election, had gradually been coming forward as the leader of the North Carolina party. He had been one of the inaugurators of the new movement, and had been a member of nearly every meeting of elective delegates until the absolute formation of the government of the new State. He was a member of the convention of fifteen which had drafted the unfortunate constitution of the State of Frankland. This change of mind may have been caused by the logic of events, but it is more probable that the change was due to his jealousy of Sevier. The two men can scarcely be compared. Tipton was indeed a brave man, but he lacked intellectual force. Envy of Sevier's popularity was the ruling motive of his character. He was vindictive, relentless, and even malignant. One of the last acts of his official life was an attempt to destroy the reputation for honesty of Sevier, at that time governor of Tennessee. He lacked the ardent generosity and fiery impetuosity of the latter, though his anger was quickly and easily inflamed. He felt peculiarly fitted for command and the leadership of great enterprises. He had experienced the bitterness of seeing Sevier, year after year, called to take the lead in all civil as well as military crises. His hatred of Sevier was Indian-like in its intensity, and his threat to have him shot, after the collapse of the State of Franklin, was made with the determination of having it carried out. He was deterred only by appeals to his reason and his self-interest. He always thought of Sevier as one who had warped his career and reaped the reward which else would have fallen to his own share. After Robertson's departure, there was none who could have contested the leadership of the frontier with Tipton but Sevier.

When Sevier, upon receipt of his commission as brigadier-general of the newly erected district, stood upon the steps of Jonesboro court-house and advised the people to return to their allegiance, Tipton stood firm to the cause of the new State. But when Sevier, yielding to the dictates of his own inclinations and the persuasions of his friends, returned to the cause which it was popularly supposed he had deserted, Tipton wavered. When Sevier was elected governor of the new State, his rage knew no bounds. He allowed himself to be hurried into extremities of resistance to the new government which frequently caused the shedding of blood and possibly loss of life. He held court at Buffalo near Jonesboro, under the authority of the parent State. On one occasion, he entered the court-house at Jonesboro, captured the records, and turned the justices out of doors. He broke up a court sitting in Greeneville, under the authority of the new State. He had a personal altercation with Sevier on the streets of Jonesboro. When elections were held for the General Assembly of North Carolina, he was elected senator in the expectation of at last entering upon a career where he would no longer be thwarted by the magnetism of manner and the brilliancy of mind which the populace loved and admired in his rival.

After the election of Tipton, the contest became more spirited, though only those in high office appear, as a rule, to have taken a tragic view of it. To the people it was rather a matter to be decided by moral influence than an appeal to the ultimate arbitrament of force. The conflicts were for the most part with the fists, frequently resulting in minor mutilations. The sheriffs of the opposing factions were selected with reference to their physical prowess. There is no authentic record of death resulting from this cause. Bishop Asbury speaks of having heard of it, but nothing more definite has come down. Still, the confusion and anarchy were no less than if there had been frequent and deadly brawls. It was a daily occurrence for one faction to rob the other of the records of their county. Many valuable papers and deeds were thus lost. Marriages solemnized under the laws of one party were not recognized as valid by the other.[1] Executors and administrators were in despair, not knowing which court to account to. No one knew where to apply for probation of wills, the approval of bonds, the recording of deeds, the paying of taxes. As a result no taxes were paid at all. The new State, needing a medium of exchange having a more widely recognized element of negotiability than raccoon and beaver skins, gave Charles Robertson

---

[1] The State of Tennessee subsequently passed an act making valid marriages contracted under the authority of the State of Franklin. This perhaps is the origin of the statement made by several writers, that North Carolina passed an act to legalize the unions entered into by the earlier settlers, or "children of the forest," who, without law or gospel, agreed to live together as man and wife. No such act was ever passed by North Carolina, and I have been unable to find any proof of the existence of such unions. Preachers were among the earliest comers, as for instance, Cummings, Doak, Balch, Carrick, and Houston.

liberty to coin $30,000 in specie. War was levied against the Indians, and all the attributes of absolute sovereignty exercised. But the difficulties surrounding the new government were steadily growing greater and more decided. The reaction was more pronounced than ever, and the supporters of Sevier's administration remarked with acrimonious chagrin that the defection was most injurious among those who had helped found the young State. Sevier finally appointed Cocke and Campbell, the most able and respected of his adherents, commissioners to treat with the legislature of North Carolina for a separation, and to devise some means of extricating the new Commonwealth of Franklin from the increasing dangers which threatened its existence. Sevier sent them with a mild and civilly worded address to the Governor of North Carolina, but in no respect wavering in his attitude of determination to preserve the separate independence of the State which had made him its governor.

Judge Campbell, having suffered some personal injury, was unable to go, but sent a kind of diplomatic document in his stead, in which he reviewed the arguments of both sides, and urged the confusion which would arise in matters of litigation that had been decided by the courts of Franklin.

Cocke, however, made his way to Fayetteville, and, according to the custom of English parliamentary usage, was allowed to appear at the bar of the House of Commons of North Carolina and plead the cause he had come to represent.

Those who dwell with pleasure only on the grand and the sublime, and who see sublimity and grandeur only in the stupendous and the overpowering, will find Cocke's appearance before the legislature of North Carolina a very tame and colorless affair. It affected only a few thousand mountaineers beyond the Alleghanies. But to the true imagination, which sees grandeur in ideas, and sublimity in the destiny of a people, it will indeed seem to be one of the finest and most suggestive spectacles in the annals of American States. Cocke's speech had been carefully prepared, and it was feelingly delivered. In itself it deserves a high rank among the forensic displays of an age fertile in orators distinguished for the force, brilliancy, and passion of their oratory. The circumstances under which he spoke were full of contrasts. Many of his hearers were fresh from the battle-fields of the Revolution, where they had vindicated the principles for which he now sued. He pleaded the cause of a people, who, from small beginnings, had grown into a commonwealth, untried perhaps, and occupying a circumscribed province, but compact, self-reliant, and eager to vindicate its right to form a new State among the republics of the western world. They had gone into the wilderness; they had met and conquered, almost single-handed and alone, the fiercest and most warlike of the tribes who inhabited the Valley of the Mississippi. They had extorted the admiration of the greatest of American orators,[1] by their unflinching courage on every field of battle and against every foe. They had risked their lives to redeem from foreign subjection those who were now refusing them the right of making their own laws and regulating their own affairs. They had been as a bulwark for the Mother State against the attacks of a foe whose craft, cunning, and bloodthirsty barbarism were the terror of the American people. He dwelt upon every point whose emphasis would appeal favorably to any passion, sentiment, or thought of his hearers, — the reasons which had actuated those who had formed the new State, the dread of Indian hostilities, the neglect of the parent State, the conditional cession. He reviewed the position of those who in North Carolina had made the cession and then retracted it and pointed out its inconsistencies — throwing the Watauga people heedlessly

[1] Patrick Henry.

away without their consent, and now demanding that they
return against their will, granting them the right of becoming a State and then denying that they were able to become
one. He dwelt upon the distance of the Franklin people
from the home government, their exposed position, the impossibility of exercising promptly and efficiently the functions of government from the capitals of North Carolina,
the failure of that State to provide the means of defense
against either internal dissensions or external dangers.
Indians were not of the number of those who issue declarations before commencing hostilities and observe the
usages of civilized warfare. In the midst of peace, in the
gathering of harvests, the war-whoop is often heard when
least expected. But two courses were open. Either let
the parent State provide with the necessary generosity for
the urgent needs of the colony they held in the trammels
of an unwilling union, or let her give them free play for
the exercise of those qualities which had won them prosperity and given them strength without external aid,
counsel, or suggestion. Judging the future by the past,
he would not hesitate to say that the first was an improbable contingency. It remained for them to decide upon
the second.

Cocke's eloquence, however, failed to accomplish the
object of his mission. He modified, perhaps, the eagerness of the sentiment which demanded expiation for the
insult to offended sovereignty, and gained a few minor
concessions, but nothing more. The General Assembly at
once passed an act of oblivion, such as had been passed
once before, and also allowed those who had suffered injuries by decisions respecting property incompatible with
justice to have their common law remedy. Certain provisions were made as to officers in the revolted counties.
Those in office at the time of the revolt who were still incumbents were continued, but all others who had accepted
office under the State of Franklin were displaced, and

their positions were to be filled by appointments. The general indignation of the older inhabitants was excited by this last clause, as those who held offices under the State of Franklin were, as a rule, those who had been most conspicuous in the Indian and Continental wars. Judge Campbell, in a letter to Governor Caswell, says: "The majority of the people of Franklin proclaim, with a degree of enthusiastic zeal, against a reversion to your State. Indeed, I am at a loss to conjecture whether your Assembly wished us to revert; if so, why did they treat the old faithful officers of this country with so much contempt? Officers who have suffered in the common cause, who have been faithful in the discharge of the trust reposed in them, have been displaced without even the formality of a trial."

Evan Shelby was to be commander of the brigade. All taxes due and unpaid in the disaffected counties since 1794 were remitted. As a measure of conciliation, this last was the happiest stroke of policy possible under the circumstances, but as a measure of statesmanship it was a fatal blunder. This was among the first instances of that remission of taxes which became a standing feature of legislative history in Southwestern States deriving their laws and institutions from North Carolina. An overflow, a severe hurricane, a pestilence, any cause was sufficient to call forth from the afflicted locality a petition to be released from bearing its portion of the general burdens of government.

CHAPTER XII.

END OF THE STATE OF FRANKLIN.

One of the first acts of the legislature of Franklin had been to erect several new counties, one of which, lying west of the north fork of the Holston, had been taken from Sullivan County and named Spencer. The General Assembly, ignoring the nomenclature of its trans-Alpine or trans-Appalachian rival, had erected the same district or division of territory into a county and given it the name of Hawkins. After the remission of taxes, the North Carolina officials in Washington, Sullivan, and Hawkins Counties, both elective and appointive, gained a decided accretion of strength, and although the Franklin organization still continued, its adherents became disheartened, and either avoided conflicts with the North Carolina or Tipton men, or entered into the contest with much less eagerness and acridity than before. In Greene County, where Sevier then resided, no one was found willing to accept a North Carolina commission, and there alone the State of Franklin held undisputed sway.

There were still elements, however, of sufficient strength to leave the crisis one of imminent danger. The North Carolina legislature had adjourned, having passed such measures as it was supposed would quiet the agitation. But no provision had been made for the contingency of a failure. Practically the attempt to quell the revolt had failed. It would now be nearly a year before the reassembling of the North Carolina General Assembly; and those whose interests were at stake, and who foresaw, with feelings of the deepest apprehension, a continuance of the disorder and conflicts of the last year, welcomed with eager satisfaction a proposition of compromise, by which means a *modus vivendi* might be established until the meeting of the next General Assembly. The terms of the compromise had not been formulated, but the sentiment in favor of a compromise of some sort was so strong that even Sevier, to whom compromise was almost a degradation, was forced to yield to the popular clamor. This willingness received a strong impulse from the fact that a more compact form of union among all the States seemed imminent. Evan Shelby, a son of the hero of Kanawha[1] and lately appointed brigadier-general of the militia under North Carolina, was made the arbitrator, upon the suggestion of Governor Caswell. He and Sevier, with other and inferior officers, met on the 20th of March, 1787, and drew up articles of compromise. There was to be a cessation of all litigations not absolutely essential. The people were to pay taxes to the officers of either government. The jails of Franklin were also to receive prisoners committed by North Carolina justices, as if committed by Franklin justices. The western counties were to send delegates, with such instructions as they saw fit, to the next General Assembly of North Carolina, and to abide by the decision of that body in the matter of separation. This was signed by both Sevier and Shelby and sent to Governor Caswell. But those who held office under commissions from the governor of North Carolina were unwilling to recognize the validity of a compromise emanating from no legal tribunal and unsupported by any display of force. Confident of ultimate victory and hoping to reap the rewards of office, they repudiated the action of Shelby, and collected taxes, issued process, and exercised jurisdiction without regard to the policy of the measure or the dangers which might result from embittered popu-

[1] The older writers frequently spelled this Kenhawa.

lar feeling. The Franklin people retaliated in like manner, and the very measures which had been expressly designed to allay popular disturbance increased the vehemence of feeling and the hostile energy of the antagonists.

After the failure of the compromise became apparent, those in military command, not knowing what to expect, and perhaps not unwilling to reap some renown in so important a crisis, consulted together to devise some means of protecting the country. Tipton, Maxwell, and Hitchings, colonels respectively of Washington, Sullivan, and Hawkins, met at the house of Shelby on the 4th of May, 1787. In a kind of memorial addressed to Governor Caswell and written by Shelby himself, but which ignored the articles of compromise, they accuse the Franklin people of what, in the impeachment of an individual, would be called high crimes and misdemeanors.[1] They request that one thousand troops be sent, and suggest that Virginia, whose border counties had been on the verge of a similar secession, would be willing to coöperate with North Carolina.

Governor Caswell's reply to this was couched in a tone of dignified rebuke, and whilst abating in no respect the position of Carolina as insisting on a return to allegiance, he points out the proper measures to be adopted, to avoid the shedding of blood, to bring about an eventual settlement of the difficulty, and to induce the discordant elements to join together against the dreaded and treacherous foe, who along the lower banks of the rivers and in the depths of the forests was plotting a war of extermination against them. This letter to Shelby, which was a fine rebuke both to his unreasonable fear and to the rhodomontades of Hitchings,[2] was accompanied by an address

---

[1] Shelby's action in this matter is inexplicable. There is no proof that the Franklin party had violated the terms of the agreement.

[2] In a letter to Shelby, of April 12, 1787, he had said, "Cocke's party are getting very insolent. I expect in a few days I shall be

to the inhabitants of the four counties. In this he urged them to unite against the common foe, to abide by and maintain the laws of the sovereignty to whom they owed allegiance, and to await with patience the time when they may have so increased in wealth and numbers as to justify a separation. He added these significant words: " It is my opinion that it may be obtained at an earlier day than some imagine, if unanimity prevail among you." This was in reality the *coup de grace*.

The Franklin, or, as it had now become, the Sevier party, which had been losing the moral support of the more thoughtful population, and with this the strength of cohesion, greeted in this address of Governor Caswell's an opening for retreat. It was published on the 21st of May, 1787. On the 1st of March, 1788, Sevier's term of office as governor of the State of Franklin was to expire. This date may be regarded as the definite ending point of the State of Franklin. It was apparent to all except Sevier that the end was near. But the native energy of his character was stimulated by the bitterness which existed between Tipton and himself. Sevier cast about for some method to restore the failing courage of his friends. The State of Georgia, as early as 1784, had turned wistful eyes towards the country beyond the Tennessee River, and especially towards the Great Bend. Various attempts by various States and land companies had been made to take possession of this region but had been frustrated by the Indians. Sevier utilized this desire to form an alliance with Georgia, and agreed with that State to unite in first putting down a threatened uprising of the Creeks, and then in occupying the Great Bend of the Tennessee River. He expected this alliance to lend strength and dignity to his commonwealth. The emissary who perfected these arrangements was Major Elholm, one of

obliged to try their number." Shelby had inclosed this with the memorial to Governor Caswell.

Pulaski's band, and a man of courage, experience, and address. In the mean time the adherents of North Carolina were growing stronger, and even in Greene County delegates were elected to the North Carolina legislature. The North Carolina county courts in Washington, Sullivan, Hawkins, and even Greene had practically exclusive jurisdiction. Sevier's alliance with Georgia put him in a condition to request the mediation of that State. The original States possessed many more attributes of sovereignty than at present, and this stroke of diplomacy was not so fanciful as it would now appear. In fact, the closing scenes of the State of Franklin finely illustrate the fertility of Sevier's resources. But all failed. A brilliant campaign against the Indians might restore confidence and unite the people in opposition to the unreasonable tyranny of the parent State. This, too, was frustrated by the action of the federal Congress, which appointed three commissioners, one each for Georgia, North Carolina, and South Carolina, to treat with the Indians and to allay hostilities. This was the death-blow to Sevier's hopes and to his government. His most intimate friends deserte dhim, and even Campbell accepted the position of judge of the Superior Court of Washington District under North Carolina. Sevier tried to induce Evan Shelby to accept the governorship of Franklin as the one man who could carry the movement successfully forward.[1] Shelby declined. Sevier, bearing up against the world in arms, cast about for some refuge, and there are reasons for believing that at this time he entertained an idea of utilizing the enthusiasm of his troops by a campaign against the Spanish possessions in the valley of the Mississippi, in order to frustrate the negotiations then pending, the prevailing impression being that Jay's project of resigning the navigation of this stream to the Spaniards for a term of years would be accepted by Con-

[1] MS. letter of Sevier in Tennessee Historical Society Library.

gress. It was in keeping with the boldness and brilliant decisiveness of his character to regard as neither chimerical nor audacious an enterprise so full of danger, and so wide-reaching in its results. In a letter written about this time, he says: "Take my word for it, we shall be speedily in possession of New Orleans." Emanating from this, a report gained currency at the national capital that Sevier designed a withdrawal from the bands of the Federal Union in order to establish a new empire in the Southwest. An investigation was ordered but nothing treasonable was discovered. It is a matter of conjecture, but perhaps the *ignis fatuus* which lured the unstable and splendid ambition of Burr to a sad and untimely end may also have danced for the first time, even though fleetingly, before the eyes of the great Tennessean.

The last session of the legislature of Franklin was held in September, 1787. Several acts were passed, one for taking possession of the bend of the Tennessee, one opening a land office and directing the officers to receive peltry instead of money. The most important was one authorizing the election of two representatives to attend the legislature of North Carolina and make proper representations.

Members were elected in all the counties to the North Carolina legislature. Greene County sent David Campbell and Daniel Kennedy; Washington County sent John Tipton, James Stuart, and John Blair; Hawkins County sent Nathaniel Henderson and William Marshall; Sullivan sent Joseph Martin, John Scott, and George Maxwell. There was one county which sent James Robertson and Robert Hays, but whose formation has not yet been described. This was Davidson County. The assembly of North Carolina, to which the above-mentioned delegates were elected, passed acts of pardon and oblivion, directed all suits under the revenue laws to be dismissed, and granted an extension of time for the assessment of property. Sevier was left a solitary figure upon the dismembered wreck of the ship of his State. His friends advised him to yield. He hesitated. His pride was strong in him, and the pangs of defeat were increased tenfold by the exultation of his implacable enemy. At one time he besieged the house of Tipton. There is no reason to believe he intended personal violence. He probably wished to subject him to the humiliation of imprisonment at the very moment of his success. But a worthier impulse restrained him. A show of resistance by Tipton, threatening the loss of life, forced him to retire. Sevier was still reluctant to yield. Having been ordered to lay down his arms, he set off on an expedition against the Cherokee Indians which occupied several months. Upon his return Governor Johnston ordered Judge Campbell to arrest him on a charge of high treason. Campbell failing to comply, a North Carolina judge issued the warrant. Sevier did not conceal himself. At first no attempt was made to arrest him. He happened to be in Jonesboro during the presence of General Martin. Tipton heard of his whereabouts, collected a small guard, and arrested him next morning at the house of a friend, where he had spent the night. Tipton, with a pistol in his hand, repeatedly threatened to shoot him, had him handcuffed and placed in prison. Sevier was sent under guard to Morganton, North Carolina, to be tried. On the way he attempted to escape and was fired upon by one of the guards. It was often said that this man had received orders from Tipton to kill Sevier during the journey, but no proof was ever produced to substantiate the charge, beyond the assertions of Sevier's friends that another of the guards informed Sevier of the fact. The rescue of Sevier in the midst of his trial by a party of his friends was one of the romantic episodes of border life. A thorough-bred horse owned by Sevier was held in front of the court-house, whilst Nathaniel Evans and James Cozby went inside. Seeing these two, Sevier realized the situation. Cozby stepped in front of the judge, and in a loud voice asked if he was done with that man, pointing towards Sevier. In the midst of the confusion produced by this unexpected interlude, Sevier made a dash for the door, sprang upon his horse, and was soon far up the mountain road, where he was joined by a party of friends. This was the end of all attempts to bring him to trial, which in fact never had any motive power beyond that supplied by Tipton's hatred. Sevier returned to his old home, and, despite a law which deprived him of the privilege of holding office under North Carolina, was elected to the senate of North Carolina from Greene County. Upon his arrival at Fayetteville, an act was immediately passed removing his disabilities in spite of the efforts of Tipton, who was present as a member from Washington, and who opposed its passage with all the relentless and narrow-minded fierceness of his nature. In the course of the debate, Amy, the member from Hawkins County, angered Tipton by alluding to the ill-feeling existing between Sevier and himself. A challenge was the result, but a duel was prevented by the interposition of friends. Roddy, a member from Greene County, reprimanded Amy for his hasty language, and alluding to Tipton's irascible disposition, suggested to Amy that he should pursue a course that would "soothe him." The day following, Roddy was selected to conduct the debate. During the discussion, Roddy unwittingly made some remark that rendered Tipton almost frenzied. He sprang towards Roddy like a panther, and seized him by the throat. During the confusion which ensued, Amy excited a roar of laughter by yelling to Roddy across the hall, "Soothe him, colonel, soothe him."

Sevier was immediately appointed brigadier-general of the western counties over Tipton's head. These counties were organized as a congressional district, and the year following Sevier was elected without opposition to represent in Congress the very district in which he had been arrested for treason. Tipton gave up the contest against his irrepressible enemy. He had neglected no weapon of attack, and he had been foiled in the use of all. He had had a fieri facias issued against Sevier's property. He had tried to capture him with the avowed intention of hanging him. He had the credit of hiring an assassin to kill him while on his way to North Carolina for trial. He had fought against his readmission to the privileges of North Carolina citizenship. But in all things he failed. From now on Sevier steps forward into the fuller life, the clearer light of state history, and his figure grows larger and in a sense more resplendent as he advances. Tipton, on the contrary, recedes. He holds office, but nothing more. Years afterwards we still find him giving vent to his implacable hatred in the proceedings against Sevier for speculating in fraudulent land warrants.

From what standpoint soever we regard the Franklin movement, the sympathies of the Tennessean verge towards Sevier's party as naturally as the sympathies of the American verge towards the ultimately unsuccessful Puritan movement in England. After all is said, Sevier was for Tennessee, and that which was treason to North Carolina was recognized and honored as patriotism towards Tennessee, when finally the State was formed. Tipton was never forgiven for his position in the struggle. Sevier was the first governor of the State of Tennessee, as much because he had been governor of Franklin as because he was worthy the honor.

One effect of the dissolution of the Franklin government was to leave the region of Tennessee which had been erected into Sevier County without any form of government. Sevier County was that part of the Indian hunting-ground which had been reserved for the Indians by the act of Carolina of 1783, and which the State of Franklin had obtained by the Dumplin Treaty. With its usual negligence and indifference, North Carolina took no steps towards any assumption of sovereignty over the country, not recognizing as valid the Franklin Treaty, and not regarding it as a matter of any importance. Thrown upon their own resources as the Watauga people had formerly been, like them the Sevier County people made provision for securing to themselves the inalienable rights of life, liberty, and the pursuit of happiness. The basis of their self-government was the company. Each company elected two delegates to a general committee who regulated the affairs of the settlement according to the laws of North Carolina. One of the articles of the association was, "United application shall be made to the next session of the Assembly of North Carolina to receive us into their protection and to bestow upon us the blessings of government." The similarity of surroundings and the coincidence which exists between what we know of the articles of association of both the Watauga and the Sevier County communities leaves little doubt that the latter, which have been preserved, were a close copy of the former. But the Watauga people, through Sevier's assistance, had gained admission to the government of North Carolina. The Sevier people failed, and were compelled to rely upon themselves until 1794, when they became a county of the Territory.

Viewed from the standpoint of that day, the attempt to form the State of Franklin was perhaps one of the most important movements in the early history of the United States, and at one time it was feared that the contagion of the example would spread and involve the country in endless turmoil and perhaps destruction. Properly to appreciate its importance, it must be borne in mind that Spain held the Lower Mississippi Valley, that her emissaries were scattered all through the Indian villages, that her trading posts were on the banks of every important river which emptied into the Mississippi, that she claimed the exclusive navigation of what might be called the very artery of American commerce, that her agents were unscrupulous, and as a rule able, and that the minds of her statesmen were still filled with dreams of a splendid empire in the beautiful and exuberant valley which receives as in a basin the fertilizing streams which are fed by the waters that fail to reach the Pacific on one side, and the Atlantic on the other. All hopes of realizing this dream as against those who spoke the tongue of England having disappeared, the possibility arose in its stead of making common cause with those not satisfied with the newly won independence, and uniting under the flag of Spain the thinly settled and rapidly growing settlements of the Southwest. The attempt to form the State of Franklin was one expression of the prevailing discontent with the existing order of things. But there is not one scintilla of evidence for the belief that it ever verged towards Spain. The implication of Blount, the territorial governor of the State, in no wise implicated the people of Tennessee. We have seen that Sevier was suspected of going to the opposite extreme. The general government at this time was weak and impotent, unable to control those who acknowledged its authority, and without any means of enforcing respect from those who defied it. If Burr had made his attempt then, it is possible that his dream of a Southwestern empire would have been in some shape realized. Such a movement after the formation, or rather after the reorganization of the United States scarcely excited a passing comment. But under the Continental Congress it was viewed with feelings of the deepest concern by all interested in even the remotest degree.

The people of western Virginia, fired by the example of their near neighbors, with whom they felt a community of interests, oppressed by three years' unpaid taxes which they hoped to evade by secession, and urged, no doubt, by the prospects of a great State of which they would be the greatest part, began an agitation of the question of secession from the parent State and a union with the new State of Franklin. Arthur Campbell, who had already figured conspicuously in the war for independence and in the invasion of the Indian country, proposed a form of government based on that of Virginia and North Carolina, with every prospect of seeing this object attained. Patrick Henry, who was at that time governor of Virginia, was alarmed by the extent of the disaffection, and at once removed from office those who favored the movement. The agitation went so far as to cause a memorial to be addressed to Congress, requesting the formation of a new State. The limits of the new State, as outlined by Arthur Campbell, were to embrace, in general terms, the western counties of Virginia, a part of Kentucky, Tennessee, Georgia, Alabama, and the northern part of Mississippi. This plan, however, never attracted serious sympathy, and fell to the ground when the State of Franklin was at the height of its prosperity. This idea has never died. In the debates at Nashville, immediately preceding the war, the proposition was frequently made that East Tennessee should be allowed to remain in the Union as a separate State. One member proposed to call the projected State, Franklin.

CHAPTER XIII.

FIRST SETTLEMENTS ON THE CUMBERLAND.

DURING the interval which had elapsed from the time when the first cabin was built upon the Watauga to the events narrated in the last chapter, in another part of the State and under circumstances of equal difficulties and dangers, another settlement had been formed and had, after years of a gloomy and bloody probation, finally grown strong and prosperous. The early history of East Tennessee is essentially the early history of Middle Tennessee. In each the beginnings were the same. In each we have the same details of Indian butchery, desultory warfare, and savage incursions. The Watauga articles of association find almost an exact parallel in the articles of agreement or compact of government on the Cumberland. In some instances the same persons figured in both — Robertson, Lucas, Tatum, and Isbell. In both we find the same self-reliance, the same niggardly neglect on the part of the parent State. In one particular alone is there a decided difference. The Watauga people, living almost in the shadow of the great range of mountains which separated their country from North Carolina, had but to ascend its sides in order to look down into the valleys and across the plains of the older State. But the Cumberland settlement was more than six hundred miles distant from the seat of government. Its forts were built upon the banks of a stream, the waters of which eventually swept past the city whose possession made the Spanish claim to the exclusive navigation of the Mississippi a tangible reality and an ever-present threat. Natchez and New Orleans, both in the hands of vindictive enemies, aliens in laws, religion, and language, were the natural markets of those who dwelt upon the Cumberland as well as those who dwelt upon the Illinois and the Wabash. The Spaniards appreciated their advantages, and they made such use of them as the short-sighted mind and the narrow forehead ever make of the accidents of fortune. This brought the Cumberland settlement in direct contact with the complications of international politics, and its growth was materially influenced by the diplomatic struggles of Europe and America. At first, too small to be of measurable importance in the scale of negotiations, it soon grew into recognition as the centre of disturbance, and became successively the object of Spanish malignancy and the cause of Spanish obsequiousness. The unrelenting ferocity of Indian vindictiveness was instigated by the agents of Mero and Carondelet, and the weapons of war were supplied from St. Augustine and New Orleans. Having sustained the integrity of its foundation, and grown beyond the power of savage warfare to destroy, the settlement was now approached with offers of gifts, and with fair words. The shallow brain, which had failed with force, now learned a lesson of Æsop, and attempted to accomplish by gentleness what it had failed to accomplish by harsher means. But through it all, against the cunning of the savage, against his ferocity and his onslaught, against all the weapons of his warfare, and not less against the bloodthirsty cruelty of the Spaniard, and in the midst of the tissues of his diplomacy and specious bribery, one mind had guided the destiny of the people of Middle Tennessee, and had proved himself superior to all attacks and above all the vicissitudes of fortune. The region of country now known as Middle Tennessee formed a part of Charles II.'s grant, and apart from the boundary lines of Indian treaties has always been included in the same geographical limits with East Tennessee. Even the Franklin people invited the Cumberland settlement to become a part of the new State. But until James Robertson, in 1779, planted corn on the bluffs of the Cumberland River, this part of the State was known to trappers and traders alone. In 1748 the same Dr. Thomas Walker whose name has already been mentioned is said to have passed through the Cumberland Gap, and penetrated to the waters of the river which takes its name from the mountain. Some historians accord Walker the honor of having given this name to the geographical nomenclature of America. After this, and during the time of its commercial ascendency in the South, France had a station on the present site of Nashville. In 1766 Colonel James Smith, in conjunction with several others, one of whom was named Stone, attempted to explore the entire region of country between the Ohio and the Mississippi. Stone River still bears witness to the expedition, which was the first authentic exploration of that region of country. The accounts which Smith brought back to the older settlements created a fury of explorations, and each succeeding year saw an increase in the numbers of those who penetrated deep into the wilderness to hunt, to trap, and to trade.

The chronicles of those times have not preserved full records of each expedition, nor perhaps would they possess more than a factitious interest if we had them. Each party came for the same purpose, each encountered virtually the same adventures, and each departed as it had come, leaving behind no vestige which remains. As yet there had been no breaking of the soil, no dropping of corn, no felling of trees. The hunter who found in the abundance of game an ample reward for the danger of its pursuit spread the fame of the region far and wide. The same glowing descriptions which caused a flood of emigration to pour over the western mountains of North

Carolina now attracted general attention to the country around the "Salt Licks of the West." Even in those days an additional interest in the new country was excited by the accounts of the natural advantages it offered for trade and commerce. In 1769 or 1770 Mansker and a party of hunters had laden boats with furs and bear meat, the chief marketable commodities of the trapper, and, descending the river to Natchez, bartered these for articles of merchandise. On the voyage downward they saw the celebrated French Lick, and all around were herds of buffaloes. The woods resounded with their bellowing and the uproar of their battles. They also saw several deserted forts, which seemed to them the unwritten legend of an extinct race.[1] Mansker returned several times after this. Once he was accompanied by Isaac Bledsoe and Joseph Drake, who gave their names to Drake's Lick and Bledsoe's Lick. Mansker's Lick was named for Mansker himself. In 1775 De Mumbreun, or De Mumbrune, built a cabin at Eaton Station. In 1777 he made a trip to New Orleans. Another party of hunters descended the Cumberland in 1777, and made their way by water to Natchez.

But in 1778 the first settler of Middle Tennessee appears in the figure of a trapper who came with a party of hunters from Kentucky to take possession of and secure permanently a part of the wilderness whose beauty and fertility were apparent to the least perceptive eye, and whose promise of future wealth found more than an earnest in the swift flowing river that ran through its midst. This was at a time when steamboats were as yet unknown, and when flatboats and canoes were looked upon as the natural means of inland navigation. But of all who

---

[1] One of Mansker's party was named Stone, and Haywood attributes to him the origin of the name of Stone River. Putnam spells this name Mansker. This is the name as signed to the articles of agreement, but in Haywood it is Mansco.

came, Spencer was the only one who had a clear and well-defined idea of the object of his mission as the fore-runner of civilization. His companions at first entered into the spirit of the enterprise, and assisted him to plant "a small field of corn." The dangers, however, which surrounded the undertaking were too great, and all but Spencer quailed before them. They returned to Kentucky, leaving him behind. It is told as a touching instance of the generosity and fearlessness of the man, that he broke his knife in two parts and gave one to Holliday, who had lost his own and feared to make the journey without one. Spencer had taken his abode in a large hollow tree near Bledsoe's Lick, which served the double purpose of protection and concealment. Here he remained throughout the entire winter. He saw no one and heard not the sound of a human voice. It is related as historically true that he passed once not far from the cabin in which dwelt a hunter in the service of De Mumbreun, and that the hunter, seeing the imprint of his enormous foot, became frightened and fled through the wilderness to the French settlements on the Wabash. This, however, is of doubtful authenticity and originated probably in later years, when the size of Spencer's foot had become one of the standing subjects of jest to the early settlers of Nashville. But in Spencer's sojourn and the small crop of corn we find the embryonic germ of Nashville and Middle Tennessee. His gigantic figure, alone in the midst of endless forests, wandering and hunting throughout their vast depths, the herald of a coming civilization, cool, courageous, and self-reliant, going to sleep at night by a solitary camp-fire, with the hooting of owls and the screaming of panthers around him and with no assurance of the absence of a deadlier foe, is one of the most picturesque in the history of Southwestern pioneers. In the early part of 1778, Spencer's hollow tree and a hunter's hut here and there on the banks of the Cumberland were the only signs of human life where Nashville now stands. Within less than a year the same place was green with the growth of newly planted corn and alive with the activity of pioneer life.

It is not always an easy task to appreciate the causes which lead to any particular train of events, and to fix clearly in the mind the exact moment of each minor departure. We see the rain, but not the rising of the mist, the toppling of the clouds, the electric spark, and the rushing together of the drops. We cannot see, or perhaps we do not try to see. As we examine the chronicles of the earlier state historians, we can easily determine the date and even the character of the first settlement of Middle Tennessee.[1] This much is of authentic record. But what led to this going into the wilderness, the various causes which gradually brought about this effect, are hidden in a mist of indistinctness, and we can only see the broader objects that enable us to infer the landscape whose details glimmer in our sight. In 1778 James Robertson was one of the most popular figures on the Watauga. He had acquired such fame as could be acquired on such a field. His defense of Fort Watauga had eclipsed the fame of the most brilliant of the frontier leaders, and his name was familiar to Richmond and Charleston. Neither honor nor riches were lacking. Why should he again face the dangers of a frontier settlement? This and numberless other questions of the same nature, the writers of those days fail to answer. One cause, in fact the chief cause, of our imperfect knowledge of our earlier history is the lack of all literary activity. Haywood's history only comes down to within twenty years of the time he wrote, and Ramsey's

---

[1] When the phrase Middle Tennessee is used, it applies to the Middle Tennessee of the present. Until the formation of the Western District, afterwards West Tennessee, all the region west of East Tennessee was known as West Tennessee.

work was published in 1853. The life of the people is clearly before us. But the individual is hidden from us. There were no Pepys, no Walpoles, no Wraxalls to tell us how people lived and spoke and acted, when off the stage of history. We have no vivid pictures, no historical groups. History deals with details. The important events make chronicles. The diary which John Donelson kept of the wonderful cruise of "The Adventure" is a solitary exception, and enables us to see with present eyes the scenes he describes. Bishop Asbury's diary contains more suggestive matter than direct information, and his observations are all made from the standpoint of a faith which, though pure and noble, destroys half the historical value of what he has left. It is therefore impossible for us to watch the gradual growth of the desire again to try the western wilds as it developed in the minds of the first who made the attempt. We cannot see them sitting by the evening fire and planning the coming venture. Their thoughts, their hopes, their desires are merely matters of conjecture. Our records of the ancient history of Tennessee are scanty and imperfect, and the first settlement of Nashville is a part of the ancient history of this State. The results we can follow closely and accurately, but at times we lose the intellectual process which produced it. The gradual enhancement of lands as the result of its occupation by communities of the white race was one of the economic truths of that day as well as of the present. It was a force whose action within certain limits was certain and invariable. Frequently, therefore, the price to be paid for land was the ordeal of Indian warfare which preceded the time of tranquillity and security which was sure to follow. It was the desire to better his condition, not the innate love of danger and hair-breadth escapes, which led Daniel Boone into the wilderness. That he was a brave man and that he possessed some of the requisites of heroic greatness, cannot be doubted or denied. But the theory which has found popular acceptation and has passed into the traditions of the present as a historical fact, that Boone was a kind of a philanthropic forerunner of civilization with a bucolic fondness for solitude and communion with nature, is without the least foundation. The immortal lines in which Byron gives to "Daniel Boone, backwoods-man of Kentucky," one of "the great names which in our faces stare," and places him among those who are "beyond the dwarfing city's pale abortions, because their thoughts had never been the prey of care or gain," are poetical enough, but they are not true. Daniel Boone was a land speculator and the agent of land speculators, and in the expressive phraseology of the present day would be called a "land-shark." He entered land enough in Kentucky to have made him wealthy if he had but known how to perfect his title. He obtained numerous grants from Spain which he lost by his negligence. The poverty of his old age, which appeals to the sentimental imagination of this generation, was not the result of indifference but of ignorance.

The earlier annals of the West and Southwest are filled with accounts of the attempts made by different men of note to gain vast estates in regions which have since become great commonwealths. Washington and Madison and Randolph are among the number. But the scheme which surpassed all others in breadth and activity was that which, according to the biographers of Boone, was suggested by the celebrated pioneer to those who composed the Transylvania company. Colonel Richard Henderson was at the head of this association, and, with the assistance of Boone, purchased from the Indians the country which lies within the natural limits of the Ohio, the Kentucky, and the Cumberland rivers. This purchase was made by Boone and Henderson at the Sycamore Shoals Treaty, held on the Watauga on the 17th of March, 1775. The price paid for what now constitutes the larger part of three

States was about $50,000 worth of blankets, rifles, beads, and other trinkets. This purchase is important in the history of Middle Tennessee as having included the Cumberland country, and as being one of the immediate causes which led to its settlement. The inducements held out to actual settlers by the Transylvania company were greater than those held out by the State. Henderson's purchase extinguished the Indian title, but according to the legislative construction of Virginia and North Carolina, it failed to vest it in him or his company. It is impossible to establish the chain of events which caused Robertson to lead a settlement to the Cumberland, but there is no doubt that the main cause was found in the desire of Henderson especially that Robertson should assist him in securing the western portion of his lands, or perhaps it would not be too expansive to say empire. The treaty and the purchase had been declared illegal and void by the governors of Virginia and North Carolina, but there still remained some hope that Henderson could perfect his title. The latter persuaded large numbers of inhabitants in the older States to emigrate to the new country, and we find Donelson and others from Virginia acting in concert with Robertson, in 1778, or perhaps earlier.

An agreement of some sort was made, the general outlines of which were that Robertson and a party under him should first go by land to the Cumberland and make ready for the arrival of the others. Corn was to be planted, cabins erected, and stockades prepared. Donelson was to come by water from Fort Patrick Henry on the Holston, by way of the Tennessee and up the Cumberland. Robertson was to leave signs at a certain place on the Tennessee which should indicate to Donelson that all was well and that he could come through the country. The wives of Robertson's party, including Robertson's wife, were to come with Donelson.

In pursuance of this agreement Robertson, late in 1778,

with a party of eight, including one negro, set out across the mountains through the Cumberland Gap, and trusting to paths of wild animals, which at times enabled them to penetrate the intricate forests, finally came to the banks of the Cumberland at the French Lick, so called from the French trading post, which had been erected there years before by permission of the Chickasaws. Immediately upon his arrival, Robertson compelled his party, who were eager to make the best of their priority of choice in order to obtain the best sites for cabins and the most fertile lands, to take the precaution of which he alone foresaw the necessity. Shortly after the arrival of Robertson's company, they were joined by another under Casper Mansker, the old trapper. The new settlers at once made ready for the emergencies of their situation, and planted a crop of corn near Sulphur Springs. Robertson, having seen the settlement well under way, started on foot for Kaskaskia, a frontier post which Colonel George Rogers Clark had recently captured, and which he made the centre of his operations against the British and their Indian allies. It was currently reported that he, as the western military representative of Virginia, had the power to sell the so-called cabin-rights which allowed to every actual settler a thousand acres of land around his cabin. The line had not been run and it was not yet certainly known whether French Lick and the adjacent territory were a part of Virginia or North Carolina.[1] Robertson made satisfactory arrangements of some kind with Clark and returned to French Lick, bringing with him a large party of new settlers. They were on their way to Kentucky under the leadership of John Rains, who, yielding to Robertson's persuasions, returned with him. Rains has the credit of "being the first man to introduce neat cattle and horses upon the west side of the Cumberland River and into Middle Tennessee." Some

[1] This was determined the spring following.

of the new settlers built a fort on the east side of the river, several miles below French Lick. This was Fort Eaton. Shortly after the arrival of Rains, came a party of South Carolinians, who were the third addition to the original Robertson party in the space of a few months. These additions became so constant as to form almost a steady stream. The most important of those which followed, and who are peculiarly worthy of mention in a history of the formation of this State, was that under John Donelson, whose trip in a boat called "The Adventure," from Fort Patrick Henry to French Lick, reads like a chapter in one of Mayne Reid's novels. The journal of the voyage which Donelson kept has been preserved, and gives a vivid and life-like reproduction of the events of the trip. The caption is, "Journal of a Voyage intended by God's permission, in the good boat Adventure, from Fort Patrick Henry, on Holston River, to the French Salt Springs on the Cumberland River, kept by John Donelson." The party consisted of "men, women, children, and negroes." Their number is not known. Among them were James Robertson's family, a wife and five children. In addition to the Adventure, which carried a sail, there were several canoes and other craft, so that the whole constituted a miniature fleet. The Adventure left Fort Patrick Henry on the 22d of December, 1779. It did not get fairly under way until the latter part of February, having been detained at various points by low water, hard frost, and running aground.

The last entry in Donelson's diary is the following: "Proceeded on quietly until the 12th of April, at which time we came to the mouth of a little river running in on the north side, by Moses Renfroe and his company called 'Red River,' upon which they intended to settle.[1] Here they took leave of us. We proceeded up Cumberland, nothing happening material until the 23d, when we reached

[1] This was the beginning of Clarksville.

the first settlement on the north side of the river, one mile and a half below the Big Salt Lick and called Eaton's Station, after a man of that name who, with several families, came through Kentucky and settled there.

"Monday, April 24th. This day we arrived at our journey's end at the Big Salt Lick, where we have the pleasure of finding Captain Robertson and his company. It is a source of satisfaction to us to be enabled to restore to him and others their families and friends, who were intrusted to our care, who some time since, perhaps despaired of ever meeting again. Though our prospects at present are dreary, we have found a few log cabins which have been built on a cedar bluff above the Lick by Captain Robertson and his company."

This diary of Donelson's is one of the most valuable documents in the annals of this State. The style is clear, direct, and in a manner unobtrusive. Although there is little color in the narrative, it brings before us in sharp outlines the wonderful adventures of his voyage. It has been frequently reproduced, but it has never lost its freshness of interest. There is nothing in Cooper to surpass it. But its chief historical value lies in the fact that it enables us actually to grasp as a tangible reality the dangers and difficulties which beset the earlier settlers of the State. The same things which occurred to Donelson and his party on water were occurring to others on land from Vincennes to the Gulf. The long and wearisome repetition of Indian butcheries and scalpings and burnings and torturings fails to give us so clear an understanding of what it meant to go into the wilderness and found a new community as this simple record of the Adventure. It is not a matter of surprise that the descendants of Donelson himself occupied a large place in the subsequent history of the State. We cannot refuse him a hearty admiration for his coolness, his undaunted determination, his unpremeditated modesty. We find in him a worthy sire of the wife of Andrew Jackson. We find in this ordeal a worthy preparation for the development of those traits which alone could invade and conquer the wilderness. The trip was productive of good results, and in one instance wrought its own retribution. With Donelson was a family which had small-pox. It was in charge of a man named Stewart. Being compelled to keep at some distance from the rest, they were captured and killed by the Indians. As a result, small-pox took hold upon the latter and caused them to die by the thousands. To this fact has been attributed the immunity which gave the Cumberland settlements time to prepare for the onslaughts which followed.

CHAPTER XIV.

JAMES ROBERTSON.

UPON the arrival of Donelson's party in their new homes, they found those who had preceded them busy with hoe and hammer. Donelson himself built a cabin and stockade on Clover Bottom. Rains, according to Haywood, " settled the lands since called Deadrick Plantation," about two miles below Nashville. A station was built on the Bluffs, and received the name of Nashborough. Early in 1779 Robertson had arrived at the Great Salt Lick with the first settlers on the Cumberland. Donelson's party arrived on the 24th of April, 1780. On the 1st of May the compact of government was drawn up, and already eight stations are mentioned as entitled to delegates among the "Twelve Notables," or "General Arbitrators." Their names are Nashborough, Gasper's, Bledsoe's, Asher's, Freeland's, Eaton's, and Fort Union. In addition to these, there were several cabins fortified with stockades able to withstand a small body of Indians. In times of great danger those who were scattered through the community collected together in one of the central stations, which were built generally in the form of a square, at the corners and in the centres between the corners of which were heavily built block-houses, with stockades running from one to the other. The block-houses were provided with loopholes. The entrance to the station was a gate, built as solidly as possible and fastened with a chain, but as much exposed as practicable to the block-houses on the sides. A single block-house built of heavy logs hewn into shape was capable of offering a good defense, and those who were able built one in preference to the more fragile but more easily erected cabins, which were built of smaller logs, generally round poles.

Among the first and most important steps taken by the new settlers was to supply that deficiency which is felt in every community, and which it is not too much to say the English-speaking people have alone been able to supply from their own resources. A form of government was devised by the settlers, and, as in the case of the Watauga Association, along the lines of precedents established by the laws of their ancestors. We find the same incidents of government in the Cumberland settlement which we found on the Watauga, and which existed in some shape or manner upon the banks of the Trent and the Ouse. The articles of agreement are a modernized reproduction of the powers and customs of the ancient court leet. The outlines and details of the compact were suggested and elaborated by Richard Henderson, the projector of the Transylvania scheme, and James Robertson. Henderson had instigated the Cumberland settlement. He had taken up his residence with the first comers and had made liberal disposition of the lands of his company, in order to attract emigration. He postponed the payments until the States of Virginia and North Carolina should have confirmed the title he had obtained from the Indians. A man of broad views and broader ambition, he aspired to found a new State on the Cumberland. He had seen much of the world, and he had a thorough appreciation of the genius of the American people. He had formed the first compact of government which was formed west of the Alleghanies, and having placed his undertaking upon what he considered a firm and republican basis, he had, with a singular mixture of audacity and patriotism, applied to be admitted to the confederacy as an independent State. This was in 1775, when the uncertainty of the impending war tried the nerves and tested the loyalty of many who had less to risk than the Transylvania company or its leader.

The compact of government was drawn up in May, 1780. More than one half of the compact is devoted to the land office. The judicial and executive power was vested in a body of notables or judges, or triers, or general arbitrators, but was not to extend to capital punishment. The members were elected by the forts.[1] These articles were signed at Nashborough, May 13, 1780. Two hundred and fifty-six names were attached. The rapidity with which the settlement spread was phenomenal even in an age when cities were built in a day, and states were made in a year. The centre of population was Nashborough. Freeland's Station was a little to the north. Eaton's Station was on the east bank of the river. Gasper's Station was several miles up the Cumberland, where the little village of Goodlettsville lies. Asher's was not far from Gallatin. Bledsoe's was near the Sulphur Springs in the neighborhood of Gallatin, and Fort Union was about six miles above Nashborough. These are those entitled to elect members of the committee of general arbitrators. But there were still others scattered at various points up and down the rivers and creeks. Donelson had a fort on Clover Bottom called Donelson's or Stone's River. The first party, which under the guidance of James Robertson had settled at the French Lick, and even the Rains party, were still pioneers. The settlement became what the adventurers of that day called a settlement only upon the arrival of Donelson's party in the Adventure.

The winter of 1779–80 was one of unprecedented severity. John Rains drove his cattle across the Cumberland on the ice. The hardships had been a terrible ordeal even to

---

[1] The provisions of this compact are elaborate and intricate and full of interest. Those wishing to examine it in detail are referred to Putnam, who gives it in full and who rescued it from oblivion.

those whom experience had inured to the tests of cold and hunger. But the intense coldness had not been an unmixed evil. The news of the settlement had spread to the Cherokees, the Choctaws, and the Chickasaws. Even the nations of the Northwest heard with apprehension and bitterness that the hunting-grounds between the Great Mountains and the Father of Waters had been seized by the insatiate pale-face. The winter, however, rendered the chase unprofitable, and the exposure too full of suffering. The warriors of the nation were compelled to seek the shelter of the wigwam. This gave the Cumberland people time to erect forts and stockades. Had an attack been made, such as that which shortly after shook the foundations of the new community, resistance would have been useless.

But by the time the mild breath of spring had awakened the sleeping life of the forests, and with it the slumbering hatred of the Indians, preparations had been made which enabled the infant settlement to develop into maturity in the midst of a succession of horrors which has no equal in the bloody annals of the Southwest. It is a profitless task to repeat the dreary chronicles of ferocity and murder and torture. The fact of the existence of these things, and that the ground was cleared, the foundation stones fitted, is sufficient. This is the prominent event, and it stands out with sufficient prominence. Haywood says the first man killed was John Milliken, Putnam says Joseph Hay. Both agree that it was in the spring of 1780, when no one suspected danger. The first death hastened the preparations for defense. The position of the settlement, separated by three hundred miles of rough and perilous travel from the nearest post, exposed it to continuous attack from Cherokees, Creeks, and Choctaws. The attacks of the enemy were more deadly because of their nature. The unseen bullet came from an unexpected quarter. There was rarely an open attack. But parties of hunters and isolated travelers were set upon. It was dangerous to leave the protection of the cabin and the stockade. In the autumn of the first year the corn crop was a failure, and a bushel of it sold for $160 in continental money. The influx of emigrants, generally welcomed as an addition of strength, was now regarded as an increase of weakness. Bread was scarce and meat was difficult to get. It was dangerous to hunt and starvation was imminent. The Indians even tried to drive the game from the country.

The butchery of the Renfroe settlement at the mouth of the Red River, which took place about this time, made the stoutest hearts quail. Scarcely a day passed that did not witness the death of some one of the settlers. Jonathan Jennings, who had escaped the dangers of shipwreck and even captivity, was killed above Nashborough. John Donelson narrowly escaped the same fate. He had planted corn on Clover Bottom and had gone with two boats to gather it, when on his return the boat ahead of his own was attacked. Only one negro and one white man escaped.[1] Among the killed was a son of James Robertson. But the last extremity still remained. Their ammunition began to run short, and the miserable pioneers, in the midst of desolation and deprivation, turned to flee from a place where death stood upon the threshold and where famine sat at their board. God's curse appeared to them to have settled down upon the hills and the valleys of the Cumberland. Every heart but one was filled with fear, every heart but one longed for escape.

---

[1] Putnam, upon what authority I have been unable to discover, says there were two negroes in the boat; "the other negro or mulatto was a free man, known as Jack Civil. He surrendered to the Indians, went with them to the Chickamauga towns, near Lookout Mountain, and then with the pirates and outlaws who settled the place on the Tennessee River, which hath acquired notoriety as Nickajack or Nigger Jack, unquestionably so named after this mulatto." This bit of philology is altogether too fanciful.

In every block-house the cry was for flight. It swept through the settlement in a day. It was just such a crisis as we meet with in all American colonies. And the man is always found, equal to the historical exigencies of the moment. In the history of Tennessee, James Robertson is what John Smith is in the history of Virginia, what the younger Winthrop is in the history of Connecticut.

Robertson is not a brilliant figure. Whatever may be the qualities of character to which the term brilliancy is properly applied, Robertson certainly did not possess them. He lacked the mental alertness, the nervous energy, the instinct of action which are characteristic of genius. His thoughts were clear and luminous, in a word, light-giving. His character was like his thoughts. He never had a flash of inspiration. He could reason well, he could act well. In the annals of the State, it is true, he rises above the mists of common-place. The light settles upon his head, but it never dazzles us. In no sense of the word was he great or talented. He lacked the far-sighted calculation and the appreciation of economic forces which made Sevier a statesman, however circumscribed his field. He lacked the decision, the quick insight, the cautious preparation, the dashing execution which made Sevier a soldier. These are his limitations. But if not great, he was admirable. There are characters whom we love but whom we distrust. There are characters whom we admire with even and impassionate serenity but upon whom we rely with utter abandon. Robertson's character was of this kind. It was well built, with solid masonry and broad foundations. He is eminently trustworthy. We are filled with a kind of joyous admiration of our humanity when we see blended in him so much modesty and so much fortitude. He possessed rather fortitude than bravery. The lack of fear was such a part of his being that we learn to take it as a matter of course.

It was a part of the times and the people. But his fortitude lifts him to an altitude. It never wavers, it never quails, it never retreats. This it is that makes him one of the great figures of our history. Under peculiar circumstances his qualities of character, although in themselves not great, accomplished results which as a rule greatness alone can accomplish. His fortitude and trustworthiness did for Middle Tennessee what the diplomacy and generalship of Sevier did for East Tennessee. He hastened its settlement by a number of years which cannot be calculated. He had from the first been recognized as the leader of the new settlement. Shortly after his arrival, he had been made colonel, an office which gave him command of the military equipment of the forts. Upon the formation of the compact, he had been elected chairman of the committee of general arbitrators. His earlier experiences in Watauga had prepared him for the position he was called on to occupy as the Atlas of the young settlement. In 1776 and later he had been commissioner for North Carolina among the Cherokees, and during his sojourn among them he had acquired the knowledge which gave him hope and strength to withstand the dangers which threatened the Cumberland settlement.

When, therefore, the question of retreat was agitated, he bore for the minute the destiny of Middle Tennessee upon his shoulders. He argued, he entreated, he commanded. He infused his own unyielding spirit into some of the hardier settlers and the task was half done. "What of the lack of powder," he said; "I will go to Virginia and to North Carolina, and I promise to supply your needs." The offer was an offer to run the gauntlet, but it was accepted. With one of his sons and a few others who were unwilling for him to traverse the wilderness alone, he departed. The incidents of the trip have not been preserved, but it was heroic, and it saved the people of Middle Tennessee. He returned, after having visited the Kentucky stations, with ample supplies of ammunition. Even the overflow which swept away the last remnant of corn in the fields and drove the game to the hills was passed over as of little moment, and all hearts were cheered by the example of one man, who, like the old Roman, had not despaired of the little republic.

It may be true there is no Providence to touch the subtile chords which control the movements of life; it may be true that the divine mercy is only manifest in the action of general laws through universal application. But there are events which bring us so close to a realization of some higher intelligence, that they well might stagger the skeptical. An event of this kind is the saving of Fort Freeland by James Robertson, a worthy instrument in the hands of the Lord. Robertson arrived from his long and dangerous trip to Kentucky in quest of powder, on the 15th of January, 1781. For weeks he had been sleeping in the very shadow of death. The keenness of his eye, the elasticity of his step, the quickness of his wit, and most of all the quickness of his ear, were the instruments which nature had given him in the unequal contest. The hoot of an owl could awaken him from the deepest sleep. The rustle of a leaf could reach his ear. Upon his arrival the settlement was stirred with a double impulse of gratitude to him, and a desire to hear what news he had brought from the eastern world. They had crowded eagerly around him to learn the fate of the Watauga people, and the fortunes of the war which shook two worlds, but whose noise rarely penetrated the wilderness that engulfed them. After the long narration and the repetition of details, the old settlers had retired, and filled with thoughts of other things, had appointed no guard to watch the fort. The moon was bright, not a cloud in the sky. The light shone full upon the square block-houses, the quadrangular space within, the upright palisades that ran from house to house. The Indians crept out from the shadow of the forest, and gliding stealthily across the intervening space, one by one, sank into the shadows of the upright pickets, until about fifty had collected together. The gate was fastened by a chain, and one, more agile than the rest, succeeded in gaining a hold upon the clasp and loosened it. The noise awoke Robertson alone of all within, and knowing the need of quick alarm, he sprang to his feet with the cry of "Indians!" As his cry resounded through the fort, the Indians had thrown down the gate and dashed in. One man rushed out only to be shot down. The settlers slept rifle in hand, and they awoke ready for battle. They poured a deadly fire into the Indians who recoiled. Their assailants were invisible and they could not return the fire. They retreated towards the gate, firing as they went. They killed a negro of Robertson's. But no further harm was done. It added one more to the many claims upon the gratitude of posterity of a brave and noble leader.

The Indians retired but with increased hatred, with a more relentless determination to subdue the infant settlement. Their chief sent messengers from village to village, along the banks of the Tennessee, through the swamps and the cane-brakes of the Lower Ohio. Their hopes were aroused, their cupidity was excited, their bravery was appealed to. But they had been cruelly decimated by Sevier and by disease. The small-pox had made havoc among them. It was difficult to collect a large army. A band such as that which under Old Abraham and Dragging Canoe had invaded the Watauga settlement would have been fatal to the Cumberland. Robertson would have been unable to repeat the glorious defense of Fort Watauga. On the 2d of April, 1781, the battle was fought which decided the fate of the Cumberland settlement. This was the "Battle of the Bluffs" so called. It ended in the complete discomfiture of the assailants, who sustained severe losses. Among the curious incidents of the battle was an attack upon the Indians by the dogs in the fort, which had been trained to this end. This created a diversion which the whites turned to their advantage. The same party of Indians returned in the evening and fired upon the fort from a distance, but were dispersed by a shot from an old swivel which, for want of lead, was loaded with gravel and stones.

The existence of the Cumberland settlement was practically assured by the "Battle of the Bluffs." Nevertheless, the dangers and the distress which surrounded the individual were in a measure increased. The Indians abandoned the hope of destroying the forts, but in the lack of organized aggression they came in small bands to lay in wait, to surprise, to kill, to scalp, and then to retreat. Those who labored in the field did so in hourly expectation of attack, and sentinels were kept on guard to warn of impending danger. If several were compelled to be in the forest or at the springs, and a conference was held, this was done by forming a small military square, each man facing outward with his rifle cocked. It was in the very face of death to pass from one fort to another. The name of a man who died a natural death has been preserved. It was Robert Gilkey.

But the law of the survival of the fittest finds its exemplification. The dangers which surrounded the settlers cultivated in them those faculties the highest exercise of which offered the greatest hope of safety. The rustling of a leaf might reach the ear of an Indian lurking in the shadow of the forests. The pioneers learned to pass through the woods even after the falling of the leaves, with the swiftness of the deer, without crushing a leaf or breaking a twig. The chances of warfare would rarely give more than one shot. That shot seldom went astray. Every sense was sharpened to the utmost limits of its possibilities. There were those who could tell by the report of the rifle to whom it belonged; the merest tyro could detect the difference between the report of an Indian gun and of a gun in the possession of a friend. The accuracy of the eye, the keenness of the ear, the quickness of the body, the alertness of the foot, the nimbleness of the hand, were weapons of defense. The marvelous tales of Cooper sink into commonplace when compared with the wonderful feats and adventures of Spencer and Edmond Jennings, the son of the ill-fated Jonathan, and Castleman and Rains and Mansker. Before the introduction of powder, the Indian's weapons of warfare and the chase were inadequate to his necessities. A natural law of existence threw him upon the resources of his wit. He became cunning, quick-witted, wily, supple of body. Quick of apprehension, he learned a lesson from the beasts of the field and the birds of the air. He could imitate the hoot of an owl, the scream of a panther, the bleat of a fawn, the gobble of a turkey, till the owl would perch above his head, the panther creep from his lair, the fawn run to meet its dam, the turkey to join its mates. The art which the Indians had been transmitting from generation to generation and perfecting through centuries of practice, the white man learned in a few years. And not only this, he went farther. Unable to determine, when he heard the sound, whether it was the imitated or the imitator, he studied the habits and the seasons of the former, and knew when to expect the voice which nature had given them. Here is a story of the brave-hearted Castleman, told in his simple and picturesque way: "It was in the dusk of the evening. The imitation of this large bird of night was very perfect, yet I was suspicious. The woo-woo call and the woo-woo answer were not well timed and toned, and the babel-chatter was a failure; and more than this, I am sure they are on the ground and that won't begin to do. 'I'll see you,' says I to myself, and as I approached I saw something of the height of a stump standing between a forked tree which divided near the ground. Well, I know there can be no stump there; I put 'Betsy' to my face — that stump was once a live Indian and he lay at the roots of those forked chestnuts. And if he was ever buried, it was not far off."

On one occasion old Mansker was "gobbled" up by an Indian, such was the current phrase. But not being certain of the turkey, he became suspicious. Approaching cautiously, he finally "located" his adversary. He was behind a tree. Knowing that as a rule the Indian only fires at close range, and knowing also that "Nancy" could talk at long range, he made no sign of fear or attempt to guard himself. He feigned to pass to the Indian's right. As he expected, the latter attempted to follow him so as to get within shooting distance. In a moment an opening in the glade exposed the skulking body. A quick aim, a word from "Nancy," and the Indian was on his way to the happy hunting ground. Castleman once heard the bleat of a fawn near him. The burden of identification, in legal phrase, was always on the owl or the panther or the turkey or the fawn. He saw a moving body and simultaneously two guns were fired. The Indian fell dead, but his bullet cut the fringe of Castleman's shirt.

CHAPTER XV.

DAVIDSON COUNTY.

The cold and sleet and bitter winds which pierced through the crannies of the well-aired cabins and blockhouses in the winter of 1781–82 again caused a discussion of the possibility of removal. The weaker began to lose heart. Murmurs of dissatisfaction were heard. But there was never a serious danger of departure. Those who so far had withstood the trials to which they had been subjected would not brook the idea. "If we fail," said one, "it must never be from cowardice." Bledsoe, the stout-hearted surveyor, the shadow of whose destiny was already lengthening toward him, pointed to the future. "If we perish here, others will be sure to come, either to revenge our death or to accomplish what we have begun. If they find not our graves or our scattered bones, they may revere our memories and publish to the ages to come that we deserved a better fate." The unfaltering rock-ribbed fortitude of James Robertson put aside the suggestion with a noble rebuke. "These rich and beautiful lands were not designed to be given up to savages and wild beasts. The God of Creation and Providence has nobler purposes in view." The powder was again running short, but the settlers resolved to use less and shoot better. Nothing less than a bear, or a buffalo, or a buck was to be shot down. The means of supplying the wants felt were on hand if only a market could be found. The skins and furs were filling the forts. The waters were low, and it was difficult to get to Natchez and New

Orleans, impossible to get to Jonesboro except by land. There was practically no method of communication with the outside world, and the Cumberland heroes spent 1782 in strengthening themselves internally. The aggressions of the savages, owing to a treaty which Robertson had made with them, were less incessant though still numerous and deadly. Frequently they turned their attention towards the houses of the settlers. The Mauldins and the Kilgores had established a fort called Kilgore's Station, on the head-waters of the Red River, but were compelled to abandon it shortly after it was erected and seek protection in the central forts. Emigration had not entirely ceased, and occasionally small parties succeeded in traversing the wilds between Jonesboro and Nashborough, as Robertson had done under circumstances of equal danger. Late in the autumn the question of desertion was again brought forward, but Robertson again gave new heart to the settlers, and they again determined to remain, this time with enthusiasm. He called their attention to the probable effect which the success of the Continental arms would have upon their fortunes. In April, 1782, hostilities ceased, and about six months later the Cumberland people heard of the close of the war which gave America its independence. Its effect was at once seen in the conciliatory attitude of the Indians. They came to hunt, they said, not to spill the blood of their white brothers.

With the advent of the new year came a revival of old hopes and a renewal of old undertakings. The Government of Notables which, almost from its formation, and certainly since the abandonment in 1781 of the different forts that elected members, had been allowed to rust in its machinery, was again furbished and put in operation. The return of many who had left in 1781 and 1782 gave new life to the settlement, and with this came the desire again to establish some form of government. On the seventh of January, 1783, the former manner of proceedings "was revived, pursuant to the plan agreed upon at our first sitting here." The forts had already been rebuilt and reoccupied, and in accordance with the design as originally planned, twelve men were elected to meet at Nashborough, namely, Colonel James Robertson, Captain George Freeland, Thomas Molloy, Isaac Linsey, David Rounsevall, Heydon Wells, James Mauldin, Ebenezer Titus, Samuel Barton, and Andrew Ewin. Robertson was elected chairman of the committee. Andrew Ewin, who afterwards became Ewing, was made clerk. Putnam has preserved the records of the Committee of Notables. They give us a fine view of the habits, customs, and modes of thought that prevailed in the Cumberland settlement. The committee exercised, practically, unlimited jurisdiction; required people to take the oath of allegiance to the Continental Congress, engaged six spies, who were to advise the settlement of the movements of the Indians, organized the militia, restricted the price of whiskey, regulated trade with the Indians, and tried all manner of cases. We find records of suits involving horses, negroes, hogs, machinery, notes of hand (one for two *cows*) and the like, which enable us to catch, in the process of formation, the ideas of government entertained by our ancestors. It is worthy of note that the caption of the records is "North Carolina, Cumberland District." The committee had once petitioned the General Assembly of North Carolina, praying them "to grant us the salutary benefits of government in all its various branches." The aspirations which filled the old Watauga people with the vain hope of becoming an independent State never obtained any foot-hold among the settlers of Middle Tennessee. A convention was held and commissioners appointed with power to "join the Franks" in their government, but nothing came of it. They stood upon too slender a foundation to think of aught but the actual present, which to them was full of danger and trouble.

After this period the growth of the settlement was rapid. The increase of population, however, for a time merely increased the powers of resistance. The danger was still great, and the chronicles of murder, mutilation, and bloody reprisal repeat the same sorry and distressing details. Land bounties, given to soldiers of the Revolution, were the immediate cause of increased emigration. In 1783 James Robertson was elected a member of the General Assembly of North Carolina, and through his instrumentality the Cumberland settlement was made a county named Davidson, in honor of General Davidson, a gallant soldier who had lost his life in the war. A court of pleas and quarter sessions was also established in the new county. A land office was opened at the same session for receiving and recording entries of land. The Henderson-Transylvania claim and title were not regarded. The original settlers or squatters were given certain rights of preëmption. Each head of a family received 640 acres, and such improvements as had been made previous to the first of June, 1780. Salt springs and "licks" were reserved to the State. The formation of the county transformed the mode of government more in name than in substance. Isaac Bledsoe, Samuel Barton, Francis Prince, and Isaac Linsey were the first magistrates, or justices of the peace. Andrew Ewing was made clerk. A court-house was located at Nashborough, and a prison built. The court-house was made of hewn cedar logs a foot square, the same which the gigantic Spencer offered to throw one by one over the bluff for a dollar a log. The court-room was eighteen feet square, with a shed on one side. Both prison and court-house, the building of which was let upon contract to the lowest bidder, were to be upon a rock-foundation. The formation of the county placed upon an equally solid basis the settlement on the Cumberland.

After the establishment of Davidson County, the current of Middle Tennessee history grows broader and deeper, and its windings more intricate, though still advancing steadily toward independent Statedom. It is an easy and interesting task to watch the gradual expansion of the original forts and observe the gradations from Nashborough on the Cumberland to Nashville, the capital of Tennessee. It was not until some years later that the Cumberland settlement was drawn by the influence of Spanish intrigue and the impulse of the laws of trade into the intricacies of a wider channel of progress and action. Occasionally, however, there is a premonitory symptom, at times a diplomatic clash. When Robertson returned from North Carolina after the adjournment of the General Assembly, he found that already many of the old forts were being rebuilt, and as the population increased, new ones added. Isaac Bledsoe built a fort at Bledsoe's Lick. Anthony Bledsoe built one about two miles distant. Charles Morgan erected one on Bledsoe's Creek. The number increased steadily, in spite of renewed Indian attacks, which fell at times like hurricanes of destruction upon the citizens of the county. The discovery of the weakness of the Continental Congress had dispelled the awe of the implacable savage.

In 1784 the town of Nashville, named in honor of Colonel Nash,— like Davidson a revolutionary hero of North Carolina,— succeeded the station of Nashborough. Commissioners were appointed to survey the plat and lay off about two hundred acres of land on the Cumberland Bluffs, near the French Lick, in lots each of one acre, with convenient streets, lanes, and alleys, four acres being reserved for public purposes. The condition of each deed to the lots was the making of certain improvements upon them within three years. The directors and trustees were Samuel Barton, Thomas Molloy, and James Shaw. The consideration, as recited in their deeds, was "four pounds lawful money and the proviso and condition that the purchaser should build or finish within three years on the lot, one well-framed log, brick, or stone house, sixteen feet square at least, eight feet clear in the pitch."

In 1785 it was enacted by the General Assembly of North Carolina that "one judge shall be commissioned by His Excellency the Governor for the time being, first being elected by joint-ballot of the General Assembly for this purpose, to hold a Superior Court of Law and Equity in the said county, to be styled the Superior Court of Law and Equity for the County of Davidson, twice in each year in Nashville, to wit, on the first Monday of May and the first Monday of November annually, to be continued by adjournment for ten days, exclusive of Sundays." The judge was allowed a salary of fifty pounds.[1] The year following the General Assembly erected a new county, taken from Davidson, and gave it the name of Sumner.

An act was passed in 1786 for the protection of the inhabitants of Davidson and Sumner counties. It was directed that a military body of two hundred men be enlisted and formed for two years' term of service, under command of major, captain, lieutenant, ensign, and four sergeants, to be elected by the General Assembly. The justices of the peace were authorized and required to lay a tax payable in corn, pork, beef, or other species of provisions for the support of the troops. A proper out-

---

[1] Haywood says "they appointed a young man of the age of twenty-four to be the judge of this court, who, upon mature reflection becoming fearful that his small experience and stock of legal acquirements were inadequate to the performance of those great duties which the office devolved upon him, chose rather to resign than to risk the injustice to suitors, which others of better qualifications might certainly avoid." This is a most improbable legend. Andrew Jackson, the young man in question, was born in 1767, and in 1785 was only eighteen years old. In addition to this, he was not admitted to the bar of Davidson County until 1789.

fit of clothing was supplied by the State as a bounty and an offset against certain stipulated quantities of ammunition to be supplied by the recruits themselves. "The officers and privates were allowed the same pay and rations (spirituous liquors excepted) as were allowed to the militia officers and privates in the service of the State." Not the least important duties performed by this corps were the opening a road from the lower end of Clinch Mountain to Nashville. The road is frequently mentioned in the early records, and each year provisions for its improvement were made by North Carolina or Davidson County. The most important of the duties of the company were to conduct parties of emigrants to the middle settlements. This frequently induced those who arrived in East Tennessee on their way to Kentucky to change their point of destination and proceed to Nashville.[1] The guard certificates which were issued in payment of these services became a kind of currency. Each day saw the arrival of new settlers — the broadening of the limits of civilization. Vegetables were grown from seeds brought from the ports of Virginia and the Carolinas, and even from Philadelphia. John Donelson, the year of his arrival, had planted cotton, and found that it grew exuberantly in soil well exposed to the rays of the sun. Corn always yielded an abundant harvest when the accidents of Indian warfare allowed it to be properly cultivated. A tobacco inspection was established in 1785. In this year also arrived the first physician, preceding by one year the arrival of the first lawyers, in Middle Tennessee, namely, Edward Douglas and Thomas Molloy. These two rode the circuit of Davidson and Sumner counties

---

[1] The fact that Andrew Jackson went to Nashville under such an escort throws some doubt upon Parton's owl story, especially in view of the fact that, according to this, the Indians allowed a party whom they had surrounded to deliberately pack, mount, and move off unmolested.

until eventually Tennessee County was erected. It is one of the distinguishing features of American history that the schoolmaster goes hand in hand with the preacher and the dispensers of justice. In 1785 the legislature of North Carolina — or rather James Robertson who represented Davidson County in the General Assembly of North Carolina — had passed an act appointing Rev. Thomas B. Craighead and others a body politic under the name of President and Trustees of Davidson Academy, and two hundred and forty acres were granted near Nashville for its support. From this origin has come the Nashville University. In this year, also, we find traces of another feature of American civilization more powerful, perhaps, than all the rest. An act was passed forbidding the distillation of spirituous liquors in Davidson County. Among the reasons assigned was the preservation of grain. Shortly after this, however, the first whiskey was distilled from raw corn, and soon the Red Heifer became one of the rallying points of the settlement. It stood upon the bluff near Spout Spring in Nashville. The Red Heifer was preceded but a few years by a corn mill and a "hominy pounder." These were run by water-power, and their invention, by a curious coincidence, originated in the brain of a man named Cartwright. Before this, hominy was made either by the hand pestle or by a so-called spring pole, worked generally by horse-power. The first application of water-power was a rude imitation of the application of hand-power. "A trough was made some twelve feet long and placed upon a pivot or balance, and was so dug out, that by letting the water run in at one end of the trough it would fill up so as to overcome the equipoise, when one end would descend and the water rushing out, the trough or log would return to its equilibrium, coming down at the other end with a considerable force, where a pestle or hammer was made to strike with force sufficient to crack the grains of corn."

This was naturally a tedious process. Cartwright "constructed a wheel upon the rim of which he fastened a number of cows' horns in such a position that as each horn was filled by water from the little stream, its weight turned the wheel so that the next horn presented its open mouth to receive its supply of water-weight and thus keep the wheel in constant revolution. To a crank was attached the apparatus for corn-cracking."[1] Two men named Henderson and Wells have the honor of being the earliest millers of Middle Tennessee. They were soon surrounded by rival establishments. By the side of some of them stood frequently the immediate successors of the Red Heifer.

Another evidence of the growth of population was the establishment of a ferry across the Cumberland, above the mouth of Sulphur-Lick Branch. Another infant industry which added to the comforts and increased the solidity of the settlements was the manufacture of salt. Up to 1789, all grants of land were expressly precluded from embracing any salt springs — commonly called licks. These were generally leased out to parties who were under contract to manufacture specified quantities. A part of the tax for the support of the guards was payable in salt. In 1789 the salt springs were ordered sold, except some reserved for public use, and those buying the licks were free to manufacture as much as they saw fit. Kettles had been brought from Jonesboro and furnaces erected as early as 1785–86. Among others engaged in this industry was the versatile Mountflorence, a Frenchman, who was noted for his thrift, his enterprise, and his politeness, and who was supposed to be in some mysterious and not very tangible manner connected with the French government.

[1] Putnam.

CHAPTER XVI.

TROUBLE WITH THE INDIANS.

But whilst the pursuits of agriculture and a small but slowly increasing trade were broadening and deepening the foundations of the future State, implacable hatred was still burning in the breasts of the ancient owners of the soil, and the rifle had not been allowed long to hang upon the gun-racks in the cabins. The treaty which Martin and Donelson, under commission from Virginia, had made with the Indians, and through which important cessions of territory were gained, had been disregarded by the United States under that custom of law which allows to sovereignty alone the right of despoiling the native tribes of America. But the same results had practically been accomplished by the provisions of the treaty made at Hopewell the 28th of November, 1785, and the later treaty of January 10. The former was between the United States and the Cherokees; the latter between the Chickasaws and the United States. The Hopewell Treaty had been received with outspoken disapproval by the Cumberland as well as the Watauga people. William Blount, then a member of Congress, declared against its ratification. Lands which the Sycamore Shoals Treaty of Henderson and the Treaty of Fort Stanwix had obtained from the Indians had been entered and settled. A great number of these settlers were declared by the Treaty of Hopewell to be upon Indian ground. Those who failed to move off were left to be punished by the Indians as they might think proper. They were allowed to arrest any person they might believe to have been guilty of a capital offense, and " punish them in the presence of some of the Cherokees in the same manner as they would be punished for like offenses committed on citizens of the United States." The region of country left the Cumberland settlement was that between the Cumberland River and the boundary line of Kentucky. The Piomingo Treaty of January, 1786, gave the Chickasaws all the country along the valleys of the Ohio and the Mississippi to the northern boundary of the Choctaws. The United States commissioners, in making these concessions, had been guided by a sincere desire to put an end to the bloody contests upon the frontier. They hoped to conciliate the Indians and to withdraw them from the influence which the whole frontier had now begun to appreciate — the malign influence of France and Spain. But they failed. Scarcely had the treaty been concluded, and before the recipients of the presents bestowed had worn the tinsel from their ornaments, the old butchery again began. Peter Barrett was killed below where Clarksville now stands, within the limits which had been reserved for the Cumberland settlement by the late treaty. This was soon followed by other attacks until the reign of terror, which the settlers vainly hoped had been forever ended as a compensation for the indignities of the Treaty of Hopewell, was again restored. One of the most determined opponents of that treaty had been James Robertson, and he inveighed bitterly against the parsimony of the mother State, which threw upon the infant settlement the burden of bearing its own expenses for self-defense and the exigencies of frontier life. As a representative from Davidson County, Robertson, in connection with Bledsoe and William Blount, an avowed friend of the Western people, had in 1786 drawn up a memorial to the General Assembly, in which he set forth in forcible and indignant language the condition of the

Cumberland settlement. He reviewed the persistent cruelty of the Indians, the number they had massacred, their threatened vengeance, and the danger undergone by those who had ventured into the wilderness and made it yield a revenue to the coffers of the State. He alluded in feeling terms to the treaty between Spain and the United States, which threatened to cut them off from all market for their produce, and the added mortification of seeing the Indians rendered more hostile by the influence of Spain itself. "We call upon the humanity and justice of the State to prevent any further massacres and depredations of ourselves and our constituents, and we claim from the legislature that protection of life and property which is due to every citizen, and recommend as the most safe and convenient means of relief, the adoption of the resolves of Congress of the 26th October last for the cession of western lands to the United States." But it was the policy of North Carolina, founded upon the dictates of self-interest, to make no outlay upon a province which in the natural course of human events would soon be beyond her control. All acts passed this session required the expenditures for the Cumberland settlement to be collected from the Cumberland people. When Robertson returned to Nashborough he found the condition of the people almost as desperate as at any time since the Battle of the Bluffs. In a few weeks after his return his brother, Mark Robertson, was killed. Filled with grief and resentment, he resolved to strike one blow that would for a time at least put an end to the daily atrocities which embittered and endangered the lives of his people. His suspicions fell upon the Indians living near the Muscle Shoals, at a place where a deep spring of cold clear water gushed forth from the hidden recesses of the earth, — now the pleasant and sleepy little town of Tuscumbia in Alabama. Not knowing the intricacies of the forests, his embarrassment was relieved by the offer of the services of

Toka, a friendly Chickasaw, and a friend of Toka. Having made due preparation, he marched out from the station with a well-trained band of one hundred and twenty men. Another party was to go by water down the Cumberland and up the Tennessee to Colbert's Ferry, a crossing place used by the Indians, with provisions, under the command of David Hay. Pushing rapidly across the country and through the cane-brakes that stood densely upon the lower banks of the Cumberland, Robertson arrived upon the banks of the Tennessee River and concealed his men until a favorable time for crossing should arrive. Finding a large canoe upon the opposite shore, a question arose as to who should swim the river to bring it back. During the discussion a plunge was heard, and Edmond Jennings, the brave and fearless son of the unfortunate Jonathan Jennings, was in the water and hidden by the darkness. Joshua Thomas, his inseparable companion, immediately followed. They soon returned with a canoe capable of carrying forty men. After some mishaps Robertson finally arrived upon the other bank with all his company. Marching towards the town, he ordered his men to preserve the strictest silence. Toka had predicted that as soon as the Indians saw them they would run to their boats at the mouth of the creek that emptied into the river some distance above the town. Robertson sent Rains to intercept them with a small body of men. Having made his preparations, the word was given, and the little band rushed into the village. The Indians were already in full retreat toward their boats, but they lost in all thirty lives. The village was destroyed, and Robertson left, taking with him a large quantity of merchandise belonging to French traders whom he had captured whilst trying to escape with the Indians. The prisoners were released and the men returned to Cumberland, without the loss of a life, laden with the spoils of the French traders. This is known as the Toka, or

TROUBLE WITH THE INDIANS. 143

Cold Water expedition. The party under Hay met with less success. It had one man killed and three wounded. Coming almost immediately upon the heels of the Hopewell Treaty, the Toka expedition created a profound sensation throughout the Southwest, and Robertson felt called on to write a justification of his course for the satisfaction of the French at Illinois. The best justification was found in a fact which he judiciously failed to mention, that the depredations were stopped, though only for a few weeks.

Robertson immediately wrote a communication to the Indians by a trader named Perrault, expressing his desire to be at peace with them and offering terms of amity. Their reply was an armed body of two hundred braves, who, separated into bands of from three to five, restored in tenfold degree the horrors of the earlier days of the settlement. Robertson hastened the formation of t battalion designed for the protection of Davidson County, and placed it under the command of Captain Evans. But it was discovered that the regularly organized troops, many of them newly arrived emigrants and recruits from the eastern settlements, were inadequate to perform the duties expected of them. They were not equal to the emergencies of Indian warfare and were therefore assigned to guard duty to escort incoming emigrants across the country over the Clinch and Nashville road. The men who were called on to meet the Indians were those who had learned the lesson of experience. John Rains and Castleman, Edmond Jennings and Josh Thomas were worth a hundred dragoons.

John Rains was given command of troops raised in the Cumberland country and made at different times three expeditions against the Indians, each of which overawed them, though only temporarily. The entire male population of the western settlement were in arms and scoured the forests in all directions. But the only good result was to drive the Indians back to their villages. The evil was merely checked for a short time. The depredations of the Indians continuing, Robertson again made ready to apply the corrective which the stern example of John Sevier had demonstrated to be alone efficacious. He invaded their country. But being met by a messenger who brought assurance of friendship, and promises to refrain from further molestation, and perhaps being also apprehensive of further complication with the Spanish, whose traders he was likely to meet, he returned without striking a blow. But upon a renewal of hostilities, Robertson and Bledsoe visited Kentucky and made arrangements for a joint invasion of the country of the Creeks. Not content with invoking the aid of Kentucky, Robertson wrote an urgent letter to John Sevier. Anthony Bledsoe also wrote to "his excellency," suggesting the destruction of Chickamauga towns as the only hope of immunity, and stating that an organized body of a thousand Creeks was reported to be on the way to the Cumberland settlement.

But Sevier was at this time no longer governor. The State of Franklin had been merged in the State of North Carolina. Nothing daunted, however, Sevier headed an expedition against the common enemy and created a diversion which prevented the threatened invasion. The last days of North Carolina's rule in Tennessee were full of misery for the people on the border. The Indians, both in the east and in the west, kept up the old system of hostilities, surprises, and massacres. The intrigues of Spain added strength and persistency to their malignancy. There was nothing to hope for from the parent State. The settlements had grown in strength and were now become restive under her niggardly neglect and chafed at the bonds which held them. The State, it is true, made no attempts to derive revenue from the new settlements, but she was also equally particular to allow none of the charges of their support or protection to fall upon herself. Recriminations ensued and bitterness of feeling. North Carolina

TROUBLE WITH THE INDIANS.

accused the frontier people of bad faith in making out their accounts. In turn the mother State was accused of viewing with cold-blooded indifference the mutilations and assassinations of her own children. The immediate prospects of separation alone prevented the Cumberland people from imitating the example of the Watauga and Nollichucky revolutionists. Separation was equally desired by those who lived on the shores of the Atlantic and in the valleys beyond the Appalachian Mountains.

CHAPTER XVII.

TERRITORY AND NICKOJACK EXPEDITION.

The immediate cause of separation was the example of the other States and the prospects held out of relief from debt. One of the leading ideas upon which the new government was founded was the assumption and payment in full by the federal government of the unpaid state debts, incurred by them during the war for independence. North Carolina, which previously refused to enter the Union, had in November, 1789, finally ratified the constitution and become a member of the new government. The act of cession was passed in December of the same year, and ceded to the United States, the strong and healthy successor of the feeble and inefficient Continental Congress, " all right, title, and claim which this State has to the sovereignty and territory of the lands situated within the chartered limits of the State," west of a line which is now the eastern boundary of Tennessee.

One condition of this cession was that all land so ceded should be considered as a common fund for the use and benefit of the United States of America, North Carolina inclusive. Certain rights of entry were reserved and provision made for the non-acceptance of the cession. One of the most important conditions was one which in the light of subsequent events was pregnant with sinister meaning: "No regulations made or to be made by Congress shall tend to emancipate slaves." It was also provided that the territory so ceded should be laid out or formed into a State or States, the inhabitants of which were to enjoy all the privileges, benefits, and advantages granted by the late Congress for the government of the Western Territory of the United States. On the 9th of January, 1790, Hamilton, the ablest and most brilliant of the members of the first American cabinet, brought forward his report on the settlement of the public debt. One of the measures advocated was the assumption of the state debts by the general government. Alarmed and excited by the rapid strides towards what they regarded despotic centralization, the anti-federalists put forth their whole strength to defeat this recommendation. It was only carried by a vote of 31 to 26, but before it had received the concurrence of the Senate, seven members arrived from North Carolina. Surrounded by friends who were eager to defeat the measures of their opponents, and perhaps persuaded that the relief from debt when so accomplished was more dangerous than the burden of the debt itself, they voted to reconsider the bill. The minority of five had now become a majority of two and the measure was defeated. Indignant at the short-sightedness which hampered the broad results of his statesmanship, and unscrupulous in the use of political forces involving no moral turpitude, Hamilton purchased the votes of the two anti-federalists from the Potomac by fixing the final site of the national capital on its banks, and thus carried triumphantly through the measures which his mature insight recognized as alone possible to place the financial policy of the young government upon a firm basis. On the 25th of February, 1790, Samuel Johnston and Benjamin Hawkins, United States senators from North Carolina, signed the deed of cession, which made Tennessee, as yet unnamed, a Territory of the United States. The act of acceptance was approved April 2, 1790, and on May 26, 1790, was passed "an act for the government of the Territory of the United States, south of the river Ohio."

The Territory being formed, it became necessary to find

a man capable of meeting the delicate requirements of the governorship. Patrick Henry, who knew the stubborn temper of the Western people, suggested and urged the nomination of Mason of Virginia. But unfortunately for Henry's nominee, there appeared a man singularly fitted for the position by his character, his affiliations with the inhabitants of the new country, his popularity among them, his knowledge of Indian affairs, and his personal intimacy with Washington himself. This was William Blount of North Carolina, who received the appointment. The choice could not have been more fortunate. It is true he lacked the thorough knowledge of Indian character which only came from personal contact and was too credulous. But he understood better than any man of his day the diplomatic relations of the Indian tribes and the United States, and was heartily in accord with those who regarded the aborigines as blocks in the path of progress and civilization. He possessed in an eminent degree the confidence of the people of the Territory. He appreciated as no man of equal knowledge of law and government appreciated the difference between the lack of social polish and the sturdy spirit of independence which, though rugged and uncouth, brooked no infringement of right and no trespass on accepted custom. He had perhaps involuntarily caught something of the Old World elegance from the foreign element which in those days thronged our larger cities and was himself on occasions as stately, dignified, and courtly as any of those who frequented the *salons* of Paris, to pay light compliments to Madame Recamier or to laugh at the saturnine witticisms of the Encyclopedists. But he also possessed the soldierly *camaraderie* that embraces all noble spirits irrespective of outward habiliments. His nomination was hailed with universal satisfaction, and the machinery of the new government started off without a jar. David Campbell, who appeared to have a prescriptive right to the position, was appointed judge. Daniel Smith was made secretary. When the General Assembly was organized, in 1794, the members of the legislative council were Griffith Rutherford, John Sevier, James Winchester, Stockley Donelson, and Parmenas Taylor. In the east the Franklinites, or "Franks," were generally appointed to office. Upon the recommendation of Blount, Sevier was made brigadier-general of Washington District and James Robertson of Mero District.

The administration of Governor Blount is undistinguished by any event of great legislative importance. A few counties were formed, among the number, Tennessee County, the act for the establishment of which had been passed by the General Assembly of North Carolina before the cession.

The seat of government was removed from Rogersville, where it had been first located, to Knoxville, and with it the "Knoxville Gazette," the first Tennessee newspaper, which had received its name in anticipation of the change. The proprietor, James White, the father of Hugh Lawson White, laid off a town which he named Knoxville, in honor of the secretary of war of Washington's cabinet. In 1792 Knox County was taken from Greene and Hawkins counties, and immediately the beginnings of a town began to appear at Knoxville, the county seat. The three leading features of Governor Blount's administration were the contests with the Indians, the gradual extinguishment of their title to lands in the limits of the present State, and the final triumph of America in the diplomatic contests with Spain.

Indian hostilities came practically if not absolutely to an end with the Nickojack expedition. The final extinguishment of the Indian title was not accomplished until many years after Tennessee had become a State. But the treaty of 1791 and its ratification in 1794 inaugurated the policy which was to control the future dealings of the United States with the Indians. Treaties, however, merely secured the results which were assured by the expedition against the lower towns. In the east, Sevier made various expeditions against the Indians, upon each of which he destroyed their towns and their cornfields. Immediately upon his return from North Carolina after his escape, he was called into active service. During his absence General Joseph Martin attempted to lead an expedition against the Cherokees, but his men, accustomed to Sevier, lost confidence and forced him to return. Scarcely had they arrived at Knoxville and dispersed when a body of Creeks and Cherokees fell upon Fort Gillespie and destroyed it. Sevier precipitated himself upon them with the flight of an eagle, and took prisoners enough to release by exchange all white captives in the Indian villages. In this way, Joseph Brown, at that time a prisoner in one of the lower towns and the future guide of the Nickojack expedition, was set free. Other attempts of the Indians to break the power of the eastern settlements met with like fate. In 1793 occurred the attack on Cavet's Station. The government at Washington had been trying to keep down all hostilities against the Indians, fearing an interruption of the negotiations with Spain. After the attack on Cavet's Station, Daniel Smith, the acting governor of the Territory, disregarded the orders of Congress and gave the permission for which the whole body of the people were clamoring — an organized invasion of their territory. John Sevier, reinforced by large bodies of troops from the three districts of the Territory, pushed immediately into the enemies' country. He crossed the Little Tennessee and burnt Estimaula, one of their largest villages. Expecting an attack from the Indians who were lurking in the woods around their deserted villages, he formed his men in two parallel lines along the banks of the Estimaula River. A midnight attack resulted in the defeat of the Indians. Sevier advanced through the fairest section of the Indian territory, burning and destroying as he went. Arriving at Etowah, an Indian village situated in the vicinity of the present town of Rome in Georgia, he came upon the retreating forces of the Indians which had been augmenting as they fled. Falling fiercely upon them with more than his usual impetuosity, Sevier put them utterly to rout and overthrew their power. This was the heaviest disaster which had ever befallen the Indians, and with the fall of Etowah came practically to an end the long line of Indian massacres in East Tennessee, which had begun almost with the building of William Bean's cabin. This was Sevier's last campaign. On his return he was met with enthusiastic applause by the people for whom he had accomplished so much, and the Cumberland settlers sent him messages of earnest gratitude.

In the west the entire administration of Governor Blount was filled with the annals of Indian warfare. On the 20th of July, 1788, Colonel Anthony Bledsoe, the brave old Indian fighter and surveyor, who had passed unscathed through all the dangers and hardships of pitched battles and frontier life, was assassinated in his own cabin. Hearing his cattle rushing by his cabin, he stepped out of his room and was shot. In 1789, Robertson, while working with several laborers in a field near his house, was wounded in the foot by a shot from a thicket of cane. In the pursuit which followed, Andrew Jackson, a newly arrived lawyer, distinguished himself by his reckless daring and cool presence of mind.[1] Danger was ever present. The fields could not be worked without

---

[1] Parton confuses this event, which took place in 1789, with the wound which General Robertson received in 1792. Andrew Jackson figured in the former. The only pursuit in the latter year was that by the Indians of General Robertson and his son Jonathan. In the the first case, Robertson was wounded in the foot, in the second, in the arm. The latter wound was a running sore for many years.

guards on the outlook. Every step was, perhaps, a step towards the grave. We still have a general order of Robertson's, dated April 5, 1789, calling on the militia to be ready to march at any moment. The low undergrowth of cane offered an almost perfect shelter to a lurking foe, and it became necessary to destroy it along the paths which ran between the various forts. In 1791, about the time of the Holston Treaty, Robertson tried to stay the hostilities of the Indians by a visit to their nation. But he soon found that the lull was merely temporary. Information came of a scalp-dance and war-orgie among the Chickamauga-Cherokees, who acknowledged no obligations of treaty. The Treaty of New York at which Alexander McGillivray, the wonderful Talleyrand of the Creeks, duped Washington and his representatives out of $100,000 as a *douceur* for himself and an indefinite quantity of blankets, dry goods, and hardware for his people, had never been regarded by the Creeks as anything more than an evidence of their *finesse* and of American credulity. Americans made treaties, gained possession of the land, and then violated the provisions of the treaties. For lands, the Creeks substituted supplies of the things they prized, and considered their policy not less laudable than that of their white brothers. In 1792 the Creeks changed their line of conduct, and actuated, no doubt, by the foreign traders, chiefly Spanish, who feared to see the trade which they found so lucrative slip from their grasp, attempted to gain advantage of the Robertson people by diplomacy. Several of their chiefs called on Robertson at Nashville, to smoke the pipe of peace in the big wigwam of their brother. The old soldier received them with cordiality. He fed them bountifully, gave them drink, and dismissed them with presents. But he kept Rains and Jennings and Castleman and other escorts in the woods. Having had some peace talks, Governor Blount became elated and wrote to Robertson, "Watts has sent me a *peace* talk, and a string of white beads. I believe he is in earnest." He saw the near end of Indian warfare. But Sevier possessed a clearer, a more penetrating vision. "The governor is too hopeful," he wrote. "He hopes against hope." Even in the midst of these friendly interchanges, Robertson continued his preparations for war, and organized anew the militia of three counties — Tennessee County having been recently added. The regular militia was distributed among the various forts for local duty. A reserve of five hundred men, exempt from local duty, was kept constantly ready to serve at a moment's notice. The military household of the district was further strengthened by the presence of a body of cavalry under Major Sharpe. Though under the immediate command of the governor of the Territory, he was required to act in conjunction with General Robertson, and being put in rank above the colonels of the district, though only a major, was the cause of one of them, Winchester, resigning.

In this year the settlers received an earnest of the friendliness of the Creeks in the murder of the three sons of Colonel Valentine Sevier, the brother of General Sevier. Valentine Sevier had settled at the mouth of the Red River, near where the hilly and picturesque little town of Clarksville now stands, and his sons, when killed, were in a boat going up Cumberland River. But filled with the courage of his race, Sevier strengthened his fortification and remained at his post. This was but one instance of the outcropping of the spirit which, over and above the question of self-interest, introduced an element of heroism and chivalric loyalty to a noble mission into the desperate struggles which characterized the founding of this State. A few months after the death of Sevier's three sons and their companions, the Indians attacked Zigler's Station, a fort on the west fork of Bledsoe's Creek. During a time when one man dared not drink from a spring unless another stood with a rifle cocked to protect him, the night guards of a large station slumbered at their posts. The Indians stealthily surrounded the fort, opened the gate, and rushed in. Resistance was useless. They killed five people and captured about twenty more. This disaster came heavily home to the settlers. Never before had so many of their friends fallen at one blow. The indignant troops clamored to be led against the common foe. Robertson refused. It was against orders, and the old settlers listened with incredulous astonishment as they were told by one who never trifled, that the governor of the Territory had forbidden any pursuit of the Indians into their own country. This meant, of course, the interdiction of all pursuit. Washington at this time was engaged in an arduous diplomatic struggle. The least jar might break the fine network of diplomatic threads in which Jay was endeavoring to entangle the Spanish authorities. The murder of a trader might bring about a refusal on the part of Spain to allow to America the free navigation of the Mississippi River. This refusal meant something which was frequently heard in the thriving young settlements of the Ohio valley, and even in the senate chamber at Philadelphia, but not from the persuasive lips of the American diplomat. On this account, for this reason, Blount was ordered by Knox, the secretary of war, to allow no offensive operations beyond the bounds of the Territory of which he was governor. Blount in turn ordered Robertson to forbid all offensive operations beyond the limits assigned the Indians by the Treaty of Holston, that is, east of the ridges which divide the waters of the Cumberland and the Tennessee. But the people chafed. One John Edmiston organized a company of his own to invade the Indian country, but was restrained by an order of Robertson which compelled him to disband his troops. In return for this, Robertson received an anonymous letter from "a citizen of the new district," who vented his spleen by wishing "Edmiston great success, and you gone from hence and a better in your room."[1] The navigation of the Mississippi River was an important question to the broad vision, the clear foresight, and the happy statesmanship of Sevier. But to Robertson, with his brother and his sons and his friends falling about him, and with the marks of two bullets on his own person, it was vague, shadowy, intangible. A burning fort and a dozen or so scalped women and children were, on the contrary, an absolute tangibility, a thing full of arguments, reasons, and conclusions. It requires but little imagination to picture the strain placed upon his sense of duty. It finally became too great and he yielded. But in both it is no difficult matter to see that he was actuated by motives which the most captious must allow to have been pure and noble. Robertson's self-containment in one thing found its reward. A Creek chief falsely reported to his tribe a threat of Robertson's: "There has been a good deal of blood spilt in our settlement, and I will come and sweep it clean with your blood." Robertson was known among all the Indians of the four nations as a man of his word in peace and in war, and the Creeks thought it best to take the initiative. From Lookout Mountain they sent friendly talks to Governor Blount, filled with assurances of goodwill and abiding friendship. Blount was completely deceived. On the 12th of September, before the arrival of the messenger with the friendly talk, he sent an order to Robertson to enroll as many men as possible for the purpose of resisting the impending invasion. On the 14th of September he sent directions to Robertson to "discharge such part of the brigade of Mero District as may be in service under my order of the 12th instant. I

[1] This, however, was merely a babbler's expression of the sentiment of discontent that prevailed generally throughout the entire community, an impatience directed not against Robertson so much as the authority that controlled his actions. Robertson himself shared the same feeling.

heartily congratulate you and the District of Mero upon the happy change of affairs. I really had dreadful apprehensions for you." On the 16th he sends an express: "The danger is imminent." Between the 14th and the 16th the lower Creek towns had declared war, and six hundred Indians had crossed the Tennessee River to wage a war of extermination. The spies reported danger before Blount's last message came. Notably, Abraham Castleman had, made a circuit of the woods of more than sixty miles, and returning predicted an impending invasion. Blount's congratulations, however, had deceived the people. Even Robertson, who had a high estimate of Castleman's woodcraft and a very low estimate of Governor Blount's, was perplexed. He sent out Rains and Kennedy in one direction, Clayton and Gee in another. The latter were never seen again. The former returned and reported no traces of Indians to be found. Castleman was good-naturedly chided for his over-caution, and John Rains looked with kindly malice at the old Indian fighter as he drily continued his preparations for an elaborate war.

Castleman was right. The Creeks, Cherokees, and Shawnees, to the number of six hundred, had stolen within a few miles of the Cumberland settlement before their presence was discovered. Their first point of attack was Buchanan's Station, which was defended by only fifteen available men. But for some cause the attack of the entire force was easily repulsed without the loss of a life in the station. One of the Indian chiefs was killed in an attempt to fire the buildings, and another was wounded. The number of killed was not known. This is one of the most remarkable incidents in the early border warfare of the Southwest. So wonderful, indeed, that even some of the pioneers believed in the direct interposition of Providence. Both Haywood and Ramsey agree in estimating the number of the Indians at about six hundred. Blount in a letter describing the attack says the Indians numbered from three to four hundred. An account of the attack, published in the Whig "Review" of 1852, which was founded on information derived from the Indians themselves, agrees with these estimates in putting the number of the assailants among the hundreds.

The repulse of the Indians by the Buchanan Station people failed to cause even a temporary cessation of their hostilities, and scattered in small bands through the settlements, they wrought more mischief than when organized. Governor Blount, who had sufficiently clear ideas of the exigencies of Indian warfare, and who among other things had a block-house built at Southwest Point,[1] organized two regiments of militia and placed them under the command of John Sevier. But scarcely had the troops been properly formed when orders came from the secretary of war to have them mustered out of service.

In 1793 another war broke out, in consequence of the killing by John Beard and his party of several Indian chiefs who had assembled at Knoxville by order of the president to arrange some dispute in reference to boundary lines. It was found impossible to get a court-martial to punish Beard. The Cherokees retaliated, Henry's Station was attacked and its inmates slaughtered. In turn a company of riflemen under Doherty and McFarland invaded the Indian country and destroyed six of their villages.

All during 1792 and 1793 the Cumberland settlement still suffered from the effects of Indian warfare. In 1793 Abraham Castleman, whom the Indians called the "Fool Warrior," with Eli Hammond and others, in direct violation of the orders of Congress and Governor Blount, crossed the Tennessee River and made a raid into the Indian country. The indignation of the frontier had gradually grown too strong for restraint. The people, in

[1] Near Kingston of this day.

the exercise of that right which in America is considered superior to all written law, the right of self-defense, began in a spirit of stern determination to make preparations for a war of retaliation and invasion. General Robertson raised troops in Nashville, Montgomery in Clarksville, Miles and Ford in the region of country between these two points. Major Ore who had been sent to Mero District by Blount with troops, immediately joined the enterprise. Kentucky was invited to lend aid, and Colonel Whitly of that State, having brought to the rendezvous a small body of troops, was given nominal command of the combined forces. The expedition at first was called Ore's Expedition. Ore was then in the service of the United States, and it was hoped this would give the expedition a certain appearance of authority. Both Ore and Robertson were acting contrary to orders. But the exasperation of the people was too great — delay was impossible. The immediate cause of the expedition was the murder of a man named Chew, with a party of fifteen, the assassination of two young Bledsoes, sons of Anthony Bledsoe, and the murder of Major Winchester one of the magistrates of Sumner County. The point of attack was the five lower towns of the Chickamaugas, of which the most noted was Nickojack. From this, the expedition received its name of the Nickojack Expedition, by which it is still known. For a long time, this expedition, which is the most celebrated of all the incidents of early Indian warfare in Tennessee, received a kind of apocryphal notoriety as being the first military exploit of Andrew Jackson since his boyish rencontre with the British officer. Ramsey gives him the credit of having planned the entire attack. But recent research has placed it beyond doubt that Jackson was not present.

There is something suggestive of the fatuitous march of events in a Greek tragedy, in the Nickojack expedition and the fate of the lower Cherokee towns. Even the element of prophecy was not lacking, and the destruction which came was terrible, complete, and directly the result of the fiercest passion for revenge. The situation of these towns caught a certain air of picturesque grandeur from the natural scenery around them. The two most important were Nickojack and Running Water. They were situated on a precipice which was all but impregnable. A deep, broad, and dangerous river ran below. Beyond were the dense forests, penetrated only by the paths which successive generations of wild beasts had made, and the tall, inaccessible peaks of the Cumberland Mountains, down whose dark and precipitous ravines it was supposed no horse could ever descend. The approach in the rear was impossible to all but friends, and the Indians exultingly boasted that "Chucky Jack" himself would never be able to reach them in their retreat. The eagle in his eerie, the panther in his lair, could not be safer. Here dwelt the fierce and implacable Chickamaugas, whose villages above had been destroyed by Shelby, and who, learning a lesson from the first surprise, had hoped to select a place where Nature herself would keep eternal guard over their women, children, and wigwams. Here, too, they had been joined by all the elements of lawlessness which had been outlawed by neighboring tribes as unfitted even for the duties which the laxity of Indian customs imposed. In addition to these had come some few of the white race — Ishmaels and outcasts from all the western world. Here they returned to rest after their labors of war. From here they could see the boats of traffic and emigration as they dropped down the Tennessee from Knoxville and Fort Henry on their way to Nashville, to Natchez, to Lance de Grace, to New Orleans, and from here they made the descents upon them which often brought them rich returns of plunder, of scalps, and of revenge. In 1788 a party of emigrants had thus fallen into their hands. It consisted of the family of a man named Brown, on his way to Cumberland. Having treacherously and by fair words gotten the party into their power, the Indians slew all but the smallest children. These were reserved for adoption into the tribe or for torture, as the accident of the hour might suggest. One of the children, a half grown boy, was held a prisoner for several years and eventually released by exchange through the instrumentality of John Sevier. Before his departure an old squaw predicted that he would live to bring back an expedition to destroy them all, and insisted on tomahawking the lad to prevent the evil. The fear of Sevier, however, prevailed. The boy of 1788 was a man in 1794, and being urged by Robertson, he succeeded in discovering a horsepath through the thick and almost impenetrable forest and undergrowth that stretched between Nashville and the lower towns.

On the sixth of September, 1794, General Robertson ordered Major Ore to destroy the lower Cherokee towns. Guided by Brown and a trusty half breed scout, the troops advanced to the Tennessee, and arrived upon its banks several miles below the mouth of the Sequatchie. Rafts and floats were rapidly and silently constructed. With the assistance of these and several hide canoes brought for the purpose, the soldiers passed secretly and swiftly over the river, in the early dawn, before the first rays of sunshine had fallen upon the tree tops above them. Some had been forced to swim, although the current of the river, which is here about three quarters of a mile wide, was strong and swift. Having all assembled upon the opposite bank, the ranks were formed and the number counted. There were five hundred.[1] The Indians were as yet totally oblivious of their danger. The troops were divided into two wings. The main body under Whitly was to make a détour and attack Nickojack above; the other, under Montgomery, below. The knowledge of the

[1] Haywood says two hundred and sixty. I follow the official report of Ore, which gives this number.

topographical features of the ground obtained from the former captive, to whom every path, every tree, every knoll was familiar, was invaluable, and alone rendered possible the complete surprise without which the expedition would, at least partially, have miscarried. Having once ascended the narrow path and gotten upon the plateau on which the town stood, without alarming its inmates, the main points of the campaign had been gained, and the details were easy of execution. The silence of death brooded over the little village. The soldiers, chiefly those from the Cumberland settlement, gazed with a sort of joyous exultation upon the unprotected homes and families of those who had often brought misery and destruction upon their homes and their families. They had come as destroyers and avengers. Two houses in a field of corn were seen. Beyond these stood the village. Here the first shot was fired, and orders were given by Montgomery to push steadily forward to the main village, about two hundred and fifty yards distant. Hurrying rapidly forward, the huts were found vacant. Whitly, hearing the firing and being advised by Brown, sent him back with a detachment of about twenty men to intercept those who might try to escape from the mouth of the creek that emptied into the river below the village. The Indians, as soon as they heard the first firing, had hurried to the landing where the canoes were fastened in the vain hope of escape. But being warned in advance by Brown, Montgomery's men hastened forward, and falling upon them slaughtered them in pitiless rage as they came upon them. Whitly, having placed his guards so as to prevent any escape to the upper towns or any reinforcements from them, came down upon them from the other side. The surprise was complete — the destruction was thorough. Running Water, a large village but strategically less important than Nickojack, was four miles higher up the river. Having destroyed Nickojack and slaughtered its inhabitants, the troops pushed forward towards Running Water, and although the inhabitants had made good their escape, they razed it to the ground. The villages higher up the river than these were small and of little moment. Their destruction could be accomplished when it became necessary. The utter annihilation of Nickojack and Running Water accomplished the objects of the raid, and the brave old Cumberland settlers recrossed the river, exultant and triumphant, flushed with victory and glutted with revenge. This was not then regarded an ignoble passion. To those who had lost a child, a wife, some relative, many friends, it became a duty, and its gratification an expiation. The Cumberland people looked forward to a long period of quiet and peace. Now that entrance had been obtained, the idea of perfect seclusion was gone. With this went all hope of continuing successfully the old system of warfare. The Indians who escaped, either joined the Overhill Cherokees or moved lower down the river.

With the fall of Nickojack the question of Indian depredations passed out of the daily thoughts of the Cumberland people. There were occasional murders and thefts of horses, waylaying of trains of merchandise, and at times captures of emigrant boats. Runners or scouts paid out of the public funds, whose duty it was to pass from settlement to settlement and keep an outlook for Indians, survived nearly to the Creek wars. But the dangers were chiefly such as were natural incidents of frontier life and an unsettled state of society, and were as frequently caused by desperadoes and lawless white men as Indians. The secretary of war wrote to Governor Blount, and Governor Blount wrote a severe letter to Robertson, when news of the destruction of Indian towns in the limits of Indian territory arrived in Washington and Knoxville. A correspondence ensued, and General Robertson offered his resignation as brigadier-general of Mero District. But here the matter ended. It soon passed from public discussion and was forgotten.

CHAPTER XVIII.

SPANISH INTRIGUES.

In Ore's report to Governor Blount of the destruction of the Cherokee towns, we find the following significant passage: "A quantity of ammunition powder and lead lately arrived there from the Spanish government, and a commission for the Breath, the head man of the town (who was killed), and sundry horses and other articles of property were found at Nickojack and Running Water, which were known to have belonged to different people killed by the Indians in the course of the last twelve months." In the same letter he says, "At Nickojack were found two fresh scalps, which had lately been taken at Cumberland, and several that were old were hanging in the houses of the warriors as trophies."

The juxtaposition of the two articles of Spanish ammunition and American scalps typifies the relative attitudes occupied by the Indians towards the two nations who then owned the region of country which is now the Southwest of the United States. By the treaty of 1762 Spain came into possession of all territory held by the French, west of the Mississippi River. By the treaty of 1783 Spain gained from England what was indefinitely known as Florida, and claimed the ownership of all the country east of the Mississippi up to the 31st degree of latitude. Succeeding the French in their North American possessions, the Spanish fell heir also to their policy. The French, in their futile endeavor to unite the North American continent, of which they owned the two extremes of north and south, connected their possessions by building forts and trading posts through the vast valley of the Mississippi. Between these they kept up a constant line of communication. In this way Du Quesne had been built, and St. Genevieve, Kaskaskia, Vincennes, Nachitoches on Red River, and St. Louis and Natchez on the banks of the Mississippi itself. The Spaniards subsequently added Lance de Grace, now New Madrid in Missouri. Du Quesne had passed into the possession of the United States, but the old trading posts still remained under the sway of the great bankrupt monarchy of the Old World. In 1783 the statesmen of Spain were filled with the same vain dreams which have raised up gorgeous visions of a magnificent southwestern empire in the minds of the statesmen of four nationalities. Indeed, this idea is almost indestructible. There is something in the geographical outlines, in the natural outlets of commerce, in the resources of the soil, which suggests almost spontaneously a great empire in the region of country drained by the Ohio, the Tennessee, the Arkansas, the Tombigbee, the Red, the Sabine, and the Mississippi rivers. From La Salle, who saw its primitive wonders and whose life was the noble offering to the sincerity of his aspirations, to Aaron Burr, the unstable and meteoric American in whom the hope was treason, the finest, the broadest, and the most statesmanlike minds of two continents have been caught by the fascination of the thought.

Spain's intercourse with the Indians was directly subservient to the scheme of extending her territory as far north as the valley of the Ohio. This was the coveted prize, but the means adopted for its attainment lie beyond the scope of a popular history of Tennessee. It is one of the romances of history. It is remarkable as being one of the few instances where diplomacy accomplished great results unaided by force. The various phases of the intellectual contest, where the keenest weapons were the wits of statesmen and the most effective feints the subterfuges of diplomats, make one of the most entertaining and absorbing pages of the world's history. But Tennessee was touched only at various points, and, in as far as its own development was concerned, in no decisive manner. A part of the present State was claimed by Spain, but none of the region then settled.

A more dangerous claim, however, was the exclusive navigation of the Mississippi River. The policy of the Spanish governors who represented that country at Pensacola and New Orleans was to attempt the extirpation of the young and growing settlements by instigating the Indians to continued hostilities, furnishing them ammunition for their purposes and playing upon their cupidity. Failing in this, the next attempt was to act directly upon the settlers themselves, first winning their friendship by allowing their commerce special privileges in the navigation of the Mississippi River, and then exciting their fears by threats of excluding them entirely from a trade which they found lucrative. The name of Governor Mero was given the Cumberland district as an expression of regard and gratitude on the part of the Cumberland people for favors extended their trading boats and the freight they carried to Natchez and New Orleans.

The question of the navigation of the Mississippi River, however, never resulted in exciting any feeling at all friendly towards Spain. Any threats to exclude the Watauga or the Cumberland people from that river aroused their earnest indignation. The intrigues of the Spanish authorities were directed towards the estrangement of the western settlements from the United States and their ultimate union with Spain. Sevier and Robertson have both been accused of complicity in these intrigues. Letters of Robertson are extant which are proof conclusive. But it is scarcely a matter of doubt that he was merely trying to placate the Spaniards in hopes of protecting the settlement under his charge. Governor Mero at New Orleans was the leading mind among the representatives of Spain in the new country, and there is reason to believe that his urbane and liberal character turned with disgust from the policy which supplied the Indians with the weapons of assassination and the means of debauchery. Up to 1792, when he was succeeded by Carondelet, a man of narrower mind and a smaller heart, he used all available weapons of diplomacy to accomplish his purpose, without the exercise of violence. Besides granting commercial privileges and exemptions, he attempted to found an American colony on Spanish soil, at Lance de Grace or New Madrid, west of the Mississippi River. He held out glittering promises to those who would break from the bondage of the weak government that languished at the American capital, either to form a separate government or to become a part of the Spanish Empire.

The policy of extermination was productive of the bitterest results to the settlements. Generally the American frontier men only felt the effects of Spanish malignancy in the acts of Indian hostilities, but occasionally they came face to face with the evil influence in the persons of Spanish traders.[1] In a letter written by Robertson and Bledsoe to Governor Caswell in 1787, they say, "It is certain, as the Chickasaws inform us, that the Spanish traders offer rewards for scalps of the Americans." The only Indian of great ability among the aborigines at that time was a Creek chief, Alexander McGillivray, who, according to an enthusiastic Alabamian, was the greatest man ever born on Alabama soil. Though not a Cherokee, his influence among all the tribes was great, and around

---

[1] Haywood, Ramsey, and Putnam speak indiscriminately of Spanish and French traders. As a rule they were of French extraction, but having come under the dominion of Spain, and having no national principles or preferences, they were, for the purposes for which Gayoso, Mero, and Carondelet used Indian traders, Spaniards.

him revolved the intrigues which involved the Indians in the struggles between America and Spain. McGillivray was one of the most remarkable products of his age. Closely connected by blood with both races, he inherited in a strangely incongruous degree the peculiarities of both. His bearing was so winningly gracious, and so frankly cordial, and his speech so clear and so fluent, that strangers meeting him for the first time could only stare at him in silent amazement. Living in the squalor of an Indian cabin, he had accumulated what the finest gentleman in Madrid would have regarded as wealth. Possessing the manners and the education of a man of the world, he took pride in cheap titles and badges of distinction which the least philosophic white man of his day would have deemed trivial if not contemptible. He hated all of the race from which he derived the better part of his blood, but he unhesitatingly and unscrupulously united with all through whom he could accomplish his purpose. His cupidity was marvelous, and was open to temptations from the things which appealed to the Indian's fancy as well as the things which excited the white man's love of gold. He lacked all idea of moral rectitude both from the Indian's and the white man's standpoint, and having accepted a bribe from the United States, he at once notified the Spanish authorities of his readiness to hear from them. In 1784 he entered into a treaty with the Spaniards looking to the total destruction of the Cumberland settlement. For ten years he never relaxed his exertions for the attainment of that object.

Robertson knew his influence among his people and the Cherokees, and knowing also the magnitude of his vanity, addressed him on one occasion a formal communication full of vague flatteries in the hope that he could be induced to exert his influence for peace. McGillivray received his messengers with lavish hospitality and overwhelmed them with praises of Robertson, and promises of eternal peace. The presents offered he graciously accepted. Nothing was changed, however, in the status of affairs.

The evil influence exerted by the Spaniards finally came to an end with the opening of the Mississippi River to the free navigation of both nations. The Nickojack expedition of 1794, and the treaty of 1795, each removed from Tennessee history a disturbing factor. But one impediment remained in the presence of Indians on the territory of the future State. These were removed gradually and at various times as required by the exigencies of progress in the making of the State.

CHAPTER XIX.

MANNERS, CUSTOMS, AND MODE OF LIFE.

A DESCRIPTION of the manners and customs and mode of life of those who inhabited Tennessee at the end of the eighteenth and the beginning of the nineteenth century is, with minor modifications, a description of the manners and customs and mode of life of those who, at the present day in the far West, are still extending the limits of civilization and laying the foundations of unnamed republics. The same general conditions exist, the same desires for self-advancement, the same longing for material prosperity and mental improvement, the same instinct of self-government. We have passed the primitive stage of our existence by a lapse of time which, compared with the period of notable change in older communities, is scarcely worthy of historical notice, but which is the interval separating youth and inexperience from age and full-blown maturity in the history of the western American States. With all the evidences of the most progressive state of civilization around us, and being in the very foremost files of time, it is difficult for us to grasp as an actual state of society that in which our grandfathers and grandmothers lived. There is but a step from the wild fox to the cotton-gin, an almost inappreciable point of time from the packhorse to the railroad. With the change in material conditions has come a change in habits of life, in social customs, in the very woof of our daily existence. But we should not forget that this change has been greater in the city than in the country.

As we pass in review the life of our near ancestors, as we look into their cabins and follow them to their social gatherings, those who know the present will be struck by the points of resemblance between the things of that day and what still remains in many of the rural districts of this State, especially East Tennessee.

The population of Tennessee in 1790 is given in the federal census of that year, as 25,691. In 1795, when the census was taken under Governor Blount, the total number of inhabitants was discovered to be 77,262. In five years the population had more than trebled. Of these only about 2,500 were in Davidson, Tennessee, and Sumner counties. The emigrants who had come in since the formation of the Territory, which had increased the impetus of inflow, were, as a rule, in better circumstances than the old Watauga heroes. They also had less dangers to encounter. Many were soldiers of the Revolution who had come to locate their grants of land. Many were families brought in by speculators who held lands they were anxious to have cleared. Many came for various other reasons. Some came from New England and Pennsylvania, traveling down the ridge along which lay the great highway of emigration. The greater number, however, came from Virginia, by what was called the Good-Spur route, passing through Western Virginia and down the Holston valley. Others came across the Stone and the Yellow Mountains. A wagon road had been opened from Burke County to Jonesboro, but it was not always possible to use wagons in traveling it. But whether on foot, on horseback, or in wagons, they came, and from early spring until late fall the road leading into Jonesboro presented the appearance of a desultory procession. Arrived here, each party rested, mingled with the people, distributed letters which they had brought, gave the latest news from the sea-board, found out the location of their lands, or the nearest and best road to the place they were seeking, and then pushed resolutely on, to Rogersville, to Greeneville, to Knoxville, or to some of the intervening forts or stations. Perhaps they desired to go to the Cumberland settlements. If so, they made their way by land over the newly opened and level road by way of the Clinch River, from the lower end of Clinch Mountain, or they embarked at Fort Patrick Henry, or Knoxville, to make the attempt by water. This, however, not so often, on account of the river pirates who made the voyage but little less dangerous than it had been during the time of the five lower towns.

Compared with the actual dimensions of the State, the portions then inhabited were but as tufts of civilization in a Sahara of wilderness and barbarous solitude. If one of the new-comers had been carried up so high as to have a bird's-eye view of the settlements, he would have seen little to please the fancy beyond the wilderness of natural scenery. In the far west he would have seen on the banks of the Mississippi where Memphis now stands a small fort filled with a few Spanish officers and soldiers, perhaps a drunken Indian in the door of a hut. Here and there he would have detected isolated wigwams reaching towards the south. Perhaps he might have seen glimpses of the Great Natchez Trace, which led from Nashville to the great trading emporium of the Southwest. After his eye had passed over miles of silent forests, fields, and streams, he would have seen an irregular collection of cabins and block-houses scattered up and down the Cumberland and along the banks of the Caney Fork, Stone River, and a few creeks that emptied into the Cumberland in the neighboring district of country. The whole settlement would not have covered much more than forty miles square, and when the mouth of Red River with its germ of Clarksville had been passed, wilderness and desolation would again have met the eye. In the extreme east the sight would have been little more gratifying. There he would have seen small wooden-house villages and palisaded cabins scattered up and down a half dozen valleys, beginning in a kind of point in Sullivan County, far away among the head waters of the Holston River, spreading out through valley and glen and along river and creek, and gradually coming again to an end at Southwest Point near the junction of the Clinch and the Tennessee Rivers. Not quite one eighteenth of the State was occupied.

If the condition of the highways of a country be taken as an index of a country's prosperity, the condition of Tennessee during these times was deplorable indeed. It is a pardonable exaggeration to say that there were no roads worthy the name. At first the line of emigration advanced to the Watauga settlements by tortuous paths leading over the Appalachian Mountains. In some places, where the forest was unusually dark and intricate, an occasional tree was blazed along the line of travel. The deserted campfires, with their heaps of ashes and broken undergrowth, assisted those who followed in the wake of more adventurous travelers. If rains or storms came, shelter was sought under a neighboring tree or ledge of rock. It was nothing unusual for a traveler to lose his way. Returning from Tennessee to North Carolina, James Robertson barely escaped with his life, having lost his way. At times the declivities of the mountains were so great that it became necessary to alight from the horse and descend on foot. The first road which was made by man was one for vehicles which ran from Jonesboro court-house into Burke County, and the chroniclers all observed that the number of emigrants with some degree of wealth at once increased in a remarkable degree. The roads which led from the various settlements were long neglected. Even as late as 1797, Bishop Asbury says sarcastically, "My horse hath the honor of swimming Holston River every time I visit the country." Nor were the rivers and ravines the only sources of danger, for many an unwary traveler received a blow under the chin from an overhanging limb, or had his knee crushed against a tree, even where the roads were best. When lost, the traveler had but three sources of comfort — chance, Providence, and the instinct of his horse, and in the absence of Indian violence it rarely happened that he failed of all three. Among the most romantic passages of our early history were the adventures which befell those who traveled from East to Middle Tennessee. Up to 1787 the usual route of emigrants was by way of the Kentucky wilderness in a direct line from the east. But in 1787 the General Assembly of North Carolina made provision for a troop of three hundred men who were first to cut a road from the lower end of Clinch Mountain in a direct line to Nashville, at least ten feet wide, and then to act as guards for bands of incoming emigrants. The starting point was Campbell's Station, and it was customary to give public notice of the time of departure.

As early as 1783, and in fact earlier, the western settlements began to turn their attention to the improvement of the roads connecting the various forts and stations. In 1783 a road which had been previously laid out was ordered cleared from Mansker's Station to Nashville. The undergrowth of cane was so great that it was dangerous to go from one fort to another, and as a measure of precaution this was gradually cleared away.

The general topography of the country was primitive and barbarous. Bishop Asbury in his Journal, makes constant allusions to the gloomy scenes through which he passes. Tyger's Valley he calls the "Valley of Distress." This he reached "after crossing six mountains and many rocky creeks and fords." The Gap he compares to "the shades of death in the Alleghany Mountains." On another occasion a Mrs. Scott was four days in traveling two miles through a declivitous thicket.

To add to the hardships which continually beset the traveler, he was frequently deprived of the comforts even of a shelter for his head. After the destruction of Nickojack, occasional log-cabin taverns were found scattered along the line of travel, and their number increased after the admission of Tennessee to the Union. But the accommodations were inferior even by comparison, and the host, as a rule, was a distiller of whiskey and kept a tippling house for the sale of his own beverages. If no tavern could be found, the traveler was thrown upon the mercy of the first human inhabitant of a cabin, and this was rarely denied. The traveler was expected to sleep on his own bedding, generally a blanket and his own clothes, receiving perhaps a bundle of straw or a little flax to eke out his rest. The beds usually given by tavern keepers to emigrants were filthy beyond description, and when the night was cold the unlucky traveler was often caught in a dilemma, one of whose horns was a bad cold, the other, the itch. There is a tradition which still survives among wags, that a traveler was once rudely ejected from one of these inns because of his objection to the towel. The irate host was unable to brook the squeamish conceit of one who objected to a towel which fifteen others had used without a word of complaint. Often as many as a dozen and even more were crowded into a room twelve by ten feet. If fortunate enough to go to bed by himself it was no guarantee that he would be without one, possibly two bedfellows when he awoke. The fare was generally sufficient to satisfy the appetite, but luxuries were not to be had. Tea, coffee, and sugar had to be supplied by the traveler. The host gave him always bread (in the earlier days made of pounded corn), butter, and milk, occasionally pork, bacon, beans, eggs, potatoes, mush, rice, and in season, a few vegetables. Fresh meat depended upon the chances of the last hunt. The tavern rates in Greene County in 1785 were as follows: Diet, one shilling; liquor, half pint, six pence; pasture and stable, six pence; lodging, four pence; corn, per gallon, eight pence; oats, per gallon, six pence.

But the seed had been sown and it fell upon good soil. Both the eastern and the western settlements throve. The question of survival was gradually being answered in favor of the fittest. People were spreading all through the eastern valleys, and from there to the middle of the future State, with the exception of the narrow strip of Indian ground which cut into it like a pair of scissors in a sheet of paper. In the forts the various phases of life came most distinctly to view, and the contrasts were most sharply defined. The log cabins were still there, but they were more scattered. The seven original forts on the Cumberland were still there — they had been necessary and might be again, but they were, with the exception of Nashville, gradually dissolving and spreading. The blockhouses still had their port-holes, their projecting roofs, their moats or ditches, but the cabins reaching out through the country were putting on a neater appearance. When, in 1777, J. W. Deadrick had built a cabin a few miles from Jonesboro, and covered it with shingles, it was regarded as a pleasant innovation. But shingles now began to vie with clapboards. Piazzas began to divide the cabins. Round poles disappeared and the logs were hewn more carefully and plastered more neatly. About 1796 frame houses began to appear. In 1800 Bishop Asbury stayed in Knoxville at the house of Francis Ramsey, the father of the historian. This house was built of stone. The public buildings showed an advance beyond the round-pole, log court-house, in which the old Watauga heroes assembled and legislated. In 1784 a court-house was ordered to be built in Jonesboro, the floor of which was to be neatly laid with plank. "Shingles were used on the roof." To the court-house was now joined a jail in the same style of architecture. In the deeds to purchasers of lots in Nashville, it was specified that they should shortly erect on the lot one well-framed, log, brick, or stone house, sixteen feet square at least, eight feet clear in the pitch. Brick and stone houses were therefore among the near probabilities, and soon ceased to be matters of curiosity. Occasionally glass windows were seen where formerly the wooden-hinge shutter had been, but these were brought from long distances and were still rare and costly. Not seldom the glass was broken by the ignorance of those who attempted to frame it.

The improvements on the inside had kept pace with those on the outside. Puncheon floors were rapidly disappearing, the plank floors were clean and dry, there was an increase in the articles of furniture. Formerly the master of the house had made the tables, chairs, benches, and boxes with his own tools. But here and there a successful trip to Natchez and back had introduced pieces of varnished furniture. On every hand were seen evidences of a new era; new clothes, new utensils and articles of luxury. Up to 1792 the commercial intercourse with the outside world had been of the most meagre description, more especially in the west. At times a peddler came through with a pack-horse or two, over the Virginia or North Carolina mountains, from Charleston, or Richmond, or Philadelphia, but he generally disposed of what he had brought in Washington, Greene, and Sullivan counties. In Nashville, the Indians or French traders were the only resource. Sometimes they came peacefully, more frequently, however, by force. It was often hinted in the letters and dispatches of those days that the Cumberland people were much more willing to organize expeditions against the Indians who traded with Natchez and New Orleans than those who did not. The Coldwater expedition had brought the settlement a rich harvest of " taffia, sugar, coffee, cloths, blankets, Indian wares of all sorts, salt, shot, Indian paints, knives, powder, tomahawks, tobacco, and other articles suitable for Indian commerce." A part of the sugar and coffee was returned to the captured traders, but none of the dry goods. As early as 1780, or perhaps a little earlier, a man named Daniel Broadhead had established a "dry goods store" at the Ohio Falls, and shortly afterwards James Wilkinson opened a store at Lexington, Kentucky. In 1783 Lardner Clark followed their example at Nashville, and kept a mixed stock of pins, needles, buttons, and the simplest dry goods for women and whiskey for the men. In 1786 a train of ten pack-horses loaded with merchandise arrived at Nashville. This was regarded as a great accession of luxury and wealth.

The necessities of their situation, however, forced the Cumberland people to extend the operations of their commerce, and we soon find them in Natchez and New Orleans, and occasionally a few at Kaskaskia and other northwestern points. Steamboats appeared on the Mississippi River in 1812. Up to that time the means of transportation on water were slow, cumbersome, and often dangerous. The keel-boat, the ferry-boat, the Kentucky-flat, were used for heavy freight. These were preceded by the pirogue, and even the skiff in which traders carried down tallow, furs, buffalo robes, deer, and hides to Natchez at first, and later, to New Orleans, and in which he brought back groceries, simple dry goods, such as chintz and calicoes, and plain domestics, hunting shirts, pins, needles, and a few articles of personal adornment. The trip from Nashville down the river and back was neither pleasant nor safe, but if successful, it was always profitable. The chief source of danger was, naturally, the Indians, incited often by the Spanish and French traders, whose jealousy of all encroachments upon their trade was always on the alert. But another source of annoyance was the so-called pirates, gangs of outlaws, and desperadoes of all nations who infested the Mississippi River, from New Madrid down, and who preyed indiscriminately upon all who fell in their way. It was first a subject of mutual suspicion between the Spanish and Americans, and each were ready to see in the other the causes of the depredations. As early as 1782 Thomas Molloy had sent a letter to the Spanish governor, denying a report which was being circulated through the western world, that the Cumberland settlement was the home of those who made the navigation of the river unsafe. In the same year the Committee of Notables laid restrictions upon those who desired to trade with the Indians, requiring a bond and previous permission. In January, the year following, one James Montgomery was bound over to appear at the next term of the court. He was suspected of being a river pirate. The most dangerous band of pirates was that under a desperado named Colbert, and "Colbert's Gang" was one of the terrors of that day. One reason for the prompt action taken by the Notables of Nashville was the desire to preserve amicable relations with the Spanish in order to enjoy the advantages of their market. This was one of the threads of diplomacy by which Governor Mero had hoped to draw the people of Tennessee into the conspiracy which was to establish a southwestern empire under Spain's protectorate. The cause of this failure was not to be found in any lack of appreciation on the part of the Tennessee people of the necessities of their commerce. It resulted, however, in keeping them constantly jealous of any action looking to their exclusion from the Mississippi River, and an invasion of the Spanish region of America was always a smouldering contingency, which the least accident might fan into flame. The people of Tennessee would not brook the Jay Treaty, and Jackson's vote against Washington in the House of Representatives was chiefly the result of the suggested terms of this treaty.

With the disappearance of Spain from New Orleans, a

new life was breathed into both settlements of Tennessee, chiefly the Cumberland, and the increase of trade kept pace with the influx of population. The pirogue now gave way to the larger boats, and constantly shipments of corn, dried beef, tobacco, whiskey, which was now being distilled on a large and increasing scale, flax, tallow, hides, skins, and furs were sent down the Cumberland, Tennessee, and Mississippi rivers, with escorts sufficient to protect them from the inland buccaneers. The journey was exceedingly slow. Seventy-five days from Pittsburgh to New Orleans was regarded as a fair voyage, and the trip from Nashville must have been in proportion. The voyage back was doubly tedious, and was not seldom made by land from Natchez to Nashville by the celebrated Natchez Trace, which was through the heart of the Chickasaw country. Generally the shipments had been the venture of several parties. The things brought back were the simplest necessities of life, including farming implements, carpenters' tools, nails, and the like. Though simple, they nevertheless rendered life more endurable, added to the accumulation of wealth, and deepened the foundations and extended the limits of civilization and refinement and social intercourse.

The prosperity of Nashville was phenomenal, and by the beginning of the century it was, both in the number of its inhabitants and the bulk of its trade, the leading city of the Southwest. One of the most marked signs of improvement was the various mills erected along the banks of the brooks and creeks. The Davidson County Court gave leave to one Headon Wells to build a water gristmill on Thomas Creek, the first in that part of the country. This was succeeded by others in rapid succession until meal ceased to be a luxury, except, perhaps, during a protracted drought. In the earlier stages of the settlement, bear's oil had been the substitute for gravy, lard, and butter. But the bringing in of hogs by the new emigrants supplied the inhabitants both with lard and bacon, which with bread now became the staple articles of food. Walnuts, hickory nuts, and wild grapes began to lose something of their importance. Another result of the growing commerce was the supply of ready money, by which the operations of exchange and trade were simplified and expanded beyond the utmost possibilities of barter. At first, rifles, cows, horses, axes, and cow-bells, the five things in greatest demand, had been the ordinary medium of exchange, and after the organization of the guards to conduct emigrants through the Indian country, guards' certificates were added to the list. This, however, embraced other things though not in such general use. Each incoming emigrant brought a little gold or silver, and the New Orleans and Natchez trade soon relieved what is now called the stringency of the money market.

In the matter of personal attire the changes were slow. There is a tradition that a "few elegant stiff brocade petticoats" existed in Tennessee before the close of the last century, but the names of the owners have not been handed down. Calico, chintzes, coarse woolen goods, unbleached linen, were still in universal use by our grandmothers, although the leathern apron and the moccasin had begun to disappear. Furbelows, flounces, and similar ornamental additions no longer occasioned surprise. With these, of course, the looking-glass appeared. The men were not less willing to profit by the opportunity of donning attire both more comfortable and more pleasant to behold. The vests, pants, and shirts, made of deer-skin, worn next the person, were discarded, and also the caps of coon-skins and other furs. The hunting shirt still remained, though not so generally worn, as likewise the leggings and moccasins. Leather thread for leathern garments gave place to cotton and flax thread.

The chief occupation of the people, of course, was agriculture, locating land, clearing it and cultivating it, growing corn, a little wheat, hemp, flax, tobacco, a few vegetables, and a very little cotton. Everybody tried to raise horses, cattle, and hogs. If any sheep had as yet been introduced, the writer has not been able to find any trace of the fact. Some of the stations had now become towns, but as yet there was no clearly marked boundary between them and the country. Still the division of labor which betokens wealth and prosperity and an increasing population was rapidly taking place. There was the farmer, the ferry-man, the tavern keeper, the distiller, the miller, the manufacturer of salt, the lawyer, the physician, the merchant, the tailor, the shoemaker, the tanner, and the blacksmith. I might even add the miner, for Jacob Kimberlin found lead in 1787 south of French Broad.

Although the struggle for life was still earnest and full of serious vicissitudes, it would be inaccurate to think of the early settlers as always beyond the cheerful influences which make more bearable even the heaviest burdens. But the relaxation was rarely carried to excess, and those festivities were most enjoyed which had a practical and useful outcome. House raisings, choppings, frolics, and corn shuckings were more popular than target shooting, throwing the tomahawk, racing, jumping, and wrestling, though all were indulged in. The only amusement of the women not enjoyed in common with the men was that of quilting. The younger generation generally amused themselves imitating the actions of their elders, and after the introduction of schools, by occasionally forcing the teacher to accord them a holiday. This was accomplished by "barring him out" until he yielded to the popular demand. If he gained entrance, it became a contest of strength, frequently ending in great personal violence. When Judge Guild was a boy, he took part in a "barring out" which terminated in letting the teacher down the well in a bucket, and burning the school-house. As the population grew, however, other amusements began to make their appearance. In 1787 a distillery which bore the euphonious name of Red Heifer was built. Patton's Still House came soon after. A road was ordered by the county court to be laid off from Clarksville to this place. A tavern was opened in Nashville, "Black Bob," for many years the centre of the habit of drinking intoxicating drinks which was so prevalent in the very earliest days of our history. Bishop Asbury's journal is filled with allusions to distillers and tavern keepers, and on one occasion he met a congregation too drunk to listen to his admonitions. Of Francis A. Ramsey he says in 1800, "It may not be amiss to mention that our host has built his house and takes in his harvest without the aid of whiskey." The records of the county court were filled with regulations fixing the price of whiskey. In 1787 the price of a dinner was set at twenty-five cents, whiskey one dollar a quart. Among the vices legislated against in the county court of Davidson County in 1784 was intemperance, nor was this the only crime committed in those days. Our ancestors were, as a rule, honest and fearless, but there were men among them who were both cowardly and dishonest. In 1784 an act of the county court refers to wicked men too lazy to get their living by honest labor, who make it their business to ride in the woods and steal cattle and hogs and alter and deface marks and brands. They were to be branded with the letter T in the palm of the hand. On another occasion it is ordered that Sam Henry be fined ten shillings for profanely swearing in the presence of the court. Even gambling was not entirely unknown. It is said that a valuable tract of land in Maury County was lost and won at the game of Rattle and Snap, by which title the place is still known. It would be a mistake to suppose that the earlier settlers were without any of the faults which usually accompany the frailties of human nature in even its most favorable surroundings. The majority were men who had come to improve their condition, to obtain land at small prices, and to "grow up with the country." They belonged to the sturdy yeoman class and were thrifty, energetic, and honest in their dealings; not a few were bankrupts who sought a new career, debtors who wished to evade their creditors. These were the first comers, the first to break the soil and to withstand the murderous onslaughts of the Indians. There were also those who had left the older communities to escape the punishment of their crimes, vicious and lawless men, adding a disintegrating element to the already lax organization of a primitive society. The inhabitants of Powell's Valley, especially, were noted for their lawless, desperate characters. It will surprise those who know the inhabitants of that beautiful tract of country, celebrated as one of the homes of Methodism, to learn that they were accused in those days of disguising themselves as Indians in order to rob emigrants as they passed through. This element, however, gradually disappeared before the influx of population and the increase of social order. They long existed, however, as pirates on the Mississippi River, as horse thieves in the surrounding country, and as highway robbers on the Natchez Trace, and were the legitimate predecessors of Murrell's band of later years.

The character of the early settler was peculiarly adapted to his surroundings and the necessities of his situation. It was but natural that he lacked those features of character which are the result of mental friction, the mingling of many people. In the matter of Christian worship and belief he was rather religious than denominational, rather practical than religious. Bishop Asbury wrote in 1797, "When I reflect that not one in a hundred came here to get religion, but rather to get plenty of good land, I think it will be well if some or many do not eventually lose their souls." His personal courage was as necessary as the Deck-hard rifle he handled with such ease of motion and precision of aim. His time was necessarily divided between the necessities of agriculture and the duties of the chase. His ambition pointed towards the future when the Indian should be exterminated, when he should be in the midst of prosperity, and all his fields yellow with harvests. His wants were as simple as his mode of life. Next to cowardice, he most despised lack of loyalty to one's friends. Drunkenness was the most contemptible of vices, and slothfulness a subject of general indignation. Having by the force of his character won all that he possessed, he had acquired a self-reliance which was apt to break into rebellion where law became irksome. Familiarity with weapons made him prone to resent insult with violence. But he never struck in the rear, and the assassin of that day, like the rapist of this, went without judge or jury. The Indian, however, he never regarded as a human being. Panthers, Indians, and bears were to be destroyed like vermin. When first we meet with him he wears moccasins, leggings, hunting shirt, and coon-skin cap. His rifle rests in the hollow of his arm. Around his waist is a leathern belt, while shot, powder, and powder horn are strung over opposite shoulders. A dog is apt to be at his heels. As the settlement advances, however, his character is modified in a great degree with his appearance. The cap goes first, then the moccasins and leggings, and finally the hunting shirt. He hunts less and works more. Perhaps he now has a negro slave or two, a couple of horses, and a few "head of stock." His family increases, also his slaves and his cattle. He loses some of his prejudice against the refinements of life. He even brooks a ruffled shirt. The earnestness of his character, kept at nervous tension during the days of Indian warfare, begins to mellow somewhat as his form grows more round. He has prospered in the new order of things perhaps better than his neighbor. He has ventured successfully a few cargoes to New

Orleans. His wealth continues to increase. He builds a frame house in which there are various rooms. It is no longer necessary for his entire family to eat, sleep, and live in two rooms, or probably one, with a curtain partition. Seated on his piazza he can see broad acres of wheat, corn, and tobacco. His son is with Doak in the east or at Davidson College; his daughters are possibly in South Carolina. During the last fall one of his horses has carried off the "sweepstakes." He is, by the way, in common with Mr. Jackson, Mr. Anderson, Mr. Dickinson, and others, very fond of the race-course. The aspect of the world has changed. As he sees one of his old friends pass, one whose lands are mortgaged and whose sons and daughters help him eke out a scanty living, it begins to dawn upon him that there are various stations in life. The idea of class is formed in his mind and the old days of perfect and noble equality among all settlers are forever past. Degrees of prosperity bring in the artificial modes of thought and the shallow and unnatural methods of life which still exist, and which belie the true spirit of republicanism founded in theory upon the universal brotherhood of all men.

CHAPTER XX.

ADMISSION TO THE UNION.

AMONG the last resolutions of the first territorial General Assembly was, "that the sense of the people be taken with respect to a new State." Governor Blount, with the political tact which was but little below statesmanship, was among the first to perceive the necessity of meeting this growing demand of the people, and at once took measures to hasten its realization. The General Assembly had been prorogued to the first Monday in October, 1795. He called it together again on the 29th day of June, 1795. A bill was passed for the enumeration of the inhabitants of the Territory. More than 60,000 free votes were cast in favor of this measure, as required by the act of cession. A constitutional convention was called, and met at Knoxville on the 11th of January, 1796. Among the members present were John McNairy, Andrew Jackson, and James Robertson from Davidson County; William Cocke, from Hawkins; Joseph Anderson and Archibald Roane, from Jefferson; William Blount, James White, and Charles McClung, from Knox; W. C. C. Claiborne, from Sullivan; John Tipton, from Washington; and Daniel Smith, from Sevier. The constitution adopted was, apart from the election of officers, substantially the one under which we now live. Ramsey says: "It is a tradition that the beautiful name given to our State was suggested by General Jackson." It may have been that Jackson, in committee, made the formal motion to adopt Tennessee as the name of the new State. But it is not true that he suggested a name which otherwise might not have been adopted. The territory south of the river Ohio was already very generally known as the Tennessee country. In Bishop Asbury's diary, under date of May, 1788, he makes an entry as in "Tennessee." The convention met in 1796. Winterbotham's "America," an old history published at London in 1795, contains a map on which the Cherokee River has given place to the Tennessee River, and the Territory is noted as the "Tennassee Government."[1]

The convention adjourned on the 6th of February, 1796. On the 28th of March following, the first General Assembly of the State of Tennessee met at Knoxville. John Sevier, of course, was found to have been elected governor. William Blount and William Cocke were elected to the United States Senate.

But for one drawback the new State would have moved off like newly set machinery, well balanced and fitly organized and adjusted, without a jar or a creak. This drawback came from an unexpected quarter, and raised a storm among those who had just been congratulating themselves on the success of the movement. Having the example of Kentucky before their eyes, Blount, McNairy, Jackson, Anderson, Cocke, and other leading members of the convention had a particular regard for what they considered the utmost possible requirements of technical regularity. Only after repeated conventions had Kentucky been allowed to become a state, and only then when it appeared that insurrection might be the result of further hindrance. When, therefore, the news came to Knoxville that in the Senate of the United States the bill admitting Tennessee as a state had been adversely reported, there was a momentary lull, followed by a storm

[1] This map, prepared evidently with great care, though not absolutely accurate, is the best I know of Tennessee at that period of its history.

that swept from Jonesboro to Nashville, carrying with it even those who had voted against it at the ballot-box. For a time the question assumed serious proportions and threatened to convulse the country. The balance of power, as a determinative principle in the admission of states, had not yet attained the full development of later years, when slavery became a deeply-rooted institution; but it was there, and derived an increased vitality, not only from the local prejudices existing between North and South, but also from the fear on the part of the older States that their power might ultimately slip from them and fall to the share of those yet to be created.

The chief ground of opposition to the admission of Tennessee was that it was "necessary for Congress to lay out and form the Territory into one or more States, and that the proof of their numbers should have been given under direction and by order of Congress, the people not being competent to give proof themselves." In the House, the right of admission was supported by Nathaniel Macon, James Madison, and Albert Gallatin. It was carried by a vote of forty-three to thirty. In the Senate, the bill passed by the casting vote of Mr. Livermore, acting president, who was severely criticised for his action. Underlying every other motive was that of party interest; the Federalists opposed the admission of Tennessee, knowing its electoral vote would be given to Mr. Jefferson in the approaching election. Chauncey Goodrich, in a letter written to Oliver Wolcott (Senior), said, referring to Livermore's vote, "It must be left for him to account for his conduct; his friends are chagrined. It is possible this act may have some serious effect." Again he says: "No doubt this is but one twig of the electioneering cabal for Mr. Jefferson."

In the mean while Governor Sevier had called an extra session of the legislature to obviate all questions as to the validity of acts done by Tennessee before the date of its formal admission to the Union. Blount and Cocke were again elected, the former in his letter of acceptance referring to the quibbles resorted to in order to deprive Tennessee of its equal share of representation. Andrew Jackson was elected to Congress. The mode of electing presidential electors was regulated. Thus finally Tennessee became a State of the Union, on the first of June, 1796.

CHAPTER XXI.

TENNESSEE INSTITUTES.

IN every organized society there are certain fundamental duties which are common to all governments. On these, which are a substratum, each nation has built a superstructure peculiarly its own. This superstructure of customs, this edifice of local institutions, makes the difference which exists among the nations of the earth. Customs and laws differ as languages differ. There is a Grimm's Law in the study of economic institutions as well as in the study of the Indo-Germanic languages. But each nation speaks its own tongue, each locality has its fine variations of phrase, each individual his peculiarities of speech. In like manner, each nation has its individual customs and laws, each precinct its traditional institutions, each town its own system of minutely varied self-government. To apply the old and beautiful illustration, the bits of glass in the kaleidoscope are the same, but each nation shakes the box and we behold each time a new arrangement of pleasing figures, delicate colors, and graceful results.

·The study of philology itself has not done more to establish the kinship of races than the study of governmental institutions. If all books and manuscripts bearing on the history of England from the twelfth century to the present time were lost, there would be no difficulty in establishing the fact that America is peopled by descendants of the same race that then inhabited England. And this is true, although the attention of students has only within the last few years been turned to the study of this subject. But even what has been done has already formulated as a general law the absolute continuity of political institutions. There are changes and modifications, re-adaptations and revivals, but rarely a new invention. The essayists of Johns Hopkins University have, in the study of New England townships, pointed out the survival of old Anglo-Saxon institutions that have been lost even in the old England of to-day.[1]

The institutions, both general and local, of American States are, with the exception of Louisiana parishes, directly derived from Anglo-Saxon and English sources. A wide breach is popularly supposed to have taken place at the Revolution, and since then we are generally supposed to have invented an entirely new and original set of laws and institutions for ourselves. It is this popular error which later investigation is rapidly breaking down.

Nowhere is the chasm popularly supposed to exist between the laws of England and the laws and institutions of this country so palpably and clearly bridged as in the case of Tennessee. In 1792 Francis Xavier Martin published, " according to a resolve of the General Assembly," " a collection of the Statutes of the Parliament of England, in force in the State of North Carolina."

The legislative authority for Martin's book is a recognition of the right by descent which the people of North Carolina and of this State have to the store of legal wisdom in the common magazine of Teutonic, Anglo-Saxon, and English traditions and precedents. An act passed in North Carolina in 1715 enacts that the common law is

---

[1] The author takes this opportunity of paying his tribute of respect to the new school of historical investigation, which, under the careful and scholarly editorship of Professor Herbert B. Adams, is introducing the same comparative methods into the study of American history which have been fruitful of the best results in Germany and England.

and shall be in force in this government, except such part in practice in the issuing and return of writs and proceedings in Westminster which for want of several officers cannot be put into execution. In 1778 we find another act on the same subject. " All such statutes and such parts of the common law as were heretofore in force and use within this Territory which are not destructive of, repugnant to, or inconsistent with the freedom and independence of this State and the form of government therein established and not otherwise provided for, are hereby declared to be in full force within this State." The courts of Tennessee have time and again decided that the common law is still in force in this State, with such conditions and limitations as we find in North Carolina.

The general organization of the machinery of state in Tennessee is directly derived from England, but those changes and modifications necessary to adapt English forms to the needs of American society which were made in the original colonies were, in our case, made in North Carolina. When the first constitution was adopted, it was practically the constitution then in force in North Carolina, and showed the influence of the colonial development of that State. In the grant of 1663 the king had been careful to reserve the colonists a voice in the fashioning of the laws by which they were to be governed. The lords proprietors themselves were not a new invention, but were merely the grantees of a monopoly differing in no legal respect from those that had been causes of contention between the English people and their sovereigns from the time of William the Conqueror. The difference was found in the monopoly itself, which, instead of being salt or woolen cloth, was land. The attempt to people this land under their supervision brought into play the same forces and factors that were and had been working in England under the supervision of chiefs, headmen and kings from the times of the earliest Angle invasions. As a governmental incident, the proprietors were foreign to anything known to English law. Indeed, they made no attempt to govern otherwise than through the regular channels. They were not the centre. This was the governor or governor-general whom they appointed, and apart from a few appointments, their interference was clearly in the nature of a revolution. One of the clearest proofs of this fact was the reserved veto power. In a manifesto issued by the proprietors, shortly after they obtained the grant, they set forth their intention of appointing a governor and council from among the colonists, "to see the laws of the Assembly put in due execution."[1] The Assembly itself was to be elected by the colonists, with the sole power of making laws and laying taxes for the common good when need should require. The council consisted of six, and subsequently twelve members. Of these, six were appointed by the governor, and six elected by the General Assembly. This was a combination of the English Cabinet and the Privy Council and the upper house of Parliament, being also a constituent part of the General Assembly.[2]

Subsequently, the number of councilors was reduced to six and these, with the governor, constituted the upper house of the General Assembly, which, before this, consisted of but one body. The House of Burgesses, whose meetings were biennial, was elected by borough franchise. The qualifications of the voters were, allegiance to the king, white color, twenty-one years of age, a year's residence in the province before voting, and the payment of

---

[1] This provision was never apparently carried out, the governors being appointed regardless of any expression of preference on the part of the colonists.

[2] This, perhaps, is the precedent which suggested to the framers of the federal constitution the device of giving the Senate a semi-executive function in the matter of appointments, treaties, etc.

at least one levy of taxes. A quorum was one half of all the members. The province itself was divided into precincts for judicial purposes and into parishes for religious purposes. The judiciary consisted of the general court, the chancery court, the precinct courts, and the courts of oyer and terminer. The judges of the general court were eight — one chief justice and seven others. The former was appointed by the voice of all the lords proprietors, and the latter were appointed by them individually, each assistant judge being also a deputy of the lord proprietor from whom he received his commission. Subsequently this right appears to have been waived by the proprietors, the number of judges being reduced to three, one chief justice appointed by the lords proprietors, and two assistants by the governor and council, who also nominated an attorney-general. The clerk was elected by the court. The jurisdiction of the court extended to all parts of the province and included all cases both civil and criminal, with the exception of cases where the smallness of the amount claimed gave the lower courts exclusive jurisdiction, which could only be when both parties lived in the same precinct. Original suits were begun by writs, served by the provost marshals, of whom there was one in each precinct, appointed by the governor. In addition to its original jurisdiction, the general court had also appellate powers for the correction of errors below. It is significant that on several occasions appeals to the king in council were refused by this court. The chancery court consisted of the governor and the councilors. The usual practice was upon bill and answer, and testimony was given only in depositions. The court of oyer and terminer, the origin of our "criminal docket of the circuit court," and of our criminal courts where such are established, was the criminal docket of the general court.[1]

[1] Two instances, in 1722 and 1729, are of record of this court being held by order of the governor and council. In each case the

Proceedings were begun either by indictment, brought in by a grand jury for the precinct where the offense was committed, or by information from the attorney-general.

Such were, in outline, the prominent features of the government originally established in North Carolina, each of which was taken in full development from England, and each of which under some name and in some guise still exists in Tennessee. It is but necessary to read an indictment in a court of oyer and terminer, or to follow the pleadings of a case in the general court, to understand the origin of Tennessee jurisprudence. There were subsequent changes, but they were, for the most part, immaterial. After the cession of the colony to the crown in 1729, the governor and a council of seven were appointed by the king. The governor and three of the council made a quorum. In 1738 the precincts were changed to counties. Sheriffs were appointed in place of marshals. The office of provost marshal of the province was abolished. Circuit courts were established, taking the place of the general court in so far as its jurisdiction was original both for the trial of civil causes and as the court of oyer and terminer. The powers of the county, formerly precinct court, were enlarged. In 1740 was passed an act to appoint able and skilful clerks for the several courts within this province and for the better securing and safe-keeping the records of the same.

An attempt made in 1754 to establish the supreme courts of justice, oyer and terminer and general gaol delivery miscarried, the acts for this purpose being repealed by proclamation. In 1762, however, an act became a law dividing the province of North Carolina into five several districts and establishing a superior court of justice in each of the said districts and regulating the pro-

person tried was an Indian. It is very likely that Indians, being as a rule the inhabitants of no particular precinct, could only be tried by a special court.

ceedings therein. In 1774 another act established courts of oyer and terminer and general gaol delivery, constituting the judges thereof a court for hearing and determining appeals and writs of error. In 1777 the State was divided into six districts, one of which was Salisbury, a part of this judicial district being the geographical district of Washington or Tennessee. Here we see the laws of Carolina in the very act of crossing the boundaries of this State. In each district was a superior court of three judges who appointed a clerk. This act also provides that all suits for breaches on penal statutes and the like, directed to be prosecuted in the name of the King of Great Britain, shall be prosecuted and proceeded on in the name of the State, in like manner as if such suits had been begun in the name of the State. Here, as in the constitution of 1776, we see the transfer of sovereignty as distinctly as if it were an estate passed from grantor to grantee in livery of seizin.

If now we examine the constitution of 1776 we shall find that it has introduced absolutely not a single feature into North Carolina institutions with which we are not already familiar. The complete breaking loose from old landmarks, the introduction of a new and original system whose salient points are antagonistic to all the despotic and autocratic ordinances of English government are nowhere to be found. It is true, a great deal that was not serviceable has been discarded, but it is merely obsolete. It is not destroyed, and at any moment the same conjunction of circumstances that rendered it necessary and useful in England may again quicken it into renewed life and vigor in America. The greatest change has taken place in exactly those institutions which are popularly supposed to have copied most nearly the English model. The Governor, Senate, and House of Representatives are as far from being the King, House of Lords, and House of Commons as a bank of clouds is from being a camel.

The King has no executive power. The Governor has. Parliament is omnipotent. The General Assembly can legislate only upon a very limited number of subjects. The King is a constituent part of Parliament; the Governor is distinctively the executive factor as opposed to the legislative. The Governor now has the veto power; the King has lost it. The sovereignty of the English people is in Parliament; with us it is in the constitutional convention, and even then with the limitations provided by the federal compact. The executive power in England lies in the hands of the cabinet. The House of Lords has certain judicial powers. The Senate has absolutely none, except in cases of impeachment. The constitution of North Carolina of 1776, which is also, with a few variations, the constitution of Tennessee of 1796, rested the legislative authority in two distinct branches, a Senate and a House of Commons, called as a body the General Assembly. The Senate was composed of representatives annually elected, one for each county.[1] Members of the lower house were to be elected annually by ballot, according to the principle of borough-representation, two for each county and one each for the six larger towns. Each senator must have resided one year previous to his election in the county that elects him, in which he must also possess three hundred acres of land in fee. Each member of the lower house must have resided one year immediately preceding his election in the county he represents, and must also have possessed in the same county one hundred acres of land in fee or for the term of his own life, for six months preceding his election. The Senate and House of Commons each have the power to elect their own speaker and other officers, and be judges of the qualifications and elections of their members. The General Assembly, by joint ballot of both houses, ap-

[1] The prevalence of the idea of proportionate representation dates from the federal constitution of 1787.

points judges of the superior courts of law and equity, judges of admiralty, and an attorney-general, who shall be commissioned by the governor and hold their offices during good behavior. The Senate and House of Commons, jointly, at their first meeting after each annual election, shall by ballot elect a governor for one year, who shall not be eligible to that office longer than three years, in six successive years. No person under thirty, and who has not been a resident in this State above five years, and having in the State a freehold in lands and tenements above the value of one thousand pounds, shall be eligible. The Senate and House of Commons, at the first session after their annual election, shall elect by ballot seven men as a "council of state," for one year, who shall advise the governor in the execution of his office. Four members make a quorum. Their advice and proceedings shall be entered in a journal to be kept for that purpose and signed by the members present, to any part of which any member present may enter his dissent. And such journal shall be laid before the General Assembly when called for by them. The governor, by and with the advice and consent of the "council of state," may lay embargoes, grant reprieves and pardons, and appoint officers to fill unexpired terms. In case of his death, he is succeeded first, by the speaker of the Senate, and in case of his death, inability, or absence from the State, the speaker of the House of Commons. The General Assembly shall by joint ballot annually appoint a treasurer or treasurers of the State, and triennially elect a secretary of state. All indictments shall conclude "against the peace and dignity of the State."

The plan of government devised for the territory northwest of the river Ohio, the provisions of which were extended to the territory south of the river Ohio in 1790, was temporary both in its nature and its effects. The entire Territory was made one district. The executive office was filled by a governor appointed by Congress, who was commander-in-chief of the militia. There was a secretary whose duty it was to keep the acts and laws passed by the legislature, the public records, the executive acts of the governor, and transmit copies of the documents every six months to the secretary of Congress. In the absence of the governor, he performed that officer's duties. There was also a court consisting of three judges having a common law jurisdiction. It was the duty of the governor and judges, or a majority of them, to adopt and publish in the district such laws of the original States, criminal and civil, as might be necessary, until the organization of the General Assembly.

Tennessee, or the Territory south of the river Ohio, lived under this scheme of government from 1789 to 1794, when the first General Assembly met. It had been provided that as soon as there were 5,000 free male inhabitants of full age in the Territory, representatives should be elected to a General Assembly, one representative for every 500. A legislative council, modeled upon the old council of the Southern States, was to be a constituent part of the General Assembly. The number of these councilors was five. These were selected by the president from ten names submitted to him by representatives, and held office for five years. The council performed generally the functions of the Senate as we now have it. Thus we see that institutionally the Senate or Upper House of the representative body in Tennessee is the lineal descendant, as well of the English Cabinet as of the House of Lords. The first session of the General Assembly under the territorial form of government was held at Knoxville, August 26, 1794. The constitutional convention met in 1796, and made such changes in the North Carolina constitution as were commensurate with the progress of democratic ideas in America, giving less power to the representatives of the people and more to the people themselves, but leaving the seed of future dissensions in the election of county officers and the taxation of land which were not healed until the constitutional convention of 1834. One of the main features of the constitution of 1796 is the appointment by the General Assembly of state and judicial officers and by the county courts of county officers. The governor is to be elected biennially by the people instead of the General Assembly. The council of state disappears. The freehold qualifications of fifty acres for voters is changed to any freehold whatsoever. The principle of proportionate representation takes the place of borough representation. A treasurer or treasurers and a secretary of state are to be appointed by the General Assembly. The provisions relating to the judiciary are drawn chiefly from the precedents of North Carolina. The judicial power of the State is to be vested in such superior and inferior courts of law and equity as the legislators shall from time to time direct. The judges are to be elected by the General Assembly and also an attorney or attorneys for the State who hold office during good behavior. The judges of the superior court are also to be justices of oyer and terminer and general gaol delivery throughout the State. Clerks are to be appointed by the courts.

The first General Assembly of the State met at Knoxville, March 28, 1796.[1] James Winchester was elected speaker of the Senate, James Stuart of the House. William Maclin was elected secretary of state. An act was passed continuing the North Carolina judiciary system and directing the appointment of superior judges. The three districts were Washington, Hamilton, and Mero, and the first judges were John McNairy, Willie Blount,[2] and Archibald Roane. In 1806 Mero district was divided into three, Winchester, Robertson, and Mero. In

---

[1] This is singular but true. The State was not admitted until three months later.

[2] Who declined.

1807 the number of superior judges was increased to four, of whom at least three were to be present at each term of court, but it was to be so managed that only one of the judges who resided in East Tennessee was to attend the courts in West Tennessee and vice versa.

This was the beginning of the sharp geographical distinction between the general divisions of the State which is a leading feature of our state government to this day. In 1809 an act was passed establishing a supreme court of error and appeals, and dividing the State into five judicial circuits, in each of which was a circuit judge having common law and equity jurisdiction, whose duty it was to hold circuit courts twice a year in each county in his circuit. The judges, both of the supreme court and the circuit courts, were to be elected by the General Assembly and commissioned by the governor. In 1811 the equity jurisdiction of the circuit court was taken away and given exclusively to the supreme court. The constitutional convention which met May 19, at Nashville, and adjourned August 30, 1834, made no radical changes in the judiciary as it was constituted at the time it met, but the sheriff, trustee, and register were to be elected by the people instead of the county court. The number of supreme judges was increased to five. These and a few other changes were the consummation of the reforms which began with the election of Carroll to the governorship.

Institutional changes since 1834 have not been of great moment, except that in 1853 the election of supreme and inferior judges was given to the people. One of the finest illustrations of the strict coincidence between English and Tennessee institutions is the history of equity jurisdiction in this State. This is something not known to the common law, having been imported into England by the ecclesiastical and Roman lawyers. It does not fit into institutions derived from the hard, inhuman Anglo-Saxon law. In Tennessee it was long a matter of dispute as to whom and to what court should be given the extraordinary powers of chancery. At first they did not exist at all; then they were given to the circuit court, then to the supreme. When it was suggested that chancellors should be appointed, great opposition arose. The discussion was flagrant when the convention of 1834 met. The question was finally settled by dividing the State into chancery divisions and electing separate chancellors. Judges of the circuit court still claim to have equity jurisdiction in many cases.

CHAPTER XXII.

LOCAL SELF-GOVERNMENT.

THE continuity of institutional development which is discovered in the machinery for the general government of the State as a whole is even more clearly exemplified when we come to an investigation of the instruments used by the people in the various local communities, and we find here especially a coherent development in the methods of local self-government, which are full of interest for those who wish to study the course of American history and the philosophy of its formation. Among other things, we shall be struck first by the fact that there is a peculiarly intimate relation between geographical divisions and the means of self-government exercised by those occupying them and then by the apparent paradox that the smaller and more decidedly differentiated the institution, the less liable to change, modification, or substitution. We shall find that the time which has elapsed since 1584 has in this domain developed nothing new. The present is the logical result of the past. The institutions of England were not made. They grew with the growth of the nation, and it would be as easy for the English and their descendants to form and carry out a resolution of being born with black eyes and crisp, curly hair and with the quick and cunning tongue of a Sevillian barber as to change their principles of government and live peaceably under forms foreign to their traditions and their education. The institutions of Tennessee are in every particular English institutions, and though embodied in constitutions and legislative enactments, they were as far from being invented by the law-making power as the principles contained in Magna Charta and the Westminster statutes from being made by the old kings and barons of England. On the contrary, these very statutes are but a kind of winnowing process, each successive one discarding what was obsolete and unnecessary, and adding fresh wheat that had ripened since the last use of the flail. Beginning with, and in fact previous to the reign of Alfred the Great, this has continued to the present time. When a new combination of circumstances has arisen requiring an expedient not in active existence, a return has at once been made to the magazine where that which had been discarded is stored up and it has always been found in a state of perfect preservation. It would be impossible in a book of this size to make anything like a thorough and satisfactory investigation of this subject. But it will not be amiss or unprofitable, at least, to imitate the earlier settlers of our State, who, being unable to build roads, blazed their way through the woods by occasional strokes of the hatchet. We shall have to be on our guard, however, even in doing so much, lest we be led astray by those who have studied the local institutions of other States. When we begin to get into the dusk of the forests it will be easy enough for us to imagine we see a great many things that in reality are not there and which are merely accidental resemblances such as we occasionally see in a tangle of vines or cluster of undergrowth.

There are two well defined systems of local government in the United States, one of which has as its centre the town, the other the county. The former is found at its best in New England, the latter in the Southern States. All others oscillate between these two, being in a measure compounded, as in Pennsylvania, or existing side by side in the same State, as in those States which were formed from the Territory northwest of the river Ohio. The township system of local government is, in its most salient features, a revival of Præ-Normanic customs and is rather an Anglo-Saxon than an English institution. The main feature is, of course, the direct action of the citizens by popular assembly on matters of local interest rather than through elected representatives. Investigations into the origin of this township system have discovered numerous details showing not merely a revival of the Anglo-Saxon tungemot, but also a resurrection of many peculiarities of Anglo-Saxon land law and official life which after a dormant existence or scant livelihood in several English shires were revived in full vigor by the Pilgrims, who were themselves a species of revival of old Saxon and Angle and Jute invaders. The leading fact to be borne in mind in the investigation of Tennessee and Southern institutions of self-government is this : that there is nothing here at all resembling anything that existed in England previous to William the Conqueror, but which failed to survive the Norman Conquest. Everything which we now find in Tennessee we also find in England. But while it or its germ may have been in existence before the date of the various charters in which the Norman kings were forced to confirm to the English their old laws and customs, yet it necessarily existed in England subsequent to that date. The survival of village communities, of land communities, of the tithing-man and the gooseherd in New England has no parallel in Tennessee. The institutions of local government in New England and the South are as distinct as two branches, though both be shoots of the same tree. There are several reasons for this marked difference between the settlements of the East and Tennessee, in the fact that the population of the former spread from towns or plantations or bodies of people, whereas the population of the latter may be said to have grown towards them. In a community of scattered families that system of government was best which regulated most successfully the large area over which they were scattered. There can be no doubt that the county organization filled this requirement. Hence the lower or smaller divisions of self-government were never called into requisition. They were practical impossibilities until a time when they were no longer institutional possibilities. Another cause of difference is found in the fact that New England was settled by different bodies of people having a common interest and generally having their lands in common, whereas land in the South was owned by non-resident corporations or proprietors, the title of which, in the main, was only parted with to individuals. The township system of New England grew up around the community of land ownership. Not only did the communal idea not exist in Tennessee and the Carolinas, but the prevailing idea was directly antagonistic. The claim of title to every acre of land in Tennessee can be traced back to the original proprietors The tenure is distinctly feudal. The customs and rights distinctive of certain Germanic stages of development found no opportunity for expansion in a system which had scarcely a trace of the allodial tenure. The contests which in New England arose between the old inhabitants and the new-comers in reference to communal land found no parallel in Tennessee. Even the proprietorship of lands which is found in the state domain subject to grant is communal in appearance rather than in fact. Here the title is in the sovereignty, not in the community. There is no doubt that there would have been a revival in Tennessee of some form of local government parallel to the town-meeting in New England if there had been any opportunity for settlements to obtain and hold in common contiguous bodies of land. When, therefore, the superior system of the North is attributed to the superior foresight of those who made it, they receive a credit not justly their due. Both are sprigs from the same stock, and adapted themselves to different circumstances in a different manner, both acting unconsciously. In the West and Northwest, it is true, the New England system has been reproduced in States of younger growth than Tennessee. But here, again, the same conditions which existed in New England produced the township also. The western township is formed about the school, and when Congress gave a square mile of land in every six square miles for a township school fund, the seed was planted. When the State gave each township corporate functions for the purpose of fostering the interests of the school, it began to germinate. Especially is this so, when we consider that that part of the population which came from New England and which finally preponderated, brought the township traditions with them. The lands given by Congress for school purposes in Tennessee were in large tracts, and each county received merely a proportionate share. It is apparent from this, that the township system was impossible in the settlements of Carolina and Tennessee, and that the causes which introduced it into the West had no existence in this State.

The centre of county government in this State is of course the county court or the court of pleas and quarter sessions. This is but an adaptation of the English quarter sessions court, which in turn was derived from the old court leets and manor courts. The court leet is the lineal ancestor of the New England town-meeting. Thus the two systems met at a common point centuries before the discovery of the continent on which both exist. In 1749 an act was passed in North Carolina enabling the justices of the several courts to provide certain law books for the use of their county courts. The titles of these law books would alone tell the history of North Carolina law. They are Nelson's "Justice," Cary's "Abridgment of the Statutes," Swinburn on "Wills" or Godolphin's "Orphan's Legacy," and Jacob's "Law Dictionary" or Wood's "Institutes." If now we seek for the origin of our county court system, we can trace it back to the old English statutes which, as already said, merely made use of that which already existed, inventing nothing new. The statutes of Westminster of 1330 prescribe that "there shall be good and lawful men in every county to keep the peace."

In 1360 a statute of Edward III. prescribed "what sort of persons shall be justices of the peace and what authority they shall have." They are to be "one lord and with him three or four of the most worthy in the county with some learned in the law," whose duty it is to look after rioters, barrators, and offenders generally. Also to "hear and determine at the king's suit all matter of felonies and trespasses done in the same county according to the laws and customs aforesaid, and that writs of oyer and determiner be granted according to the laws and customs aforesaid." Here we see the shaddowy outline of the county court. This very act gives them jurisdiction of one matter which they still retain: "to inquire also of measures and also of weights." In 1391 they were given power to redress forcible entries on real estate, also a species of jurisdiction which the Tennessee justice has. Being descended from the hundred reeve, the criminal jurisdiction predominates, and for a time all increase of power and authority is in that direction. In 1411 they were required to arrest rioters, and in 1483 they were allowed to "let to bail," and three years later a limitation was added to this power, allowing this privilege to two, one to be of the quorum. In 1530 these justices of the peace, who had been gradually gaining in authority, were empowered to lay a tax for the building of bridges and repairing of highways, another power which they have possessed to this day. Among the powers granted to the lords proprietors by the charter of 1663 was, "to erect and make so many manors as to them shall seem meet and convenient, and in every of the said manors, to have and to hold a court baron with all things whatsoever which to a court baron do belong, and to have and to hold views of 'frank pledge' and 'court leet' for the conservation of the peace and better government of those parts." These courts, however, which necessarily presuppose a population sufficiently large to perform the duties required, were never established. The circumstances did not justify a revival of old forms, and it was found necessary to adopt the forms then in existence in England. In 1679 John Harvey, "governor-president of the council and commander-in-chief of the forces in Albemarle County," granted a commission of peace for the precinct of Berkely to his "well beloved and faithful George Durant, Alexander Lillington, Ralph Fletcher, and Caleb Callaway, Esquires."

Locke's fundamental constitution provided for a court in each county, consisting of the sheriff and four justices, one from each precinct, appointed by the palatine's court, and a precinct court consisting of a steward and four justices. The precinct courts were to be held quarterly and had jurisdiction of all offenses not punishable with death, and of all civil causes whatsoever.

These provisions of Locke may have tended to strengthen and render more decided the power and jurisdiction of justices of the peace, although those appointed in 1679 by Governor Harvey are evidently not the same officers provided for in Locke's constitution. Later, the justices of the peace in North Carolina were appointed by the governor, and the council insisted, only with their consent. By the constitution of 1796, justices of the peace in Tennessee were appointed by the General Assembly. During the earlier days of storm and stress, the militia was, in many cases, the nucleus of local self-government both in Tennessee and other Southern States. Justices of the peace were appointed at first according to the captain's companies in each county, not exceeding two for each company except in the case of the county town. Not more than three were to be appointed for the company embracing this. The constitution of 1834 divided the counties into districts, not more than twenty-five in each county, or four for every hundred square miles. Each district was to elect, by popular vote, two justices of the peace and one constable, except the district in which the county town is. This, three justices of the peace and two constables.

The single justice of the peace appears to have had certain judicial powers in civil matters involving forty shillings or less, at a very early period in the history of North Carolina. The precinct court, the sessions of which were quarterly, was composed of all justices of the peace in the precinct. This court occupied a position about midway between our present county court and the circuit court. It required three justices of the peace, one of them to be of the quorum, to hold court. The officer who served their writs was the sheriff, or, previous to 1738, the provost marshal. It was not until 1734 that the precinct court had the power of taxation. In that year an act directed "that the justices of the aforesaid precincts shall have full power and authority to appoint a place for a church, court-house, and prison; to tax all taxable persons in the said precincts for raising a sum of money sufficient to defray the expenses of the above public buildings." It is curious that the first instance in our history of local taxation was that which the vestries in North Carolina were allowed to levy for the support of the ministers, and also to purchase glebes and to build churches. The parish as a unit of local self-government plays an important part both in English and New England history, and in the latter was an influence in the development of the township system. In North Carolina, however, the parish and the vestry never possessed great influence. An act in 1701 established the Church of England in the Province of Carolina, and some attempts were made to organize under it, although against the bitter opposition of the Quakers. In 1715, however, a second attempt was successful. The Province was divided into nine parishes, a parish to each precinct except in the case of Chowan and Pasquotank, which contained two each. Twelve vestrymen were appointed in each parish, who elected two of their number wardens. The wardens were the executive officers, and could levy a double distress to collect the parish taxes, namely, a poll-tax of five shillings or less, for the minister's support, and the same for purchasing the glebe and building churches. These were levied by the vestry. The vestrymen were at first appointed by the General Assembly, but in 1741 their election was relegated to the people. The church establishment lasted until the adoption of the constitution of 1776. It never gained a foothold in Tennessee.

In 1738 an act enlarged the powers of the county court, the name having been changed from precinct court. In 1741 their criminal jurisdiction as individual officers was increased. The county court was also in this year required or allowed to levy a tax to build court-houses, prisons, and stocks in every county. In 1754 an act for establishing county courts and enlarging their jurisdiction and settling the proceedings therein was repealed by proclamation, the General Assembly and Governor Dobbs being in a state of perpetual hostility and disagreement.

In 1760, however, an act to establish inferior courts of pleas and quarter sessions in several counties in North Carolina was passed, and two years later their civil jurisdiction was extended to all matters that did not exceed fifty pounds proclamation money. In 1764 they were empowered to direct the laying out of public roads, to establish and settle ferries, and to appoint where bridges shall be built, and to clear navigable rivers and creeks. In 1777 an act was passed for erecting county courts, for holding sessions of the peace, and also appointing and commissioning justices of the peace and sheriffs in and for the several counties and the District of Washington within this State.

In 1777 the "act establishing courts of law and for regulating the proceedings therein" became a law, and this, as already said, is the basis of Tennessee jurisprudence to this day. By this act, the justices of the county courts of pleas and quarter sessions, or any three of them, are given jurisdiction of matters above five pounds and of petit larceny, assaults and battery, trespasses, breaches of the peace, and all inferior misdemeanors, and are given full power to keep and maintain the peace in their respective counties. Matters of five pounds and under are determinable before any individual justice of the peace, with right of appeal reserved to the court of pleas and quarter sessions, now to the circuit court. In 1785 an act extended the jurisdiction of the county court to all actions of trespass in ejectment, formedon in descender, remainder and reverter, dower, partition, and trespass *quare clausum fregit*. The same act extended to simple justices of the peace jurisdiction of all debts and demands of ten pounds and under, where the balance is due on any specialty, contract, note, or agreement for goods, wares, and merchandises sold and delivered, or work or labor done. The act of 1786, for raising troops to protect the inhabitants of Davidson County, directed the justices of the peace to levy a tax payable in pork, beef, or other species of provision, to support them. It is unnecessary to follow the development of the county court beyond this. The county court of to-day is in all essential particulars the county court of North Carolina, which in turn was taken bodily from the English quarter sessions court. The county officers, the sheriff, the constable, the coroner, all three of them bearing names that were once high in honor and strong in authority, are lineal descendants of what has gone before, and could in like manner be traced back to the time when America was unknown to the people among whom they performed their official functions. There has been constant growth, modification, change, and even exchange of duties and responsibilities. The most careful analysis and comparison could not, without the aid of historical investigation, find in the coroner of Tennessee any very decided resemblance to the coronator of the time of Henry II. But the functions of the coroner of to-day were surely performed in that day, and the coronator has grown into the coroner by historical processes as undoubted and as natural as those which carry the tree back to the acorn. Even the county ranger and the city pound-master are remnants of Anglo-Saxonism. When the Tennessean of to-day forces his neighbor to erect his share of the common fence, he is merely doing what his ancestors did even before they migrated to England. When the overseer of roads calls on those living on the highways to meet him on a certain day in order to work the roads, he is following a precedent that was old in the days of the Heptarchy. The hue and cry can still be raised in Tennessee, and if any man is called on by an officer in pursuit of a felon to assist in his arrest and refuses to give aid, he is liable to a fine. When the people of Memphis held the successive meetings which began with the abolition of the city charter and ended with the compromise of the city debt, and passed the resolutions which each time were embodied in laws by the state legislature, they were but reviving a custom of their race, the first record of which is found in the Germania of Tacitus. In short, it would not be difficult to multiply examples of this kind. There is nothing in the State to-day the importance of which is greater than a recognition of the fact that the institutions under which we live are the result of growth. They can be changed. In fact, the urgent need of a total revision of our entire machinery becomes more apparent each day. But if the changes are to be made successfully they should be made with due regard to the nature of our institutions. Above all things, the fact should be kept clearly in mind that the most brilliant parts and the most liberal understanding are powerless to do more than to change, mend, or modify. Nature alone can make the leaves of a tree, and time alone can make governmental institutions.

CHAPTER XXIII.

RELIGION IN TENNESSEE.

A HISTORY of the early days of the settlement of this country which did not take note of the first steps of its religious development would be as defective as a history of England which omitted all mention of Wiclif, or of France which passed over in silence the massacre of the Waldenses and the expulsion of the Huguenots. There is no factor of our intellectual development which worked with so little disturbance, which brought about such important results. The whole social organization of this State is tinged with the ideas which came from the influence exerted by the pioneer preachers in much the same manner and to almost the same extent that our political institutions are affected by the bias given them by the school-teacher and the lawyer. The Bible and the rifle went hand in hand. The chapel arose in the wilderness with the school-house. The chancel which six days of the week during certain seasons of the year was occupied by the man of law, was on the seventh and for the rest of the year occupied by the man of God, whose congregations at first brought their rifles as a protection against sudden assaults by the Indians. Religion in this State was coeval with immigration. The Presbyterians at first had every outlook to obtain a complete ascendency in the religious thought and life of Tennessee. Internal and schismatic dissensions alone opened the way for the Methodists, who availed themselves of the opportunity with zealous enthusiasm and liberal proselytism. Southwestern Presbyterianism springs directly from the Scotch-Irish race, whose predominant influence can be traced through all the Southwest. The Protestants of Ireland, who had come from Scotland, had begun to seek in America a refuge as early as 1729. From this time on, the stream had poured continuously across the ocean, increased at various periods by the struggles and rebuffs of the unfortunate Stuarts. Presbyteries had been formed in Ireland as early as 1642, and as the Scotch-Irish came to America, they brought with them the Solemn League and Covenant, the Confession of Westminster, the gloomy and stern doctrines of Calvin. They settled through the western district of Virginia, along the base of the Blue Ridge. John Caldwell, about 1736, brought over a colony from Ulster, that settled in Charlotte County, Virginia. These various settlements soon reached to Georgia and the Carolinas along the fertile regions of the Yadkin and Catawba. Another accession of Presbyterians came direct from the Highlands of Scotland and settled on the banks of the Cape Fear River. Large bodies of colonists settled in Pennsylvania, but soon the stream turned south and came pouring steadily into Virginia, settling along the Potomac and in the Shenandoah valley. From here they pushed on southward until they met those who were already established on the Yadkin, the Dan, the Haw, and the Catawba. Here they also met the other moving stream which came by way of Charleston. Uniting, like the waters of the Missouri and the Mississippi, they swept on, branching out in an overwhelming flood, until it poured over the mountains into Tennessee and over a thin skirt of Kentucky.

As they went they built churches, they established congregations, they formed presbyteries. The spirit of undaunted resistance to the encroachments of civil power flamed out on all occasions, as at the Alamance, and came to a head as at Charlotte in Mecklenburgh County, when the members of seven Scotch-Irish Presbyterian congregations planned and enunciated the declaration of independence, the inspiration for which had been drawn from Alexander Craighead, who strikingly exemplified the religious zeal, the independent sturdiness, the earnest opposition to illegal usurpation which distinguished the Scotch-Irish Presbyterians. In 1740, during the time of a renewed spiritual enthusiasm, which had been brought about by the celebrated Whitefield, Craighead was accused of irregularities. These irregularities consisted of too great vehemence and fervor in his admonitions. In the division which took place, and which was not healed until 1758, he was a member of the New Brunswick Presbytery and arrayed himself with the "New Side." Craighead was next a member of the Hanover Presbytery, formed in 1755, and for many years the centre from which radiated the religious influence that held sway in the Southwest. Shortly afterward he removed to what soon became Mecklenburgh County. A pamphlet from his pen in 1743, on the political rights of the people, which had been condemned by the synod of Philadelphia as calculated to "foment disloyal and rebellious practices and disseminate principles of disaffection," paved the way for the Mecklenburgh declaration of independence.

In 1788 the Presbytery of Abingdon, formed in August, 1785, was united to the Synod of the Carolinas. Here we see the first introduction of Presbyterianism into Tennessee, for the Abingdon Presbytery lay almost entirely in this State. It was first upon the ground and its ministers were leading figures in the State. They were men of strong characters, and the minds of men had not yet been turned to spiritual affairs. Besides this, they were practical school-teachers. Subsequent events alone prevented the complete ascendency of the Presbyterians in Tennessee and the Southwest.

In 1772, a few years after the erection of Bean's cabin,

one, perhaps two, churches had been established by the Wolf's Hill or Abingdon settlement. The pastor was the Rev. Charles Cummins, a member of the Abingdon Presbytery. When Knoxville was laid off, a lot was reserved for the site of a church, which was subsequently built in 1810. The first minister who came to live in the State, who was at the same time the first and most prominent teacher in Tennessee, was Samuel Doak. His parents, Samuel Doak and Jane Mitchell, emigrated from the north of Ireland and settled in Chester County, Pennsylvania, from whence they removed to Augusta County, Virginia. They were both "Old Side" Presbyterians. In August, 1749, Samuel was born. Having received a thorough rudimentary education, he entered Princeton College in October, 1773, and remained two years. He returned to Virginia and married Esther, the sister of Rev. John Montgomery. He was for two years tutor in Hampden Sidney College, in Prince Edward County. Here he also studied theology. He was then licensed by the Hanover Presbytery, preached for a while in Virginia, and removed to Sullivan County, and in a short while to Washington County. Here he purchased a farm. He built a church, perhaps the first in the State, on his own land. He built also a school-house, which was not only the first in Tennessee, but "the first literary institution that was established in the great valley of the Mississippi." He also founded Salem Congregation. He took some part in the Revolutionary War, and was a prominent member of the Franklin convention.

In addition to Doak, among the earlier preachers who came to the State were Samuel Houston, Hezekiah Balch, Samuel Carrick, all of Scotch-Irish descent and all members of the Hanover Presbytery. About this time, Thomas B. Craighead, a son of Alexander, fixed his residence at Spring Hill, not far from Nashville, and at once began that long pastorate which has made his name illustrious among the sons of Tennessee. He was a graduate of Princeton, and had been early ordained by the Presbytery of Orange. He began his ministerial mission in Kentucky. From there he removed to Tennessee. A church built of rough stone was at once erected for his use, and for a time he combined the work of teacher and preacher. He was a man of stern character, indomitable will, and varied learning. His diction was clear, elaborate, unadorned, and often wearisome He possessed none of the pleading sympathy and humane fervor that distinguished the pulpit oratory of M'Gready, and of the great Methodists of his day. He was tall and straight as an arrow, his features were cast in strong lines, his complexion was rough and ruddy, his eyes were blue, his hair sandy. His enunciation was clear and precise. His general bearing was dignified. In 1805 his orthodoxy was suspected, and he was examined by the Synod of Lexington on thirty-one questions. His answers were satisfactory, though sometimes obscure. At a synodical meeting at Lexington in 1806, he preached a sermon which was considered flagrantly heterodox. He was at once brought before the committee of bills and overtures, of which he himself had recently been elected chairman. This procedure resulted in Craighead's making an explanation, and the moderator dismissed him with an earnest entreaty to be more circumspect. Some years later he published a sermon on regeneration with an address directed to the synod, which was regarded as smacking strongly of what was known as "New Light" sentiments. He was also accused of encouraging Shakerism, and of Pelagianism. In 1810 he was summoned before the Presbytery of Transylvania. He refused to obey and at the next meeting was suspended from the ministry. He spent many years in writing letters, sermons, and pamphlets, and prosecuting appeals to the General Assembly. But not till 1824 was he reinstated. He was earnestly opposed to the course of those who eventually founded the Cumberland Presbyterian Church. The dignity of his character, the unyielding severity of his mind, rendered him averse to all emotional display. This in no wise lessened the kindness of his affection or the sincerity of his faith. "He was," said Philip Lindsley, "the most spiritual, heavenly-minded person I ever knew."

From the first, the seeds of discord were implanted in the soil of Tennessee Presbyterianism. The members of the Abingdon Presbytery in 1788 were Charles Cummins, Hezekiah Balch, John Cossan, Samuel Houston, Samuel Carrick, and James Balch. Doak joined in 1793, Gideon Blackburn in 1794. In 1790 Houston was dismissed. In 1791 Cossan took issue with the presbytery upon some point of discipline. In 1792 the General Assembly determined, in answer to a question from the Synod of the Carolinas, that those persons who professed a belief in universal salvation through the mediation of Jesus Christ should not be admitted to the sealing ordinances of the gospel. In 1796 it was repeated to the synod that great excitement had prevailed in Abingdon Presbytery, and that Charles Cummins, Edward Crawford, Samuel Doak, Joseph Lake, and James Balch had withdrawn and formed an independent Presbytery of Abingdon because Hezekiah Balch had published some articles of faith which greatly scandalized many members of the church. The matter having been brought before the presbytery, Balch apologized for certain abusive epithets, explained his utterances as in accord with the confession of faith, and was suffered to go without further discipline. Hence the secession of the Independent Presbytery. This procedure was subsequently condemned, but the dissatisfaction being great, a commission was appointed before whom the Independents appeared, and they renewed their submission. They were then reinstated. Abingdon Presbytery was divided into two; Doak, Cummins, Lake, and James Balch being members of one, Abingdon; and Hezekiah Balch, Cossan, Carrick, Henderson, and Blackburn being members of the other, Union. The charges against Balch were renewed before the new presbytery, and he was eventually removed. In 1799 Thomas Bowman was suspended by the Abingdon Presbytery for unsound doctrine. "The subject of his dispute was the extent and manner of the offer of the gospel." The synod reinstated him.

It was evident that the time was ripe for new life, new vigor, a more liberal dispensation, a less doctrinal essence of Christianity. This came as naturally as the Reformation, as the Presbyterian Covenant itself, as the Wesleyan reawakening of the slumbering and torpid spirit of the Church of England. Indeed, the Cumberland Presbyterian Church is to the Presbyterian what the Methodist Episcopal is to the Episcopal Church. The great learning, the deep piety, the dauntless self-sacrifice of the Presbyterian ministers could not be doubted. But their passion and fervor throve only in the midst of danger and persecution. The white heat of their faith as an active force in human life appeared mitigated and tempered in those surroundings of individual liberty and freedom of worship for which they were prepared to battle with such intrepid fortitude and resolute audacity. Disputes involving points of doctrinal belief and questions of discipline were constantly arising, and differences of opinion and variations even in non-essentials were frequently punished with the extreme rigor of ecclesiastical censure. The spiritual life of the Southwest was growing daily narrower and harder. The organization and temper and general spirit of the church was peculiarly adapted for a revival of activity and vigor. The so-called revival that in the early part of the seventeenth century spread from Antrim throughout Ulster and then to Scotland, and the visits of John Whitefield to this country had made this apparent. But this new light had soon flickered out: so completely that the son of Alexander Craighead, one of the leaders of the early revival, was the most determined opponent of the last. The forms remained, but there was no vitality — no flashing of the electric sparks of human sympathy — no trumpet calls to repentance — no attempts to touch those wonderful recesses in which are hidden the tears, the loves, the desires, the pains, the raptures, the tremors, the passions, and the joys of every human heart.

The reawaking Christian energy which ushered in the nineteenth century and which introduced a new method of spiritual propagandism and enlightenment into American Christianity was due to a man whose name has almost been forgotten by the great body of the people. This was James M'Gready, who was born in Pennsylvania, of Scotch-Irish parents. When young, he was removed to North Carolina, and was under the pastorate of John Caldwell. He was, as a boy, of a naturally grave and serious disposition, and was early destined for the ministry. He thought himself devout and a true Christian. But he accidentally overheard a remark made by one whom he respected, that he had not a spark of religion in his heart. He was aggrieved and surprised. He thought over what he had heard. Light began to dawn upon him. Returning to North Carolina he commenced preaching in earnest. In 1790 he married, and took charge of a church in Orange County. He was accused of "running people distracted, diverting their attention from the necessary avocations of life, and creating unnecessary alarm in the minds of those who were decent and orderly in their lives." A letter written in blood ordered him to leave the country. His church was attacked. His pulpit was set on fire. In 1796 he removed to Kentucky. Here he took charge of three congregations in Logan County — Gaspar River, Red River, and Muddy River. He infused new life into them. The people were aroused. His reputation spread. His influence grew. People came miles and miles to hear him. The walls of sectarianism were thrown down. He joined with Methodists in the work of reviving the love of Christ. William M'Gee, a Presbyterian, was located first at Shiloh, near Gallatin, Tennessee, then on Drake's Creek, in Sumner County. His brother, John M'Gee, was a Methodist. In June, 1800, the two brothers assisted M'Gready at the Red River meeting-house, where the great revival fully developed itself. The crowd was enormous, and many were compelled to sleep in the open air under the trees. It was noticed that some had brought tents and food. This suggested the idea of a camp-meeting. The next month the first camp-meeting the world had ever seen was held at Gaspar River church in Logan County, Kentucky.[1] The spirit spread wider and wider, farther and farther. A peculiar physical manifestation accompanied these revivals, popularly known as the "jerks." They were involuntary and irresistible. When under their influence, the sufferers would dance, or sing, or shout. Sometimes they would sway from side to side, or throw the head backwards and forwards, or leap, or spring. Generally those under the influence would at the end fall upon the ground and remain rigid for hours, and sometimes whole multitudes would become dumb and fall prostrate. As the swoon passed away, the sufferer would weep piteously, moan, and sob. After a while the gloom would lift, a smile of heavenly peace would radiate the countenance, and words of joy and rapture would break forth, and conversion always followed. Even the most skeptical, even the scoffers who visited these meetings for the purpose of showing their hardihood would be taken in this way. As the inspiration spread, the demand for new preachers was greater than the church could supply. In

[1] There is a conflict of opinion as to the date of the first camp-meeting. Flint's *Geography*, p. 147, gives Cane Ridge, Tennessee, 1799. The weight of authority is in favor of Gaspar Creek, 1800.

this demand the Cumberland Church had its origin. David Rice, the leading member of the Transylvania Presbytery, visited the Cumberland country. Convinced that the revivals were doing great good and appreciating the lack of preachers, he suggested that laymen possessing the proper qualifications for carrying on the work should be selected to apply for membership in the presbytery. Alexander Anderson, Finis Ewing, and Samuel King applied and were licensed to exhort. During the revival, the Cumberland country, as it was called, was a part of the Transylvania Presbytery, but in 1802 this was divided, and Cumberland Presbytery established. It was composed of ten ministers, of whom five favored and five opposed the method of the revivals. The various stages by which the Cumberland Church was evolved from the Cumberland Presbytery are too long to be given here in more than outline. The licensure of the young men to exhort excited adverse criticism. A difference upon doctrinal points acted as a dividing wedge. M'Gready, Hodge, M'Gee, Rankin, and M'Adow, accepted the Westminster Confession of Faith in so far as they believed it agreeable with the Word of God, by which they excluded the doctrine of fatality. In October, 1804, Craighead, Bowman, and Donnell wrote a hearsay or common-fame letter to the synod, protesting against the actions of the revival members of the Transylvania Presbytery. After some time, and in an irregular manner, the synod passed what amounted to a vote of censure on the course of the revivalists, and appointed a commission to investigate the matter. This commission censured the admission of the young men as irregular, and required them to submit to another examination touching their qualifications. They refused to submit, upon the advice of M'Gready, Rankin, Hodge, M'Adow, and M'Gee, who were thereupon cited to appear before the synod. The revival preachers formed themselves into a council. Subsequent attempts to effect a reconciliation failed. The Cumberland Presbytery was dissolved, and its members joined to the Transylvania Presbytery. On appeal to the General Assembly, they advised a review of its own proceedings by the synod. This was done, but their proceedings were confirmed. In 1810, at the residence of Samuel M'Adow, in Dixon County, Tennessee, it was proposed to establish a new and independent presbytery. This was done on the 4th of February. By 1813 the number of presbyteries had increased to three, and in October of that year the first synod of the Cumberland Presbyterian Church was formed. In 1829 the first General Assembly met at Princeton, Kentucky. Since then it has spread over the entire nation, and is especially powerful and influential in the Southwest. It is worthy of remark that M'Gready, in whose exertions the new church had its origin, never joined it. He made peace with the Synod of Kentucky and remained in the Presbyterian Church.

Among the causes of censure alleged against the revivalists in the Cumberland Presbytery was too strong a leaning towards Methodism. Hawe, a Methodist preacher, had been received, and, it was charged, without renouncing his previous views. On the records of the Cumberland Presbytery were mentions of Finis Ewing's "circuit," "a device borrowed from the Methodists." The mode of licensing their preachers had been suggested if not borrowed from Methodistic usages. The Methodist Church at this time furnished undoubtedly the vitalizing influences among the great body of people. These influences have never waned. That element of the Cumberland Presbyterian Church which gave it force and vigor was derived from the church of Wesley and Asbury. In 1785 the Methodist Church of America was placed upon an independent footing. In 1783 the first Methodist preacher came to the Holston circuit, which embraced East Tennessee and a part of Virginia. This was Jeremiah Lambert, who was followed by Henry Willis, Mark Whittaker, and Mark Moore. At the end of the first year Lambert returned sixty members. In 1787 the Holston circuit was divided into two, the Holston and Nollichucky. The next year two more were added. In 1787 Benjamin Ogden went to the circuit of Nashville, which was yet a small station struggling to preserve its existence. He was born in New Jersey and was twenty-two years old at the time of his advent. He had been a soldier in the Revolutionary War. After Yorktown, he had joined the Methodist Church, and was at once appointed to carry the gospel of salvation to the wilds of the far West. For a long time services were performed in the county jail at Nashville. In 1811 a small brick church was built, but being too far away it was in 1818 succeeded by another on Spring Street, of which John Johnson was pastor. In 1818 Nashville was made a separate charge. The number of traveling preachers in Tennessee at that time was thirty. The growth of the Methodist Church was rapid and wonderful.

The observant traveler who passes through Mexico and who sees the little shrines upon the roadside, the smooth-faced priest, or the mendicant friar with pendent rosary and bare feet upon the streets, the cathedral in the cities, and the cross upon every shrine, need not be told the religious life of the people. In like manner, the signs of Methodism, though in a measure now giving way before the incoming tide of a general laxity of faith, are equally apparent to him who studies the history of the present. What the Catholic Church is in Mexico, the Methodist Church is in Tennessee. To follow its steps would be foreign to our purpose, but it would be impossible to understand the inner life of the people and the organization of society unless we know the great instruments which first gave bent to the religious impulse of the early settlers. Perhaps it would be proper to say instrument, for without doing injustice to the able and learned successors of Craighead, and without overlooking the Tennesseans who added a powerful branch to the already numerous Protestant denominations of America, it may be said that the religious life of the State is to this day the direct outcome of the exertions of the early Methodist itinerants. Other denominations have followed in the wake of civilization. The Methodist circuit riders led it. What the friar, the adventurous padre, was in the early days of Mexican settlement, the circuit rider has been in this State, and the evidences of his work and influence are upon every hand. The Sunday of to-day is the Sabbath which we inherit from him. The silent theatre, the houses from which the sound of music and mirth are banished, the empty streets, the calm stillness of the day, in these things we see the signs of his influence. The career of the circuit rider both individually and collectively renewed in a great degree the romantic memories of the mediæval church militant. There were indeed no glittering panoplies, no burnished helmets, no silken banners, no dappled palfreys, and no vows of celibacy. But the resemblance, in spite of the saddle-bags and the raw-boned horse, is apparent and suggestive. The circuit rider was the embodiment of a sacred and enthusiastic zeal which held in light esteem both the dangers and the allurements of this world. And indeed he was a man whose like has not often been seen. His limitations were decided and palpable, but they were not repulsive. He was bigoted as a Christian, but tolerant as a churchman. He believed in the Bible with a literal faith which in the present days of Renan and Strauss seems to have disappeared from the face of the earth. He could not grasp symbolic meanings, and he felt no impulse to search for them. The nearness of Christ to man, the illuminating grace of God, the infinity of His love and mercy, the sanctification of the soul by faith, were actual and real facts to him. His God was a personal God, a being of infinite wisdom but also of infinite vengeance against him who had been called and who had not hearkened. The catholicity of his tolerance embraced all churches but the Roman Catholic. To him the cross was the emblem of Popish blasphemy, of the iniquity which masked as religion, as that religion that forbade the reading of the book of life, and encouraged the idolatrous worship of graven images. He regarded Wesley as the greatest instrument the Lord had raised up for the work of salvation. The Methodist Church offered him the safest and the fairest road to eternal grace. This could indeed be attained through other Protestant denominations, but with less assurance to the sinner and with less of the divine dispensation of spiritual light and life. He was a strict observer of the austerities of life. He preferred coarse fare, he would wear nothing but the plainest habiliments. This came from the ideas of what both he and his spiritual charges thought required by the censure of the ordinary frailties and vanities of human existence. He trusted in Providence for both food and raiment, and this was made manifest by the gifts from members of his congregation. His yearly stipend was rarely more than eighty or one hundred dollars. If no other method was found, the influential members of the church gave a festival, the proceeds of which were devoted to buying him the necessaries of life. His manners were not polished, but they were far from rude. They were simple and sincere, and were filled with a deep sympathy that warmed the hearts of his associates. He was plain of speech, however, though if he wounded the vanity of his hearers he never wounded their sensibilities. These were his chief limitations. He was narrow, sectional, and bigoted, unpolished, beyond the grasp of any but Christian fellowship, taking a hard, austere, and almost terrible view of the world as it is, having real sympathy alone with the world as it should be or as he would make it. Religion to him was the goal of existence; all other interests were greater or less temptations that drew away from the path to that goal.

But his virtues were great. Even his imperfections were such as appeal to the purest impulses of every heart. The religious, or more accurately the emotional zeal which has shed the blood and destroyed the empires of so many generations of the human race, in him was purified, tempered, and in a manner brought into harmony with the spirit of a more liberal civilization. His determination was the determination of the fanatic, but it was directed towards construction, not destruction. His was the work of saving souls, not the work of preventing others from having them damned. He had a clear conception of what he was called on to perform, and the frantic zeal which brought Latimer to the stake, and the undying faith which sustained him when there, were not deeper or more unwavering than the zeal and the faith which sustained the circuit rider in his labors in the wilderness. It is not a figure of speech to say that his path was beset with death, and that for months at a time the penances of a Trappist monastery were but as luxuries compared to the daily trials of hunger and thirst and sleeplessness which fell to his lot. He would ride for days at a time, through any inclemency of weather, through any degree of heat or cold, to keep an appointment to preach the Word to those who hungered for the Lord. The last rain perhaps had swept a bridge away. A tribe of hostile Indians were prowling through the forests which he would have to penetrate. A heavy fall of snow had obscured the trail that led through the intricacies of a swamp. It was doubtful if he could procure food for man or beast for days, and it was vain to try to carry a sufficient supply. It was impossible to procure a guide across "the Forks" of some range of hills, thickly covered with ravines and with dangerous defiles. Starvation and all the forms of death lay thick around and before him. The stoutest heart might have quailed, the most unflinching sense of duty might have wavered. The rational mind might have justly demanded a greater degree of equality between the magnitude of the thing to be accomplished and the difficulties and dangers attending its accomplishment. All of these things gave him not a moment's pause. Herein was manifest the grandeur of the circuit rider's character. His mind was not the mind of a rational man, as we estimate rationality. His profession of faith and his wish for salvation were sincere to the full extent of their importance, as he estimated it. Religion was a real and a tangible thing to him. The simple, unhesitating sincerity of his faith was grand, it was wonderful, it was sublime. The manifestations of a spiritual world around him were as the fluttering of doves about a cote. Traveling through the forest, his eye would fall upon a tree stricken, scarred, and blasted by lightning. The Spirit of the Lord would speak to him, reminding him of his unworthiness and pointing to the tree as a token and a sign. Straightway he would alight, and, kneeling with uncovered head, he would pour out his heart in the most abject terms of humility and the most exquisite expressions of humble and child-like dependence and love. He himself was an instrument of the Lord, not figuratively, but in absolute literalism. As a rule, the Lord had called him, and he had at first refused to heed. Finally, after many spiritual conflicts in many particulars, not unlike those of Mahomet when yet a driver of camels, he had obeyed. At once the light had come to him, the shadows had been lifted, peace and a flood of rapturous emotion had filled his heart, and he was prepared to wrestle with the Lord for the salvation of souls. His was a sacred function, and the least duty of his mission was of importance in his eyes. And all the dangers of physical pain and even death were but of small moment to one who could see with rapture-lit eyes a world of eternal happiness open before him, a world full of strange and beautiful sights and the calm peace of eternity, a world in which there would be only perfect happiness found chiefly in the singing of endless psalms of praise to the great and infinite Jehovah, and with crown of gold and harp in hand mingling in the glittering ranks of seraphim that surround his central throne, the earnest of the divine pleasure in his accomplished work ringing in his ears and echoing in the words that had greeted his entrance through the uplifted gates of gold, "Well done, thou good and faithful servant."

And it must not be supposed that he recognized in this the Christian mythology with which Milton, as with sunlit and gorgeous clouds, has obscured the tranquil heavens of the religion which the God of Israel gives the faithful who believe in Him. On the contrary, he believed these things as an integral part of his religion, and though he knew the Bible from lid to lid, he would not have hesitated, if questioned for the proof of this faith, to refer to that. This was the character of the circuit rider. Is it wonderful that he should have accomplished great results? The Jesuit type, waiving a discussion of the moral aims of the two orders, may have been finer, more coherently organized, broader in scope, having a more self-conscious end to attain; it may have been a more delicately adjusted instrument for the achievement of a more complex object. The early Methodist Conference itself was of coarser grain than the Order of Jesus. But this was the utmost and all. The circuit rider in all things else was adapted to the object and end of his mission in a degree of equal excellence. He merged the individual completely in the work, he lost all sense of personal interest in the craving to advance the interests of others. He was willing to meet death for the attainment of the smallest of the tasks set before him. He was willing to forego all personal comfort as a part of the daily life of which hunger and thirst were incidents. Luxury he had never known or seen. When his work was with the wild, the desperate, the hardy, and the dangerous, he went among them without a moment of hesitation, without a quiver of fear. He led a life of solitary self-communion, of mental solitude. He voluntarily resigned all the things which make the sum and the substance of the world's happiness, — the peace and comforts of home, the house filled with love and laughter and the prattle of childish lips, the settled mode of life, the ambition of self-advancement. And he did this without an effort of self-abnegation, without oaths, adjurations, and vows of celibacy, without any of the up-bolstering that comes from a feeling of human fellowship even in a colorless and a cheerless cause. To the circuit rider, this was a matter of course. Without probation, without any aid beyond that of his own spiritual exaltation, he stepped at once into a mental atmosphere of cold and solitary elevation and created a new life in the new world, apart from the new world activity around him, not for his own worldly good or the gratification of his ambition, but that good might come to others.

As the church increased in numbers and influence, the pioneer of religion, the one who had hewn for it a way through the primeval forests, either pushed forward with the advance line of civilization or yielded to the mellowing influence of a more genial state of society. As villages developed into towns with souls enough to repay an exclusive charge, the saddle-bags and the saddle were exchanged for a settled habitation. Sometimes he married, and from the first marriage had practically destroyed his usefulness as an itinerant. He is now familiar to us only in tradition. The discipline of conference assignments of duty, which carry with them change of habitation, still suggests his noble activity in the early days of Tennessee history.

CHAPTER XXIV.

SCHOOLS.

The history of the common schools is, in the main, the history of public lands in Tennessee, and the history of public lands in this State is the history of confusion. This confusion, which is much too intricate to unravel in a short space, originated in the Act of Cession, and more than three hundred acts have been passed upon subjects growing out of the relation between the public schools and the school lands of the State.

The first school in Tennessee, in fact "the first literary institution established in the great Mississippi Valley,"[1] was founded by Samuel Doak. In 1788 the legislature of North Carolina incorporated this under the name of the Martin Academy, Doak being president. In 1795 Martin Academy became "Washington College at Salem, Washington County," Doak still remaining as president, a position which he held until 1818, when he resigned in favor of his son. Doak has been described by one who knew him as a "a rigid opposer of innovation in religious tenets, very old school in all his notions and actions; uncompromising in his love of the truth and his hostility to error or heresy; a John Knox in his character, fearless, firm, nearly dogmatical and intolerant, but no one has been more useful to church or state." Doak was thoroughly identified with the earlier history of Tennessee, having been a member of the "State of Franklin" Con-

[1] Monette.

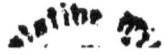

vention. He was also a soldier of the Revolution. He was peculiarly adapted to his environments, and his influence was felt throughout the State. He turned the minds of the hardy mountaineers towards intellectual improvement, and the thoroughness of his methods gave a bent to the school system in the eastern part of the State which it retains to this day.

In 1785 Davidson Academy was established in Davidson County by the legislature of North Carolina. However, but little is known of its first development beyond the fact that the State made a valuable donation of lands near Nashville to encourage its founders. In 1803 the General Assembly appointed Thomas B. Craighead, James Robertson, Daniel Smith, Andrew Jackson, and others trustees of a college "proposed" to be built on this tract of land, to be called Davidson College. Craighead was elected president. In 1794 Blount College was founded near Knoxville, of which the "liberal, tolerant, and refined" Samuel Carrick was president, and in the same year Greene College at Greeneville was established by Hezekiah Balch, who was the first president. It is worthy of remark that the first four prominent educators of Tennessee, Doak, Craighead, Carrick, and Balch, were all of Scotch-Irish descent, and members of the same presbytery. The Bible and the school-book were borne together across the Alleghanies by men in whose veins flowed the blood which had withstood the oppression of three centuries.

An act of Congress of 1806 may be said to have set the common-school system on its feet. The four colleges then in existence and a few private schools here and there[1] had till then supplied the absolute requirements of the people for rudimentary instruction. But the State was unable to give assistance. In 1801 the State Senate, in

---

[1] James Menees had opened a private school at French Lick during the eighties.

answer to a petition of the University of North Carolina, adopted a resolution in which it says: "Tennessee, in her present condition and infant state has not arrived at the period when her revenues will even authorize a loan to patronize the seminaries of learning already established within the limits of her own State." By the act of 1806 Congress set aside one hundred thousand acres of public land in one tract for the use of academies in Tennessee, one in each county. Six hundred and forty acres were required to be located for every six miles square in the territory ceded to the State of Tennessee, to be appropriated to the use of schools for the instruction of children forever. The same act appropriated another tract of one hundred thousand acres, the proceeds of which were to be applied to the support of two colleges, one in East and one in West Tennessee. In East Tennessee, Blount College was united with the new college. In West Tennessee, Davidson College was consolidated with the one about to be established there, and Cumberland College was the result. Academies were established in twenty-seven counties.[1] This congressional grant of lands was entered by occupants, and act after act was passed granting relief to them and laying off other lands for the use of the schools. Each new accession of territory from the Indians was at once drawn into the maelstrom of confusion.[2]

The advantages to the State which would flow from a thorough system of public instruction were fully appreciated from the first, and the messages of all the governors are filled with suggestions looking to their upbuilding and improvement. The first definite plan attempted was by the act of 1829. County courts at the first or second

[1] Only one female academy appears to have been founded — Fisk's Female Academy at Hilham, in Overton County.

[2] Those who wish to investigate this complex episode in state history are referred to the Journals of the House and Senate from 1817 to 1833. It is curious and interesting. See especially the report signed by James K. Polk, November 27, 1824, House Journal.

term after January 1, 1830, were to appoint commissioners to meet at regimental musters on the third Saturday in April, 1830, to divide regiments into school districts and make registers of names of heads of families. The justice of the peace was then to give notice and hold an election of five trustees, who were to organize themselves into a board, the chairmen of which were to meet at the court-house on the first Saturday in June to choose commissioners for the county. This bill gave existence to the common-school system of Tennessee, and this is the germ from which the present organization has grown.

In 1837 a report to the General Assembly throws a striking light upon the condition of the public schools at that time. "The subject of education has never yet received in Tennessee that attention which it so vitally merits. Appropriations, it is true, have been made to the support of the common schools, but the system adopted under that name has heretofore proved inefficient and by no means equal to the expectations of those who first established it. While this has been the case in the common-school system, a prejudice has prevailed against the higher institutions of learning, academies and colleges, neither of which has consequently ever received much from the munificence of the State." This report takes strong grounds against entirely free schools, advocating partial self-taxation. A great drawback to the improvement of the public schools was the lack of any proper head. The superintendent was merely an agent to look after the school funds, and there was no unity of action or spirit among the schools themselves. The fund itself was a prey to the vicious and the unprincipled. "It has been," says a report in 1839, "time after time plundered by a thousand hands." In some cases, sheriffs who collected school funds failed or refused to pay them over. Robert H. McEwen had been elected to the recently created office of superintendent of public schools in 1836 and reëlected in 1838. He loaned large sums of the school money to private individuals, particularly one John Scott, with whom he was connected in business. McEwen was sued and a receiver appointed, but heavy losses ensued. McEwen was succeeded in 1840 by R. P. Currin, who gave way in 1843 to Scott Terry. The constitution of 1834 provided that the common-school fund should be "a perpetual fund, the principal of which should never be diminished by legislative appropriations." It was this wise provision which has kept alive, even under the most unfavorable circumstances, the vital spark of public instruction. The establishment of the bank of 1838, one object of which was to increase the public-school fund, but partially accomplished its purpose. The act itself was passed by a combination of the friends of internal improvement and common schools, but was earnestly opposed as inexpedient by Neil S. Brown, who took an active and leading part in the discussion of all measures affecting the welfare of the public schools. On the 19th of February, 1836, an act was passed making it the duty of the superintendent of public instruction to prepare plans for the improvement and organization of common schools. Under this act some changes of minor importance were made in the organization of the schools, and the first scholastic year began in July, 1838.

In 1845 was passed a measure which manifested for the first time a correct understanding of the true principle of common education. This was the introduction of the feature of self-taxation for the support of common schools. The State was divided into districts, each district was to levy or not levy a tax by the vote of all qualified voters, and the secretary of state was to pay each district an amount equal to that raised by itself. Two years later, Governor Neil S. Brown recommended that county courts be allowed to levy a tax on the whole county. Speaking of the previous attempts to establish common schools, he says in the same message: "Yet this effort for popular education has slumbered and languished and pined, and exists now rather as a memento of the past than as a living system for future growth and expansion." One great good accomplished by the unceasing agitation of this question before the war was the gradual strengthening and spreading of the appreciation and estimate of the advantages to be derived by the people from a public-school system. In 1848 a long step forward was taken in the establishment of common schools in the city of Nashville, according to plans proposed by J. H. Ingraham. This was also an additional factor in the process of development by which Nashville has become the educational centre of the Southwest.

More than to any other one cause the credit for this is due to Dr. Philip Lindsley. Cumberland College, incorporated in 1806, opened its doors in 1809, with James Priestly as president. In 1816 it was closed for want of funds and Priestly resigned. The original grant of 50,000 acres had been unavailable. Congress had directed that it be laid off in one body and not sold for less than two dollars an acre. But the legislature of Tennessee located the grant in detached parcels in the region of country south of French Broad and Holston rivers, and sold it on credit for one dollar an acre. Even of this, but a small part was eventually received. In 1837–38 the General Assembly allowed the University of Nashville 11,520 acres in the Ocoee district, which had just been acquired from the Indians, in lieu of all claims against the State for principal and interest. In this way the sum of $40,000 was realized. But this was long after Priestly's resignation. In 1820 an attempt was made to reopen the college, but Priestly's death in 1821 frustrated it. In 1822, and again in 1823, Philip Lindsley of New Jersey was offered the presidency but declined.

In May, 1824, it was again offered him and this time he accepted. In 1825 Cumberland College became the University of Nashville. Lindsley had been thoroughly trained at Northern universities, especially Princeton. The motive which actuated him in leaving an established career in the North for the troubles and trials of a small, thinly-settled community was undoubtedly noble and high-minded. It was his ambition to build up a great Southwestern rival to Harvard, Yale, and Princeton. In his Baccalaureate Address, entitled, "The Cause of Education in Tennessee," delivered at the first commencement in 1826, he unfolded his plan. Lack of means alone prevented its consummation. He undoubtedly raised high the standard of pedagogic excellence. He ennobled teaching as a profession. He liberalized the tone of the entire Southwest, and his influence was strong and widespread. Up to 1848, 398 regular graduates and 1,500 undergraduates had gone out from Cumberland College and the University of Nashville. It was remarked that at one time there were twenty-eight members of the United States House of Representatives who had graduated at that institution.

The present is the child of the past, and the imperfections of the earlier period have come down and been perpetuated. The condition of the mass of the people as regards education in Tennessee is mortifying and even disgraceful. The losses entailed by the war and the burdens of general and local taxation have been but a bare justification. But the highest duty which a community owes its children, higher than every duty not the result of moral obligation, is the rudiments of an education. The time has come for Tennessee to readapt itself to the progressive spirit of the age, and offer those who are within its limits the advantages without which civilization itself is but a state of more galling bondage. The fact that our resources are insufficient does not lessen the weight of the obligation. The greatest, the gravest duty which now impends is that of teaching Tennessee children, all of them, irrespective of age or color, the simple art of the alphabet and the multiplication table.

CHAPTER XXV.

SEVIER TO CARROLL.

THE election of John Sevier to the governorship was practically without opposition. In fact, political contests as we now know them were of more recent development. There were no local issues involving interests within the State upon which men could align themselves, and in national politics all were Jeffersonians or Republicans. The certainty of Tennessee casting its electoral vote for Jefferson caused the bulk of the opposition to its admission, and, in fact, Adams was only elected by a majority of three votes. The term Federalist had not yet become a by-word and a reproach. The nucleus for a division upon national questions existed. Such men as John Overton and John Haywood, men of thought and patriotism, were attracted by the ingenious speculations and were impressed by the brilliant services of Alexander Hamilton. The Tipton party was still sullen, still sore, and still alive. The unsettled negotiations involving the navigation of the Mississippi River left the whole Southwest a smouldering fire. But the Excise law of 1791, which aroused the fierce opposition of innkeepers and distillers scattered throughout the valleys of East Tennessee, and who were the bulk of the Tipton faction, retarded the feeble beginnings of organized opposition to Sevier and to Jefferson. The storm which followed the Alien and Sedition laws of 1798 swept the last remnants of federalism from Tennessee, and the purchase of Louisiana by Jefferson obliterated its traces. The Whigs, the next anti-Democratic party in Tennessee, were cut off from the Federalists of the eighteenth century as completely as the French Republicans of to-day from the Girondins of the Revolution.

Sevier was elected to fill for the first time the first office in this State. The course of public affairs offered no occasion for the display of administrative skill or executive ability. Nothing was called for beyond the routine duties with which every man of ordinary application can render himself conversant. Sevier's residence was several miles from Knoxville. Unable to support the manner of living which had distinguished the elegant administration of his predecessor,[1] Governor Sevier affected the opposite extreme, and while losing nothing of the portly dignity which always marked his personal bearing, the studied simplicity of his life gained him additional popularity among the people over whom he ruled. He was reëlected for three successive terms, when the limitations provided by the constitution rendered impossible his continuance in office. In 1801 Archibald Roane was elected, and served until 1803, when Sevier was again a candidate for reëlection. The contest between Roane and Sevier was purely personal. Sevier's popularity was unbounded. The only hope of compassing his defeat was to break the influence of his name. An attempt was made to sully his reputation. At this distance and from the scanty material which survives, it is difficult to determine exactly how far the attempt was successful.

In 1792 he and Landon Carter owned in partnership land warrants for 128,000 acres, and by an agreement made August 1, 1792, Sevier bound himself in the sum of 700,000 silver dollars to perfect the title, by laying them on lands "as valuable as present circumstances will permit." After titles in fee simple shall have been acquired, "in John Sevier's or any other person's name,"

[1] The new State had but $3,145.64 in the treasury.

Sevier is to convey one half of what was left, after paying expenses, to Landon Carter.[1] Ten years after the date of this agreement, during the canvass against Roane, it was discovered that a large amount of fraudulent land warrants were in existence, and it was charged that John Sevier was deeply implicated. Andrew Jackson was on the bench at the time, and at once arrayed himself against Sevier. Among the latter's most earnest political friends were the Donelsons, a sister of whom was Jackson's wife. This defection, especially in so conspicuous a character as a superior judge, damaged Sevier in the eyes of the public. It also embittered him. His bitterness was enhanced by an appearance of flagrant ingratitude, for Jackson owed his original appointment to Sevier.

The contest between Roane and Sevier was acrimonious and the latter often referred to Jackson in his speeches. Roane was a lawyer, had been a judge, also a teacher, in which capacity he had given instruction to Hugh L. White, was fond of polite literature, and had an affable demeanor, though at times he was abstracted in manner. But he was not the man to cope with the hand-shaking and buoyant-hearted Indian fighter of the Nollichucky. Sevier was elected by a vote of 6,786 to 4,923. Shortly after Sevier's inauguration, Jackson was holding court at Knoxville. They met October 1, on the public square. Proceedings had already been instituted by John Tipton in the General Assembly to investigate the land-warrant affair. With this impending, Sevier, upon seeing Jackson, denounced him violently as one who had instigated the calumnies of his enemies. Jackson retorted, and among other things, referred to his public services. Sevier scornfully replied that he knew of no public services that he had performed, except to run off to New Orleans with another man's wife.

[1] The MS. agreement is in the Historical Society Library at Nashville.

The two men had many points in common. Both had a gracious and a winning suavity of speech and gentleness of manner when calm. Both were subject to frantic outbursts of fury. And both, when enraged, were like madmen. They stormed. They blustered. They swore loud and boisterous oaths. Their faces and lips grew white. Their eyes glistened like melted glass. And like wild beasts, the first impulse of each was to strike, to wound, to tear. But each had also a reserve of prudence that was rarely extinguished even in the most extravagant paroxysms.

Jackson's anger flamed out at the reference to his wife, and he made desperate efforts to reach Sevier, but was restrained. Jackson, seeing his antagonist with a drawn cutlass, and having only a cane himself, prudently yielded to the remonstrances of the bystanders. The next day he sent a challenge. Sevier returned a mocking reply, accepting for any time and place "not within the State of Tennessee." Jackson insisted on the meeting taking place in the neighborhood of Knoxville, since the insult had been passed here. Sevier declined. "I have some respect," said he, "for the laws of the State over which I have the honor to preside, although you, a judge, appear to have none." A vigorous correspondence bristling with threats and expletives ensued. It would have perplexed the best special pleader in England or America to determine what point of difference was at issue between them at any given time. Finally, Jackson, in a note dated October 10, 1803, expressed his willingness to meet Sevier at Southwest Point, any time between Tuesday afternoon and Wednesday at midday. This proposition Sevier again rejected as not coming within the conditions previously raised. Jackson then agreed to meet him in Virginia. Sevier refused to open the note containing this proposition. Jackson, in pursuance of a previously uttered threat, published Sevier as "a base coward and poltroon —

he will basely insult but has not the courage to repair the wound." Jackson went to Southwest Point, but Sevier did not appear. Returning, he met him and a company of friends. Jackson had prepared a note setting out his wrongs and demanding reparation. Seeing Sevier he sent this forward. Sevier refused to receive it. It was returned to Jackson. Enraged, Jackson charged upon him with his cane. Sevier dismounted. Pistols were drawn. But Jackson had lost all stomach for the fight and Sevier had never had any. Friends interfered. After some wrangling an indifferent peace was patched up between them. In 1791 Sevier had seventeen children alive. Sevier's death at Jackson's hands meant also Jackson's death at the hands of Sevier's sons, who were proud, brave, and devoted to him. This undoubtedly had much to do with the hair-splitting niceties of the correspondence by which a meeting was successfully evaded.

During the contention between Jackson and Sevier, Tipton and other members of the General Assembly of his faction prepared an address to Jackson expressing their entire confidence in him and approbation of his official acts. David Campbell, one of the superior judges, had been impeached for receiving a bribe from a litigant. This, it was thought, might possibly besmirch Jackson in the eyes of the general public, although Campbell was declared not guilty by a vote of 9 to 3.[1] In the House, Tipton pressed with unflagging energy the investigation of Sevier's speculations in land warrants. A special committee was appointed composed of Jesse Wharton, William Martin, John Menifee, David Campbell, subsequently withdrawn for James Scott, Samuel Tipton, and John Tipton. John Carter, entry taker of Washington

[1] Campbell never recovered from this blow. In 1809 he and James Trimble were candidates for the judgeship of the second circuit. Trimble was unanimously nominated on the first ballot.

County and also one of the witnesses to the agreement between Sevier and Landon Carter, had deposited with Governor Roane certain documents relative to his office. These Roane delivered to the speaker of the House of Representatives, and these were the material for the investigation which followed, and which kept Sevier in hot water while it progressed. The Senate appointed a similar committee. Sevier was called on to deliver up such papers from Carter's office as had been deposited with him. On the 8th of November, the committee reported that 165 of 175 papers purporting to be locations, each containing 640 acres, were in John Sevier's name and written in his hand. Of the other ten, a majority were in the names of members of Sevier's family. Upon these, warrants had been issued by Landon Carter to John Sevier to the amount of 105,600 acres, and on these grants for 46,060 had been obtained. All of these entries were founded in fraud, and in some cases sixty different grants had been issued to different individuals. The report concludes in these words: "From the foregoing facts, founded on the testimony herewith accompanying, the committee are of opinion that warrants to the amount of 105,600 acres of land have been fraudulently obtained by John Sevier from Landon Carter who acted as entry taker in said office, on the file of papers purporting to be locations and grants surreptitiously obtained from the secretary of North Carolina, to wit: James Glasgow by said Sevier on said fraudulent warrants, to the amount of 46,060 acres." A motion to reject the entire report was lost, and another motion to amend the report so as to have it merely set forth the facts without attributing any design to or interpreting the motives of John Sevier was carried. It is worthy of note that Sevier's friends voted even against this. This is the evidence. It is too meagre to establish definite conclusions. Our whole system of land-laws was a labyrinth to our forefathers, as it is to us.

Large land speculations were daily events. The charges against Sevier involved forgery. In the absence of more conclusive evidence, his character, his popularity, the love his neighbors bore him, his achievements during long years of service are of themselves sufficient to overthrow the most conscientious skepticism. But join to this, that he was twice elected, even after the investigation, to the same high office, that at the end of his last gubernatorial term he was elected to the State Senate, that in 1811 he was chosen a representative in Congress and served as a member of that body until his death, and he should be acquit even in the eyes of those prone to accept the most sinister interpretations of all complex human transactions. His hold upon the people of Tennessee appeared to grow from year to year. The impression was wide-spread that he would serve as governor for life, with such intermission as constitutional restrictions made necessary. In 1807 William Cocke announced himself as a candidate for the governorship. Cocke had long held an honorable and conspicuous place in Tennessee. He had been one of the earliest pioneers. He had been prominent in the State of Franklin. He had been one of the first senators from Tennessee. But so hopeless did it appear to contest the election with Sevier that he was forced to withdraw. He was at once assailed as having had some secret end in view. On the 13th of July he wrote a letter to the editor of the "Impartial Review" in which he denounces the report that he had offered himself as a candidate for governor in order to deter others, and had then retired by arrangement with "the present governor to secure an election to that office at the time the constitution prohibits his further services."

Sevier not only possessed great popularity, he deserved it. He harmonized with the times and the people. His tall and commanding figure, his intelligent features, his skill in all those manly exercises which were the only accomplishments of a turbulent era, his bravery, his intellectual force of character, placed him naturally at the head of affairs. But more than this, he possessed perhaps every qualification which could contribute in an essential degree to the success of a politician. He made himself at home in everybody's house and made everybody at home in his house. Even when governor, his house presented at times the appearance of an inn. His horses, his ammunition, his camp equipments, his provisions, his purse, he placed at the disposal of his friends with lavish generosity. He was fond of mingling with people, and his amiability and cordiality rendered him irresistible. He knew enough of human nature to serve his purposes, which were always noble. He had a manner of forcing the opinions of those whose agreement he desired. Not by fluency of speech or cogency of argument, but by the prestidigitator's trick of ostensibly allowing one to draw one card at hap-hazard when in fact a sleight-of-hand has effected the substitution of another. This he accomplished by withholding an expression of his own views and then assuming them to be the opinions of his associates, at the same time approving them with quiet flattery. One who knew him said: "He made many a man, a veritable fool upon some favorite topic, believe himself a real Solomon."

But the basis of Sevier's character was laid in sincerity, in truth, and in honor. He was loved because he had a loving heart. The gentle word, the quick sympathy, the open hand, the high purpose, the dauntless courage, the impetuosity, the winning suavity were the wings and the turrets and the battlements of a magnificent and harmonious structure. Energy, ability, and determination can accomplish many feats, and cunning can simulate many effects. But the tender and the true and the loyal heart is beyond their power. This may not be counterfeited and its deficiency cannot be supplied. The most beautiful trait of Sevier's character was the exquisite sweetness of his disposition. No man was ever more deeply beloved in the circle of his family, and Sevier's was very large. He was the boon companion of his boys, some of whom were almost as old as he, for though he was only thirty-five when the battle of King's Mountain was fought, he had two sons present. At home he was the companion of his wife and the playmate of his children. A delightful glimpse of his family life is given in a letter written to him in 1791, by a correspondent who says: " I more sincerely wish you an hour's chat with Mrs. Sevier and a romp with one of your little girls than all the honor you could obtain by destroying ten Indian tribes." [1]

In 1815 he was appointed by President Monroe to locate the boundary lines of the Creek territory, and died in Alabama on the 24th of September. His grave has been neglected, and is now said to be covered with weeds and wild growth. Various attempts have been made at various times to induce the General Assembly to have his body brought to Tennessee. But so heedless and so indifferent have been the members that as yet no steps have been taken. Some have excused the failure on the score of economy. This excuse is a confession of shame. Those whose minds are so contracted, whose sensibilities are so frigid, whose souls are so torpid that they are not inspired by the glorious passages in the history of their State may find in such a plea of specious parsimony ample justification. But it will not fail to excite the ridicule and contempt of Tennesseans who are proud of their past history, and whose imaginations are fired by the contemplation of the glorious achievements which have made the history of Tennessee more brilliant than the history of any other Southwestern State. Of all whose fame was attained within the limits of this State, the most illustrious, the most conspicuous, the one whose name was and de-

[1] MSS. in Historical Society Library.

serves still to be the most resplendent was John Sevier. So long as his bones are allowed to remain among strangers, so long as the children of Tennessee are allowed to grow up in ignorance of his noble character, so long as no worthy monument commemorative of his rare genius and his stormy career has been erected to his memory upon the beautiful grounds that surround the capitol of the State, every right-thinking Tennessean should feel that he stands belittled in the eyes of the world and that he deserves the contemptuous scorn of every mind that can rise above the coupon or the breeches pocket.

At the end of Sevier's last term, Willie Blount was elected and reëlected for the constitutional limit of three terms, and if there was any opposition it was not chronicled. The influence of the Blount name and his friendly relations with all factions probably prevented it. He was on intimate terms with both Sevier and Jackson, and had written the former an urgent letter in the latter's behalf, just before Sevier appointed him judge. He had been private secretary to his brother, and the popularity of the latter, which had not been affected by the impeachment, was in a measure transferred to him. From 1791 to 1796 he had performed most of the duties of the territorial secretary, had been offered a judgeship of the superior court, was a licensed lawyer, a trustee of Blount and Cumberland colleges, and in 1807 a member of the General Assembly. During his administration occurred the Creek War, and his hearty support of Jackson rendered possible its vigorous prosecution. On his own responsibility he raised $370,000 at the time of Jackson's greatest urgency, and in return he was thanked by the president, three secretaries of war, and the General Assembly of the State, as well as by Jackson, whose friendship he enjoyed until his death in 1835.

The governorship of the State after the war came to be regarded as a more desirable prize. Blount had gained a national, though a transitory, reputation. In 1815 we find five gubernatorial candidates, of whom, with the exception of Foster, little is known beyond a dry catalogue of the offices they held. Jesse Wharton had been appointed senator to succeed George W. Campbell, who became secretary of the treasury in Madison's cabinet. A few days before the election in 1815, Wharton resigned his seat in the senate in order to be a candidate for the governorship. He had been among the earliest settlers in Tennessee and had served in Congress and was an able lawyer. It is probable the Sevier party had not forgiven his action during the investigation of 1803. Robert C. Foster came to the State in 1800, when eighteen years old, and had been several times speaker of the House of Representatives. Robert Weakley was also one of the earliest pioneers, had been a member of the convention that adopted the federal constitution, was frequently a member of the General Assembly and once of Congress. Thomas Johnson came to Tennessee in 1788, was a member of the convention that adopted the federal constitution, took part in the Nickojack Expedition and the Creek War, was a member of the Constitutional Convention of 1796, and frequently a member of the General Assembly of North Carolina and Tennessee.

The successful candidate in 1815 was Joseph M'Minn. He was a farmer from Pennsylvania, had been in the Revolutionary War, came to Tennessee and settled in Hawkins County, had held several offices, and in 1807 was speaker of the Senate. He had been reared under Quaker influences, and was a man of plain demeanor, had a sound education, avoided display, and was fond of work. He and his wife had often been seen working together in their fields. It is remarkable that he announced his candidacy just one month before the election, after circulars had been issued by all the other candidates, in response to a "call," signed "your fellow citizens." It was the custom for candidates to issue circulars, announcing their candidacy, emphasizing their devotion to the "Republican party," and indulging in vague platitudes upon the functions of government. In the solicitation addressed to M'Minn, by his fellow citizens, this custom is frowned upon. They state their belief that "the modern practice of every office-hunter sticking up his own name as a candidate to be inconsistent with the genuine principles of Republicanism." When the votes were counted, exclusive of Roane County, M'Minn had 15,600 votes; Weakley, 7,389; Wharton, 7,662; Foster, 4,184, and Johnson, 2,987.

M'Minn thus had much less than a popular majority, and encouraged by this, Foster was again a candidate in 1817, but was overwhelmingly defeated. Foster held various minor offices after this and was a man of prominence in the State. But he was one of those irreproachable persons in whom Tennessee is and has been rich, who, by the universal agreement of their fellow citizens, would adorn every high position, but who are never called upon to occupy any. In 1819 M'Minn was opposed by Enoch Parsons, who received a very small vote. M'Minn served three terms.

In 1821 took place the hotly contested struggle between William Carroll and Edward Ward. Robert Weakley came forward at the beginning, but withdrew in June. The conflict of 1803 had derived its vigor from purely personal inspirations. But that of 1821 had an underlying significance. It was the hostile clash between two opposing systems, which had slowly grown up until mutual encroachments had rendered inevitable a struggle for the mastery. It was in the nature of a revolution. Privilege had expanded into usurpation, and presumption had then called forth resistance. In 1821 resistance stepped in and curtailed the original cause of contention. This election anticipated the Constitutional Convention of 1834, and emphasized the necessity for reforms which took place long after. The constitution of 1796, in spite of Jefferson's extravagant assertion to the contrary, was unrepublican and unjust in the highest degree. It was framed by land owners, and every large land owner of that day was a land speculator. A monstrous provision was inserted that "all lands shall be taxed equal and uniform in such manner that no one hundred acres shall be taxed higher than any other, except town lots, which shall not be taxed higher than two hundred acres of land each." The bulk of the most tillable lands, and those nearest Nashville, Knoxville, Jonesboro, and Greeneville, were in the hands of a few men, and this system of taxation enabled them to hold them. It was an entail law in disguise. In addition to this a supreme and despotic power was given the General Assembly, whose members were nearly all drawn from that class which had the leisure to be candidates and the means to be successful, for there were election expenses even in those primitive times. All judges, state attorneys, and justices of the peace were elected by the legislature. Those who had the means could readily go to Knoxville, or Nashville, or Murfreesboro, and see to it that justices of the peace acceptable to them were appointed. In turn, these justices of the peace composed the county court, who elected the sheriff, coroner, trustee, and constables. The county court had large jurisdiction, and could impanel juries and decide cases in ejectment, the most important of all in a community where land is the foundation of nearly all wealth. When we consider now that the judges and the state attorneys and the justices of the peace held office during good behavior, and until impeached by the General Assembly that appointed them, it is at once apparent that the most comprehensive ingenuity, exercised with a view of devising a plan by which as little power as possible shall be placed in the hands of the many, and as much as possible in the hands of the few, could not suggest any improvement in a system whose perfection of organization had left unutilized no expedient consistent with the forms of republican government. It surpassed the Athens of the kings. It put to shame the rotten borough system of England. The whole State was one "Old Sarum."

Ward represented those who favored and profited by this system. Carroll represented those who opposed and those who were oppressed by it. Each possessed attributes of character which emphasized and exemplified the conflicting ideas. Ward came from Virginia, where he had been a candidate for Congress, and it was at first whispered and soon openly charged with malicious satisfaction by his enemies that he had been defeated as a Federalist. He had great wealth, and lived in a style of sumptuous extravagance, entirely out of keeping with the simple and homespun life around him. He had received a thorough education and was a man of learning. His bearing was dignified. His manner was restrained. His character was austere and unbending. He was represented to be cold-hearted and selfish. He rarely attended the rough country festivals, where the combined influence of general mirth, pretty eyes, wild dances, and a jug with a corn-cob-stopper broke down utterly all the conventionalities behind which, as behind a hedge, sensitive and formal natures hide themselves. He had been a presidential elector, and voted for Monroe, and was speaker of the Senate in 1817.

Carroll bore the impress of a widely different mould. He was born near Pittsburgh, Pennsylvania, in 1789, and was intended for a mercantile career, but removed to Nashville in 1810, and opened a nail store, the first in the State. He had a tall, athletic figure, refined face, and graceful bearing. He was fond of studying military tactics, and in 1812 was elected captain of the "Nashville Uniform Volunteers." He was at first a favorite with

Jackson, who treated him with great consideration. In 1813 he was made brigade inspector of the command sent by the United States to defend the lower Mississippi River, and the same year was elected major of militia. When Jackson received the appointment of major-general in the regular army, Carroll was elected major-general to succeed him in the command of the Second Division of Tennessee Militia. After the return from the lower Mississippi, Carroll fought a duel with Jesse, the irascible and volcanic brother of Thomas H. Benton. It appears to have had its origin in the prejudice against interlopers, which is characteristic of fools and school-boys. It would have been remarkable if Jackson were preoccupied when pistols were being primed. He acted as Carroll's second, who shot Benton in a part not generally exposed to hostile fire by brave men. Out of Jackson's action in this matter grew the encounter between him and the Bentons. When the trouble was brewing on the eve of the meeting in Nashville, Carroll left town, pleading pressing business, and carrying with him Jackson's sneer that he wanted no man to fight his battles. Shortly after the Creek War began, Carroll entered service with his reputation for valor badly besmirched. His duel with Jesse Benton alone gave him grace. When the war was over, Carroll returned to Nashville. He had proven himself a good tactician, a good drill master, a clear-headed commander, quick and full of resources. But above all he had made a reputation for cool, desperate bravery and hard fighting, equaled only by Jackson himself and John Coffee. After the war, Carroll appears to have turned his attention to trade again, and in 1818 the first steamboat floated under the Nashville bluffs. It was owned by Carroll, who, probably to propitiate his old commander, named it "Gen. Jackson." Jackson apparently remained unsoftened, for he was an active friend of Ward's, voted for him and urged his claims. Cordial relations were, however, subsequently reëstablished between them.

Carroll's natural disposition was frank, open, and cordial. He was always at his ease, and was always ready to enter into the spirit of any occasion, especially at the country dances which were so distasteful to Ward. When he met one of his old soldiers, he always stopped him for a shake of the hand, and generally knew his name. It was urged against him by Ward's friends that he had allowed his note to be protested. This was an unfortunate accusation, for it developed the fact that he had become bankrupt by going security for his friends. There was a popular uprising for Carroll. He was toasted at every banquet, and cheered at every barbecue. The grand jury of Montgomery County "presented" him as their preference. The battle raged in the newspapers, and this is remarkable as the first local contest in Tennessee in which the newspapers openly advocated the cause of different candidates. The "Nashville Whig" supported Ward. The "Nashville Clarion" supported Carroll. The claims of each were violently assailed, and hotly defended, generally by open letters. In one letter headed derisively, "Hurrah for Ward," the latter is praised as being a wise man, because like the wise man in the proverb, he had changed his opinion. Having been a Federalist in Virginia, he had become a Republican in Tennessee. On the Fourth of July, the "Clarion" published a letter in which "A Big Fish" gives his reasons for not voting for Carroll: Because he is of humble but poor parents. Because it would be a shame for the son of an old Revolutionary farmer to rule over "the quality" of the State. Because he has never learned Latin and Greek. Because, as a boy, he had plowed and had been handy at reaping, log-rolling, and country weddings, all of which is coarse and vulgar. Because he is not rich and did not stay at home during the war. Because, if elected governor, he would be unable to support the dignity of the State with fine dinners, splendid carriages, liveried servants, state balls, etc.; because he does not carry himself with sufficient dignity and austerity, but will heartily shake the hand of a ragged fellow soldier, thus doing away with the distinctions of rank. Because, if elected, he would not shake off his old friends. It was well enough for low-born loons like him to fight the battles of his country, but the nobility ought to have the honors and rewards. The actual votes for each candidate make a fitting climax to this long score of derision. Carroll received 42,246 votes, and Ward 11,200. Carroll's majority was the largest ever given in this State before the war, and he broke the strength of what would now be called the bureaucracy.

The contrast between Carroll and M'Minn is especially marked. The latter was, in all things, a conscientious and painstaking officer, but he was essentially a man of the present tense, and he possessed none of the powers of combination which enable more gifted minds to forecast the future. Carroll had not only seen much of the world, he had also profited by his experience. His position on the public questions which came up for discussion during his long administration was often very far from being the popular position, but it is remarkable that no other governor ever had so much influence over the legislatures to whom his messages were addressed.

CHAPTER XXVI.

BANKS OF TENNESSEE.

THE financial history of Tennessee, which really began under M'Minn's administration, is instructive, though elaborate and intricate. But even the broad outlines are full of interest, and throw much light on the progressive development of the State.

The Nashville Bank, chartered in 1807, was the first bank incorporated in Tennessee. Among the reasons urged for its establishment were the accommodations which it was expected to extend the State in anticipation of uncollected revenue. The amount of its stock was limited to $400,000. It entered into operation several years after incorporation. The affairs of the bank prospered, and it was long one of the soundest financial institutions of the Southwest.

In 1811 it was feared that the State would lose the advantages of a sound and sufficiently abundant circulating medium, through the extinction of the United States Bank, which Congress had refused to recharter. To remedy this evil, and also to reap the large profits supposed to flow from banking operations, it was proposed to establish a State Bank, of whose constitutionality no doubt could arise, and the Bank of the State of Tennessee, at Knoxville, was the result. Judge Hugh L. White was made president, and continued in office until 1827. It was due to his conservative management that this bank weathered all the financial storms which wrecked so many Southern and Southwestern banks. It never failed to redeem its notes in specie. During the War of 1812 the whole country, thrown by the Embargo Act upon its own resources, was compelled to turn its attention to home industries. The demands of trade, agriculture, and manufactures gave an impetus to banking that called many new enterprises into existence. In addition to this, the prominent part taken by Tennessee in the War of 1812 and the Creek War, under the impulse of local pride, caused the State to put forth exertions in furnishing supplies that strained its resources to the utmost. The Nashville Bank was especially liberal in advances, and one of the excuses offered by its directors when subsequently embarrassed was that its difficulties all dated from the loans it had made during the period of the war. In 1815 were incorporated the Fayetteville Tennessee Bank, the Holston Tennessee Bank, at Jonesboro, and the Franklin Tennessee Bank. They were in the main modeled upon the State Bank. In 1817 the name of the Holston Tennessee Bank at Jonesboro was changed to the Eastern Bank of Tennessee, and all three were allowed to become branches of the State Bank. In 1817 a general banking act established banks at Gallatin, Carthage, Rogersville, Nashville, Kingston, Columbia, Maryville, Shelbyville, and Murfreesboro. All of these banks were established for the public benefit and to ease the stringency of the money market which followed the importation of foreign goods after the peace of 1815. Each of them could issue bills and notes. The charter of each was so worded as to allow it to become, if accepted by the Nashville or State banks, branches of these institutions. It was generally supposed that the peace of 1815 would bring on a state of prosperity hitherto unknown to the people of the country. But instead, various causes, whose influence could not be clearly estimated at the time, produced a financial crash that for years clogged the financial industries of the country. The multiplication of state banks on every hand during and immediately following the war, the issues of which were not based on any sound foundation, and could not be converted into specie, drove out of circulation all the gold and silver in the country. It rapidly made its way to New England, whose banks had never suspended specie payment, to the strong boxes of cautious old men and the stockings of still more cautious old women.

The refusal to recharter the United States Bank in 1811, and the winding up of its affairs had caused about $7,000,000 of specie to be transported to England to pay the foreign stockholders. The heavy importation of English goods still further increased the drain of gold to that country, and, besides destroying the sale of American manufactured products, caused nearly every shop in America to close or to be run at a loss. There was a general lack of confidence in all those transactions where confidence is an essential ingredient of prosperity. The banks of New England distrusted those of Philadelphia, and these again distrusted the banks of Louisville and Nashville; the people distrusted the banks, and the banks distrusted the people. A traveler from Nashville to New York was either compelled to pay a ruinous price for New England exchange, or he was compelled to have the value of his money computed in the local currency by an elaborate process, whenever he stopped for a night at an inn. The profits of this process were among the emoluments of the broker, who, like the tavern keeper himself, the barber, the blacksmith, and the man of livery, was one of the necessary institutions of every town.

A general suspension of specie payment took place throughout the entire country, except New England, about 1814. It is to the honor of Tennessee that its two leading banks struggled on without resorting to this expedient until 1819, and that even then the State Bank, under the management of the illustrious White, refused to suspend but continued to redeem its notes in specie without a single interruption. But, on the whole, suspension was unavoidable. When it came, however, it brought with it an unexpected stringency. The charters of the banks had limited the quantity of bills and notes that could be issued, and these of themselves were not sufficient to supply the necessities of trade. The notes of other than Tennessee banks had totally disappeared. This scarcity of circulating medium would have been oppressive in a community free from debt and engaged in the ordinary transactions of daily exchange and trade. But it was disastrous to a community such as Tennessee then was, having little or no reserved capital, heavily in debt, and at the end of a speculative and expansive era. Governor M'Minn, in 1820, speaks of a "general pressure, unexampled in the history of our government." Various remedies were suggested to relieve the depression and to make "money matters easy." Among the number was the suggestion that the State Bank and the Nashville Bank should consolidate, and a law was passed for this purpose. Indorsement and stay laws were passed forbidding execution to be issued upon a judgment in less time than two years, unless the creditor agreed by indorsement upon the execution that he would take the notes of banks in the State at par. Governor M'Minn suggested that this remedy, usually called "property laws," be tried in Tennessee, which was done. Under his administration, and upon his suggestion, was exhibited the strange paradox of a democracy exhibiting the most pronounced features of the so-called parental or patriarchal form of government. Another suggestion made by him in his message to the called session of 1820 produced results which were prolific of many evils to the State. This was the establishment of a loan office.

In 1817 the legislature of Tennessee passed an act taxing heavily any bank established in this State by any authority other than the laws of this State. This was done in order to prevent the establishment in Tennessee of a branch of the United States Bank, newly chartered. A town meeting was held at Nashville to protest publicly against the passage of this law. Among those who took a prominent part at this meeting were Felix Grundy and William Carroll. In anticipation of the establishment of a branch of the United States Bank despite this law, Andrew Jackson recommended two names, one for president and one for cashier, to William Jones, president of the United States Bank. Grundy wrote a private letter, suggesting certain names as a fit directory. These facts were subsequently used with telling effect against both Jackson and Grundy by White, during the days of his candidacy for the presidency.

The management of the United States Bank refused to establish a branch in a state where the will of the people had been expressed in opposition. A strong sentiment became general in favor of some measure for the "inflation of the currency." Governor M'Minn suggested "the issuance of treasury certificates circulating upon the faith of a public responsibility and resting for their final redemption on the sale of lands in the Hiwassee District, as well as upon the ordinary revenues of the State." These certificates were to be put into circulation through the agency of a loan office. The capital stock was fixed at $1,000,000, in bills payable to order or to bearer, all of which "shall be emitted on the credit and security of the borrowers, and the whole to be warranted by the State on the proceeds of the sale of its unappropriated lands, the interest of the money arising from the sale of lands south of the French Broad and Holston." Loans were to be made to citizens upon bills of exchange, notes, and real and personal property, the former to be secured by indorsement, the latter by mortgage and power of attorney to confess judgment. The rate of interest was six per cent. per annum. Notice must be given before calling in more than ten per cent. of the amount loaned. One agency was to be established in each county, and the amount loaned in each county was to be determined by the relative amount of taxes paid into the public treasury for the year 1819. The name of this institution was to have been "Loan Office." The bill establishing it was prepared in the main by Felix Grundy. It is not known whose audacity suggested the device, but the caption of the bill on its passage was changed to "An Act to establish a Bank of the State of Tennessee." White afterwards charged that this was done in order to give the new bank the influence of the confidence reposed in the State Bank already in existence. This charge was made in the United States Senate when Grundy was present, and there was no denial. Another episode which occurred during the discussion of this measure was the remonstrance against its establishment. This was signed by sundry citizens of Davidson County. Among the number was Andrew Jackson, who aroused the ire of some of the legislators by remarking that "any member who voted for it would perjure himself." In a protest entered on the House Journal, two members speak of "that most chimerical of all political schemes of the State of Tennessee."

From the first the new bank was a failure, and in 1821 Governor M'Minn was forced to acknowledge that it had not met the expectations of its friends. In 1821 William Carroll was elected governor. It is scarcely probable that the loan office of 1820 would have been established if Carroll had been elected two years earlier. With the exercise of that clear judgment and sound practical view of things which distinguished him, he discards in his first message the make-shifts which had been resorted to by the previous administration. He puts aside the "property laws," the "replevin and stays laws," the "indorsement laws," and the issuance of large quantities of paper money as totally inadequate. Instead he recommends economy and industry. He urges as prompt a return to specie payment as the circumstances will permit. He disposes of the proposition to unite the Nashville and State banks by an unanswerable syllogism. "Their strength consists in their solvency; if they are solvent and continue so, they have nothing to fear. If they are unsound, a union of unsound parts can never make a perfect whole." In place of this, he suggests a thorough examination of all the banks, and the appointment of a day for the resumption of specie payment. A law was at once passed in accordance with these suggestions, and the first day of April, 1824, was appointed. The effect of Carroll's message was in every way beneficial. It aroused the people of the State from a lethargic dependence upon the hope that the General Assembly would do something to relieve their distress, and it set them to work. In his message of 1822, Governor Carroll says: "I am happy in having it in my power to say that the pecuniary embarassments of the country have been greatly diminished by the industry of our citizens and the surplus produce of last year." A slight depression in 1823 again alarmed the pessimists, and a law was passed directing the banks to loan out, as soon as received, all moneys received from the sale of public lands. A unique resolution, adopted in 1823, is peculiarly characteristic of the times, and gives a striking illustration of the force of Governor Carroll's influence. The resolution recommends the members of the next General Assembly "to appear in clothing entirely of domestic manufacture," and the people of the State generally are advised to "manufacture their own clothes and live within their means and not go in debt."

In the spring and summer of 1825 the price of cotton and tobacco went up very considerably, and as a result brought a great influx of capital back to the State. In addition to this, there had been a steady inflow of population from the older States since the crash of 1819, in consequence of which there was a constant widening of the area of cultivation and increase in the aggregate products of the State. In 1825 Governor Carroll finds it "pleasing to reflect on the happy and prosperous condition of the State." "Our citizens . . . have been relieved by economy and their own exertions and not by the passing of laws interfering between debtor and creditor which never fail to injure the interests of both." "Our population," he adds, "is increasing with astonishing rapidity."

On the first of September, 1826, about a year and a half later than the time appointed, all the banks in Tennessee, except the Nashville Bank and its branches, resumed specie payment. There were not wanting voices to exclaim that it was bad policy to resume at that particular time. The good results which flowed from this were enhanced by the establishment of a branch of the United States Bank at Nashville, the previous law having been repealed. The Bank of Nashville, however, was seriously crippled. Its notes in 1826 were at a discount of 37½ per cent. Its management, in pursuance of the policy of straightforward honesty which had distinguished it from the first, decided to wind up its affairs, which was accordingly done with but small loss to any one.

The failure of the Nashville Bank increased a suspicion which had become current that the new State Bank was in trouble. It was now patent to all that, in so far as the object of its creation was concerned, it was a pronounced failure. It had not benefited the State. It had not benefited the citizen. It was estimated that debtors paid from twelve to twenty-five per cent. for every dollar they borrowed, and that the State gained only three per cent. net on the money invested in the bank even when honestly conducted. Between the adjournment of the General Assembly in

1827 and the reassembling in 1829, three hundred judgments against debtors of the bank had been recovered at Nashville alone. In 1829 Governor Carroll said: "As, however, the avowed causes which induced the legislature to establish the Bank of the State of Tennessee have happily passed away, a fit occasion seems to present itself to inquire whether a due regard to sound policy and to the best interests of the country does not require that measures should be adopted to settle the affairs of the institution by calling in the debts due to it with as little delay as possible, taking care not to injure or oppress those who are indebted to it." In pursuance of this suggestion, a resolution was passed directing the committee on banks "to inquire into the policy and expediency of closing the concerns and finally winding up the business and repealing the charter of the Bank of the State of Tennessee." The committee went earnestly to work. The managers of the bank became frightened. On January 3, 1830, the capital was startled by the announcement that gross irregularities had been discovered in the State Bank, and that the cashier, Joel Parrish, was a defaulter for a considerable sum. Being pressed by the committee, Parrish conceived the daring design of making away with the books of the bank in order to destroy the only evidence upon which he could be convicted. He and the clerk were arrested, but not until the books had been secreted.

The amount of the defalcation was discovered to be very nearly $200,000, a large part of which had been drawn out by friends of the cashier who had nothing to their credit. The clerk had embezzled about $15,000. The latter obtained an entire release by giving a lien on real estate. Parrish eventually returned the books of the bank upon an agreement that he should not be criminally prosecuted. Close investigation revealed the fact that the agencies, especially those in West Tennessee and in the Western District, were in a worse condition than the main bank.[1] New officers were elected and were instructed to bring the affairs of the bank to a speedy close. A law was passed directing the funds of the bank remaining after payment of all indebtedness to be turned over to the board of public-school commissioners in the various counties.[2] In 1833 the committee appointed to report upon the winding up of the affairs of the bank estimate the probable losses in closing up the bank's business to be about $153,344.05. The whole profits from the beginning amounted to $341,639.62, and the entire expenses had been $153,884.26, leaving a balance of $187,755.36, or very little more than enough to cover the estimated losses.

The next financial venture of Tennessee was the Bank of Tennessee, chartered December, 1831. This charter was repealed in October, 1832, by the same act that established the celebrated Union Bank. The capital stock was to be $3,000,000, of which the State was to take $500,000, issuing bonds therefor. The State was to receive a bonus of one half of one per cent. on the capital stock and interest on deposits of state funds. Profits arising from the state stock, the bonus, and the interest on deposits, after the payment of the bonds, were to go to the common schools. In case of a violation of the provisions of the charter, the directors voting for it were made responsible in their private property for any loss or damage, and next the stockholders to the amount of their stock. Suspension of specie payment was expressly forbidden, and holders of notes who had demanded and been refused specie were entitled to recover ten per cent. interest from the date of the demand. The notes of the bank were receivable for all dues to the State. The public faith of

---

[1] Andrew M'Millin, cashier of the Knoxville branch said : " With but few exceptions the agents in East Tennessee have acted with strict integrity and have managed their agencies only with a view to the interests of the institution."

[2] Also those of the old State Bank.

the State was pledged to the redemption of all debts of the bank in proportion to the amount of the state stock. Proper limitations were placed upon the power to inflate the currency. The charter of the Union Bank showed a distinct advance in the knowledge of the proper relations which should exist between State and bank. In 1856 the stock of the State was transferred to the Bank of Tennessee.

In 1833 the Planter's Bank was chartered upon the model of the Union Bank, as also the Farmer's and Merchant's Bank, except that the State had no stock in the latter. The former was designed as a Middle Tennessee Bank, with headquarters at Nashville, and the latter as a West Tennessee Bank, with headquarters at Memphis.

Up to 1838 the three subjects which chiefly engrossed the attention of those who confined their attention to state affairs, were the public schools, the banks, and internal improvements. As yet, however, the last, although a matter of constant discussion and even legislation, had been compelled to stand upon its own footing. Especially was it true that it had not become in any manner entangled with the financial institutions of the State. On January 19, 1838, this limit was overstepped, and, undeterred by the experience of the previous experiment, the legislature chartered the Bank of Tennessee, "to raise a fund for internal improvements and to aid in a system of education." The faith and credit of the State were pledged for the support of the bank, to supply any deficiency in the funds specifically pledged and to give indemnity for all losses arising from such deficiency. The capital stock was $5,000,000, raised from the whole school funds, the surplus revenue deposited by the federal government and in such sum in specie or in fund convertible into specie at par value as may be necessary to make up the balance. The governor was directed to issue $2,500,000, of state bonds for the benefit of the bank. Twelve directors were to be nominated to the General Assembly by the governor, "more than one third of whom shall in no case be merchants." Fortunately for the State, William Nichol was elected president, and Henry Ewing cashier. With but slight intermission, either Nichol or Cave Johnson was president of the Bank of Tennessee until Isham G. Harris became governor. Another provision in the charter designed for the benefit of farmers, and which subsequently caused much trouble, was one forbidding the bank or its branches to discount more bills of exchange than notes and bills single. Of the dividends, $100,000 were to go to common schools; $18,000 to academies, and any deficiency was to be made good by the State. The bank might not owe at any one time, exclusive of deposits, more than twice the amount of its capital stock. The notes of the bank were receivable for taxes. Discounts were to be apportioned annually among the counties in proportion to the number of qualified voters. Of the bonds ordered to be issued, $1,000,000 were sold in New York at par, and the bank reaped a double profit by assigning to each branch its pro rata and authorizing it to draw at the usual rate of exchange and receive the bills of the new bank, thus giving them circulation at par. Another problem which met the new bank on the threshold of its existence arose from the fact that the other banks had suspended specie payment. If paper, payable on demand, had been issued, it would have been possible to issue but a small amount of notes beyond the actual quantity of specie on hand. On the other hand, was it possible or even honest to issue paper redeemable on demand with the express intention of not redeeming it on demand? The problem was new and its solution, though novel, was successful. Post-notes were issued payable in twelve months, and the faith of the bank was pledged to redeem them in specie whenever the other banks resumed, either before or after maturity. The president of the bank reported that no inconvenience resulted from the experiment. Specie payment was resumed in January, 1839.

The principal bank and three branches were to be located in Middle Tennessee, two branches in East Tennessee, and two in the Western District. An eager rivalry arose among the various towns for the location of the branches. Thirty-seven places presented petitions and excitement ran high. The contest over the location of the capital was not more determined. The selection finally made caused great dissatisfaction among the disappointed, and for a long time traces of bitterness remained. It was supposed that the location of the bank would have a decided effect upon the future prosperity of the town selected. The branches ultimately went to Rogersville, Athens, Shelbyville, Columbia, Clarksville, Trenton, and Somerville. The most flourishing towns at that time in West Tennessee were Jackson, Randolph, Brownsville, Memphis, and La Grange. At a later date, branches were established at Sparta, Knoxville, and Memphis. One of the chief reasons for chartering the Bank of Tennessee was the stringency of the money market. The crash of 1832 had brought ruin to or seriously crippled nearly every one of the Southern and Southwestern banks, the issue of whose paper had been entirely out of proportion to their capital. It is to the honor of Tennessee that every one of its banks came triumphantly through the crisis. But it was at the expense of the debtor classes and by the suspension of specie payment, a practice which the example of the Bank of England and custom had made one of the ordinary expedients for financial depressions. The Bank of Tennessee failed to alleviate the stringency caused by the curtailment of discounts on the part of the other banks. The aggregate circulation of the Tennessee banks in 1836 and 1837 was about $5,000,000. In 1842 this had sunk to $1,200,000. Had the intention of the legislature been carried into effect, much of the suffering of that period would have been obviated. But the surplus federal revenue which had been deposited with the Union and Planter's banks and the Memphis banks had by these been loaned out, and being required to turn over this sum — in all it amounted to $1,356,746.41 — to the State Bank, these institutions found it necessary to restrict their operations and call in their loans. Instead of inflating the currency, it caused a contraction at the most critical period. In addition to this, only $1,000,000 of the bonds of the State issued for the benefit of the State Bank could be sold at par as required by law. The rest, $1,500,000, were subsequently destroyed by the governor in pursuance of an act of the legislature.

From the first the dissatisfaction was wide-spread and general. Governor Cannon, in 1839, said: "The bank has failed to effect the amelioration of our pecuniary affairs that its authors anticipated. . . . There is probably not another law to be found among our statutes that has more signally failed to fulfill the wishes of the legislature." Another one of the curious financial experiments of that day was a still further attempt to unite banking and internal improvements in the Southwestern Railroad Bank. The act chartering this institution was passed in December, 1837, and its object was to confer banking privileges on the stockholders of the Louisville, Cincinnati, and Charleston Railroad. The distinctive feature of this enterprise, which was chartered by three States, was that each share in the bank should be inseparably connected with a share in the railroad company, never to be transferred without it. Every person owning stock in the railroad company was entitled to one share in the bank for each share in the railroad company, and forfeiture in one worked a forfeiture of the corresponding share in the other. This bank actually went into operation, and in his message of 1841 the governor mentions this as the only bank that had not suspended specie payment. The failure of the railroad, however, carried with it the failure of the bank.

Early in the forties the State Debt for the first time began to be a subject of disquietude. In 1842 the stock banks of the State were ordered to dispose of their real estate and receive in payment stock of the banks or bonds of the State. In 1844 it was found necessary to lay a heavy tax on personalty by an act with the significant title, "To preserve the faith and credit of the State and to avoid reducing the amount distributed annually under existing laws for the support of common schools." In 1846 a sinking fund for the gradual extinguishment of the State Debt was created. The profits of the Bank of Tennessee were inadequate to the demands upon it. The necessity of curtailment became apparent, and it was found necessary to relieve the bank by a sale of the State's interest in the stock banks. From now until the war, the history of the Bank of Tennessee is intricately interwoven with the history of the State, at times dragged into the arena of politics by partisan prejudice, but being always preserved by the judicious management and undoubted integrity of William Nichol and Cave Johnson. Nearly every governor of the State, from the time of its establishment to the election of Governor Harris, recommended that its affairs be wound up, but it lived through it all.

In 1852 the Free Banking Act was passed which contained the germ of the present national banking system. Any one with a capital of $50,000 was allowed to do a general banking business and issue circulating notes to be secured by bonds, worth par in the market, to be deposited with the comptroller, who was required to issue notes countersigned, numbered, and registered in a proper book kept for that purpose. Subsequent amendments were added, and the whole act was repealed in 1858, but not until several banks had organized under it. The General

Banking Act of 1860 placed a wise restriction upon banks and banking operations, and, had it come sooner, would have prevented not only the speculative mania that hampered the legitimate industries of the State, but would also have prevented the reckless waste which turned the blessings of internal improvements to curses, the evil effects of which still clog heavily the wheels of our industrial enterprises. The capital stock of all banks was required to be paid in coin; it was not to exceed $3,000,000 or go below $300,000; the circulation was not to exceed twice the amount of its specie bonds. Monthly statements were to be made to the comptroller of the State. A suspension of specie payments worked a forfeiture of the charter. Individual liability of stockholders extended to the amount of their stock until the original subscription had been paid in full. A supervisor of banks was to be appointed by the governor and confirmed by the senate.

During the war, a part of the bank's funds was used to advance the cause of secession. In addition to this, $3,000,000 of bonds were issued to assist the confederate government, and the seeds of litigation were sown which still flourish in healthful vigor. The issue signed by G. C. Torbett, and known as the Torbett Issue, was the chief source of contention. One of the first acts of the Brownlow régime, after gaining control of the State, was to pass certain amendments to the constitution, one of which declared void all notes and bonds issued on or after the sixth day of May, 1861. In his message of April, 1865, Governor Brownlow suggests an investigation into the affairs of the "three old banks." He regarded all as insolvent, and recommended that they be closed up and made to redeem their issues, and that no future state banks be chartered. In February, 1866, an act was passed requiring the governor to appoint six directors to wind up the business of the Bank of Tennessee. The

Free Banking Act was repealed (the previous repeal applied only to banks to be organized after the date of repeal), and the banks were ordered into liquidation, saving only those which should place their notes at par with United States treasury notes within sixty days. In April, 1866, the board of directors of the State Bank made an assignment of all the assets of the bank to Samuel Watson as trustee, who proceeded to wind up the bank in chancery. In 1866 he reported the entire assets of the bank to be about $16,000,000, including worthless claims. The case continued almost up to the present time. When the available assets were finally distributed to note holders *pro rata*, provision was made for issuing notes for the balance, which were receivable for taxes. The United States Supreme Court had already decided that the issues of the bank were receivable for taxes, despite legislative enactments. An attempt was made in 1869 to convert the notes of the bank into bonds, but this failed. The holders of the notes were finally paid in full. But those who had money deposited with the State Bank have never received any return. Even those who find in the Brownlow régime a justification for the settlement at fifty cents on the dollar of that part of the State Debt issued to railroads, can and do offer nothing against the validity of the claims of those who deposited their money with the Bank of the State upon the faith and credit of the sovereign State of Tennessee.

Since the war the financial history of Tennessee, apart from the State Debt, has been, in the main, the financial history of the rest of the Union. Apart from a few so-called exemption charters, obtained during the disastrous period following the close of the war, the banks of Tennessee rest upon a healthy and just basis, always subject to the scrutiny of the State. Their complete severance from the State, the necessity of regular reports, and the inability to issue notes are the historical sequence of the financial experience through which Tennessee passed prior to the war. A new spirit of commercial conservatism has come in, bringing with it the possibilities of a new era of expansion, growth, and enterprise. Until a knowledge of the history of the various Tennessee banks shall have been lost to the people of this State, it is not probable that the State as such will ever again attempt to depart in any radical degree from its proper sphere into the fields where great rewards only come to individual effort, guided, watched, and guarded by the jealous eagerness of individual self-interest. The financial history of Tennessee has colored and influenced the whole commercial complexion of the State. Radiating from the banks of the present, the true spirit of business life has permeated the entire social structure. Business has laws of its own for violations of which it has its own punishments, unknown to the code. The commercial prosperity of a community can be gauged by the extent of the reign of these laws. Before the war, this spirit was practically unknown. Beginning with the Southern planter, but few in practice drew a sharp line of demarcation between the exactions of business and the amenities of social life. The custom of indorsing notes indiscriminately for friends was universal, and a refusal frequently brought about a rupture, at times a personal clash. A bill too often presented aroused anger and indignation. A gentleman's credit was supposed to be above suspicion, and, resting upon this supposition, liberties were taken with the goods of merchants and the bills of doctors that would now stamp a man as having no credit at all. In every respect, the business organization of the present is sounder, broader, and better than before the war.

CHAPTER XXVII.

INTERNAL IMPROVEMENTS.

INTERNAL improvements in Tennessee, which have played an important part in its history, were at first confined to the making of roads and turnpikes and the building of jails, court-houses, and stocks. The roads leading from Tennessee to Virginia, Georgia, and Kentucky were matters of inter-state regulation and enterprise. Resolutions, memorials, and messages were constantly interchanged. Very soon attention was turned to river navigation, and the pages of the earlier statute books are crowded with enactments allowing mill-dams and fish traps to be erected in certain creeks and rivers, or requiring them to be removed. At first, matters of this kind were subjects of local regulation. In 1804 an act was passed empowering the county courts of the State to order the laying off of public roads, establish and settle ferries, and to appoint where bridges should be built. In 1811 Governor Blount laid before the General Assembly an act passed by the New York legislature providing "for the improvement of the internal navigation of the State of New York," which had been sent by the authorities of that State with the request that the legislature of Tennessee be formally requested "to instruct representatives in Congress to advocate such measures in relation thereto as shall be before Congress." This was the beginning of the great canal. This memorial in effect turned the attention of the State in the direction of internal navigation. In November of this same year, in a resolution addressed to the Tennessee delegation in Congress, they are directed to obtain " free navigation of the boatable waters between this State and Mobile, to establish a road from East and one from West Tennessee to Mobile, to be kept up by turnpikes and ferries at proper points to be kept by white people, and to have the Natchez Trace kept in repair." In 1813 the governor of Tennessee is authorized to open a correspondence with the governors of the States of Alabama and Georgia, on the subject of internal improvement. A correspondence had already been opened with the governor of Alabama in reference to removing the obstructions occasioned by the Muscle and Colbert's Shoals in the Tennessee River. Governor M'Minn, in his message of September, 1817, said: "I will submit for your consideration the propriety of turning your attention to improving the navigation of our rivers, either by incorporating navigation companies for a definite number of years with the right to charge toll, or by such other means as your wisdom may suggest."

One of the first steps taken in pursuance of this policy was the appointment of a board of managers for opening the navigation of the rivers, who, however, beyond a meagre report or two, accomplished nothing. The general policy of internal improvement, however, was rapidly gaining favor, and the success of the Erie Canal was to the entire country an index-finger that pointed towards the goal of assured prosperity.[1]

In 1819 Governor M'Minn again urged on the General Assembly the subject of improving the navigation of the rivers and roads in the State. A joint resolution empowered him to appoint one or more fit persons to examine and explore the navigable rivers of the State for the pur-

---

[1] The contest between Clinton and Tompkins for the governorship of New York in 1819 was a wager of battle between those favoring and those opposing internal improvements. The success of the former gave a renewed impulse to the policy.

pose of reporting to the next General Assembly on the obstructions which existed, and the probable expense to be incurred in removing the same. The idea of the General Assembly was to appropriate immediately $500,000 for this purpose. In 1821 Governor M'Minn submitted to the Treasury Department of the United States an elaborate report prepared by himself, on the navigable waters of Tennessee. He also suggested a canal uniting the Holston and Tennessee to the Mobile, it being not more than eleven miles from Hiwassee to Connasauga. He also urged upon the United States the necessity of free navigation through the Muscle Shoals in the Tennessee River.

The constitutional questions involved in the relation of the federal government to internal improvements gave rise to long debates, acrimonious discussions, and exhaustive investigations. Out of the mists, however, Henry Clay emerged as a body of light, and taking as his basis one of the pentateuch of Democratic authority, the report of Mr. Madison to the Virginia General Assembly, replying to the resolutions passed by some of the States in reference to the Alien and Sedition laws, he evolved the principle of internal improvements as a part of his broader scheme or plan known in American politics as the American system. The objections raised against the participation of the general government in such works, which culminated in Mr. Monroe's celebrated veto message, but emphasized the necessity of such works and compelled the strict constructionists to look to the efforts of the individual States. Clay's speeches of March 13, 1818, and January 16, 1824, were widely circulated and read. As yet no comprehensive plan had been formulated in Tennessee, but evidences of the demand were not wanting. In 1825 Robert H. Dyer was loaned $3,000 for three years for the purpose of cutting a canal from the Forked Deer River to the Mississippi. In the same year the governor was authorized to appoint a suitable person to act with the United States engineers in the survey which was about to be made of a route through the State for the Great National Road. All of these measures bore but little fruit at the time, but they indicated and encouraged the general drift towards works of this kind, and were the forerunners of the subsequent mania or bubble. This tendency was further illustrated by the readiness of the legislature to grant special inducements to those who established manufactures of any kind, by the purchase for the State of the patent right of Eli Whitney and Phineas Miller in a machine or new invention for cleaning cotton, commonly called the ".saw gin,"[1] and by the number of lotteries authorized to be drawn for public and local purposes. Among the first, if not the very first, instance of a legal sanction being given to lotteries in the Southwest, was the law of 1794, "to raise money to cut a wagon road from Southwest Point to Cumberland settlement." Lotteries were as common as church festivals of the present day. In 1825 the town of Franklin was allowed to procure a town clock in this way. In 1826 alone, lotteries were allowed for the benefit of Cumberland College, to improve the navigation of Forked Deer River, to build a masonic hall in Knoxville, to enable certain parties to make salt in Bedford County, to remove obstructions from Caney Fork, and to encourage the establishment of cotton manufactures in White County.

As early as 1823 a standing committee on internal improvements had been appointed in both houses of the state legislature, and the accession of Governor Carroll, who was a warm advocate of internal improvements, gave additional strength to the movement. In 1825 a joint resolution urged on senators and congressmen to use their best exertions " to procure a survey of the route between the Hiawassee and Coosa Rivers, by civil engineers

[1] This was the "cotton gin."

of the United States, appointed to survey and lay out a road from Washington to New Orleans, and to report whether it is practicable to unite the waters of the Hiawassee and Coosa Rivers by a canal." In 1825 the committee on internal improvement submitted a report on the Great National Road, in which they recommended the line that would run through the centre of the State to a point on the Mississippi River at Memphis, there to be discontinued, as the rest of the journey to New Orleans could be made by water. Commissioners were actually appointed by Tennessee and Alabama to examine the Muscle Shoals in the Tennessee River with a view of making the river at that point navigable. They reported that "this could be done at much less expense than has heretofore been thought necessary."

The difficulties, however, in the way of a regular and systematic plan of operation were found almost insurmountable. The difficulty was in deciding upon the points of commencement. Local jealousies were aroused. Each little community clamored for recognition. Political influence came into play. Even the attempt to encourage private investment in turnpike stock failed. But the principle itself flourished, and although the way had not been found, the will was there.

The very scruples which made the strict constructionists deny the power of the general government to undertake works of internal improvements, forced them to an acknowledgment of the necessity that the States themselves should adopt measures for this purpose. Great works of this kind were in progress on every hand.

In 1829 Governor Carroll said in his message, " In many parts of our country the great work of internal improvement is advancing with astonishing rapidity. The New York canal is in successful operation. The Pennsylvania Canal, four hundred miles long, is nearly finished. The Baltimore Railroad, the Chesapeake Canal, the canal uniting the waters of Lake Erie with that of the river Ohio, and numerous other improvements of less magnitude, but of great value to the internal trade of the country, are in a state of vigorous progression, and will in a few years be entirely completed. With these bright examples before us does it become Tennessee to be idle?" In compliance with the spirit of the age, and in obedience to a general demand from all parts of the State, the General Assembly devised the first systematic plan of internal improvement in Tennessee. This is the plan of 1829.[1]

According to this, a board of internal improvement was appointed consisting of six commissioners, two east and two west of the Cumberland Mountains, and two west of the Tennessee River. One hundred and fifty thousand dollars of the unappropriated funds from the sale of the lands in the Hiwassee district were set apart; $60,000 for East Tennessee, $60,000 west of the Cumberland, 30,000 for the Western District. The governor was *ex-officio* member of the board. In 1831 the number of commissioners east of the Cumberland Mountains was increased to three and made a separate board for the purpose of removing obstructions to navigation in the Tennessee and Holston rivers and their navigable tributaries, and the $60,000 already appropriated were turned over to them. This same year was established a board of internal improvement for the mountain district of Middle Tennessee, one for Caney Fork, and one for Obed's River in Overton County. Also, in counties west of the Tennessee River, the county courts were directed to appoint three suitable persons, residents of the county, boards of county commissioners of internal improvement. Special acts were passed creating boards of internal improvement for Giles, Davidson, Rutherford, and Bedford counties.

The constitution of 1834 directed that an effective system of internal improvement be established throughout

[1] The act in reality was passed in 1830, January 2d.

the State. The plan of 1829 had not worked well in practice. But little support had been extended by private citizens, and local jealousies were so strong that the plan failed to accomplish definite results.

The next plan was that of 1835, passed February 19, 1836, for the construction of railroads and turnpikes and known as the Pennsylvania Plan. The principal feature of this scheme was the formation of corporations or companies for the prosecution of individual enterprises. After two thirds of the capital stock had been subscribed and its payment secured by others, the State was required to subscribe to the other one third, for which bonds were to be issued. In 1839 the State was required to subscribe one half and citizens the other half. One third of the directors were to be appointed by the State. Under the operation of this law, $66,666.66⅔ were issued to the Nashville, Murfreesboro, and Shelbyville Turnpike Company, $125,000 to the La Grange and Memphis Railroad Company with a lateral branch to Somerville, $45,000 to the Gallatin Turnpike Company, and $40,000 to the Lebanon and Nashville Turnpike Company. This was the first faint beginnings of the State Debt. The interest on the bonds issued by the State was to be paid by the company and deducted from any demands that might subsequently accrue to the State upon its stock. In 1837–38 this scheme was still further amplified by the formation of the Bank of Tennessee, which, among other objects, was to aid in establishing a system of internal improvement in the State. The bank was required to provide for the interest of the bonds from its own profits in addition to the dividends accruing to the State in internal improvement companies. Should this be insufficient, the governor was to notify stockholders in the company for whose stock state bonds had been issued, who were compelled to pay in on unpaid stock enough to meet the interest, under penalty of forfeiture of charter. The State retained a lien on the works of the company for the amount paid in by it. This was frequently known as the Partnership Plan. The State bore all the burdens, and was unable to protect itself against the negligence and fraud of its partners.

Governor Polk, in his message in 1841, said: "Indeed, our whole internal improvement system, as at present organized, is so very defective as to demand your anxious and unremitting consideration." The amount of bonds issued under the act of 1835–36 was $265,666.66⅔, bearing 5¼ per cent. interest, and under the act of 1837–38 was $300,000 for navigation and $599,500 for internal improvement companies, bearing interest at five per cent. Charters of incorporation were too readily granted, and works of no importance were undertaken for the purpose of obtaining state aid, which, by a judicious system of estimates, was, in many cases, made sufficient to accomplish the whole work. It was almost impossible to persuade the inhabitants of any locality that any work of local utility was not for the general good. The number of charters obtained was so great that $4,000,000, the amount to which the state subscriptions in all internal improvement companies were limited, would not have been sufficient to pay for one half of what was actually applied for. The failure to comply with the requirements of law on the part of the stockholders alone protected the State. Even the law itself was so ambiguous that no two agreed upon the same construction. An act was passed January 25, 1840, repealing all laws authorizing the governor of Tennessee to subscribe for stock in any internal improvement company on behalf of the State. This was spoken of as a dissolution of partnership. Provision was made for a careful investigation to determine whether the requirements of the statute had been complied with. This was used *in terrorem* to force many companies to surrender their charters, and in a great measure accomplished its purpose.

The financial crash of 1837 was one of the causes which forced the State to withhold aid from internal improvement companies. But the most potent was, no doubt, the inability to devise a plan that would accomplish the result effectively and economically. In the mean time, railroads, as a means of transportation, had passed beyond the experimental stage, and the popular desire for national advancement had turned enthusiastically in that direction. It had become a mania, and as such raged with unabated fury until the beginning of the civil war. As attention was more steadily turned towards railroads, canals and the navigation of rivers received less consideration. An occasional reference to schemes that had once been much in the public eye is found, but nothing more. Governor Cannon in 1835 urges the construction of a canal from Savannah on the Tennessee River to Big Hatchie near Bolivar, which would shorten the distance of steamboat navigation about four hundred miles. So little interest was taken in the improvement of the rivers that $300,000 appropriated by an act of 1841 were never spent, on account of a disagreement between the board and officers of the Bank of Tennessee.

The first railroad chartered in Tennessee[1] was the Memphis Railroad Company, in 1831. This title was, in 1833, changed to the Atlantic and Mississippi Railroad Company, which was to run from Memphis to Pulaski, there to connect with another railroad which it was supposed would be constructed by Alabama from Florence.[2] One of the next roads chartered was the La Grange and Memphis Railroad, which received $125,000 from the State. It was perhaps this that enabled it to build the six

---

[1] The first built was the Nashville and Chattanooga Railroad.

[2] I can find in the statutes no act chartering the Memphis Railroad Company. The date is given in the act which changed the title. The act refers to December 17, 1831, and again to December 12, 1831, as the date of the first act.

miles which were actually constructed in 1837. Railroads from New Orleans to Nashville, from Memphis to some point in Virginia, from Memphis to Charleston, from Charleston through the eastern part of the State to Cincinnati and Louisville, were the main topics of discussion.

Perhaps the largest, certainly the most conspicuous railroad enterprise of that day was the Charleston, Cincinnati, and Louisville Railroad. For several years it was a matter of interstate diplomacy and negotiation. The messages of the governors and the statute books of the States are filled with mentions of it and references to it. In Columbia, Greeneville, Charleston, Cincinnati, and Louisville meetings were held, speeches were made, and resolutions were passed. Tennessee was the last State to pass the act of incorporation. The governor was directed to subscribe $650,000 in behalf of the State, and $32,000 in bonds were actually issued. Most of these were subsequently returned and the subscription canceled, but new vehemence had been given to internal improvements or, as it had now become, the railroad mania. But it was not without significance that the State was compelled in 1846 to meet a deficit of interest on the bonds.

In 1845 was held the great commercial convention at Memphis, over which John C. Calhoun presided. The object of the convention was to bring together the friends of internal improvements for mutual discussion. It was here that Calhoun came out for the improvement of the Mississippi River, declaring it to be a "great inland sea." The immediate outgrowth of this convention was the building of the Memphis and Charleston Railroad. The history of this enterprise forms an important chapter and played an important part in the making of Tennessee. It is worthy of being detailed at some length.

In those days a certain efficacy was attached, in the popular mind, to a railroad, entirely independent of the greater ease of locomotion and facilitated transportation of freight which came with it. Even so clear-headed a man of business as Marcus B. Winchester seemed to think that the advantages that flowed from a railroad stretched themselves along its rails foot for foot. In a letter written in 1834 he says: "If the Jackson company owned the property and some about the upper end of the town of Memphis they would have every inducement to string their road through our town from north to south, which would regenerate, it seems to me, every part and portion of it." In the eyes of most Americans of that day, the town that was so fortunate as to come within the influence of a railroad was like an Indian village with a powerful medicine man. With ideas such as these, it is not surprising that so ambitious a place as Memphis was eager to have a railroad. Capital, as political economists use the phrase, had not turned its attention in this direction. The motive power then was a compound of agriculture and sentiment. Roads were built, not from accumulated savings, but from the proceeds of a discounted incoming era of prosperity. The method of proceeding was for various local companies to be formed, each of which built, or expected to build, a fragment of road designed to connect with other fragments until a through line, as it is now called, was finished. In this way the La Grange and Memphis Railroad and the Tuscumbia, Courtland, and Decatur railroads had been begun and had failed. As its name indicated, the Memphis and Charleston Railroad was designed to connect these two cities.

The public discussion of this question elicited a general enthusiasm, and it became the leading topic of the day. The most prominent statesmen, politicians, merchants of Tennessee and Georgia and South Carolina became its warmest advocates, and men like Hayne, who had gained national fame in his brilliant debate with Webster, and Jones of Tennessee took a leading part in advocating this enterprise. Jones added to his already brilliant reputation by the force and eloquence of his speeches.

For more than a year he canvassed West Tennessee, North Mississippi, North Alabama, Memphis, New Orleans, and Charleston. The corporation of Memphis subscribed $500,000. The largest individual subscription was that of R. C. Brinkley, $15,000. Jones was elected president, and George W. Smith, secretary and treasurer. He was soon succeeded by Sam Tate. The road was divided for working purposes into two sections. The eastern division extended from the Alabama line to Stevenson, where it connected with the Nashville and Chattanooga Railroad, and the western to Memphis. In 1851 the letting of the contracts began. Soon after this, Jones was elected to the United States Senate. He in turn was succeeded by A. E. Mills of Huntsville, and under Mills the lines contracted for under Jones were finished. The first track laid was at the crossing of Union Street in Memphis, on April 1, 1852. But after the contracts for the rest of the work had been let, the treasury was exhausted. An added embarrassment was the failure to get a charter through the Mississippi legislature allowing the right of way across the northeast corner of the State, owing to the opposition of the friends of the Mississippi Central Railroad. In order to overcome this hostility, Mills and Tate for their road agreed to subscribe $125,000 of the capital stock of that concern. When submitted to the board of directors of the Memphis and Charleston Railroad this contract was indignantly rejected, some of the directors declaring they would resign before accepting a charter on such disgraceful terms. At this time Tate, who lived at Memphis, was the only acting officer on the western division, Mills living at Huntsville and having charge of the eastern division. Even the warmest and most hopeful friends of the enterprise now began to despair of its completion. The one ray of hope, however, was the fact that one man had demonstrated an executive ability and comprehensive grasp of affairs that gave promise of substantial results. This was Sam Tate, the secretary and treasurer, and even he had sent in his resignation to take effect on the first day of April, 1854, on which day there was to be a general meeting of stockholders at Tuscumbia, Alabama. The object of the meeting was to consider the rejection or acceptance of the contract which Tate, since its former rejection by the board, had again entered into with the Mississippi Central Company. After a stormy debate the contract was accepted. Mills resigned the presidency, and Tate the secretaryship. The latter was then offered the former position but declined. Nothing could more distinctly emphasize the difference between the two stages of development in railroad building of that day and this than the fact that for several days the presidency went absolutely begging. Finally, after great persuasion, Sam Tate was induced to accept the position. Tate's first action was decisive. He made an accurate estimate of what money was still needed to complete the work. Already $2,000,000 had been spent. He decided that $1,600,000 would still be necessary. A stockholders' meeting was at once held at Huntsville, before which Tate laid his statement of the affairs of the company. All his recommendations were at once adopted. He declared that $400,000 were necessary to complete works then in process of construction. This, as he pointed out, could only be raised by the stockholders subscribing for that amount of the bonds that were to be issued. It would be impossible to get Northern capitalists to invest in so doubtful a security. Tate's reputation had gone before him, and he gained the implicit confidence of all with whom he came in contact; $312,000 were at once taken, and he was urged to proceed with this amount. But he refused on the ground that he could not regard it as honorable to speculate at the risk of men whose bread depended upon their daily labor. After the adjournment of the stockholders, Tate, with an energy that filled with enthusiasm all who came in contact with him, at once set out in a buggy to visit the largest stockholders to persuade them to increase their subscriptions. On all sides he proclaimed that he had money on hand sufficient to pay off at the next pay-day, August 15, 1854, and that if the $400,000 were not assured by that day, he would give notice to suspend work. He postponed the pay-day until the twentieth of August. After a long and arduous journey up and down the beautiful and fertile valley through which the Memphis and Charleston Railroad now runs, he drove into Huntsville on the evening of the eighteenth of August. He was met on the public square by an immense throng of citizens who had followed his course with enthusiasm, and who now greeted him with cheers. Standing in his buggy, he announced that his subscription list still lacked $13,000. In a moment this was subscribed by four of the bystanders, and amid cheers not unlike those that greeted Fourth of July orators during the earlier part of this century, Tate announced that the road would be a success. He promised at the time to have the road completed by the 1st of April, 1857. It is worthy of remark that the last spike was driven on the 27th of March, 1857. His calculations had missed absolute accuracy by only four days.

When the road was completed, nearly 25,000 people visited Memphis, upon the invitation of the railroad company, to celebrate the successful completion of so important a work, and also to witness the marriage, as it was called, of the waters of the Atlantic Ocean and the Mississippi River. This ceremony consisted in pouring a hogshead of Atlantic water into the Mississippi River amidst the booming of cannon and the shouting of the people. The building of this road not only rounded out a period in Tennessee history; it was also an epoch in the history of the Southwest. The completion of the great sub-Alpine tunnel did not affect the commercial intercourse and development of France and Italy more decidedly than the completion of the Memphis and Charleston Railroad affected the intercourse and development of the entire Southwest of the United States. The completion of this road gave us the Tennessee which we have now.

In 1848 an attempt was made to establish a new system of state aid to railroads. The distinctive feature of this plan was that the State indorsed the mortgage bonds of the companies, instead of issuing its own. The State was secured by a lien on the whole stock of the company and on the road fixtures. Curiously enough, however, these bonds sold for less than par, whereas the bonds of the State were at or above par. This plan proved to be not more satisfactory than the other. Its most glaring defects were the failure to devise means by which the State could examine into the financial condition of the corporations whose bonds had been indorsed, and the failure to reserve to the State the power of legislating to protect its interests. In addition to this, being an indorser and guarantor of the bonds issued, the ability of the State to protect itself depended on the actions of those over whom it had little control. Still another grave disadvantage was the fact that the lien for the protection of the State depended upon the deed to be made by the company instead of public act or statute. In 1749–50 an attempt was made to correct these defects. The State was to issue its own bonds and have vested in it the title to the roads to secure the debt created for their benefit, and individual stockholders were required to accept and ratify the act. But again the legislature failed to provide measures by which information could be obtained of the condition of the companies, and also by which the State could legislate as a sovereign instead of resorting to the courts as an individual.

The act of February 11, 1852, was passed to avoid the defects of all previous enactments. Under this act, the

State Debt was contracted, and had it not been for the incompetency of the so-called "Brownlow régime," immediately after the war, when a large majority of the voters of the State were disfranchised, the success of the act would have been unmixed with evil. The bonds of the State were issued in its sovereign capacity, for the payment of which its credit was pledged, and without involving itself in any relation of trust or partnership. The manifest intention of the law-makers was to float the bonds at or above par by pledging the credit of the State for their payment, which would not have been done had any question of the primary liability of the companies been entertained. It was the intention, an intention altogether reasonable and well founded at the time, to provide means by which to save the State from all loss, if possible, and certainly to reduce this loss, if any should occur, to a minimum. The war could not be foreseen. The losses could not have been avoided. Had it not been for the war and the Brownlow administration, the debt of Tennessee would doubtless have been paid in full. The act of February 11, 1852, was called an act to establish a system of internal improvements in this State. It required each railroad company to have a *bona fide* subscription to its capital stock sufficient to grade bridges and prepare for the iron rails the whole extent of the main trunk line. The governor was to exact a rigid compliance with these terms. After this had been done and thirty miles of the road at either terminus prepared, the governor was to issue $8,000 a mile in six per cent. state bonds, to be used in procuring rails and equipments alone. The State was to be invested, upon the issuance of these bonds, with a first lien or mortgage upon the section so prepared, without a deed of the company. Other sections of twenty miles each were to be treated in the same way. After the completion of the road, the State was invested with a prior lien or mortgage on all its interests, franchises, equipments, etc. The company was to deposit in the Bank of Tennessee, fifteen days before due, the interest on the bonds as satisfactory evidence that the same had been paid. Upon failure, the governor was to take charge of the road, and place it in the hands of a receiver until the interest in arrears should have been paid. If the company failed to pay the bonds when they fell due, the State was to take possession and dispose of the road to protect itself. Five years after the completion of the road, one per cent. per annum upon the amount of bonds issued was to be set apart by the company and used to retire the bonds of the State, which bonds when retired were to be a credit on the debt due the State, and these bonds were to be held and used as a sinking fund for the payment of bonds issued. Semi-annual reports were to be made under oath by the president of the company. The State reserved the right to enact all such laws as might be deemed necessary to protect its interests and secure it against loss.

An act was passed February 8, 1854, amendatory of this act of 1852. This act increased the amount per mile to be issued to $10,000, and provision was made for issuing bonds for building bridges. On February 17,[1] the length of the sections after the first thirty miles was decreased from twenty to ten miles, and on January 19, 1855, the grading of ten mile sections was to be taken in lieu of completing them. On February 21, 1856, the the sinking fund was increased to two per cent. On March 20, 1860, an act to provide for the equalization and investment of the sinking fund directed that the money and bonds paid to the sinking fund commissioners should be passed direct to the credit of the party paying them, and operate as a release to said party for that amount on the debt due by them to the State, and the sinking fund was still further increased to two and one half per cent.

[1] By an act to amend the charter of the Memphis and Somerville Turnpike Company and for other purposes.

The war prevented the good effects of this law from being felt, apart from the retirement of a small part of the debt.

The total amount of bonds issued to railroads alone before the war was $14,841,000.[1] As soon as the war closed, what is now called a raid was made on the treasury. From April, 1866, to December, 1868, a period which has been described as "a carnival of revelry and corruption," at a time when every industry and enterprise had been paralyzed by the war, and when, by the loss of slaves, the assessed value of the taxable property in the State had sunk from $388,936,794 in 1860, to $225,393,410 in 1867, $14,393,000 were issued to railroads, $113,000 were issued to turnpikes, besides $4,941,000 issued under the act of 1866 to fund the war interest, and $2,200,000 under the act of 1868 to fund past due coupons. This increased the debt of the State in two years, $21,647,000. In addition to this, by an act passed May 24, 1866, incorporating several turnpikes, the stock of the State in the East Tennessee and Georgia Railroad, amounting to $425,000, was turned over to them. This and the $113,000 issued between 1868 and 1870 succeeded in building twenty miles of turnpike, as officially reported by a committee of investigation. A large part of these twenty miles was built by private subscriptions paid in work.

On the 25th of February, 1869, an act was passed to liquidate the State Debt contracted in aid of railroad companies. This act was passed in the interest of the railroads, who were represented by strong lobbies at the capital during the pendency of the bill. It allowed them to

[1] Add to this $3,000,000 issued in 1833 and 1838 to the Union Bank and the Bank of Tennessee, $1,323,000 issued to turnpikes from 1836 to 1854, $1,166,000 issued between 1848 and 1860 for building the Capitol, $30,000 issued July 19, 1856, for the Agricultural Bureau, and $48,000 on March 29, 1856, for buying the Hermitage, and the entire State Debt at the beginning of the war, exclusive of the repudiated Confederate loan, was $20,408,000.

cancel their indebtedness to the State by paying in bonds of the series issued to them. The State was to receive, at par, bonds quoted in 1869 as low as 40½. That provision of the law, however, which required bonds of the same series as those issued to be paid in acted as a restraint on the railroads, and the act of January 2, 1870, was lobbied through the legislature which allowed them to pay the State, in liquidation of the principal of the debt, any of the legally issued six per cent. bonds of the State, without regard to series or number. It was anticipated that questions of the validity of the post-bellum issue of bonds would be raised. The acts of 1865, 1866, and 1867, the last being the "Omnibus Railroad Bill," had been passed under circumstances of such notorious fraud and so clearly in defiance of law, that as soon as the Brownlow and Senter régime was overthrown, steps were taken to repudiate those bonds which were issued contrary to law. A committee was appointed by the legislature of 1869–70 to investigate the railroads and the bonds issued to them. But the work of the committee had scarcely been begun when a movement looking to the reconstruction of the State began to assume shape at Washington. The ground upon which reconstruction was urged was the belief that the Brownlow and Senter bonds would be repudiated. Mr. D. B. Thomas, speaker of the Senate and Mr. W. O'N. Perkins, speaker of the House, went to Washington, and by their assurances saved the State from what would have been the disaster of reconstruction. It became necessary to abandon the line of policy mapped out by the committee, according to which the validity of the bond-issuance was to be tested by proceedings at law.

The railroads hastened to take advantage of the laws of 1869 and 1870. It is a remarkable circumstance that of the $14,841,000 issued to railroads before the war, up to 1880 $5,330,000 had been canceled, and of the $14,393,000 issued to railroads since the war, $11,258,000 had been canceled. More even than this. Of the ante-war bonds, a part was retired before the war and a part was paid, November 17, 1865, by the Louisville and Nashville Railroad. Under an act of 1871, for the sale of insolvent and delinquent roads, eleven roads were sold for $6,698,000 and the amounts paid in by the railroads under the acts of 1869 and 1870 was $14,787,600. The total amount of the State Debt in January, 1879, according to the report of James L. Gaines, comptroller, was, including interest, $27,008,480, represented by 21,005 bonds outstanding, of which 10,067 were issued before the war to banks, turnpikes, and railroads, to build the Capitol, to buy the Hermitage, and for the Agricultural Bureau, and 10,938 issued since the war, of which 113 were for turnpikes, 3,135 for railroads, 2,254 under the Funding Act of 1866, 569 under the Funding Act of 1868, and 4,867 under the Funding Act of 1873.

The constitution of 1870 put an end to the possibility of any further internal improvements as a political or economic scheme at the expense or with the aid of the State. It enacts that "the credit of this State shall not hereafter be given or loaned to or in aid of any person, association, company, corporation, or municipality." The State Debt was long a political issue in Tennessee. It passed practically out of politics with the compromise of 1882, which settled the so-called State Debt proper, the Capitol, Hermitage, Bank, Agricultural Bureau bonds in full, and the rest of the debt at fifty cents on the dollar, with three per cent. interest. The war interest was repudiated.

CHAPTER XXVIII.

CARROLL, HOUSTON, AND CONSTITUTIONAL CONVENTION.

THE period which intervened between the first election of Carroll and the Constitutional Convention of 1834 is one of steady progress. During this period of thirteen years, Carroll was governor eleven. This was an era of reform and growth, and nearly every step forward was taken at the suggestion of the brave old warrior. His overwhelming victory in 1821 emphasized his popularity with the people, and in 1823, and again in 1825 he was elected without opposition.

In 1827 Willie Blount, Newton Cannon, and Sam Houston were candidates for the governorship. The vote cast for Blount was contemptibly small. Houston was elected by a large majority. His administration was successful, his recommendations conservative. Houston's career, even before he was made governor of Tennessee, was not without a touch of romantic diversity. He had been brought up among the East Tennessee mountains, and on the banks of the beautiful stream which gave its name to the State. As a boy, he had been a familiar inmate of the wigwams of a small settlement of Cherokees in the neighborhood of his mother's cottage. Here he had tasted the pleasures of that undisciplined mode of life which seems to have a strong fascination even for those reared in the lap of luxurious indulgence. When a mere boy, Houston entered the army, fought with desperate bravery through the Creek War, won the applause of General Jackson, was made a lieutenant in the regular army, resigned, studied law, was elected solicitor-general of the Nashville district, removed to Nashville, was elected adjutant-general in 1821 over Newton Cannon, to succeed William Carroll, and was elected in 1823 and 1825 a member of Congress. Cannon was known to be lukewarm in the cause of Jackson. Houston was known to be his ardent partisan. This may have influenced the final result, both in the contest of 1821 and again in 1827.

Houston had a tall, commanding figure, an imposing bearing, an affable demeanor, and popular address. As solicitor-general he had displayed oratorical talents of no mean order. Oratory, or rather public speaking, had not yet been developed to the extent which has since made it the distinguishing feature of American political life. The passionate eloquence of Patrick Henry had been adapted to times of danger, to a turbulent and troubled period. The incisive discourse of Franklin, the luminous exposition of Hamilton, the philosophic reasoning of Jefferson, the persuasive declamation of Fisher Ames, were adapted to the deliberations of men engaged in the serious occupation of making laws for nations. Clay and Webster were just rising through the morning mists. There were no orators in Tennessee. Houston, it was then thought, would be a great orator. Perhaps a more favorable field for the cultivation of his talents might have accomplished this result. His first efforts, considered as first efforts, were full of promise, which, however, was never realized. Perhaps there is something which unfits the man of action for words. Houston was certainly a man of action. Indeed he was a great man, though his claim to this title rests upon his achievements after he left Tennessee. In January, 1829, Houston married a Miss Eliza Allen, daughter of an influential family in Sumner County, and a member of "the quality." In April of the same year Houston's wife left him and returned to her father's house, after Houston had written to the father requesting him to bring about a reconciliation between him and his wife. The first information that came to the public was Houston's resignation, which took place on the 16th of April. He at once abandoned the State, went to the Cherokee country, to the wigwam of an Indian chief who had adopted him when a boy. From here he drifted to Texas where, fortunately for his fame, he found a proper field for the display of those strong and admirable qualities of mind which, united to a steadfast character and a high purpose, made him great despite his puerile affectations and his robust vanity. The cause of separation was at that time a mystery, and the lapse of time has in no wise lessened it. Houston, even when deepest in his cups, never suffered a word of explanation to escape him. He always protested that the virtue of his wife remained unimpeached. The most plausible and satisfactory explanation appears to be this: Houston was spirited, sensitive, and vain. The young woman had been driven to the marriage by the importunities of her family, who were ambitious, and who saw, as they imagined, a brilliant career opening for Houston. Her affections had been won by another lover of less pretension and promise. She yielded to the wishes of her friends. The marriage took place. She was cold. Houston was importunate and passionate. Suddenly he discovered the truth. She did not love him. His suspicions were aroused, and he suspected more than the truth. Reproaches and recriminations followed. An explanation took place. Houston saw the real truth. He tried to effect a reconciliation. He wrote the letter, already mentioned, to her father, to enlist his services. She remained obdurate, and returned to her father's house. Houston, who was fond of dramatic effects, determined to resign. This he did in a dramatic manner, and surrounding himself with a cloak of mystery, he left the State. This explanation is consistent with Houston's character, with the ordinary transactions of daily life, with what we know of the event, and most of all with the letter which Houston wrote before his wife left him. In this he says: "Whatever had been my feelings or opinions in relation to Eliza at one period, I have been satisfied, and it is now unfit that anything should be adverted to." Again, "Eliza stands acquitted by me. I have received her as a virtuous, chaste wife, and as such I pray God I may ever regard her, and I trust I ever shall. She was cold to me, and I thought did not love me."

Houston was succeeded by the speaker of the Senate, General William Hall. Hall was born in Virginia, and came to Tennessee when young, had been sheriff of Sumner County, brigadier-general of the fourth regiment of state militia during the Creek War, — at various times a member of the state legislature, and in 1823 speaker *pro tem.* of the Senate. When elected to the Senate in 1827, on the eve of Jackson's election to the presidency, all eyes appear to have been turned toward Hall as the proper man to be speaker. He possessed the important qualification of being an intimate friend of Jackson. Houston in his letter of resignation speaks of him as one who has been "the consistent friend of the great and good man now enjoying the triumph of his virtues in the conscious security of a nation's gratitude." As soon as elected, William Carroll had written to him, "I have no hesitancy in saying you ought to be speaker of the Senate. If you give authority to mention your name, I feel confident that there will be no opposition, to produce which, my best efforts shall be directed." Robert C. Foster also urged him to be a candidate, and he was elected without serious opposition. He served as governor until Carroll was again elected, which was in August of that year.

Carroll was reëlected without opposition in 1831 and 1833. During his last term the second Constitutional Convention of Tennessee assembled.

The Constitutional Convention of 1834 marked an era in the making of the State. The admission of Tennessee to the Union brought about generally that condition of affairs which is said to make a people happy at the expense of the historian. The epic stage of our development was during the turmoils and wrangles of Indian warfare, incipient secession, and civil agitation. With the end of these came the end of striking episodes, tragic climaxes, and events that influence a people's destiny. From 1796 to 1834 we see the gradual expansion of the area of cultivation, the steady inflow of immigration, the building of cabins, the widening of settlements, the formation of new counties, the laying off of new county seats, and the building of schools, churches, and courthouses.[1] While this is going on among the people, we see their representatives first at Knoxville, then at Murfreesboro, and then at Nashville, where the permanent seat of government was finally located in 1843, attempting to devise legislation to help forward the material interests of the commonwealth. The primitive and clumsy machinery of state government is gradually improved. The most complex problem of all, involving the highest functions of legislation, just laws firmly administered, is vigorously undertaken. Always, however, and even to this day, without a complete or entirely satisfactory solution. The cultivation of the soil brings gradually increasing wealth, and the planting of corn, cotton, and tobacco, as it spreads, carries with it the curse of slavery and the seeds of future disasters. The beautiful blue-grass regions of Middle Tennessee and an abundance of water, draw the attention of the thrifty to stock-raising. New inventions gradually creep in and a better mode of agriculture. The increasing power of the press brings with it a widening of mental vision, a humanizing of passions

---

[1] The Penitentiary was built in 1831. The State Capitol, begun in 1845, was finished in 1855.

which, in subsequent years, finds practical expression in the establishment of asylums for the afflicted. Comforts become generally diffused and luxuries follow comforts. In the homely phrase of the day, Tennessee is fairly out of the woods. On all sides are pleasant visions, beautiful landscapes, fast-flowing streams, thriving towns, thrifty plantations, a happy, prosperous, industrious, and, in the main, virtuous population.

The changes in the organic law of the State accomplished by this convention have already been described under other heads. It was a fit culmination that it should be held during the administration of Carroll, whose election had opened the way for the changes in the official organization of Tennessee, and whose influence had created the impulse which resulted in a radical reform in other branches. Among the signs of the times were the impeachments of Judge Nathaniel W. Williams and Judge Joshua Haskell. Feeling secure in their seats, many of the judges had become so high-handed and overbearing, and in many cases so neglectful of their duties, that a general protest went up from the people as well as the bar. The experiment of filling judicial seats with officers *quam diu bene se gesserint* was not a success in Tennessee.

The four ablest governors of Tennessee before the war were John Sevier, William Carroll, James K. Polk, and Andrew Johnson. But John Sevier earned his reputation before he became governor, and Polk and Johnson, after they had been. None of them had an opportunity of displaying any species of statesmanship, even in so circumscribed a sphere. Carroll was more fortunate. The opportunity was offered and he seized it. In his circular issued in June, 1821, he set his face against the recently organized Loan Office or Bank of Tennessee, which Felix Grundy had pushed through the extra session of the legislature. In his first message he took a decided stand against all the relief and stay and replevin laws, by which, acting on the suggestion of Governor M'Minn, the General Assembly had hoped to cure the financial and commercial evils of the State. He urged, instead, rigid economy and retrenchment by the people themselves. He called attention to the inefficiencies of the judicial organization of the State and the confusion resulting from a lack of sharply defined jurisdiction among the courts. He urged the repeal of the law which gave the county and circuit courts concurrent jurisdiction, and suggested the establishment of district courts of equity. He advised the establishment of a penitentiary, and the abolition of such barbarous methods of punishment as the pillory, stocks, branding, and the like. He dwelt upon the importance of a system of general education, internal improvements, and a more thorough organization of the state militia. Many years elapsed before all these reforms were accomplished, but it is due to Carroll's liberal-minded appreciation of the necessities of the times, and his unwavering obstinacy in pressing them that they were at last achieved. All his messages from the first to the last returned repeatedly to the charge. If we divide our state history into ancient and modern periods, the credit would fall to Carroll's lot of having foreseen and ushered in the latter. He was essentially the reform governor of Tennessee.

At the Constitutional Convention of 1834 appeared representatives from a division of the State which had heretofore attracted little attention. They now came in numbers sufficient to demand and to enforce consideration. Although having been open to emigration only about fifteen years, its growth had been so rapid and yet so quiet, that the older communities of East and Middle Tennessee could scarcely realize and were loath to acknowledge that they were threatened with a rearrangement of political power. This division of the State was West Tennessee, at that time known as the Western District.

CHAPTER XXIX.

WEST TENNESSEE.

THE history of West Tennessee has never been written. Its real history begins at a time when the troubles which attended the formation of the State were at an end. The treaty of 1818, by which the Chickasaws lost their interest in the soil of Tennessee, is the beginning of the history of this part of the State. This groups itself for the first part of its development around Jackson and Brownsville and then around Shelby County and Memphis. The inflow of population was of two kinds — that which gradually spread like waves on ruffled water, approaching from the east, and that which came down the rivers. In an interesting account of "The Chickasaw Country lately ceded to the United States," written in 1819 for the "Raleigh (North Carolina) Register," by Calvin Jones, he says: "There is not a white family nor a trading house in the country, unless a store at Fort Pickering near the Mississippi line should be on the north side of it, a fact of which I am not well informed. . . . In 1784, all that portion of country which I have described as lying between the inundated lands and gravelly ridges, together with some parcels on the elevated banks of the Mississippi at or near the mouths of the rivers which empty themselves into it, were surveyed by Judge Harris, General Roberts, and Henry Rutherford of Nashville, in tracts of 500 to 5,000 acres each. Five years ago these lands were selling at from twelve and a half cents to twenty-five cents an acre, and within a few months they have been sold in Raleigh at fifty cents. I once witnessed a conveyance to the late Governor Williams of 640 acres, very favorably situated on the Obian (sic), given in exchange for an indifferent gig-horse. The average value of all these lands is now ten dollars an acre, and many tracts are worth double that sum." Those who first came to this country were surveyors and land speculators who, according to an old chronicler, were stopped by no difficulty. By an act of the legislature, the priority of location was decided by a lottery.

Hickman County was organized as a county in 1808, two years after the first settlement on Pine River by Adam Wilson. The first county seat was Vernon, but was succeeded in 1824 by Centreville. Lewis County was organized in 1806 and Wayne County in 1820, five years after the first settlement at Buffalo Creek by Frederick Meridith. Perry, which at that time included Decatur, was organized in 1820.[1] Humphreys, which includes also the present limits of Benton, was organized in 1810. The first county seat was Reynoldsburgh, on the east bank of the Tennessee, which is now a deserted village more desolate than sweet Auburn itself. In 1838 the seat was removed to Waverly. The first settlement in Carroll County was made by John Woods, Thomas Hamilton, and others on Clear Creek near where McKenzie now stands. Huntingdon, the county seat, was built on ground donated by the heirs of Memucan Hunt, whence the name.

The first settlement made in Henry County was in 1819 by Joel Hagler, John Stoddurt, and Jones Williamson near where Manley's Chapel now stands, or stood a few years ago. The county, named for Patrick Henry of Virginia, was organized in 1823, and Paris was founded the same year. Hardin County, which is partly in West and partly in Middle Tennessee, was organized in 1820. It

---

[1] The county was sometimes organized a year or two after the passage of the act authorizing its establishment.

was named in honor of Captain John Hardin, a Revolutionary hero. The first settlement was made at the mouth of Horse Creek by James Hardin. Henderson County, organized in 1822, was first settled by Joseph Reed, a few miles east of Lexington, which was founded the same year. McNairy was established in 1823 and named for Judge John McNairy. It was organized at the house of Abel V. Murray. Purdy, the county seat, was founded in 1824. The first settlers upon the territory that afterwards became McNairy, were the Murrays, McAlpins, Sweats, Gillespies, Beattys, and Kirbys. Gibson County was organized in 1823 and named in honor of Colonel Thomas Gibson, who had gained distinction under Jackson in the Creek War. The first settlement was made by Thomas Fite and James Spencer near Trenton in 1819. Gibsonport was laid off as the county seat, but the name was changed to Trenton in 1825. By the act of 1823-24 Gibson, Fayette, Hardeman, Haywood, Dyer, and Tipton became separate counties and commissioners were appointed to lay off county seats. The first county court of Fayette was organized in 1824 at the house of R. G. Thornton, about a quarter of a mile south of the north fork of Wolf River. Somerville was laid off as the county seat by the commissioners appointed for that purpose. The commissioners were Henry Kirk, Daniel Johnson, Hamilton Thornton, William Owen, and John T. Patterson. The immigration to Fayette County in 1825 was very great. One author says enthusiastically of it: "Settled by men of enterprise, intelligence, and wealth, it early took a stand among the most favored counties in the district noted for the refined, cultivated taste and good morals of its citizens." In 1837 William Lewis issued the first number of the "Somerville Reporter." La Grange, one of the principal towns of Fayette County, at first attained great prominence. It carried on a lucrative trade with the Indians of North Mississippi and was for a time a substantial rival of Jackson. In 1828 it had sixty houses, two hundred and forty inhabitants, four stores, two taverns, and twelve mechanics. The final completion of the Memphis and Charleston Railroad, to which it had looked for growth and prosperity, had an opposite result, and it yielded to the commercial supremacy of Memphis.

The first county court in Dyer County was organized in 1824, and was named for Colonel Henry Dyer, who served in the battle of New Orleans. The first building, put up in 1824, was a double log cabin with a dirt floor. Dyersburg was made the county seat.

The first settlement in Hardeman County was made by Colonel Ezekiel Polk, his son William, and son-in-law, Thomas McNeal, and Colonel Thomas J. Hardeman in 1823 near Hickory Valley. The county court was organized at the house of Thomas McNeal. The county seat was named at first, Hatchie, but was changed in 1825 to Bolivar, in honor of Simon Bolivar, "the Liberator of his Country," a name as familiar to the ears of our grandfathers as that of Kossuth to our fathers or Garibaldi to our own.

The first settlements in the territory which afterwards became Tipton County were made by General Jacob Tipton in 1821, by Jesse Benton below the third Chickasaw Bluffs, by H. Yarbrough on Indian Creek, and by Henry Turnidge and others on Big Creek. The county was named for Captain Jacob Tipton, who fell in St. Clair's defeat near Fort Washington in 1791, and who was the father of General Tipton. The county court was organized in 1823 at the house of Nathaniel Hartsfield, about one mile south of Covington. Covington, the county seat, was located on lands donated by John C. McLemore and Tyree Rhodes. The constitution of 1834 having provided for the formation of a new county out of territory lying between Hatchie and Forked Deer, Lauderdale was established in 1835, leaving Hatchie as the north boundary of Tipton County. The proximity of Tipton County to the Mississippi River and the bluffs within its limits gave it great prominence in the annals of settlement and the struggle for precedence which make up the early history of West Tennessee counties. Jesse Benton's place was a general landing for emigrants who came by river, and soon became a distributing point for the adjacent country. Benton's Trace still remains in local geographical nomenclature. Randolph soon became a flourishing town. Indeed, at first all indications pointed to its future success in the contest for commercial mastery which geographical position forced upon the two towns, Randolph and Memphis. Like Memphis, it was situated upon one of the Chickasaw Bluffs and at the mouth of a small inland stream. But Big Hatchie was navigable as far up as Bolivar, and Randolph carried on a lucrative trade by water with many of the newly established counties east of Hardeman. It became at once the shipping point for all the western counties except Shelby and Fayette. This was during the internal improvement mania, and a plan was suggested which, if carried out, might have enabled Randolph to carry off the palm in its contest with Memphis. This was to connect the Tennessee and the Hatchie by means of a lateral canal or drain. This would have given Randolph the trade of the fertile sections of country through which the Tennessee runs, and would probably have given it the greatness which has fallen to its rival. The governor of Tennessee recommended the project to the General Assembly, but nothing came of it. In 1834 the "Randolph Recorder" was issued by F. S. Latham, who soon afterwards sold out to A. M. Scott and removed to Memphis. In 1836 or 1837 the "Randolph Whig" was established by the McPhersons, but was soon discontinued. In 1836 Randolph shipped 40,000 bales of cotton, and in 1839 from 20,000 to 25,000. Some time in the thirties Randolph established a bank. In 1833 a semi-weekly stage was started by James Brown from Jackson to Randolph. A great drawback to the growth of Randolph was the A. M. Cambreling suit, involving the title to 1,000 acres of land, on part of which Randolph was located. This prevented the growth of population, and was not settled until 1835. The removal of the Indians and the settlement of North Mississippi helped Memphis, and finally a few steamboats that navigated the Hatchie began to unload at Memphis. The foresight and liberal policy of John Overton caused Memphis to prosper rapidly, and by the time the Memphis and Charleston Railroad was built, the leading merchants of Randolph had removed to the lower town.

The last attempt of Randolph to regain its earlier importance was in 1852, when, by a bare majority of the voters in the county, it was decided not to move the seat of justice to that point from Covington. A Tipton County institution, which exerted a beneficent influence upon the development of the western part of the State, was the Mountain Academy, founded by the Reverend James Holmes, of which it is chronicled that it "was long noted as the best in West Tennessee, and hundreds of youths were instructed and trained there, who became eminent as teachers and professional men. The name of James Holmes, D. D., is more intimately connected with West Tennessee as an educator and instructor of the young, both male and female, than perhaps any other man living."

Haywood County, named for Judge John Haywood, the historian, was organized in 1824, and the first county court met at the house of Colonel Richard Nixon. The first permanent settlement was made by Nixon about four miles east of the present site of Brownsville, on Nixon's Creek. Nixon had blazed a way through the cane from Jackson in Madison County. Brownsville itself was laid off in 1824 and the jail was built in 1825. In 1824-25 public roads were cut out from Brownsville to the county seats of neighboring counties. Being accessible to small steamboats, Brownsville did a large receiving and forwarding business for the surrounding country. It was the second town west of the Tennessee which carried on a regular trade in merchandise with the adjoining country. The first and most important was Jackson.

Madison County was organized in 1820, and named in honor of James Madison. The first county court met at the house of Adam R. Alexander, about two miles west of where Jackson now stands. The first settlement recorded was made in 1820 near the old Cotton Grove neighborhood, by John Hargrave and the McIvers family. Shortly afterwards, John Bradbury settled on Spring Creek. Seth O. Waddell settled "the Sixteenth District" the same year. The most important settlement was that made by Adam R. Alexander, William Doak, Lewis Jones, and others near Jackson. Jackson has been described by one who knew it in its earliest infancy as "the abode of ease, elegance, and refined social enjoyment, the home of the enterprising and intelligent, the beautiful and cultivated, the seat of learning and temple of law." He calls it the first habitable town in West Tennessee. "It was here the first courts of law were organized and the first academy of learning established, and it gave birth to the first newspaper published in West Tennessee." Jackson was for many years the centre of activity in the western portion of the State. The fact that it published a weekly newspaper made it politically conspicuous. The "Pioneer" was established in 1822, but soon died and was succeeded by the "Gazette," which was edited by E. Begelow and published by Charles D. McLean. The first number appeared on the 29th of May, 1823, and continued until 1831, when it was merged in the "Southern Statesman." Jackson was the centre of the political activity of the Western District and then of West Tennessee, and it was here that the fight between Crockett and the friends of General Jackson, after he became president, was hotly waged. Robert I. Chester, who still enjoys the fruits of a long life well spent, was postmaster and a warm friend of Jackson. McLean and the newspaper men generally were opposed to Crockett, and the struggle gained in fierceness from year to year. Indians still came here to buy their supplies, and on Saturdays it was no unusual sight to see all mingling on the streets together, Indians, boatmen, hunters with bear and coonskin caps, herdsmen on small Indian ponies, slave drivers with short lariats, lawyers, doctors, and merchants. The first court-house at Jackson, which was laid off in 1822, was built by John Houston " of round logs, with dirt floor and daubed chimney." The judge's bench was made of puncheons. The first dwelling in Jackson was built by Thomas Shannon in 1821. As Memphis grew, Jackson, as well as Randolph, receded, but it still retains its position as the second town in West Tennessee, distinguished by the thrift and enterprise of its inhabitants, the thoroughness of its schools, the beauty and comfort of its houses and the activity of its politicians. It is worthy of note that the first cotton in West Tennessee was grown in Madison County, and that the first gin was brought to Jackson from Nashville in 1821. The plank used in building the first frame house in Jackson was brought on a keel-boat from East Tennessee and up the Forked Deer.

Shelby County, of which Memphis is the county seat, has but little history which is not also a part of the history of Memphis. It was organized May 1, 1820, at the house of William Lawrence where the county court met until a court-house was built. The first magistrates were William Irvine, chairman, Jacob Tipton, Anderson B. Carr, Marcus B. Winchester, Thomas D. Carr, and Benjamin Willis, Jr.; Samuel R. Brown was sheriff; Thomas Taylor, register; Alexander Ferguson, ranger; William

A. Davis, trustee; Gideon Carr, coroner; John P. Perkins, solicitor; William Bettis and William Dean, constables. The first frame building was built for Benjamin Fooy by Zaccheus Joiner, and was occupied by old Isaac Rawlings. The first steamboat that landed at Memphis was the Ætna.

Weakley County was organized in 1823 with Dresden as the county seat. Lauderdale was organized in 1836, and was named in honor of Colonel James Lauderdale, who fell at the battle of New Orleans. The first settlement was made in the Key Corner by Benjamin Porter and Henry Rutherford, who came in a flatboat from Reynoldsburgh in 1819-20. In 1789 Henry Rutherford, a son of General Griffith Rutherford, had been employed by certain North Carolina landholders to locate their grants. He descended the Cumberland to the Forked Deer, and then went up that stream until he came to high land, where the Cole Creek Bluffs are intersected by the former stream. Landing here, Rutherford made a mark in the shape of a key on a sycamore tree as a starting point. From this the whole section of country of which Tipton, Dyer, Haywood, Lauderdale were parts, was known as the "Key Corner Settlements." In this region Crockett attained his celebrity as a bear hunter. A son of Benjamin Porter, named Benjamin T. Porter, was born, lived, and died in the same house.[1] The change in the territorial limits of counties is strikingly illustrated by the fact that he lived successively in three counties. Ripley was laid off as the county seat of Lauderdale County. Obion County was organized in 1824 at the house of W. M. Wilson. Since then, Benton, Decatur, Crockett, and Lake have been established.

[1] There is a conflict of authority as regards the first name of Porter. One account gives it as David T., and his father's name as David.

CHAPTER XXX.

MEMPHIS.

MEMPHIS occupies a geographical position that thrusts upon it a peculiar prominence, which only those familiar with the Mississippi River can appreciate. The stranger who first sees Memphis from the deck of a steamboat readily understands the cause which has made it one of the leading cities of the Southwest. Hundreds of miles below the Chickasaw Bluffs is a highly interesting but rarely broken series of forests, canebrakes, sandbars, and masses of willow trees. The muddy waters of the river, when at a low stage, lap the crumbling banks that yearly change as they yield to new deflections of the current. When the spring floods come, however, the banks disappear, and the water pours over the low marshy land for miles back. It has been found necessary to run embankments practically parallel with the current in order to confine the waters of the river in its channel. Even where the banks are above high water mark, they are of a treacherous sandy soil, and at any moment the constant working of the current may cause, not square yards, but acres of land to disappear beneath the flood. The same conditions exist above Memphis, except that on the Tennessee side the overflow is not so wide-spread. For purposes of habitation the difference is not great. From Cairo to Memphis but three eligible places exist where a city might have been built. These are the so-called Chickasaw Bluffs. These bluffs differ from ordinary banks, both in their height above the river and in the fact that the same formation runs back into the country, forming a kind of plateau suitable for all the purposes of civilized habitation.

There are in all four bluffs which still bear the name of the original owners, the Chickasaws. Memphis stands upon the fourth. The four Chickasaw Bluffs have a history which reaches back to the earliest days of American colonial history. They played an important part in the political history of three great European powers. Here was the centre of the history of a people who, long since banished, have attained prosperity and enlightenment in the wilds of the far West. The Chickasaws were one of the great tribes, perhaps the greatest. Their country extended through what is now Mississippi to Natchez. It is a conjecture that De Soto crossed the Mississippi River at these bluffs. If so, the Casique or head man of the tribe of Indians who opposed his passage had his seat of government at Memphis. More than one hundred years later La Salle, desiring to enter into amicable relations with the aboriginal inhabitants along the banks, was forced by geographical considerations to build his fort here. He gave it the name of Prud'homme. This was probably in 1682. In 1714 the successor of Prud'homme was built by the French, Fort Assumption. About this time the centre of the Chickasaw government appears to have been transferred to the region of country in which were the Chickasaw Old Fields in North Mississippi. For reasons by no means difficult to explain, the Chickasaws, in the contest between the French and English for the possession of the Mississippi valley, always favored the latter. The cause of this preference was that they saw a great deal of the French and very little of the English. In 1739 Fort Assumption was seized by the French for the double purpose of avenging a previous defeat and of exterminating the tribe whose stubborn vindictiveness was an obstacle in the way of the French plan of uniting the North and the South by a cordon of forts. The attempt miscarried, and the expedition, worn away by sickness and deadly epidemics, returned to Natchez, Canada, and New Orleans. After Fort Assumption came Fort San Ferdinando de Barancas, built by the Spanish governor-general, as a move in his desperate attempt to build up the great Southwestern Empire of North America. During the war between France and Spain, in 1794, the Spaniards seized the Chickasaw Bluffs, previously abandoned by them. Washington, who was president, at once protested, "The act of the Spaniards in taking possession of the Chickasaw Bluffs is an unwarrantable aggression, as well against the United States as the Chickasaws, to whom the land belongs."

As soon as the United States came into possession of the Mississippi valley, General Pike immediately occupied the old Spanish fort. Several years later General Wilkinson took command. He at once dismantled Fort San Fernandino at the mouth of Wolf River, and built Fort Pickering lower down, naming it in honor of Timothy Pickering. The local designation of Fort Pickering remains to this day, having been kept alive by various attempts to make it a rival of Memphis. The fourth Chickasaw Bluffs are about ten miles north of the southern boundary of the State of Tennessee, and hence lay within the grant of Charles II. to Clarendon and his associates. This was also claimed by the French and the Spanish in turn, and was within the limits of the Crozat grant of Louis XIV. Even so late as 1763, when the treaty of Paris was made, the boundary lines of Louisiana and Florida were not definitely known. The purchase of Louisiana from Bonaparte in 1803 settled all questions of boundaries, in so far as Tennessee was concerned, between the United States and foreign countries, and left the Indian alone to be dealt with. By the treaty of October 19, 1818, made by General Andrew Jackson and General Shelby with the Indians, all of the land north of latitude

35° and east of the Mississippi River was ceded by the Chickasaws. This settled the southern boundary line of the State. According to the terms of the original grants, the constitution of North Carolina, the cession of the Southwestern Territory to the United States, and the constitution of Tennessee, the 35° of latitude was to be the boundary line of Tennessee.

By a strange coincidence the territorial limits of the Memphis region of country have always been in doubt, and the struggles between Spain, France, England, and the United States find a parallel in the contests which were long waged by the earlier settlers and proprietors. In March, 1819, James Brown, an old surveyor who survived the war between the States, extended the southern boundary line of Tennessee, beginning at the northwest corner of the State of Alabama. The line ran to the lower end of President's Island, about four miles below Fort Pickering. A few months later the official line was run by General James Winchester. About 1832, when Memphis had become a prosperous village, the Indian chiefs in North Mississippi became dissatisfied with the Winchester state line, claiming that it had been falsely run. It was many years before the line was again run. It was long supposed by those who did not live there, that the new town was in Mississippi. As late as 1832 Memphis is spoken of as "a town in the northwestern angle of Mississippi, upon a high bluff which used to be called Fort Pickering."[1] The people of Mississippi claimed the town with zealous enthusiasm for several years. To settle the dispute an engineer was appointed to take new observations in accordance with which the line was run. One of the Tennessee commissioners was Judge Austin Miller of Bolivar. It was discovered that the real line of the 35° of north latitude was about four miles farther south than the Winchester line. This settled the

[1] *Encyclopedia Americana.*

question in a manner altogether unexpected by those who had raised it.

When the town of Memphis and the county of Shelby were first organized, the virgin wilderness bore scarcely a trace of the human hand. The foundations of both city and county were laid under the shadows and around the roots of forest trees and in the midst of tangled undergrowth. The old block-house still stood in Fort Pickering and a few straggling "shanties" clustered around a large and primitive structure known as the Public Warehouse, sometimes called Young's Warehouse, in the neighborhood of Wolf River. Between these two were thick canebrakes and a heavy and luxuriant growth of timber through which a narrow footpath ran from Fort Pickering to Wolf River. A wolf tax of six and one fourth cents was levied in Shelby County in 1822. At this time the only semblance of a road leading to the Chickasaw Bluffs from the interior was the so-called Cherokee Trace. A trail ran from the bluffs to the Chickasaw Old Fields in North Mississippi, where it connected with the Great Natchez Trace. The chief avenues of ingress were the Mississippi River and its tributaries, the chief means of transportation, flatboats, pirogues, and broad-horns.

Memphis properly begins with the Rice and Ramsey grants. John Rice was an energetic trader of the earlier days of Tennessee history, and even so early as 1780 made trips to Natchez and New Orleans. During one of these trips his attention was attracted by the advantages offered by a high and accessible bluff to river commerce. In 1783, with shrewd foresight, he entered in John Armstrong's office at Hillsboro, North Carolina, 5,000 acres of the best land on the bluffs. Having obtained his warrant, the survey was made in 1786. The price paid was ten pounds for every 100 acres. In 1791 John Rice was killed near the present site of Clarksville. His will bequeathed his brother, Elisha Rice, this grant. In 1794

John Overton bought from Elisha his interest in this grant for the sum of five hundred dollars and immediately transferred one undivided one half to Andrew Jackson.

But there existed still another and equally important grant of land upon the great bluffs known as the Ramsey Grant. In 1783 John Ramsey entered a tract of 5,000 acres of the North Carolina western lands. The year following a warrant was issued to him. Some time subsequent to this he assigned a small interest in this warrant to John Overton, and in 1823 grant No. 190 was issued to John Ramsey and John Overton, for a certain 5,000 acre tract of land, beginning at the southwest corner of John Rice's 5,000 acres, on the banks of the Mississippi River. The Rice grant was registered in the recorder's office of Shelby County in 1820, but for some reason never satisfactorily explained the Ramsey grant was not recorded until 1872. The date of Ramsey's death is not definitely known. His will has never been recorded in Shelby County and his title to property which is worth millions of dollars has never been extinguished by any deed or written instrument known to the law of Tennessee.[1]

In 1819 a law was passed by the Tennessee legislature for the laying off of the lands just acquired from the Indians, into ranges, townships, and sections. Grants obtained from North Carolina were to be reserved — all the rest was to be thrown open to sale.

In January, 1819, John Overton, Andrew Jackson, and James Winchester, the proprietors of the Rice grant, entered into an agreement to lay off a town on the Rice tract. In May of the same year, the first conveyance of a lot in Memphis was made. The town, therefore, had its birth some time in the early part of 1819. The origin of the name is not remote when we consider that the ancient city of the Pharaohs also stood upon the banks of a

[1] His will is said to be of record in Chatham County, North Carolina.

great river that in many respects resembles the Mississippi. In a description of Memphis published in a Philadelphia paper in 1820, the Mississippi River is called the American Nile. To the Memphian of the present, who sees about him the activity, the enterprise, the broad streets, the huge buildings that indicate a large and prosperous city, the contrast between the two, so far separated by time and distance, is not so striking. But for many years it was a subject of ridicule to those who saw but a few straggling houses perched upon the bluffs. Samuel Lover satirizes the name in an invocation to the Shades of Pisostris.

The new town was laid off some time in 1819 on the Rice grant, and at the time the contest which subsequently arose between the owners of the two grants in reference to the boundary line did not exist. Some years later, when Overton had the Rice grant again laid off according to the survey of 1786, the question came up for settlement. Overton discovered to his mortification that by beginning about one mile below the mouth of Wolf River, according to the terms of his grant, the most attractive and finely situated body of land on the entire bluffs lay beyond his limits. John Rice, in selecting the mouth of Wolf River as a determining point, left out of consideration or was ignorant of the variations which take place in the currents and banks of all streams which run through alluvial soil. In 1786 Wolf River flowed into the Mississippi at a point at least one half mile lower down than it did in 1819. The exact point cannot now be determined but it was probably between Jefferson and Adams streets. The plat made at the time of the original survey, represents the banks of the Mississippi south of Wolf River as running in a decidedly southwestern direction and out into the space which is now under water. As a result, Wolf River was forced inland until it struck the base of the bluffs, along which it skirted for a short distance until its waters broke into the current of the Mississippi. At this time there was a batture about the mouth of Wolf River not unlike that which now exists except that it extended farther out and lower down. In 1819 this had been swallowed up by the Mississippi, and the banks south of Wolf River had greatly caved and pushed the mouth of the smaller stream upwards. The mile below the mouth of Wolf River as it was in 1786 and in 1819 made a vast difference in the quality of the tract of land conveyed by the Rice grant, and the owners were anxious to establish the fact of the change. Naturally the Ramsey grant people were anxious that the mouth of 1819 — the Rice grant people, that the mouth of 1786 — should be taken. The former proved, among others, by the testimony of Jesse Benton, that there had been no change since 1819. The latter proved that previous to that date there had been a change of debouchement. Benjamin Fooy, who had been living on the Chickasaw Bluffs or on the opposite side of the Mississippi River since 1795, swore that it was three hundred yards higher up. The southwestern point of the Rice grant was eventually fixed at or near the point where Beal Street runs into the river. From there it runs east and a little north as Beal Street diverges from a straight line.

The description of the Ramsey grant called for the meanders of the Mississippi in establishing the western line, but strange to say in the Rice grant no mention is made of the Mississippi at all. In the original plat, a waving line was made where the Mississippi River should have been called for. This was the source of great trouble and dissension to the future citizens, and played an important part in the litigation which ensued after the formation of the so-called mud-bar in front of Memphis in the thirties.

Among the first steps taken by the new projectors of Memphis was to give deeds of gift to some of the old settlers for the purpose of making a beginning of the town and from charitable motives. Lots were thus given to Peggy Grace " in consideration of the long residence of old Mr. Grace at the Chickasaw Bluffs." Pat Meagher was also given a lot. On the 22d of May, 1819, the proprietors entered into an agreement with John Henry Fooy, son of Judge Benjamin Fooy, to convey to him any lot he might select in the town then being laid off, on condition that said lot be purchased by Fooy or his agent at the public sale of the first lots sold. Fooy selected lot No. 53, on the corner of Mississippi Row (Front Row) and Sycamore Street. It is not known what fabulous price he may have ostensibly given for his lot, but he set an example which has found successful imitation even in our own day. The lot, however, brought him no good and was ultimately involved in litigation.

The number of lots sold at this public sale was very small, but Overton was by no means discouraged. With wise foresight the proprietors looked to the future for their reward, and they laid the foundations for a large superstructure. In one respect alone did they calculate falsely. They laid off into streets and squares too small a portion of their land. They expected Memphis, when it had grown to be a great city, to be as densely populated as the cities of Europe. They failed to make allowance for the spacious habitation which the American demands. This is the reason why the upper portion of the town is so evenly laid off whilst the suburbs are but little more regular than Boston itself.

They laid off four squares for public purposes, Court, Exchange, Market, and Auction squares. The promenade, subsequently the cause of violent dissensions, was laid off on the bluff, and was designed for a public pleasure ground. A burying-ground was laid off north of Poplar Street which was, for the first decade, the southern limit of the new town. The strip of land fronting the river and running from Jackson Street to where the Bayou empties into Wolf River was made a public landing, the ferry privileges, as it was afterwards asserted, being reserved.

The first feeble steps towards the making of a town have been partially preserved in the records of the court of pleas and quarter sessions. In May, 1820, Joseph James was allowed to keep an ordinary or house of entertainment in "the town of Memphis." Thomas H. Parsons, Charles Holman, Joshua Fletcher, M. B. Winchester, John C. McLemore and William Irvine were appointed a jury of review to mark out the best and nearest route for a road from the town of Memphis to the county line in the direction of Taylor's settlement situated on Forked Deer. William Irvine is allowed to keep a ferry across the Mississippi. At the August term of the same year patrolmen are appointed for the county, among the number being Russell Bean, the first-born of Tennessee and the hero of the Jackson anecdote. Three indictments are found at the same term of court, one of them against Paddy Meagher for retailing spirits. Paddy, probably having no exculpatory evidence, set the precedent for a long line of equally shrewd successors in that he disarmed judicial severity by pleading guilty and throwing himself upon the mercy of the court. It may have been that his offense was not regarded as a decided departure from the straight path, or the value of money may have been at a great premium, for he was only fined one dollar and costs. It was also ordered at this term that Thomas Carr be authorized and empowered to contract with some workingman to build and erect a temporary log court-house, jury-room, and jail on Market Square in the town of Memphis. One hundred and seventy-five dollars were appropriated for erecting the same. The May term in 1821 was held in the court-house in the town of Memphis. This was a building procured instead of the one ordered to be built at a previous term of the court, since the order itself was rescinded.

At the May term in 1822 commissioners were appointed to lay off and establish a public road from Memphis to the settlement on Big Creek and Loosa Hatchie and thence to the Forked Deer River. One of these commissioners was Jesse Benton, the brother of Thomas H. Benton and the implacable foe of Andrew Jackson, whose name at this time was frequently mentioned in connection with the presidency of the United States. Jesse qualified as justice of the peace at this same term of court. Commissioners were also appointed to lay off a road to R. G. Thornton's settlement on Wolf River, thence to Fowler's Ferry on Big Hatchie. In August, 1823, the court appointed a venire for the circuit court to be held for the first time in Memphis on the fourth Monday of October. When the court of pleas and quarter sessions met in 1825 a change of the county seat was not contemplated by the members of the court as a bare possibility even. Memphis had been actually laid off, and although the number of inhabitants was not large, improvements of a substantial nature had been made. But the overwhelming advantage which the Memphis of to-day has over the Raleigh of to-day did not exist at that time. There were no roads and no railroads, and the bulk of the interior commerce was carried on upon the inland streams, Hatchie, Wolf, Nonconnah, and others. When, therefore, a plan was made for the transfer of the county seat from Memphis to a point some miles inland upon a branch of Wolf River, it was very far from being even remotely as preposterous as such a scheme would now seem. The state legislature having appointed commissioners to fix the seat of justice in the counties west of the Tennessee River, the county court of Shelby County, whilst in session, were startled by a report signed by James Fentress, Benjamin Reynolds, William Martin, and Robert Jetton, stating that they had located the seat of justice for the county of Shelby on Sandelin's Bluff on the north bank of Wolf River.

The details of this plot, for such tradition tells us it was, have been lost. We only know that it excited vigorous opposition among those who had purchased lots in Memphis and especially among the proprietors. It was most likely a blow aimed at them. The court appointed commissioners to obtain a perfect title to the lands for the new county site, lay off a town, and advertise and sell the lots according to law. Among the commissioners were Robert Fearne, a pronounced enemy of the proprietors. In January, 1827, $555 was appropriated for the building of the court-house at Raleigh.

The change of the county seat had no ill effect upon the growth of Memphis — perhaps the contrary. It caused an increase in the area of cultivation, and added to the means of communication. A firm entitled James Brown & Co. started a line of post coaches drawn by four horses between Memphis and Raleigh, which was soon extended to Somerville.

The chief street in the new town was Winchester, and the central point was at first Anderson's Bridge. Gayoso Bayou, now dry except for occasional puddles and the last rain, was then a running stream, the water of which was clear and pure. (On the map of 1827 it is called Gayoso Creek.)

In 1824 the three firms who carried on the business of the city were Winchester and Carr, Henderson and Fearne, subsequently Lawrence and Fearne, and Isaac Rawlings. The leading spirits in the new community were M. B. Winchester and Isaac Rawlings. The latter had a store at Anderson's Bridge which was the camping ground for Indians and in-coming emigrant trains. As long as this class of trade was most lucrative, Rawlings thrived. But Winchester, a late arrival, had a decided advantage, having been made postmaster as soon as the town was well under way. He built what was at that time the finest house in Memphis on Front Row just below Jackson Street. He also made roads — streets were out of the question — which rendered both the landing place on the Mississippi River and his own place of business more accessible. When the flat-boat trade became the source of commercial prosperity, and especially after the disappearance of the Indians, Winchester became the leading merchant of the town.

These two men are interesting figures in the history of Memphis, not merely because they were present at the founding of the city, but also because they represented the two opposing tendencies which in turn have had such a powerful effect upon its development. Rawlings was a man of cautious temperament, suspicious of innovation, well satisfied with the existing order of things unless working to his disadvantage, adverse to change, rough, blunt, and without mental discipline or cultivation. Winchester had a quick mind, a clear judgment, a spirit of restless inquiry, ever eager for advancement, constantly in search of improved methods, prone to be led astray by theories and abstractions, refined, well educated in books as well as in knowledge of the world, lacking only a leaven of the practical common sense that was the distinguishing feature in the character of his rival. Rawlings was conservative; Winchester was liberal. Their commercial rivalry was not diminished by the fact that Rawlings was a Whig and Winchester a Democrat. Rawlings had once been a sutler in Jackson's army, and had been at the bluffs longer than any one then living. He was among the first appointed magistrates. He predicted the failure of the effort to make a city on the Chickasaw Bluffs. His attitude of antagonism was perhaps confirmed by his rivalry with Winchester. His vanity, which was remarkably robust, received daily blows from the decrease of his importance as his rivals in trade grew more numerous and successful. After a time he began to realize that, contrary to his predictions, Memphis was growing, and indeed rapidly. He determined to change his site, and bought a lot of ground on an alley which subsequently, through his intercession, became Commerce Street, and built him a store, with many muttered revilings against the folly of people and their fondness for new things. But the current of trade had set towards Winchester and could not be changed. There is a tradition that Rawlings marked the price on his goods, and in spite of all competition and the general decrease of prices refused to sell under his marks. It was said he had on hand at the time of his death goods purchased years before.

In 1826 Memphis was made an incorporated town by the action of the legislature, although the limits of the new corporation were not defined. When the news reached Memphis there was a general outburst of alarm and indignation, especially from those most hostile to the proprietors. One of the characteristics of Memphis is the readiness with which it vents its spleen in an indignation meeting. The first of a long series was held when the news of the incorporation came. The presiding officer was Isaac Rawlings. But the meeting developed the unexpected fact that those most violently opposed to the incorporation were those who lived farthest from the centre of business. It was therefore proposed that these should be left out. The change as suggested was adopted by the meeting. It was discovered when too late that the land left out belonged almost entirely to the proprietors, who were thus the chief beneficiaries.[1]

[1] The only authority I have been able to find for this episode is the author of the *Early History of Memphis*, James D. Davis. It may be and probably is largely apocryphal. Davis says that the change of boundary by which the complainants were left out of the city limits was ratified by the legislature. I can find nothing in the

According to the terms of the charter, seven aldermen were elected, who in turn were to elect one of their number mayor. Winchester was postmaster at the time of the passage of the new charter, but he was immediately chosen mayor. Perhaps no better proof of his reputation for strict integrity and unbiased fairness could be given than this. Though looking after the interests of those who were regarded as the natural enemies of the inhabitants of Memphis, he was yet chosen to the office having at the time most influence over their immediate welfare. During Winchester's second term of office, the corporate powers of Memphis were increased.

Among other changes was a restriction which prohibited the mayor from holding a federal office. Winchester refused to resign his postmastership. This opened the way for Isaac Rawlings, who succeeded him in March, 1829. This singular and almost grotesque figure made one of the best mayors who ever presided over Memphis from M. B. Winchester to D. P. Hadden. He was long known as the model mayor. Rawlings was vain, stubborn, self-willed, and imperious, impatient of contradiction and conservative to a fault. But he was also honest, clear-minded, law-abiding, determined to be obeyed, and economical. He took the duties of his position in earnest, and rigorously enforced the law, preserved order, looked after the disbursement of the public funds with scrupulous care, and was remarkably energetic. His prejudice against the city appeared to die away after his exercise of power. He served two terms, from March, 1829, to March, 1831, retired for two years, was reëlected in 1833, and served three successive terms until 1836. He was a candidate for the Constitutional Convention of 1834, but it was during the height of Jacksonian Democracy and he was defeated. His last appearance was almost dramatic. Hav-

records to justify the statement. There was probably some foundation for the tradition, as Davis wrote from memory.

ing weathered the storm of Democratic ascendency for many long years, he had himself carried in an easy-chair to cast his last vote for Harrison and Tyler. He was suffering from a mortal disease, and waited eagerly but confidently for news of the election. When it came he remarked, "Now I can die happy," and very shortly afterwards expired.

From 1820 to about 1833 Memphis was still an experiment. The natural advantages which it then possessed belonged in an almost equal degree to Fort Pickering below and Randolph above. There was as yet no white population in Arkansas and Mississippi to draw together the nucleus of a town as a depot of supplies. The region which was inhabited was that which stretched back towards Jackson and the Big Hatchie country, and for the purposes of navigation and trade Randolph was not less convenient than Memphis. That Memphis became the city and not either Fort Pickering or Randolph is due mainly to the wisdom of one man, John Overton. The other proprietors exercised merely a passive ownership. The terms upon which Overton conveyed one half of the Rice grant to Andrew Jackson are not known. But the latter disposed of his interest long years before the dream of Overton, which dated from his purchase of Rice's land in 1794, began to be realized. Jackson sold to John C. McLemore, in 1823, his last remaining interest (one eighth) in the grant. The other three he had already sold to the Winchester brothers. The fact that he had an interest in the Rice grant was made the cause of much severe criticism at the time of the treaty in 1818. Those who had already settled on the Chickasaw Bluffs, especially a few of his old soldiers, expected to have their rights recognized, some of them having purchased from the Indians. These lost sight of the fact that the Rice grant had already been surveyed and located. In order to spare himself these criticisms, for at this time he was no longer in pecuniary stress, he sold his interest to John C. McLemore. The other proprietors were, besides Overton, who still had his one half, William Winchester, who owned one eighth, and Gen. James Winchester, who owned one eighth in his own right and one eighth as trustee for the children of a deceased brother. William Lawrence and M. B. Winchester were agents of the original proprietors. The final division of unsold lots took place in 1829. But during all the time that Memphis was still an experiment, John Overton was the only one of the proprietors who did anything to advance its interests, and he did everything. From the first he had looked into the future far as human could see, and he had literally seen all the visions of the world and the wonders that should be. He not only foresaw the future of the Chickasaw Bluffs as a city, but he also appreciated the minor consequences that would flow from founding a city there, and turned them to his own advantage. He exercised the minutest care in perfecting his title. He not only bought the Rice grant from Elisha Rice, but also obtained quitclaim deeds from all possible distributees in case no will existed. The reason of this was that John Rice's will, though in his own handwriting, was not attested.

Overton possessed neither brilliancy of mind nor striking greatness of character, but he was a man of singularly sterling qualities and had a remarkable aptitude for business. He possessed in a fortunate degree that peculiar combination of practical caution and liberal temerity that alone carries great undertakings to a successful termination. Having foreseen what was coming for Memphis, he mapped out in really a marvelous manner the line of its development. He devised the general policy which controlled the proprietors in their dealings with the inhabitants. It was his eye that watched with microscopic care every point, and it was his ingenuity that turned it to the advantage of the infant town. He used his influence with the general government to secure the establishment of a mail stage-route from Memphis to other points. The commercial contest between Memphis and Randolph was decided in favor of the former by several factors, one of the chief of which was the line of tri-weekly mail stage-coaches from the East to Memphis by the way of Nashville, Charlotte, Reynoldsburg, Jackson, Bolivar, and Somerville, which the postmaster-general established at the intercession of Overton in 1829. After Jackson became president, he also succeeded in having a weekly mail, carried on horseback, established between Jackson and Memphis by way of Brownsville, Covington, and Randolph. When a hospital is to be built he is ready to furnish the ground free of charge, but he uses his generosity as a means of preventing its being built in a wrong place. When a possible purchaser goes to Memphis, he writes to Winchester, "Make him pleased with the place by polite attentions." One of the most active opponents of the proprietors was Fearne. Fearne's partner was Robert, a brother of William Lawrence. Overton advocated making Robert joint agent with William in order to soften Fearne's opposition. When the town was fairly on its legs, he remitted none of his care, and his letters, even during this period, were filled with minute directions as regards the laying of corner-stones, the grading of streets, the opening of alleys, the laying off of graveyards and the like. As a matter of course he was a friend of Jackson. But he was ever anxious for Memphis to emphasize the part that it also was Jackson's friend. He, as all other friends of Jackson, knew that these things did them no harm with the imperious old soldier. When the " Globe" was started at Washington, he wrote to Winchester, sending him a copy, and requesting him to procure half a dozen subscribers from among the friends of the administration. "Tell your editor Phœbus to get the paper and extract from it fully, for rest assured it is and will be ably conducted." The next sentence has a touch of unconscious irony. "Besides, in these intriguing corrupt times, it is absolutely necessary for the support of correct principles." When Van Buren is rejected by the Senate he wants an indignation meeting held in Memphis. Hearing that a majority of the people of Memphis will vote for Crockett for Congress, he is filled with indignation. "But for the present administration, it would not have risen as it has. Don't your citizens sometimes think of this? What administration was it made it the great road leading east and west throughout the United States to Mexico by the establishment of three stages a week, besides speaking of it as it deserves? Is there no consideration of these things? Besides giving the public printing of the United States to the editor of your newspaper?"

In 1833 the postmaster-general makes Memphis a distributing point. While in the North he hears that a Clay organ is about to be established in Memphis. He is even told by those who watch affairs minutely that Winchester himself, though a federal office holder, is not in high favor with the administration. He is suspected of secret leanings towards the corrupt enemies of good government, namely, the Whigs. He tells Winchester plainly that the enemy of an administration so capable of doing a small town injury and the agent for the proprietors cannot be the same person. He subscribes liberally for the establishment of a newspaper. As the various suits involving his proprietory interests arise, he attends to them in all their details with unflagging interest. He is an unwearying letter-writer. His style is charming by reason of its clear, direct simplicity and pure, wholesome English. He has a trick of at times repeating his words that accomplishes the purpose of emphasis admirably. In one letter he says, "I pray you — I pray you, look after this." In another he writes, "Do not, I beseech you, do not let this be known." Being old and garrulous, towards the last he writes very long and reiterative letters, but always clear, full of eminently judicious advice and suggestion.

In addition to the difficulty which besets all new towns, Memphis labored under an unusual and decided disadvantage in the feeling of antagonism that existed on the part of the inhabitants against the proprietors. This feeling of hostility was a well-recognized fact. Overton, in 1831, says: " Particularly where the people have manifested so much hostility as those about Memphis have." As a rule the inhabitants were wrong. Those who came in at first, generally, had no money. They bought lots on long time, and were rarely able to meet the first payment. From 1819 to 1829, when the first era of decided prosperity set in, the inhabitants rather regarded themselves as patrons of the proprietors whom they were accommodating by living in their town. Overton had seen to it that the new town was well advertised. So early as 1820 the " Portfolio " of Philadelphia published a long and glowing account of it. Inducements were held out to *bona fide* settlers. Long leases were frequently given to those who would clear the soil and build cabins on it. A typical lease is one made to Samuel Gibson. Overton leased to him the place on which he was living for the term of six years from January, 1826, on the following conditions: He was to clear and cultivate at least thirty acres of land, build a good log cabin, plant out and take care of one hundred fruit trees to be furnished by Overton. He was to leave about ten acres of woodland around the spring. The timber outside the clearing is only to be used for the improvement of the place. At the end of said term of six years, Gibson is to return the said place to Overton in good farming order and well fenced.

In 1826 a newspaper was established at Memphis, to which the proprietors, at the instigation of Overton, subscribed liberally. This was Thomas Phœbus's " Memphis Advocate." The chief business of the " Advocate " was to urge the claims of General Jackson for the presidency, and to call universal and unceasing attention to the peculiar advantages offered by Memphis to settlers. These were both themes agreeable to Overton, and he wrote a great deal for the new paper. Those who came in answer to such direct invitations as those contained in the Memphis papers felt as if they were going rather upon the judgment of the proprietors than for their own satisfaction. One of the main causes of discord was the cutting of timber. On this point, Overton was particularly sensitive. When it became necessary, the inhabitants, in a manner very far from clandestine, cut down and used for fuel the trees most conveniently situated near them. Winchester wrote the proprietors that he was helpless to stay the destruction. Overton, who could be bitter as well as prudent, wrote to him that the destruction must be stopped. He advised hiring a man by the month to guard the woodland. He also directed Winchester to hire teams, and as soon as the wood was cut by the depredators, to haul it to town and sell it. Public sentiment eventually corrected the evil.

But soon a new element of discord was thrust between the inhabitants and the proprietors, involving greater interests than the loss of timber. The origin of this went back to the time when the town was first laid off and certain tracts of land designated for public purposes. The Promenade was the broad strip of land between Mississippi Row (now Front Row) and the river. A part of this is now occupied by the custom-house. This had been intended for a public promenade or park. The bluffs at that time ran out to the river, not having been cut away to make a wharf or cut through by streets. There was no way of getting to the river from the lower part of the town. The growing flat-boat and steamboat trade of the now thriving little town rendered it difficult to get along without a landing lower than Jackson Street. At this juncture it was proposed that the city should take the responsibility of cutting a street through the promenade. Having been appropriated for public purposes, of course it could be disposed of as best suited the public. This stated the case from the standpoint of the citizens. Overton, returning from New Orleans and landing at Memphis in 1828, found the street already cut. He at once addressed a protest to his agents. This was the beginning of the entanglement that was not ended till nearly twenty years later. The fact that the promenade was directly upon the river added a disturbing element to the contest. The privileges were becoming valuable, and these of course went with the ownership of the land. It is possible that these questions would have been amicably settled had not the Mississippi River in one of its freaks injected a still more perplexing and discordant factor. This was the celebrated batture or mud-bar which, like Aaron's serpent, swallowed up the rest.

In 1828 the water of the Mississippi River was higher than ever known before. One of the inevitable results of high water is that it completes changes already begun by the action of the current in ordinary years, and begins changes which perhaps would not otherwise begin for many years. From 1786 to 1828 the mouth of Wolf River had been going steadily up stream. Previous to 1811, the year of the great earthquake, the mouth of Wolf River had been about the foot of Jefferson and Adams streets. Around and above it was a bar. Upon this bar the Indians had at one time built cabins, and in 1782 Benjamin Fooy, by command of Governor Gayoso, had here quartered Spanish troops. He cleared a few acres of the willow and cottonwood growth that covered it, and raised corn. The Indians had also at one time a quarter mile track upon which they tested the speed of their ponies. The bank north of the mouth of Wolf River ran in a northwesterly direction, and was at that time constantly washed by the action of the current. The earthquake of 1811 is supposed to have created changes which sent the current of the river against this bar. It soon disappeared, and for many years the narrow strip of ground above Jackson Street was the only landing above Fort Pickering. According to the statement of Jesse Benton, a north course from the point of intersection of the Mississippi and Wolf rivers in 1786 would run over what was the current of the Mississippi in 1821. This shows very clearly, if correct, that the Mississippi above North Memphis had at one time been much farther west than it was before 1811, that it had worked its way towards the east, bending into the country above Wolf River, and had then again shifted its bed towards the west where it now is. It is now, and has been since 1828, about where it was in 1786. The overflow of 1828 caused the westward movement and left a kind of bar or harbor at the mouth of Wolf River, which was not in the direct flow of the current. The rapid rush of a vast body of water by it, however, created an eddy which in turn gradually formed, by the settling of sediment, a hard and compact bit of earth. This remains to this day and by municipal geographies is called the navy yard.[1] In the earlier days it was called by the accurate and the polite, the batture. To the great public, however, it was known only as the mud-bar. The winter of 1831-32 is given as its historical date. It had taken a little over three years to form, and the distinction of having discovered that it had formed is claimed by James D. Davis, the author of the "Early History of Memphis."

It is not going too far to say that a profound sensation was created among the inhabitants of Memphis when the

---

[1] Within the last few years, the current appears to have set in towards the point as it did in or previous to 1811, and unless prevented by the engineering skill of those who have the work in hand, it is probable we shall have a repetition of the events of that year.

formation of the mud-bar became known. Only those who had recently arrived were ignorant of what a bar meant, or of the difference between a sand-bar and a mud-bar. The effect of the mud-bar upon the river commerce was primarily bad, but ultimately good. The great necessity of a landing convenient for steamboats and accessible for the citizens of Memphis caused various attempts to be made to remedy the damage done to navigation. A wooden wharf was built by W. A. Bickford for a company from the foot of Winchester Street to the edge of the mud-bar. In a few years, however, this proved futile. The Memphis and La Grange Railroad agreed to build a kind of earthen quay from the foot of Washington Street, but failed. An attempt was made to run a wagon road from Market Street diagonally across the bar, striking the water at a point about opposite Poplar Street. This was stopped by Winchester. It was then run straight across from the foot of Market Street, but a change in the river soon rendered this unserviceable.

For some months after the forming of the mud-bar, it was a matter of hot discussion as to who owned it. But no active steps were taken to settle the question. In May, 1834, the Supreme Court of Tennessee, in the case of the Mayor and Aldermen of the City of Memphis v. Wright, decided that the mayor and aldermen were the representatives of the original proprietors and as such had vested in them all the right to dispose of or apply to any use they might think proper, the public promenade and squares which existed in the proprietors originally. The lawyer who represented Wright in this case, which had arisen in reference to some ordinance affecting the river landing, was R. C. McAlpin. In August of the same year, we find him trying to induce the corporate authorities to make a conveyance of the public promenade to trustees for the benefit of the railroad. The question of right was to be decided by an agreed case. This case appears to have attracted McAlpin's attention to a new way of settling the mud-bar case, and in this year we find McAlpin, John D. Martin, and several others laying their warrant on this geographical windfall, through the land office of Colonel Tipton of Tipton County. W. D. Dabney tried to obtain a warrant for a part of the river front that was below the mud-bar, but the only claim of serious importance was that of Martin and McAlpin and their associates. As soon as they obtained the grants they made application to the county court for the right to establish a ferry. The question of wharfage was left in abeyance for the present. The ground upon which Martin and McAlpin based their claim was the fact that the Rice grant did not call for the water's edge. The course given undoubtedly marked the meanders of the river as it had been when originally surveyed. This the claimants admitted, but contended that inasmuch as the course had been laid down specifically, it would not shift with the river. The western boundaries of the Rice grant, therefore, had been left by the receding of the river, and new formations as a result became the land of the State and as such could be granted. The proprietors, on the other hand, contended that the specifications of the grant called for the water's edge, and, as a matter of fact, went to the channel of the river. The phrase, "beginning one mile below the mouth of Wolf River," could mean nothing else than beginning on the bank of the Mississippi River. More than this, the first line of the Rice grant had in some places actually caved in, and although the alluvial deposit extended west of where the line had been at one time, yet originally the line, apart from the river meanders, had been farther west than the western line of the bar just formed. More even than this, the Rice tract had been processioned and resurveyed in 1820, and the certificate of the survey called for the river's edge. These were the two sides of the question as between the proprietors and the warrant holders.

The city's claim involved the question of the promenade as just mentioned. The details of the contest are not only long and comparatively uninteresting, but had but little effect upon the making of the city itself. When the question of the ferry rights was brought before the supreme court, they decided that they belonged to the proprietors and had never passed from their possession. This somewhat disheartened the McAlpin claimants. At this juncture the United States came forward and raised a storm of laughter by proposing to buy a large part of the mud-bar for a navy yard. The idea was first broached in a letter published in the "National Intelligencer" over the name of "Union Jack." When the "Enquirer" of Memphis republished this letter it excited among the clear-headed Memphians merely an expression of amusement. This was followed by other communications to the press signed "Harry Bluff," who was the celebrated Commodore Maury. Finally the plan began to assume shape. In 1843 a committee of naval officers, three in number, were sent to inspect the premises and especially to report on its fitness for a naval depot and dockyard. The people of Memphis, with a shrewd eye to the main chance, carried out Overton's idea of making them pleased with the place by polite attentions. The report was favorable, and it was decided to locate a navy yard upon the mud-bar itself. This brought about a compromise between those who were contending for its ownership. The proprietors submitted the following proposition: All parties should donate to the United States such part of the bar as was necessary for the navy yard. The rest should be sold and the proceeds divided in such manner that the proprietors should receive one half, the city one sixth and the warrant holders one third. The proprietors agreed to give the space between Poplar and Washington streets for a centre landing, and to allow all cross streets and alleys to be extended across the promenade to the water's edge. The question of wharfage was to be submitted to the arbitration of three able jurists to be selected by the governor of Kentucky. This proposition was accepted, and Seth Wheatley, whose glib tongue had once defeated old Isaac Rawlings for the mayoralty, was appointed trustee to carry it into effect. This changed the popular name of the mud-bar to that of Compromise Addition to the city of Memphis, and was the end of the contest between the city and the proprietors relative to the promenade and between all parties relative to the ownership of the mud-bar.

The fate of the navy yard is soon told. It dragged its slow length along for many years, beset on one hand by unwillingness, on the other by incompetency. When the question of sectional preference was injected into the debate upon internal improvements, the Memphis navy yard was at once flung into the face of the Southern members. F. P. Stanton, the member from the Memphis district, found it each year more difficult to obtain the necessary appropriations for continuing the work in a proper manner. Eventually the subject became a matter of jest. Those whose untimely fate it was to be doomed to the mud-bar of Memphis on the banks of a muddy inland stream, whilst their companions were on the high seas enjoying the tropical splendor of the East or loitering around the beautiful bays and harbors of the Mediterranean, were not reticent in expressions of disgust. They too ridiculed the navy yard. A commission was sent by the navy department, who returning made an unfavorable report. At length, in 1853, at the suggestion of ex-Governor James C. Jones, at that time in the United States Senate, the government cut the knot of its entanglement with the Memphis mud-bar by donating it back to the city.

CHAPTER XXXI.

SOUTH MEMPHIS AND FORT PICKERING.

ONE of the peculiar manias which obtained in the early days of Southwestern history was that of city-building. A favorable location on a river bank, a railroad, and a map of the city with streets laid off and a public outcry of lots was supposed to constitute the necessary ingredients for the making of a town. The fundamental error was prevalent that a city drew population. The necessary antecedence of population was not known. Overton was the solitary exception among those who made the experiment. He looked to the gradual growth of the surrounding country and a distant future. The law which directs the currents of city movements, and which acts slowly and almost imperceptibly but surely upon the causes which decide its fate, was entirely ignored. The undercurrent of prejudice, of local preference, of pride, the apparent shifting of the stream of population which, like that of a river, is only indicated by its results, these and many more determining factors were unknown to the city-maker's philosophy. One of this kind was Robert Fearne, the wily and energetic intriguer, on whom Overton kept a constant and suspicious eye. He originated and developed the South Memphis scheme, and so successfully that his city eventually obtained a charter of incorporation, though after his own disappearance from the scene. In July, 1827, he issued a prospectus under his seal as proprietor of a certain tract of land, in which he undertook to accommodate himself to the wishes of many citizens.

The tract of land in question was 414 acres, being the northern part of the Ramsey grant. His proposition was to form a stock company under the name of the Memphis Auxiliary Company. He was to issue eighty shares, retaining five himself and selling seventy-five. The stockholders were to appoint commissioners to attend to the necessary details of surveying, selling, etc. In September, 1828, he made the agreed conveyance to five commissioners. Here the project halted for many years. Some of the commissioners left the State, among them Fearne himself, and others refused to act. In 1838, after some legislation, new commissioners were appointed who carried out Fearne's original ideas. In 1846 the town of South Memphis was incorporated by the legislature. Union Street was the northern boundary of the new town. Subsequently the southern line was extended to Jackson Street to include Fort Pickering. Town officers were elected. Sylvester Baily was elected mayor. There were eight aldermen. This was the culmination of the up-town and down-town rivalry which characterized the history of those days.

When the act of 1826 was passed, no limits were prescribed for the new town. In 1832 Jefferson Street was made the southern boundary. There is a tradition that the bitterness which existed between Pinch and Sodom surpassed that of Carthage and Rome. The origin of these nick-names has been preserved. Pinch is the survival of a term of ridicule applied by Craven Peyton, one of the earliest Memphians, to those who lived upon the banks of Cat-Fish Bay, a lake-like body of water north of Jackson Street filled with cat-fish, dead and alive. These people were poor and Peyton spoke of them as Pinch-Gut. In the course of time the appellation was applied to that part of the town and then eventually to the entire north part of Memphis. Sodom was the name given by the Pinchites to South Memphis to indicate their utter abhorrence of the place. The geographical application of Pinch shifted. In Memphis it was confined to all the town north of Washington Street. But it gradually crept south until it was generally recognized as extending to Market Street. Those who lived between Market and Adams repudiated the term. The city was at that time divided into three wards of which that was the third. The other two, being in a majority, overrode the third ward in the matter of municipal improvements and appropriations of city funds so ruthlessly that it finally became almost a personal matter between those who represented these wards in the city council. This feeling of exasperation was encouraged by Sodom. One of the chief causes of complaint was the refusal of the council to allow a street to be cut to the river through the bluff for the convenience of this part of the city. It was wittily remarked by one of the wags of that day that if he wished to turn a man of sense into a jackass, the first thing he would do would be to make him an alderman. This observation was caused by the action taken by the board of mayor and aldermen in reference to the landing. In 1837 a large wharf had been built from Winchester Street across the bar for the purpose of a steamboat landing. But the increase in the bar made it difficult for large boats to land at this point. A steamboat captain let his boat land several hundred yards lower down where the water was deeper, but was promptly ordered by the indignant rulers to return to the proper landing. The absurdity of this proceeding became more apparent in view of the fact that there was much more freight than the boats could handle. A heated discussion arose, which ended by the captain dropping his boat below the city limits. This encouraged the South Memphis people, and filled them with sanguine hopes of soon outstripping their rival. But it had the good effect of bringing the first and second wards to a better sense of public duty. The third ward was divided into three, thus giving them a majority in the city government. The South Memphis people, who had always taken sides with the oppressed ward, saw in this a victory for themselves. The steamboats had been in a measure forced to their wharf. They hoped to see the inhabitants of the third ward district come to them in like manner. It is a common and amusing illustration of the potency of prejudice that the Sodom people imagined they could accomplish this end by making the name of Pinch cover all the region from Market to Adams Street. Their belief appears to have been that this part of Memphis proper would resort to any expedient to escape the reproachful term. But in so far as it had any effect, it rather consolidated the contending factions. A still more efficacious cause of a mutual drawing together was, in addition to the removal of absolute grievances, the desire to retain the lucrative trade of the flat-boats, the landing of which extended all the way from Wolf River to Adams Street. South Memphis maintained a separate corporate existence for three years only. In December, 1849, it and Memphis became an incorporated town of six wards, governed by a mayor and twenty-four aldermen, under the name of the city of Memphis.

Another rival of Memphis was Fort Pickering, now its southern suburb. At one time its rivalry became a serious matter. This was due to railroad expectations. Among the railroads projected during the mania for internal improvements was the La Grange and Memphis Railroad. This became the subject of discussion about 1831. The enterprise appears to have taken shape at La Grange itself. La Grange was not far from the Indians in northern Mississippi, and it hoped by building a road to the Mississippi River to attract enough trade to make it a great inland city. Such were the extravagant ideas of those days. As soon as the building of this road became a matter of general discussion, it was suddenly discovered in Memphis that the fate of that place depended upon its becoming the western terminus. Even before the first cross-tie was laid, the enterprising thought of the community was already looking to the ultimate extension of it to the eastern seaboard. In 1834 Winchester mentions the fact that the stock of the Jackson Company was taken and that the Columbia Company have agreed to unite with them. This was designed to be a Middle Tennessee road, and was the germ of the idea which, after two ante-bellum failures, is at last being pushed to completion. The contest for the western terminus was primarily between Randolph and the country north of the Big Hatchie, and secondarily between Memphis and Fort Pickering. The first was soon settled. The second was long and hotly waged. Fort Pickering has long since ceased to offer any rivalry to Memphis. Now that the latter has waxen into a comely city, Fort Pickering has pursued that line of development which makes it a necessary complement of the larger place. But during the first years of the thirties it was still a rival and indeed a formidable rival. In 1836 Winchester wrote, "So far as our immediate prosperity is concerned, it matters little whether the railroad terminates at Fort Pickering or at some point above us — say Randolph or Fulton. In either event, the young Memphis must be merged into its greater rival." Comparing Memphis and Fort Pickering, he says: "As a town site, it is not probable that we have anything the advantage over Fort Pickering. As a landing, that place has decidedly the advantage over the one we now use." But his fears were groundless and were not shared by Overton. The idea of making Fort Pickering a rival of Memphis had been entertained for some years, and more especially by one of the proprietors of Memphis — John C. McLemore. In the La Grange railroad, McLemore thought he saw his opportunity to build up a town in which he would have as great a preponderance over Overton as Overton had over him. The latter owned 181 acres of the Ramsey grant and McLemore 995. The connection of McLemore with Memphis had from the first been a disadvantage. He possessed great energy, but he had a speculative turn, which loaded him with a heavy debt at the very time when he could have been of greatest service to the infant town. He left the management entirely to Overton, and could rarely be persuaded to go to Memphis after its incorporation. When the first real prosperity of Memphis set in, about 1830, there was an active demand for lots, and public sentiment insisted upon the proprietors supplying the demand. Overton, writing on the 29th of January, 1832, said: "All future sales, at least for some time to come, are likely to fall entirely on my unsold lots." McLemore on the 24th of November, 1831, writes to Winchester, "Now, while the judge is willing to sell, you must find purchasers. I will urge the judge to instruct you to sell, and when the instructions reach you, act — get the property out of his hands — it is his interest as well as the town's that he sell. He is getting very infirm and can't last long. My lots are not for sale at present prices." Overton's confidence in McLemore was unbounded. On the 20th of December, 1832, he says: "He is certainly a most excellent man, and his exertion is far beyond one in ten thousand. He is so honorable a man and of such indefatigable industry that I have no doubt that he will come out."

But Overton with his usual caution appears towards the last to have begun to feel uneasy about McLemore and Fort Pickering. Still, old and infirm as he was, the indomitable will and sagacity of the old man asserted itself, and for all McLemore's indefatigable industry and his scheming letters to Winchester, he was outwitted. Having crushed Randolph, he, at the last, let fall the weight of his hand upon Fort Pickering — to this day it feels the blow. In 1830 he proposed to McLemore that they should mutually grant to each other the right to establish ferries at Fort Pickering. Shortly after this, the scheme to "make Fort Pickering a city" began to assume tangible shape. On the 12th of May, 1832, the old man writes triumphantly to Winchester, "I think with you, that even if they were to begin the execution of the project of laying off lots, etc., to-morrow, they can't affect Memphis materially. It is too far advanced to be arrested in its progress now. Putting off a year or two making a town below will be better. So much so that none but a simpleton would think then of it. Especially as I own nearly half the landing at Fort Pickering and that the best part of it." The year following Overton died.[1]

There was a sale of lots at Fort Pickering, which did secure the terminus of the La Grange railroad. But the collapse of the road ensued, and with it the collapse of its rivalry to Memphis, which had already been placed beyond danger by its founder.

[1] His death was characteristic. An eye-witness wrote, "I heard him request Doctor Hogg to say to General Jackson that he died like a man and a soldier, so you see he clung to the general to his last moments."

CHAPTER XXXII.

JOHN A. MURRELL AND THE REIGN OF DISORDER.

Strange as the statement may sound, one of the most important events in the making of Tennessee was the hanging of five men in Vicksburg in July, 1835. To perceive the relation which this event bears to the history of this State, it is necessary to understand the general state of society which existed during the years just preceding. One of the most striking contrasts to be met with in the study of American institutions is the ease with which a thorough system of laws is introduced and the difficulty of having them enforced. The relation between the ministers of law and the people upon whom they are to be administered is so personal and intimate, that it is impossible to obtain that rigidity which is a characteristic of European countries. The enforcement of law and especially criminal law, therefore, depends rather upon the character of the individual than upon the general system. The result is a laxity which offers direct inducement to law-breakers. Where the population is sparse, and in regions of country where the interval between a state of nature and civilization is in process of being bridged, this laxity attains its highest development. The pioneers who open the way are, as a rule, brave, honest, uncouth, but quick to repel the invasions of others by a prompt resort to violence. They may be said to clear the field. The first growth is generally one of tares, and then comes the labor of the husbandman.

After the departure of the Indians from Tennessee, as

the country rapidly settled up, the field for brigandage in the State was a peculiarly favorable one. The state of society was generally rough, and the newly introduced laws frequently failed to command respect. The thief, the robber, the horse-stealer, the negro-runner, the highwayman, the burglar, and the counterfeiter profited by the opportunity, and a reign of lawlessness began. But it was frequently tempered by lynch-law, and was overridden at times by superior force. It was the glory and the boast of a native Tennessean to have organized these scattered elements of recklessness and crime into a "noble band of valiant and lordly bandits," as Murrell styled his following.

It is beyond the power of historic research to separate the false from the true in all that has come down to us about John A. Murrell. Still all that we know is equally characteristic of the times, and if all did not happen, it can be as truthfully asserted that it all might have happened. Murrell was born in Middle Tennessee in the earlier part of the century. His mother was a woman of evil disposition, and taught him his first lesson in vice. By the time he was of age he had become a confirmed evil-doer, and formally adopted robbery as a profession. He soon became noted among the fraternity of "speculators," as all of that profession were called by themselves, for the boldness and success of his ventures. The distinguishing feature of his methods was their thoroughness. After the commission of an offense, nothing was stickled at to prevent detection. He knew no degrees in crime, and regarded murder as in no wise more heinous or repugnant than the theft of a watch. He never robbed a man, unless by stealth, without killing him, and he never robbed by violence where the person robbed could not be killed. The following incident, told in his own words, gives an idea of his methods: "While I was seated on a log, looking down the road the way I had come, a man came in sight riding a good-looking horse. The very moment I saw him I determined to have his horse if he was in the garb of a traveler. I arose from my seat and drew an elegant rifle-pistol on him and ordered him to dismount. He did so and I took his horse by the bridle and pointed down the creek and ordered him to walk before me. We went a few hundred yards and stopped. I hitched his horse and then made him undress himself, all to his shirt and drawers, and ordered him to turn his back to me. He asked me if I was going to shoot him. I ordered him the second time to turn his back to me. He said: 'If you are going to kill me, let me have time to pray before I die.' I told him I had no time to hear him pray. He turned around and dropped on his knees, and I shot him in the back of the head. I ripped open his belly and took out his entrails and sunk him in the creek. I then searched his pockets and found four hundred and one dollars and thirty-seven cents and a number of papers that I did not take time to examine. I sunk the pocket-book and papers and his hat in the creek. His boots were bran new and fitted me very genteelly, and I put them on and sunk my old shoes in the creek to atone for them. I rolled up his clothes and put them into his portmanteau, as they were quite new cloth of the best quality. I mounted as fine a horse as I ever straddled, and directed my course for Natchez in much better style than I had been for the last five days." Having met with some congenial spirits in New Orleans, men possessing, like himself, a certain degree of force, Murrell conceived the design of organizing "a clan." As subsequently developed, the plan of organization appears to have been the formation of a kind of general central committee, called Grand Council of the Mystic Clan, to direct the operations of local thieves and robbers called strikers. These latter were not admitted to the general meetings, and were simply tools in the hands of Murrell and his council. The strikers executed the plans of their superior associates, running most of the risk and dividing the profits with them. The central place of meeting was an enormous cotton-wood tree in Mississippi County, Arkansas, said to be still standing. There existed among them a system of signs and countersigns and the usual paraphernalia of a clandestine association formed for deeds of secrecy and violence. After the organization had been placed on a proper basis, Murrell, who had hitherto led a roving life, married the sister of a former confederate, and bought a farm near Denmark in Madison County, Tennessee. Here he lived in apparent quietude, but in reality carrying on the most extensive and elaborately devised schemes of rapine and plunder.

Murrell was undoubtedly a character for whom nature had done much. He possessed a quick mind and a remarkably pleasant and gentlemanlike address. He had great natural adaptability, and was as much at ease among people of refinement as among his clansmen. He had a certain frank, cordial manner that enabled him at times to convert his bitterest enemies into his warmest admirers. He was not altogether unread, and had made a special study of criminal law in order to avoid its dangers. He knew enough of theology to palm himself off as a minister of the gospel, and at one period of his life attempted medicine with some degree of success. He frequently assumed the disguise of a preacher in order to pass counterfeit money. He had a cool, clear-headed judgment, and was utterly without fear, physical or moral. His ascendency over his men never waned, and they were ever ready to sacrifice their lives in order to save his. Within the ranks of his clan, he was just, fair, and amiable. He was a kind husband and brother and a faithful friend.

Murrell had a nefarious ambition that took a pride in his position and in the operations of his followers, independent of the love of gain. He was vain and eager to lead. As a soldier he would have been a brilliant, though probably a temporary success. His conceit was the only weak spot in his armor, and it was the cause of his downfall. During the period of Murrell's reign there was no security to life or property in West Tennessee. The favorite operations of his clan were horse-stealing and negro-running, so called. The latter was accomplished by promising the negro freedom in the North if he would leave his master, accompany his new friend, and allow himself to be sold several times on the way. The negro consenting, the runner carried him through the country, selling him in the daytime, recovering him again at night, and pushing on until another favorable opportunity presented itself. It required a certain address to gain the negro's confidence, and this Murrell possessed in a supereminent degree. But he never failed in the end to murder the negro, open his stomach, and sink him in water deep enough to hide all traces. This was in obedience to his rule that no man should live who could implicate him without implicating himself. His only violation of this rule, which was caused by his vanity, caused his detection.

The man who brought Murrell to justice was Virgil A. Stewart. Stewart himself gives a detailed account of this transaction, which is so filled with glaring inconsistencies and even contradictions that it is safe to accept only that which coincides with known facts. Stewart was a young Georgian who had removed to Madison County, Tennessee, when young, and from there had gone to the Choctaw purchase in Mississippi. Before Murrell settled in Madison County, Stewart, being on a visit to Denmark, was told by a friend that he suspected Murrell of having run off some of his slaves. Hearing of Murrell's intended departure, Stewart followed him, made his acquaintance on the road in the disguise of a horse-hunter, and wormed himself into Murrell's confidence by playing upon his vanity. Murrell eventually gave him a history of his life and an insight into the character, organization, and workings of his clan. Stewart accompanied him to the celebrated cotton-wood tree in Arkansas, and was present at a meeting of the Grand Council. Returning, he had him arrested and was the instrument of having him sent to the Penitentiary, from which he emerged an imbecile and an invalid.

Among the assertions made by Stewart was that Murrell had revealed to him a plan which he had originated for a general insurrection of the slaves on a day appointed. He represents this as in a manner the climax of Murrell's ambition — the scheme nearest his heart. There may have been a scintilla of truth in this, as some members of his band were arrested and confessed that such a plan existed. It is probable, however, that Stewart elaborated the idea in order to attract attention, for notoriety was the breath of his nostrils. Another statement of Stewart's which is preposterous on its face was that many men high in social and official life were members of the gang. They were used by Murrell to give an air of respectability to any impeached member, to laugh down rumors of the existence of such an organization and to help the clansmen escape the toils of the law. But in spite of having received and published a list of Murrell's gang, the name of no one high in social or official life was ever produced.

Murrell's conviction in 1834 acted as a great clarification of the atmosphere. It discouraged the marauder class and it gave heart to the citizens. So strong had the clan been, that no one was willing to run the risk of needlessly offending them.[1]

In Memphis their most unrelenting enemy, M. B. Winchester, had felt the weight of their anger in slanders that eventually drove him to his cups. Isaac Rawlings,

[1] This probably was the grain of truth in Stewart's statement in reference to the members who stood high in the esteem of the public.

who was mayor at the time of Murrell's conviction, and who had enforced the law where he could find transgressions, without regard to consequences, was only protected from personal violence by the fear of lynch-law. But the members of the lawless class were bold, defiant, and insolent.

The towns upon the river banks were peculiarly exposed to evil influences. The rivers were almost exclusively the channels of trade, and the entire traffic of the lower Mississippi valley passed by Memphis and the places farther south. New Orleans was the great Southern mart or emporium, and the products of the Valley States were brought down to New Orleans as to the market of the world.

The forms of the boats used would baffle any attempt at accurate classification. Everything that could be made to float was forced into service. Those chiefly used by people whose circumstances permitted choice were the barge, the keel, and the "flat" or flat-boat, also called Kentucky-flat or broad-horn. Pirogues, canoes, skiffs, and dug-outs still remained as relics of earlier days, but were only adapted to light work. The keel was a slender and rather stylish looking boat, capable of carrying about twenty tons. The barge was a heavy, ponderous wooden structure with a hulk raised above the surface of the water, and was not unlike a schooner of the present day. It had a possible capacity of very nearly one hundred tons. The flat-boat or "broad-horn" was the one in most general use. It was easy to make and was sufficiently durable and cheap. At the end of a voyage it was generally sold to saw mills. The barge and the keel were occasionally worked up stream, by means of tread-mills, sails, and ropes tied to trees so as to pull along the bank from tree to tree, but the greatest speed gained was about ten miles a day. From New Orleans to Cincinnati in three months was a good trip. The flat-boat never attempted to do more than float with the current. The life upon the river would appear to the steamboat traveler of to-day as phantasmagorical. On the large barges two or three families with all their household effects, poultry, produce, hogs, horses, mules, and cows would sometimes embark, intending to change their place of habitation. On the keels, pleasure-seeking parties would sometimes descend the river on a jaunt to New Orleans with the expectation of returning by land. There were bedrooms, a dining-room, and a platform for dancing. The fiddle, flute, banjo, and bones furnished rhythmical and appropriate accompaniment. At each large village or town a landing was made, followed by a sojourn of several days. On the flat-boats traveled those who were lower in the scale, the needy, the desperate, and the adventurous. It was made by fastening together logs as large as could be procured, erecting two immense paddles at both ends or sides, sometimes both, making a rough flooring and building a roof. The necessities of the maker decided its length. Upon this, the poor man with his family would live for months, drifting leisurely down when it suited his convenience, and occasionally stopping over to make a crop on shares for some one living upon the banks. His chickens, pigs, cow, dogs, wife, and children lived together in daily association. More frequently, however, these flat-boats were tenanted by the rough elements of society, carrying the produce of the year to market, eager for amusement, generally well supplied with whiskey and fire-arms. At times several of them would fasten their rafts together. As a rule the sober, staid citizen who undertook a trip of this kind down the river threw off all restraint, and became as boisterous as the most hardened. When two flat-boats passed each other, a continual fire of jest, taunt, insult, and ribaldry was exchanged, sometimes ending in blows, pistol shots, stabs, and death. Occasionally a raft would be seen to drift by vacant and apparently deserted. The fate of the former proprietors was easily guessed. Fish-like they preyed and were preyed upon. When a crowd of these aquatic rovers found themselves together in a town, they instinctively banded together against the stationary being as a natural enemy. The fights between flat-boat men and citizens were often fatal.

An incident of this kind occurred in Memphis in 1842, and marked a distinct advance in the progress of law and order. The damper cast upon the gamblers by the events of a few years before had not spread to the flat-boat men, and in the vernacular of that day "they took the town" when they liked, and flatly refused to pay the city fees for wharfage. Their trade was valuable, and the subject was not pressed until William Spickernagle was elected mayor in 1841. He determined to have a more vigorous administration of law, and appointed the proper man wharf-master, who rigorously collected the wharfage fees despite threats and bloody noses. In 1842 Edwin Hickman, the successor of Spickernagle, carried out the policy of his predecessor, and continued the same officers in power. In May, 1842, about five hundred-flat boats were at the Memphis landing, and among the flat-boat men was one named Trester who had heard of the change which had taken place in Memphis. He had previously passed down the river and landed at Memphis without paying the fee. He cut himself a heavy haw stick set with knots, which, as he said to the wharf-master himself, he had cut on purpose to use on any one who tried to make him pay for landing where he pleased. The wharf-master swore out a warrant and placed it in the hands of G. B. Locke with orders to serve it. Being resisted, Locke obtained the assistance of a detachment from the Memphis Guards, a local military company, and again started for the river. Seeing the uniforms and the bayonets, Trester pushed out from the bank, and being pursued, resisted and was killed. For a day, a pitched battle between the flat-boat men and the city of Memphis was imminent, but was averted. This event had a salutary effect upon the flat-boat men, in so far as Memphis was concerned, and they never again attempted to "take the town."

During the latter years of Murrell's life in Denmark, the lawless elements of society in the South and Southwest undoubtedly had the upper hand of the law-abiding. The best citizens lived in apprehension. But it is only the kind heart and the liberal mind which is not made insolent by success. The very fact of their mastery carried with it the proper corrective. This was administered on July 6, 1835. Vicksburg had been overridden by gamblers almost from the time of its inception. A great many of them had their headquarters there, and a stream of them was continually flowing through Vicksburg to and from New Orleans. The citizens had grown very restive under their domineering, but were afraid to take a stand against them. On the fourth of July, 1835, the usual national festivities were being celebrated by the citizens, when a drunken gambler, in imitation of many successful examples, undertook to "run the meeting." He was at once put under arrest and only released in the evening. When discharged he not only uttered insolent threats against his imprisoners, but immediately armed himself to carry them into execution. He was then seized, carried to the outskirts of the town, given a coat of tar and feathers and dismissed. The gambling "fraternity" were deeply incensed and were loud in their denunciations. The blood of the citizens being up, they issued a notice to all professional gamblers to leave the town in twenty-four hours. On the morning of the sixth, committees previously appointed examined the gambling houses and burned all the gambling devices they could find. By this time most of the profession, being frightened, had left the town. A few desperadoes alone remained, and having armed themselves, collected together in a house used by them for gambling purposes and refused to open the door. The door was broken down by a mob of infuriated citizens with Dr. Bodley, a prominent and popular physician, at their head. The gamblers fired and he fell dead. Several shots more being exchanged without results, the citizens made a rush and obtained entrance to the house. They captured three of the inmates in the house and two others who had escaped from the building, and hanged the whole five. Their names were North, Hullams, Dutch Bill, Smith, and McCall.

The moral effect of this act cannot be fully appreciated by any one not familiar with the current literature of that day. The news swept like wild-fire throughout the Mississippi valley, and was eagerly discussed by every fireside, at every cross-roads store, and on every stage coach throughout the South and Southwest. Coming on the heels of Murrell's conviction, it gave heart to the lovers of law and order. Committees were formed in every community from Cincinnati to New Orleans that had suffered from the thief and the cut-throat, and general notices were issued for specified classes to leave in twenty-four hours. Few, if any, lynchings took place, but an end had been put to organized crime in the Southwest forever.

CHAPTER XXXIII.

RISE OF THE WHIG PARTY.

FROM December, 1834, to the loss of Tennessee by Polk in 1844, may be called the decade of partisan fury, though the era of partisan activity continued to the time of the war. The contest between Carroll and Ward in 1821, and that between Bell and Grundy for Congress in 1827, was spirited and full of fire. The gubernatorial struggles between the Browns, Trousdale, Campbell, Johnson, Gentry, Henry, Harris, Hatton, and Netherland were obstinate and vehement, but all were tame when compared with the terrific encounters of these ten years. Then every election was the coming together of the Numidian lion and the Arachosian tiger. During this era the Whig party came into existence in Tennessee. In 1834 it was not merely in a minority in Tennessee; it was, as a political organization, absolutely unknown. In 1840 it carried the State overwhelmingly for a Whig candidate for the presidency. The history of its gradual development and of the period of its ascendency in the State is curious and instructive. Between Jackson and Buchanan, the Whigs carried Tennessee at every presidential election. The Whig leaders of Tennessee repelled with indignation the charge that their party had its origin in opposition to Jackson. But such was the fact. Carroll was the only prominent candidate who was opposed by Jackson who did not subsequently become a Whig. The Republicans held undisputed supremacy in Tennessee long after Clay's secession and the annunciation of his American system. Jackson was nominated by the legislature of Tennessee on the 20th of July, 1822, for the presidency of the United States. Between the period of the War of 1812 and this date his influence had become paramount, and as far as personal influence, unaided by the machinery of party conventions, could control the politics of a state, he controlled the politics of Tennessee. His prejudices were strong. He was devoted to his friends. He hated his enemies, and he was suspicious of those who were indifferent. His final election to the presidency made him politically omnipotent. Those who were excluded from his good-will were excluded from all preferment, not resting upon the direct vote of the people. The politicians of Tennessee have always been singularly tractable to authority, and the people have always been remarkably intractable. Jackson was an old man, and during a long and tempestuous life he had contracted many debts of personal gratitude. He became president; these were now to be liquidated. There was room for no new men, a class of politicians who are frequently hated as much in our day as in Cicero's. Young, ambitious spirits were not wanting to see that there was no place for them, unless a new order of things could be inaugurated. During Jackson's second term, circumstances arose which opened up the possibility of revolution. The number of those willing and able to lead in this movement had been steadily increasing. Not only were the Jackson men supreme, they were intolerant. Jackson not only proposed to reward his friends, but to punish his enemies. As Crockett said, "to turn against Jackson was the unpardonable sin." Naturally there was much mutiny.

One of the ablest of those who were driven into the Whig ranks by the intolerance of Jackson and his friends, was Newton Cannon. He had been born in Guilford county, North Carolina, educated at a public school, and removed to Williamson County, Tennessee, when quite young. He entered the Creek War as a private, was elected captain and then colonel of a regiment of volunteer mounted riflemen. He was in two engagements and bore himself bravely. His term of service having expired, he returned to Tennessee before the end of the war, and on this slight circumstance was founded the charge of cowardice and desertion subsequently made by the "Nashville Union." Before the Creek War Cannon had attracted Jackson's attention. He was on the jury that tried Magness,[1] the father of the man who shot Patton Anderson. Jackson, a warm and enthusiastic friend of Anderson, spared no exertion to have Magness convicted. He was acquitted. Jackson shook his finger in the face of the obstinate young juror, and said, "I'll mark you, young man." During the Creek War fresh fuel was added to Jackson's prejudice. In a letter which appeared on the fourth of July, 1821, in the "Nashville Clarion," the writer asks, "Is it not known that he and Colonel Cannon have not been very friendly since the Creek War?" In 1814 Cannon made his appearance on the political field as a successor to Felix Grundy, who had resigned his seat in Congress. With the exception of the 15th Congress, when he was a commissioner to negotiate a treaty with the Chickasaw Indians, having been appointed by President Monroe, Cannon remained in Congress until 1823, when he voluntarily retired. Whilst in Congress he excited the indignation of Jackson's friends by denying some statements in the life of Jackson begun by Reed but finished by Eaton. He also voted against maintaining the military establishment as Jackson desired. He addressed a letter of explanation to Jackson which the latter, such was the currently accepted rumor, trampled under foot. When Cannon was a candidate for governor in 1827, against

---

[1] Parton, in his *Life of Jackson*, vol. i. p. 344, in relating an incident that occurred at the trial of the son, spells the name Magness. In Cannon's speech it is spelled Magnus.

Blount and Houston, Jackson's sympathies were avowedly for either as against him. Naturally Cannon was not in high favor with the national administration which came into power the year following.

David Crockett was another Lucifer of republicanism who became one of the morning stars of Whiggery in Tennessee. Perhaps it would be true to say that Crockett was the first prominent Whig in this State. He was born in East Tennessee, and was reared in the narrow circumstances of those times, without education or the means of intellectual cultivation. He moved to Elk Creek near the mouth of Mulberry. From here he entered the army and served in the Creek War. It is probable, though borne out by no direct proof, that Crockett contracted a prejudice against his commander during these campaigns which made it an easy matter for him, when elected to Congress, to array himself against Jackson. As early as 1823 he voted for John Williams and against Jackson for senator. Returning home he again removed to Shoal Creek in Giles County, where he became colonel of militia, and was elected a member of the General Assembly. Having suffered some reverses, he again removed, this time to the banks of the Obion, where he was in 1823 again elected to the state legislature. In 1825 some practical joke in the town of Jackson spread the report that he was a candidate for Congress. Angered by the implied ridicule, he at once came forward and made a vigorous canvass. Though defeated, he laid the foundations upon which he was elected in 1827. When he entered Congress it was as a Republican. But his indignation was aroused during his second term by the course of the administration towards the Cherokee Indians in Georgia.

His violent denunciation of Jackson's perfidy incensed the friends of the president. When he returned home to seek a reëlection, he found that the storm had been raised. He himself says, " he was hunted like a wild beast, and in this hunt every little newspaper in the district and every little pin-hook lawyer was engaged." Crockett was defeated by a small majority. In 1833 he was again elected, after a stubborn contest. He voted with the Whigs for a protective tariff, for internal improvements, to renew the charter of the United States Bank, while Bell was still dealing his heaviest blows against the American system. He signed the letter of the 19th of December, 1834, calling on White to be a candidate for the presidency.

Jackson's defeat of General John Williams for the Senate, in 1823–1824, embittered his adherents. He had been in the Creek War and was very popular, especially in East Tennessee. Scattered here and there were men like McNairy and Jesse Benton, in whom old wounds still rankled. Indeed, Jesse Benton's hatred of Jackson was so fervent, so malignant, so active, and so futile that it became amusing. It was suggestive of the burlesque representations on Vaudeville stages of Ajax defying the gods. In 1824 he was a candidate for elector in the Western District. If elected, he promised to vote for Crawford. If it should be necessary to change his vote, for Clay. He wrote a letter to the editor of the "Whig," proposing to examine the lives and conduct of presidential candidates. "All I ask is that the people shall have light. I owe a duty to my God and to my country, which I will discharge." Being refused the privilege of performing this duty through the columns of the "Whig," he published a pamphlet. This contained thirty-two specifications. It was extensively copied by the organs of the Adams, Clay, and Crawford factions. It created a great commotion in Tennessee, and elicited answers from Mayor W. B. Lewis and others. But no one proposed to bring the implacable pamphleteer to terms.[1]

[1] In the *Old Times Papers* by James D. Davis, a fight between Jesse Benton and Jackson at the Old Bell Tavern in Memphis is mentioned. Jackson appears to have had the advantage. Parton does not refer to this. Davis says he had it from Jesse Benton himself.

In 1827 John Bell and Felix Grundy were pitted against each other for Congress. Both were avowed friends of Jackson, Grundy perhaps a little more vociferous than Bell. Grundy was then fifty years of age, twenty years older than his competitor. Born in Berkeley County, Virginia, he had removed, when two years of age, to Brownsville in Pennsylvania, and the next year to Kentucky. Here he received a substantial education, studied law, and was admitted to the bar. He was a member of the Constitutional Convention of Kentucky in 1799, for several years a member of the General Assembly and was on the supreme bench of that State. In 1807 he removed to Nashville. In 1811, and again in 1813, he was elected to Congress. He sprang at once into national prominence. His support of the war measures was energetic and effective. The Federalists denounced the war as one instigated by "Madison, Grundy, and the Devil." He resigned in 1814 and devoted himself to law. The Southwest has never produced another criminal lawyer of equal fame. He had a figure which was strikingly graceful and commanding, an open, refined face, a disposition of great affability. These personal qualifications, joined to a mellow flow of words which was impressive and which sparkled with antitheses, distinguished also by occasional bursts of pathos that never failed to move the sensibilities of the jury, gave him an unvarying tide of success, the very momentum of which rendered him eventually invincible. He is said to have defended but one man who was afterwards hanged. The traditions which still linger among lawyers of some of the trials in which he played a part, show him to have been quick of mind, full of stratagems and wiles, and not overscrupulous in resorting to any method or expedient that was likely to save the neck of his client.

Bell, on the contrary, was a very young man, just thirty years of age. He had been in the legislature at Nashville, having served one term in 1817, declining a reëlection. Devoting himself to law, he had established a reputation as a man of strong mind and solid parts. He had enjoyed the advantages of a classical education, and during the interval between 1817 and 1827 he had pursued, in addition to his practice at the bar, such studies as strengthened his powers and cultivated his tastes. He possessed an intellect of extraordinary vigor, broad in its scope and catholic in its sympathy. He tended too much towards speculative generalities, which detracted from his talents as a partisan leader. He was not without subtlety, and he could map out a plan of action with consummate skill. But he lacked the quickness of resolution and the dashing execution necessary in the guerilla warfare of political contests. His eloquence showed marks of polish, and his talents for speaking had been assiduously improved. On the stump, his powerful logic, his comprehensive discussion, his thorough grasp of the political questions of the day, his terrible invective and noble and elevated tone of oratory made him the delight of his audience. On the floor of the lower house at Washington, all of these qualifications lifted him as an orator high above the head of every Tennessean who was his colleague during his active term of service. But he was not a master of the arts of rhetorical bushwhacking which make the debater. He was too composed, too slow in his movements, he required too elaborate preparation, he moved in an atmosphere too rarified. He was a prominent figure in the lower house, it is true, but he never gained the ascendency to which his eminent abilities justly entitled him. In 1841 he was appointed by Harrison secretary of war, but resigned the same year. For six years he was out of public employment. Had his career closed here, it would have been an evil thing for his fame. But in 1847 he was a member of the legislature, and after protracted balloting he was elected to the United States Senate, of which body he was a member for the next twelve years. Here was the proper arena for the display of his talents. Here his eminent abilities, his melodious rhetoric, the philosophic bent of his virile mind, the serene dignity of his bearing, and the perspicuous quality of his logic shone with unclouded brightness. Here he was a distinguished figure in a body of which Henry Clay, Lewis Cass, Salmon P. Chase, Stephen A. Douglas, John J. Crittenden, William Pitt Fessenden, John P. Hale, Benjamin F. Wade, Charles Sumner, Judah P. Benjamin, Jefferson Davis, and Andrew Johnson were members. His nomination by the Constitutional Unionists, in 1860, for the presidency was a natural climax to a life whose greatest intellectual triumphs had been gained in attempts to accomplish what divine foresight alone could see was impossible, the attempt to make fanaticism and moral right work in harmonious traces with self-interest and constitutional warrant.

When Bell and Grundy were candidates against each other, the latter apparently had every political advantage, joined to long service and a national reputation. General Jackson electioneered actively for Grundy and voted for him. Bell was elected by an overwhelming majority and took his seat, feeling sore and mutinous. Jackson had offended the ablest mind which Tennessee has ever produced, after his own and Andrew Johnson's. Grundy was elected, however, two years later, to the Senate, to succeed Eaton. It was charged that Jackson's preferences were consulted in this matter. In 1829 Jackson took the oath as president of the United States. He appointed a cabinet. The man who, outside of Tennessee, had been most instrumental in making him president, was Martin Van Buren. In 1831 Jackson determined that that man should succeed him as president. He discovered that it was necessary to have all the political forces of his administration act in harmony and move in concert towards this common point in order to accomplish it. His election had been a rebuke to the system of using the patronage of the government for ulterior purposes. The method heretofore pursued was for the president to appoint to the secretaryship of state the successor apparent. Adams's appointment of Clay had created the " bargain intrigue and corruption" storm. Jackson now allowed himself to be seduced from the true theory of his political career. But he contrived to draw a specious veil over his plans by ostentatiously establishing the rule that no member of his cabinet should be a candidate for the presidency. His attention had already been drawn to a possible candidate from Tennessee; a man of unblemished reputation, of distinguished merit, and of the highest talent. Jackson proposed to net two birds at once by turning Van Buren out of the cabinet and by drawing Hugh L. White into it. White refused. Jackson accepted this as a confirmation of his suspicions. He at once set in operation the entire force of his influence, but in vain. White had been his life-long friend, his stanchest supporter, his warmest adherent, his most trusted adviser. But unlike most of his compeers, White never lost his manly individuality of character. He was Jackson's friend, not his dependent, and he obeyed unhesitatingly the dictates of his own conscience. During the debate on the tariff difficulties in 1832–33, Jackson sent for White, and requested him, who was speaker of the Senate *pro tem.*, not to put Clayton of Delaware on the committee to which would be referred the bills pending on this subject. Having already ordered his name to be entered on the "Journal" as a member of the committee, White refused. This strengthened the estrangement between Jackson and White, an estrangement which gave this State to the Whigs and embittered the last days of the two great Tennesseans.

Viewed as a political organization, the distinctive feature of the Jacksonians was a proscription never dreamed of by those who laid broad and deep the foundations of our government in tolerance, individual freedom, and brotherly love. In 1823 the "Nashville Whig" published some letters signed "Boone" and "Viator," in which Jackson's candidacy for the presidency was discussed in a temperate and a conservative tone. This was at once held up as evidence of hostile feeling, and a large number of subscribers adopted that method of punishment which is the delight of narrow minds and the amusement of newspaper men. They refused to continue taking the paper. As Crockett said, to turn against Jackson was the unpardonable sin.

During the year 1833 the availability of White as a successor to Jackson became more patent. In Tennessee, Van Buren was unpopular in the highest degree. The Democrats saw in White a worthy successor to Jackson and the Whigs saw in him a high-minded statesman who would be unwilling to debauch the public service. In the autumn of 1833 the legislature of Tennessee desired to put him in nomination, but desisted at his earnest request. In the spring of 1834 Jackson, in a conversation with an intimate friend of White's, suggested that White should be vice-president on the ticket with Van Buren, and that after the latter had served eight years, White could then succeed him. Jackson also offered White a seat upon the supreme bench. White indignantly rejected every overture. It is probable that he would never have been a candidate, but some time in 1834 Jackson uttered the characteristic threat that if he did become a candidate for the presidency, he would be rendered odious to society. White determined at once to come forward regardless of all consequences. On the 19th of December, 1834, the members of Congress from Tennessee, with the exception of James K. Polk, Felix Grundy, David Crockett, and John Blair, met to consider White's candidacy. Luke Lea stated that Polk had promised to support White, and

James Standifer answered for Grundy and Blair. Of Crockett there was no doubt. The next day the meeting addressed a letter to White, who replied, consenting to become a candidate. In the winter of 1834 the legislature of Alabama put White in nomination.

The issue was now joined. At once the stream of obloquy began to rise. The "Globe" made a furious onslaught on White, as a tool in the hands of one deeper and more designing than himself — one whose foul and deep-laid scheme it was to defeat Jackson's administration and strengthen the hands of his enemies. This of course was John Bell. Up to this time the rivalry between Polk and Bell had been purely personal. Bell, during the contest for the speakership in 1834, and his friends as a rule, protested that he was "as good a Jackson man as Polk himself." Polk had long desired to see Bell assume a position of antagonism to Jackson. The open warfare of the "Globe" which was certainly in harmony with Polk's desires, if not under his immediate direction, finally drove Bell into opposition, and removed from Polk's path the only enemy he feared in Tennessee. Jackson himself, who had used the machinery of a convention to force Van Buren on the Republican, now occasionally called the Democratic party, as vice-president, determined to resort to the same means to make him president. In February, 1835, he wrote a letter advocating a national convention to nominate candidates for president and vice-president. In May the convention was held at Baltimore, and Van Buren was nominated. Tennessee refused to appoint delegates, and its vote was cast by one man, a chance bystander named E. Rucker, and Ruckerize became one of the political commonplaces of the day. A systematic plan for the purpose of destroying White's influence in Tennessee, without the hearty support of which he was lost, was then devised. When White's candidacy was announced, the two Nashville papers at once declared for him. Letters were to be written for use in Tennessee, by Jackson. Bell was to be defeated for Congress. A Van Buren man was to be elected governor. White was to be defeated for the Senate. Jackson himself was to enter the canvass personally in Tennessee. A new paper was to be established at Nashville to oppose White and to denounce him as a Federalist. The contest was to be narrowed down to Jackson and White, and Van Buren was to be left out of the discussion. The most important of all these designs was to leave Van Buren in the background and to bring on the struggle as between the two Tennesseans. Bell, who hoped indeed to see White elected, but who hoped above all things to break the supremacy of the Jackson men in the State, managed the White canvass in so far as it had any management. He proclaimed on all hands the warmth of his and White's friendship for Jackson. The "Republican" called repeated attention to the fact that Bell had supported all of Jackson's measures, that he had voted against the tariff of 1832, for the compromise of 1833, and the Indian and anti-nullification policy of his administration. In a speech made at Nashville, on the 23d of May, 1835, he frankly declares his design: "Opposition to the administration of General Jackson is the course the worst enemies of Judge White desire his friends to adopt. They are so anxious on this point that they appear determined to put Judge White and his friends in opposition whether they will or not. But, gentlemen, the friends of Judge White will adhere to General Jackson and his administration from consistency and respect for their own characters and because they will be supporting their own principles."

In August, Jackson traveled through the State and inaugurated the campaign. He proclaimed in public that White was a red-hot Federalist, and that he was as far from his administration as the poles are asunder. Donelson in Washington had incautiously declared that White's candidacy for the presidency would be made a contest between him and Jackson. Blair of the "Globe" predicted that Judge White would be "as effectually and entirely crushed by General Jackson as if the foot of an elephant had been placed on him." The "Globe" studiously avoided the reiterated charge that Jackson was for Van Buren. Jackson wrote two letters to a man named Gwin, a parson, to be used against White. In the second, written on the 8th of August, 1835, he says in reference to the first Gwin letter, "I wrote it immediately on seeing the article in the 'Republican,' and intended it as a rebuke of what I considered an unwarrantable use of my name to subserve the views of factious intrigues, seeking to undermine the course of Republicanism and to defeat the result of the leading measures of my administration." This was intended to repel the assertion made by the "Republican," that Jackson would prefer White to Van Buren. He wrote other letters of like substance to Willie Blount and one to Felix Grundy which Cave Johnson was in the habit of reading on the stump during his canvass.

The "Union" was established by the Jackson party at Nashville, and was edited with an energy of personal vituperation never before witnessed in Tennessee. It poured a steady stream of denunciation and doggerel against Bell and White and their adherents. About this time the name of Whig began to be applied to the White men. A toast at a dinner given to Jackson in August denounced the "new-born Whigs," a phrase recently coined by Jackson, and the "Union" called White's supporters, "White Whigs." But all these extraordinary exertions resulted in no measure of success. The press of the State was overwhelmingly for White — the proportion was seventeen to seven. The Jackson men failed to make the issue between White and Jackson, and the people of Tennessee were filled with a profound veneration, a deep-seated affection, an earnest and almost sorrowful sympathy for the pure and noble character who had been caught in the toils of a wild and frenzied fight of factions. White meetings were held in almost every county, and the support of Tennessee was pledged with increasing and spontaneous enthusiasm.

The first conspicuous failure in the Jackson programme was the result of the August elections. The return of John Bell was peculiarly galling. Caucus after caucus was held, letters were written, extravagant promises were made to induce some one whose standing and reputation gave some promise of success to come forward against him. But his defeat of Grundy had taught the politicians in his district a lasting lesson, and no one fit and available could be found. The towering genius of John Bell was not of the sort that could so easily be hawked at in its pride of place and killed. He had no opposition.

More than this. The candidates for the governorship were Governor Carroll, Newton Cannon, R. G. Dunlap who soon retired on account of ill health, and W. H. Humphreys who was for White, but who made no figure. Carroll was outspoken for Van Buren, though protesting that the presidential question should not be made an issue in this canvass. In 1834 the Constitutional Convention met. Under the old constitution, Carroll, having served three terms, was not again eligible. But his supporters declared that the new constitution, although not changing this rule, entirely abrogated the old, and that Carroll stood in the attitude of one who had never been governor. So great was his popularity that the leading White organs conceded his election. Newton Cannon, who had been chairman of a White meeting in Williamson County, and was personally obnoxious to Jackson, attacked Van Buren and declared his decided preference for Judge White. The leading White men took no open part, but Cannon was elected by a majority of about 7,000. So strong and uncompromising was the feeling for White, that Polk avowed on the stump his individual preference for White. He even went to extreme lengths and attacked the Baltimore Convention. He declared that the proceedings of that body had no more obligatory force on the party than the recommendations of any other equally respectable men. The White candidates carried the State by a large majority. When the legislature met, E. H. Foster, an outspoken White man, was made speaker of the House by acclamation. The Jackson men seemed unable to grasp the drift of things. The second day after the members assembled, each one found on his desk a copy of the "Globe's" extra edition, franked by Jackson himself and containing violent and almost scurrilous attacks on White's course during the last session of Congress on the Expunging Resolutions. The same day White was re-elected to the Senate by an almost unanimous vote. The motion to instruct him to vote for the Expunging Resolutions was laid on the table by a vote of 50 to 22. On the 17th of October the legislature, by a vote of 60 to 12, recommended White to the country as a man eminently qualified to fill the office of president.

The overthrow of White's enemies in Tennessee was complete. Almost the only victory of the Jackson men was the defeat in 1835 of Bell by Polk for the speakership. The Van Buren organs spared no exertions to drive White into the Whig ranks. From his candidacy dated the Whig party in Tennessee, but he never became a Whig himself. He was an independent in the highest sense of the word, steadfast in his principles, and sacrificing nothing to party expediency. Such men as these rarely become great statesmen, but they exemplify a noble phase of human character. To the charge of having abandoned his principles, he retorted that he stood firm, that it was Jackson that had abandoned his. He excited deep indignation among his old friends by supporting the bill to prevent federal interference in local elections. He pointed to the fact that he had taken this same position in 1826 and that Jackson had been elected on this issue. In a speech delivered at Knoxville on the 5th of April, 1827, while still a warm friend of Jackson, he had defined his views on all the leading questions of the day. In the matter of internal improvements he said: "I think not only that the United States do not possess this power, but further, it ought never to be surrendered to them." In a speech delivered in the Senate in the very heat of the canvass, he said: "I have been one of those who do not believe the federal government has the power to carry on a system of internal improvements within the States." He said of protection in 1827: "To give protection to a certain extent, I have never doubted the power of the federal government; but this, like every other power, ought always to be exercised for the good of the whole." These views he never changed. In 1833 he discussed the national bank idea: "I hold that, by the constitution of the United States, Congress has no power to create a bank, and having no power to create it, we have no power to continue it beyond the time of its limitation." As late as August, 1838, after all his leading supporters had gone over to the Whig party, he still held fast to his ancient moorings. He was comparing the views on this subject held by Van Buren and himself. "He is against a national bank and so am I." He held, as Jackson had once held, that Congress could create a bank of deposit and transfer. The only specific charge that White had changed his views on this subject was based upon Bell's celebrated Cassidy letter,[1] in which, referring to White's position on the bank question, he remarks that it would be unprecedented and do him a great injury to declare beforehand that he would put his veto upon any measure whatsoever. The only variance between the views of

---

[1] Written May 11, 1835, to Charles Cassidy of Bedford County, Tennessee.

Jackson and White not founded upon Jackson's desire to be succeeded by "the heir apparent to the government," as Crockett called Van Buren, was that upon the bill to prevent federal influence being exerted in order to affect the result of popular elections. On the 16th of February, 1835, White, in the Senate, reviewed his course in the matter. He not only established the fact that he had not changed, but proved unanswerably that the change was in Jackson, who had abandoned his earlier professions on this subject. Upon Benton's Expunging Resolutions, the difference was not political but personal. When Benton first introduced his resolutions to expunge from the Journal of the Senate the vote of censure passed upon him for removing the deposits from the United States Bank, Jackson saw at once that this could be made a test question as between his friends and enemies. Properly used, it could change the complexion of the Senate which was hostile, and it offered an additional weapon in his attempts to make Van Buren his successor. After all, the whole question was a veritable mist without weight or substance. But White, with characteristic disregard of appearances, at once declared it was unconstitutional to mutilate the records of the Senate by the literal destruction or expurgation of the offensive vote, and that a rescission and a repeal would accomplish exactly the same result. This position he maintained with unwavering courage, and in reality the question was eventually settled in accordance with his views. The Jackson papers, however, ignored this, and persisted in placing him among the foes of Jackson, the Federalists, the enemies of good government. Both White and Jackson agreed upon the distribution of the sales of the public lands. In his letter of resignation of 1839 he defines his position on this question: "When a bill was introduced having such a distribution as that spoken of for its object, I voted against its passage and in favor of the veto of the chief magistrate, on the ground that no such distribution ought to be made until the public debt was all paid." In his message of 1829, Jackson, anticipating the time when "the application of the revenue to the payment of debt will cease," had suggested its distribution among the States for purposes of "internal improvements."

When the subject came up again several years later, White voted for the distribution. The debt had all been paid. The attempt to implicate White and Bell and subsequently the Whigs with the Nullifiers was regarded as unworthy serious refutation.

The Van Buren-White-Harrison campaign was long, arduous, and exciting, but lies beyond our scope. White was overwhelmingly defeated, receiving the votes of Georgia and Tennessee only. In addition to this, he was voted for by the Whigs of Alabama, Mississippi, Louisiana, Arkansas, and Missouri. Jackson had the mortification of seeing Van Buren lose Tennessee by 10,039 votes. In the Hermitage polling district, White received 43, Van Buren 18 votes. The defeat of White paved the way for the Whigs in Tennessee. Even then, the defeat of Van Buren by another candidate would have cemented the breach, and probably have left them in as hopeless a minority as in Alabama. But Van Buren was elected. The leading measure of his administration was the Sub-Treasury Bill. This was opposed by White in the Senate, who regarded it as a step toward a treasury bank or a national bank owned and operated entirely by the government, with power to issue currency and as increasing the power of the national executive. In 1839 Newton Cannon was again a candidate for governor. He was opposed by General Robert Armstrong, one of Jackson's most intimate friends and a pronounced Van Buren man. The popular exasperation was still undiminished. Cannon was reëlected.

Cave Johnson was a member of Congress from 1829 to

1845, when he was appointed postmaster-general by Polk, with the exception of one term. This was from 1837 to 1839, when he was defeated because of his opposition to White, the year preceding. Polk was saved by local pride in his prominence as speaker. Grundy was beyond the reach of popular displeasure. A notable indication of popular sentiment was the election of Washington Barrow, editor of the obnoxious "Republican," as a member of the legislature from the Hermitage district. In a speech in the State Senate on the 18th of October, 1837, Anderson of Davidson County, discussing the election of a United States Senator, declared that he " was proud of the good old name of Whig, and that he accepted the title for himself and party." The Whig party was now fairly established in Tennessee. It was strengthened by the contest in 1839 between James K. Polk and Newton Cannon for the governorship. Jackson experienced deep mortification over the loss of Tennessee. He regarded it as a prodigal son, eating the husks of Whiggery. He was anxious to have the State redeemed. It was agreed that Polk should make the race. If elected, he was to be put upon the ticket in 1840 for the vice-presidency. This part of the programme failed. Polk was nominated by the Tennessee legislature and supported by the Jackson interest, but the antagonisms were too strong in the convention and no nomination was made for that office. But in this way attention was drawn to him as "presidential timber."

CHAPTER XXXIV.

POLK AND CANNON.

THE charge made against Polk in 1844 that he was an unknown man was merely a campaign dodge which has been so often repeated that it has been popularly accepted. In truth Polk was an unexpected nominee, not an unknown one. He was as prominent in his day as Mr. Carlisle is in ours. He was as prominent as Mr. Clay in 1824. He was more prominent than Mr. Lincoln in 1860. He was more prominent than Mr. Hayes in 1876. His career had been one full of gradual growth and coherent expansion. He had filled several positions and all of them well and with honor. Reared under the influence of Jeffersonian traditions, he had naturally attached himself to Jackson. He was well educated and graduated with the highest honors. He was a rare example of a school-boy whose early promise found future fulfillment. He was clerk of the state Senate for several terms and then a member of the legislature. In 1825 he was elected to Congress, and was continued in office until 1839, when he voluntarily withdrew to enter the canvass for governor. In Congress he had been speaker for two terms, defeating both times John Bell, a personal as well as a political enemy, for they did not speak. Polk was a fine illustration of what can be accomplished by the union of a sound mind, discretion, and great energy. He could not be said to have possessed brilliant parts — he was not an orator — he had none of that broad grasp of intellect with which men who lack industry often supply their deficiencies.

But he had a mind of singular force, and his industry was both methodical and persistent. He was one of the first politicians of his day. He appreciated public sentiment and knew how to guide it, when it could be guided, to evade it or to follow it when it could not be guided. As president his administration was perhaps the most brilliant before the war. The very order of mind which rendered it impossible for him to inaugurate any of the great questions and lines of public policy to the solution of which were called the ablest diplomatic talents of the day, rendered it possible for him to select fit instruments for the accomplishment of the works whose importance he fully appreciated. In state history he deserves a credit which has never been fully accorded him. He was the first great "stump speaker." He taught the art, not of popular oratory, for he was not an orator, not merely of a thorough discussion of public questions, but the art of popular debate. Polk was always full of his subject, ready at retort, sophistical, quick to capture and turn the guns of his enemy against him, adroit in avoiding an issue whose result must be unfavorable, thoroughly equipped with forcible illustrations, humorous anecdotes, and a ridicule which ranged through all the changes from burlesque to wit. After the canvass of 1839, which brought into play upon a broader field the powers which Polk had long utilized and which kept him in Congress fourteen years, " stump speaking " became a distinct political accomplishment, which some of the most brilliant orators, Clay for instance, never possessed; which, on the contrary, some of the politicians of third rate power, Governor McNutt of Mississippi for instance, possessed in an eminent degree. But Polk taught the art.

> "Most can raise the flowers now,
> For all have got the seed."

In politics he was something more than a friend of Jackson — he was his follower. Jackson tolerated no independence, and Polk avoided any clash of judgment with assiduous caution. In 1836 the State of Tennessee was overwhelmingly for White. The most prominent Democrats in the State were White, Bell, Grundy, Polk, Johnson, and Catron. Bell alone had the sturdy determination to sustain White, and even his courage was strengthened by the known prejudice of Jackson. Grundy, Polk, and Johnson all intended at first to support White. They had given evasive answers to the invitation of the Tennessee delegation to attend the meeting of December 19; so evasive that they had been reckoned among those friendly to White. But an interview with Jackson at once changed their attitude. They declared they were for White in case White was nominated by the convention. Very shortly after this, Jackson wrote the first Gwin letter suggesting a convention, and very shortly after this the convention nominated Van Buren, as men with less foresight and political sagacity than these three had foreseen. Jointly with Jackson, they did as much to defeat White as they could without danger to themselves. They were ably assisted at home by John Catron. These were the four great pillars of that phase of Jacksonism which involved political management.

Catron was perhaps the ablest of the four. He was certainly more sprightly and agile. He was a self-educated lawyer who had been placed on the supreme bench of Tennessee. But he was uncouth, full of eccentricities, and overbearing. He says of himself as a lawyer: "I got on very well but often with an arrogance that would have done credit to Castlereagh." In a judge this arrogance was offensive and vicious. The greatest incident evil of the many advantages which flow from civilized government is the insolence of office, and Shakespeare's phrase fitted Catron well. He was very unpopular and when last a candidate was defeated. But he was an unswerving Jackson man. In 1829 he wrote a series of brilliant and plausible letters against a United States Bank, which were extensively copied, and which were not without their effect in Jackson's "war on Biddle's Bank." He pursued White with all the malignancy and force of his rugged wit and crushing satire. He had his reward. Of the four pillars of Jackson in Tennessee, it is worthy of note that Grundy and Johnson both became cabinet officers, Polk became president, and that Catron became a United States supreme judge.

In 1839 the controversy was for the first time between the Whigs and the Democrats. The latter granted consistency to the old Whigs, but denounced the "New Whigs," such as Bell and Foster, with as much bitterness as the Republicans of the present time denounce the so-called mugwumps. In our day we have seen the additional vigor with which an October election is conducted in a presidential year in a doubtful State. It was understood that the election in 1839 in Tennessee was to be the first skirmish of the presidential battle of 1840. Tennessee was a doubtful State. The Democrats selected the man of all others best fitted to carry it — a selection concurred in by Jackson and Van Buren. Prentiss, the brilliant Mississippian, refused to concur in the vote of thanks at the close of Polk's term as speaker on the ground that this would be used for political purposes in the approaching struggle in Tennessee. Newton Cannon was accepted by the Whigs and came forward as a Whig candidate, the first in the history of the State. He attacked Polk for his course in 1836 and as being supported by federal patronage. Jackson he denounced as a despot. But the advantage was all on the side of Polk. Cannon had rather a slow, ponderous delivery, not adapted to the new tactics of his opponent. Polk was Napoleon in the Italian campaign, and Cannon closely resembled the Austrian generals. The Democrats had a compact organization, and "the hurrah boys," a phrase which came into vogue during this canvass, were all for Polk. He had a definite line of policy, and he was for Martin Van Buren for president. Cannon still hoped to receive the votes of many Democrats who would be alienated by an outspoken preference for Clay, although White openly announced that as between Van Buren and Clay he would vote for the latter. Polk ridiculed Cannon for his indecision in announcing his preference for president. White's pronounced opposition to the sub-treasury scheme hampered Cannon in his efforts to win lukewarm Democrats. He was also accused of having neglected the interests of the Tennessee Volunteers who had taken part in the Florida War.

A notable addition to the Democratic party was the advent of Jeremiah George Harris upon the field of Tennessee journalism. The "Union," heretofore a small weekly, was enlarged and issued three times a week. Harris came from New England, New Bedford, where he had edited the New Bedford (Mass.) "Gazette," which had been strongly tinctured with abolition sentiments. Having charged Bell with leaning towards the abolitionists, the most fatal of political heresies at that time, the "Nashville Banner" procured files of Harris's paper and published extracts strongly squinting towards abolitionism. But Harris was a born fighter. Having been brought to Tennessee for the purpose of fighting the battle of Democracy, he was often called "Dugald Dalghetty." He had learned from George D. Prentice the art of writing pungent paragraphs that stung and irritated. He dealt largely in personal abuse and ridicule. Let those who accuse the present stage of journalism of being characterized by vituperation, read the files of the Tennessee papers from 1839 to 1860. The "Union" was for many years the leading Democratic newspaper in the Southwest. Harris was a terse, vigorous, rough writer, and wielding the party whip, he could lash the Democrats into a phrenzied fury. He seemed utterly impervious to even the most scurrilous assailants. He had a cut of an eagle with wings widespread which he was in the habit of putting at the head of any issue of the "Union," containing news of a Democratic victory. Judge Guild has preserved an amusing story about this eagle, told him by Felix Grundy. News was expected of an election in an adjoining State. While the mail at Murfreesboro was being assorted, a leading Whig, peeping through a window, exclaimed: "It's all over; there is Harris's infernal buzzard in the mail."

Polk opened the campaign on his side by an address to the people of Tennessee, perhaps the ablest political document which appeared in this State up to the time of the war. This was the beginning of the custom, which was subsequently carried to great length, of discussing national questions in local elections. Polk defended this procedure on the ground that the objections urged against his election were based on difference of opinion on national questions.[1] In this address, he reviews the course of the Whig leaders, deduces their origin from the Federalists, and defends those who had refused to support White, accusing his supporters of a desire to overthrow Jackson in Tennessee. This address caused a great stir among the Whigs. Bell, especially, denounced it bitterly, saying it was "a tissue of the foulest calumnies and falsehoods he had ever seen published since the sun shone in the heavens." It had a powerful effect on the people. On the stump Polk completely demolished Cannon. He ridiculed him so effectively that Cannon abandoned the joint debate on the score of a press of official duties, but was compelled by party friends to resume. Polk was elected by a majority of 3,000 votes, and the Democrats had a safe majority in the legislature. The breach between the faction of the Democratic party which had

[1] In 1839, after Polk's election, a committee on federal relations was raised by the General Assembly.

refused to support White and that faction which had supported him, was widened and rendered impassable by the course of the Democrats in the legislature who instructed White and Foster, the successor of Grundy, to vote for the Sub-Treasury Bill and other measures favored by Van Buren's administration, in order to drive them from the Senate. In this they were successful and both resigned.

CHAPTER XXXV.

THE FIRST WHIG VICTORY.

The issue of the "Republican Banner" announcing the result of the election of 1839 called for increased exertions and a more thorough organization among the Whigs to rescue the State from giving its vote to Martin Van Buren and his odious administration. "Let the din of preparation be heard throughout the Whig ranks in Middle Tennessee." On the 25th of October a great Whig dinner was given at Island Springs, just below Nashville. Bell made an elaborate speech, cheering the Whigs and denouncing Polk's address. Clay was invited to visit Nashville. The Whig party was now thoroughly rooted in Tennessee soil. An illiberal party management and a despotic use of party power had, in five years, made doubtful a State which had been regarded as the focus of democracy.

The Whigs were desperately in earnest. Whilst their opponents were still rejoicing over their victory, the Whigs were making preparations for the most marvelous political contest which had ever taken place in the Southwest. Through one of those queer revulsions by which nature endeavors to equalize the forces of the world, a revolution took place in the relative position of the parties. The Whigs now had all the advantages of discipline and earnest determination which came from the loss of a skirmish preceding a great decisive battle. The election of 1839 was the Quatre-Bras of the Waterloo of

1840. The enthusiasm grew from day to day. Whigs meeting each other in the streets spoke of the next ensuing election as if their personal fortunes and the fate of the Union depended upon the result. The Whigs drew hope from a comparison of the votes cast in 1837 and 1839. Cannon, the first year, received 52,660, the second, 52,899. Armstrong in 1837, 32,695 and Polk in 1839, 52,899. Thus Polk had been elected by an increase from votes which had been wanting at the polls in 1837, but had not gained by accessions from the Whigs.

The enthusiasm with which the Whigs went to work alarmed and terrified the Democrats. The Whigs of Davidson County met on the 7th of September for organization, and county after county followed this example until the whole State had been put in the condition of an army or of a secret organization. The Democrats accused them of having secret conclaves, grips, and passwords. The "Union" denounced their organizations and committees as "new and strange fermentations in the body politic to be put down by all lovers of peace and social order."

The Whig National Convention met at Harrisburg on the 4th of December, 1839. The Whigs of Tennessee, whose origin dated from the opposition to the convention that nominated Van Buren, refused to send delegates. Harrison was nominated, and for a moment the Whigs of Tennessee whose hearts were set on Clay threatened to rebel. But the tide of popular feeling was running high, and soon all resistance gave way and "Tippecanoe and Tyler too" were taken up with a rush. The Whigs in 1840 advanced no general principles upon which they proposed to administer the government, but relied upon attacks on the party in power, upon phrases and catchwords, upon emblems and monster processions, upon ridicule of Van Buren and glorification of Harrison, upon brilliant speeches and imposing spectacles. Every party to be successful should have a plan of action as well as a plan of attack. The Whigs of 1840 had but the second, and though successful, they crumbled to pieces.

In February, 1840, a monster demonstration at Columbus, Ohio, suggested the plan of campaign. This was followed by the Young Men's Convention at Baltimore on May 5, which, we are told by a chronicler of the day in words of overpowering eloquence, was "all the imagination could conceive of beauty, grandeur, and sublimity." The very next day, at the same place, the Democratic Convention, of which Governor William Carroll was chairman, met and nominated Van Buren, but made no nomination for vice-president, to the sincere regret of the Whigs in Tennessee, who expected it would be Polk and who hoped to defeat him. The Democrats, who saw little to attack, at first imagined they would have little difficulty in overthrowing the Whigs. But it was Don Quixote's charge upon the wind-mill. In May a Whig festival was held at Clarksville. There were parades of military companies, and a procession in which a log-cabin drawn by four horses figured. A live coon was on the top of the cabin. These were the emblems of the Whig candidate. Some Democrat had spoken of Harrison as an old Hoosier who might get along very well as a clerk whose ambition would be satisfied with a log-cabin and a barrel of hard cider. These were unlucky phrases for the Democrats. The Whigs at once adopted them as battle-cries. Governor William Carroll made a speech in which he belittled Harrison's military ability. This was violently denounced at a meeting held at Tippecanoe where about 20,000 people were present. Tippecanoe clubs were formed in all parts of the country, and in June a delegation of Indiana Whigs came to Tennessee to present the Nashville Tippecanoe Club with an Indian canoe, a cage containing a coon, and other Whiggish emblems. The day of their arrival, a log-cabin had been put up on Market Street, built by the personal exertions of Bell and other prominent Whigs. The "Banner," describing it, quoted the refrain of an old negro song: —

> "Pussum up a gum-tree
> Cooney in the hollow."

Harris of the "Union" replied in three stanzas of doggerel which were among the briskest and raciest songs of the campaign: —

> "Whiggies to the rescue,
> Cooney in a cage,
> Go it with a rush, boys,
> Go it with a rage.

> "Mum is the word, boys,
> Brag is the game;
> Cooney is the emblem
> Of Old Tip's fame.

> "Go it, then, for cooney,
> Cooney in a cage;
> Go it with a rush, boys,
> Go it with a rage."

It is characteristic of this contest that the Whigs seized at once upon lines which were written in derisive ridicule and made a campaign song of them. In May came the news that the Harrison men had carried Virginia and various other States, and the Whigs, as they passed the office of the "Union," yelled to the editor to "fetch out the buzzard." Jackson was again dragged into the struggle, but in vain. He wrote a letter indorsing Van Buren and speaking of Harrison as the "representative of Federalistic principles in the present contest." But this shibboleth was no longer potent. He, Governor Polk and Adam Huntsman, who had defeated Crockett for Congress, visited Lexington, Tennessee. When Jackson arose next morning, he saw near the inn a "liberty pole," from which a Harrison and Tyler flag was flying. Both he and Polk made speeches. Polk, who, without making a regular canvass, neglected no opportunity of speaking for Van Buren, was presented by the grand jury of Sevier County as a nuisance. Both parties had their ablest men forward, but the Whigs outshone their rivals. White, who had agreed to support Harrison, was put on the Whig electoral ticket but died. Bell met A. O. P. Nicholson in East Tennessee. Foster, smarting under his recent resignation, canvassed the State from end to end, " from Carter to Shelby," a phrase which was first applied to Polk's canvass against Cannon. Wherever Foster went, he was received with unbounded enthusiasm, being frequently met by processions and greeted by ringing of bells and the huzzas of the people.

Among the most startling events of this year was the defection of Eaton, the intimate friend and adviser of Jackson, from the Van Buren cause. When he announced his intention of supporting Harrison, a change which he justified on the score that he had seen the disastrous results of a hard money system in Spain, to which country Jackson had sent him as minister in 1836, there was a burst of indignation among the Democrats, and it was openly predicted that Jackson would refuse to receive him. In a speech delivered just before the election, in which he made an earnest appeal for Harrison and the Whigs, he said " he had heard it intimated that General Jackson would not recognize him as a friend on his return to Nashville," but that their meeting had been as cordial as at any time before.

The most notable political event of this anomalous contest was the Whig Convention held at Nashville on the 17th of August, 1840. It was first suggested at a Whig Convention at Little Rock, and was originally designed to embrace merely the new, or the Western and Southern States. The idea was accepted and swept like a fire from place to place, until it was universally adopted and the day selected. The Whigs of Muskingum County, Ohio, made an enormous ball painted in variegated colors, and covered with mottoes among which was one that had become a battle-cry for the Whigs, "Keep the ball rolling." This was sent to Nashville and arrived just preceding the time for the assembling of the convention. On the 12th of August, the "Nashville Whig" formally announced that Henry Clay himself would be present, and fears were entertained that the crowd would be larger than could be accommodated. The procession was to form at seven o'clock on Market Street and march to Walnut Grove. Marshals were appointed to keep order. They were to be mounted and were to wear black hats, blue silk sashes with rosettes on the shoulder, and were to carry white batons. The day was clear. Not a cloud was in the sky, and the sun rose resplendent. It was such a pageant as had never been seen in the Southwest before, as has been seen but once since then, — four years later, when a distinguished Tennessean was to experience the humiliation of seeing one more gorgeous assemble for the purpose of doing honor to a rival candidate for the presidency. Fourteen States had each a general state banner, and indeed the immense throng fluttered with banners of all sizes and kinds and colors, generally of satin. Conspicuous in the parade were the "Straightouts," a military company of Tennessee, dressed in dark blue hunting shirts, trimmed with white coon-skin caps and copperas breeches, suggestive of the early pioneer life with which the fame of General Harrison was intimately connected. They bore three banners. The first was of plain white upon which was the motto, "One Presidential Term and Fair Wages for Labor." The second represented an eagle with wings outspread, bearing in its talons the words, "Harrison and Reform," and underneath, "In Hoc Signo Vinces." The third was of blue muslin on which was a game-cock with the inscription, "A loud crow Chapman," in allusion to the phrase of "Crow, Chapman, Crow," one of those senseless absurdities in which the political phraseology of that day is peculiarly rich. The "Straightouts" were followed by a general committee on arrangements. Next came the Arkansas delegation whose banner bore David Crockett's immortal saying, "Be sure you are right, then go ahead." The Missouri banner represented a buffalo "roused to the claims of an early friend," in reference to Harrison's course during the contest over the admission of Missouri to the Union. Madison County, Alabama, in which party feeling ran unusually high, sent a large delegation and a banner on which was a fanciful design, representing the Goddess of Liberty hovering over "Old Tip's Cabin," and underneath the significant phrase, "Day is Dawning," in allusion to recent Whig gains in Alabama, which then as now was overwhelmingly Democratic. Illinois and Mississippi both sent large state satin banners. The banner of Indiana, which had just given an enormous Whig majority, displayed a huge ball on which were the words, "The Ball in Motion. Indiana 10,000 Majority." Ohio displayed an eagle, bearing in its talons "For President, the Farmer of North Bend." Kentucky, the State of the founder of the Whig party, who was to be orator of the day and who excited as much wildness of enthusiasm in Tennessee as in his own State, was largely represented. In addition to two richly uniformed and caparisoned military companies, many counties were represented by large delegations. The banner of one county represented "Little Matty" flying from the White House, another, a portrait of Harrison. New York showed a pair of scales, with Van Buren going up on one side and Harrison coming down on the other, with the motto, "Weighed in the Balance and Found Wanting." New England's device was,—

> "From hill and from valley
> From mountain and glen,
> We come to the rescue
> Of our country again."

Pennsylvania represented a fox following a lion — Jackson was the lion. Tennessee, of course, formed much the largest part of the procession. The chief banner represented on a blue ground a stately "Seventy-four" under full rig, pointed towards the White House and Capitol, which was seen dimly in the distance. The state banner, which was satin fringed with crape, displayed a device representing the tomb of the great Tennessean, recently deceased, around whose memory clung the same atmosphere of unruffled serenity which distinguished him living, and whose unbending and exalted independence of character had opened the way in Tennessee for the party which was proud to number his name among those which had made it illustrious. The great Ball from Ohio was there, elevated upon wheels, and beside it strode the oak-like figure of Porter, the Kentucky giant.[1] The rear was brought up by numerous county delegations from Tennessee and Kentucky. Robertson County, Tennessee, sent an immense painted canoe on wheels. Maury County, in which Polk lived, sent as an ominous threat, a likeness of Hugh L. White, and the noble lines in which he resigned his place in the Senate.

The procession began to move at ten and arrived at the grove about twelve. E. H. Foster was elected chairman, and vice presidents were appointed from eleven States. Foster made the opening address, and almost before he closed cheers and shouts began to rise in stormy succession until the air trembled with the noisy clamor. On the stand beside Foster sat a tall, spare figure, with a face whose features, far from symmetrical, have been rendered almost as familiar to us as to our fathers. Whatever may have been the measure of his statesmanship or the excellence of his celebrated American system, there was certainly no doubt about the splendor of his fame, the vigor of his intellect, the gentleness and sweetness of his char-

[1] He was said to be eight feet tall.

acter, the magnificence of his oratory, the importance of his services to the party which he had founded, or the nobility of ambition which had cemented it for this contest by his generous self-sacrifice. When he arose, the audience, as if electrified, arose with him. The applause rose and swelled like the roar of the waters at Niagara. Hats were thrown in the air. Men acted as if possessed, some of them embracing each other as in transports of rapture, others with tears in their eyes choking with emotion. In those days the fever of political frenzy had spread even to the women and many were present. They were as ungovernable in their emotions as the sterner sex, and several fainted, overcome by an excess of zeal and enthusiasm. Clay stood for a moment and gazed with kindling eye upon the frantic spectacle. Then he lifted one hand, and in a little while the silence was so deep that the crying of a child on the outskirts of the crowd could be heard by all who were present. Clay's speech was neither very brilliant nor very profound, but it was suited to the occasion. It was a ringing denunciation of the abuses which had crept into the government under the administration of the "military chieftain" whose rugged impetuosity had so often borne down his own finer and more elastic talents. It was full of alarums and drum-beats to victory and the blare of trumpets. On the whole, perhaps, it was a little more dignified, a little more thoughtful than the type of heated iron and hissing water which elected Harrison and accomplished what the Whigs vaingloriously declared "was the greatest moral revolution of the age." After Clay, on this and succeeding days, came J. J. Crittenden of Kentucky, Balie Peyton, the knight-errant of Tennessee politics, and others, men of greater or less brilliancy, whose reputations still remain as traditions only — traditions which are but the beads and wrought flowers upon the skirts of history.

After this convention the Democrats began to lose heart. Their last effort was a trick, a shallow, disgraceful trick, such a trick as the censorious are fond of declaring a disgrace to the political life of this day. It is not without comfort to us to reflect that an accurate knowledge of our forefathers reveals to us the same errors of unreasoning passion and unjust prejudice in their methods of thought and action which we deplore in ourselves in anticipation of the verdict of our children.

General Harrison made several speeches in Ohio during the few months immediately preceding the election. In one of these he said the people had an inalienable right to petition for redress of grievances, even for the abolition of slavery, if they regarded that an evil. He was at once denounced as being an Abolitionist, a charge which was daily repeated in Democratic journals. During the latter days of October, the "Nashville Whig" gave notice to the Whigs that some treachery was designed and to be on their guard. On the 2d of November the treachery was made apparent. Handbills were scattered broadcast containing a letter of Harrison's to Arthur Tappan, the undaunted fanatic, declaring himself an Abolitionist. If this had been true, Harrison would have lost Tennessee and every Southern State. The "Union" at once issued an extra edition containing the letter. But the "Whig" was not less enterprising than the Democratic organ, and it appeared the same day in flaming headlines publishing a letter of denial by General Harrison. Van Buren received 48,289 votes; Harrison, 60,391. It was said there was not a sober Whig in Tennessee the day the result was announced. The "Straightouts," in high glee, went to the lodgings of the editor of the "Union," gave "Three cheers for Jeremiah George," and called on him to show himself. Harris came forward and good-humoredly "acknowledged the corn." The crowd cheered him again and left. The asperities of political warfare were moderating since the time when a mountaineer with hard knuckles and a big fist made it a rule "to lick on the spot any man that said he did n't vote for Hugh White."

CHAPTER XXXVI.

POLK AND JONES IN 1841.

A STRIKING characteristic of the politicians of that day was their stoutness of heart, and the din and tumult of 1840 had not died away before the Democrats began preparations for 1841. On the 10th of December, 1840, Dr. Felix Robertson distributed a circular in which he suggested the plan of an organization for the following year. Five men were to be appointed a corresponding committee in each county, and these were to select three Democrats in each civil district to distribute documents and get voters to go to the polls. The Whigs were not less alert. An old Whig still living [1] has described the thoroughness of the Whig organization during the three years, 1841, 1843, and 1844, as surpassing anything ever before witnessed in the Southwest. Not only were the ordinary committees appointed, but each civil district was placed under a kind of political martial law. Those voters who were unalterably attached to the Democratic or the Whig parties were polled. Those who were doubtful were turned over to some Whig friend or neighbor to be persuaded, wheedled, and argued into voting the Whig ticket. All who were halt, maim, or blind were each assigned to some individual whose duty it was to procure a vehicle and bring them to the polls. Tennessee had now become and for many years remained as prominent in the politics of that day as New York in the politics of our day. Jackson's residence in the State, and the fact that

[1] Colonel Sam Tate.

the Whigs had carried it over his opposition made it conspicuous as a battlefield. Nashville, through the various conventions which met there, became a gathering place for the Southwest. Here were arranged many of the plans of campaign, and here often were concocted the schemes and plots by which shrewd and subtle managers controlled the actions of their parties. From Tennessee came some of the ablest leaders among the Whigs and Democrats of the United States. From now until 1850 the biographies of the candidates for the governorship appeared in all political papers and their utterances were quoted. The messages of the governors were generally reprinted in full in the Eastern papers.

The contest between Polk and Jones in 1841 was followed with keen interest by the Democrats, who hoped to find some indication of the " sober second thought of the people " asserting itself after the frenzy of 1841, and by the Whigs to see if their hold upon popular favor gave promise of being permanent. The contest of 1843 was conspicuous as preceding 1844. The canvass of 1841 turned chiefly upon national issues. This was now and long continued a matter of course. James K. Polk was the Democratic candidate, and James C. Jones was the Whig candidate. The leading question was of course the bank. The Independent Treasury scheme had at last become a law in 1840, but was promptly repealed in 1841, and the rest of the session was spent in vain endeavors to establish a National or Fiscal Bank of the United States. Polk favored the reëstablishment of the Sub-Treasury System and Jones a National Bank. He twitted Polk with a change upon this subject which was more apparent than real. In so far as the abstract question of a National Bank was concerned, neither party in Tennessee had what is called a straight record. Clay had opposed this measure in 1811, and Grundy had favored it in 1814. The petition for a branch at Nashville which was signed by William Carroll, John C. McLemore, and other leading Democrats was used by the Whigs in this as in other campaigns. Indeed, the Democrats were somewhat hampered by a diversity of opinion within their own ranks upon the question of a bank. There was a small but very determined body of voters who acted with the Democrats on all other questions, but who had been converted to the National Bank idea. The leadership of the party at once "read them out of the party." In vain they called attention to Madison's and Jackson's earlier record. The party organs insisted upon their "going where they belonged," into the ranks of the Whigs.

The "Knoxville Argus" was one of the Democratic organs. It denounced bank Democrats as Federalists. "The 'Post' says we are reading 'Bank Democrats' out of the party," declared the "Argus." "We are doing no such thing, for bank men, whether they call themselves Democrats or not, are not in the party. Their only appropriate place is in the federal ranks. We will have nothing to do with them — we will hold with them no political communion."

On the other hand, the position of the Whigs upon the tariff was uncertain and indirect. Indeed, it was not till this canvass that the Whigs came out boldly for even a moderate degree of protection. Even so late as 1839 Ephraim H. Foster denounced the protective tariff system as one "that steals from unconscious purses." Bell had said in 1832, "It is scarcely necessary to say that I regard what is called the American system, the great idol of the majority, as the direct and baleful cause of the present distracted condition of the country." It was not till the forties that the Tennessee Whigs became protectionists, and even then they rarely went beyond the doctrines of Jackson's Coleman letter, and Polk's Kane letter. Gentry was the only Whig who voted for the tariff of 1842. The Democrats were not without flaws in their party record. The Whigs were a protective party with occasional free-trade utterances, and the Democrats were a free-trade party with occasional protective utterances. When a small amount of revenue was to be raised, the Whigs favored a protective rate. When a large amount of revenue was to be raised the Democrats favored a protective rate with discriminations within certain broad landmarks. In Tennessee the bulk of the people were opposed to high duties, and this compelled the Whigs to handle this subject with extreme caution.

Upon the subject of internal improvements the Whigs generally had the advantage. Jefferson, Jackson, and Polk himself had at some time or in some measure squinted at a system of internal improvements at the expense of the general government. Boasting of his consistency, Polk said: "I challenge the newspaper press of the State to pick out the act — the single act upon which I have changed my principles." Jones called attention to the fact that when a member of the General Assembly of Tennessee, he had, in a report on internal improvements, referred to the "propriety of such works being constructed by the State or general government." Again in a circular dated the 10th of May, 1825, he said: "A judicious system of internal improvements, within the powers delegated to the general government, I therefore approve." When twitted by Jones concerning these things, he evaded it by saying that if such things were necessarily to be, he favored Tennessee getting its share.

The White-Van Buren-Jackson contest of 1836 was discussed in detail again, and this led to a discussion of the origin of the Whig party. Polk made a searching and skillful argument proving that the Whigs were Federalists with but a change of name. He reviewed at length the bargain, intrigue, and corruption charge of 1824, and paid exalted tribute to the public services and private character of General Jackson. The only question of state policy drawn into the canvass was the "Sterling Bond" charge upon which Jones based a demagogic appeal to the prejudices of the people. After the State Bank was chartered, Polk as governor suggested that the interest on a certain number of the bonds to be issued for that enterprise should be payable in pounds, shillings, and pence in order to negotiate them abroad, as Jones said, "to sell them like sheep in the market." The suggestion was practical and sensible. It strains our credulity to know that upon this ground Jones attacked, and in a great measure successfully attacked, Polk's patriotism. The Democrats, in order to offset the prejudice flowing from this preposterous affair, made a counter-charge to this effect, that Jones in 1839, when a candidate for the state legislature, had advocated the same idea, and, out-Heroding Herod, gave as a reason for this that he had just sold his farm and expected to be paid in state bonds. The falsity of this charge was clearly proven. The Whigs were also charged with having condoned the defalcation of Robert H. McEwen, the superintendent of public instruction. Jones accused Polk of using the patronage of the State Bank, and Polk accused Jones of being supported by the private banks, who hoped to break down the state banks.

But the election in 1841 turned upon other things than questions of public policy. It was in a large measure a revival and a continuation of the preceding year. The Whigs found a candidate peculiarly adapted to their needs. Immediately after their great success in 1840, the fruits of victory were taken from them by the death of Harrison and the refusal of Tyler to act in harmony with the party to which he owed his election. The approaching dissensions were not yet apparent when Jones was nominated. Still in the national party they grew and increased in bitterness during the canvass in Tennessee. It was due to the Whig candidate that the spirits of the

Whigs were not chilled by adversity, disappointment, and deferred hope. This candidate was James C. Jones, or as he is popularly called, even to this day, Jimmy Jones. When nominated, the Democrats ridiculed him as a man of yesterday "unknown to fame." Jones had all the attributes and all the antecedents of a popular hero. He was born in 1809, in Davidson County, near the Wilson County line, and almost within sight of the Hermitage. He was a delicate child, and being compelled to leave school on this account, he turned his attention to farming. Plowing and the hard work of a farm restored his health and replenished his stores. He married at an early age. As a married man he was as striking a contrast to Polk in this as in other things. Polk had no children at all, Jones welcomed a new one nearly every year. He took no part in politics until 1839, when he was elected a member of the legislature from Wilson County. As a member of this body, he gained neither applause nor blame. The ardency of his Whig sentiments was soon established, for even as a candidate for the General Assembly he advocated the nomination of Clay by the Whigs for the presidency. The first time attention was drawn to him as a public speaker was in January, 1840, at Nashville, where a large meeting of Whigs assembled to ratify the nomination of Harrison. In 1840 he was one of the Whig presidential electors, and within a week after his return from the legislature he began making speeches for Harrison and Tyler. His canvass gave him the reputation of being a strong, effective stump-speaker. "He can hold a crowd well in hand," it was said, "and handle his opponent with ease." The Whig Convention that met at Murfreesboro on the 5th of March, 1841, met with the knowledge of the fact that their nominee would be called on to face the ablest stump-speaker in the Southwest — perhaps in the United States. Some one must be found who could "stand up before Polk." As by inspiration, Jones was suggested and unanimously nominated. His task was before him. He was to "get after Polk." The Whigs, in speaking of Jones's nomination, frequently confessed that "Lean Jimmy was nominated to get after Polk, and he went straight for him." They canvassed the State twice, in 1841 and in 1843, and the excitement of the two contests is still a tradition among Tennesseans. Polk had laughed Cannon from the stump by anecdotes, by ridicule, by burlesquing his manner of speaking, by confusing his mind, by the most ingenious perversions of his views, aided by a thorough grasp of political questions and masterly discussion of current issues. He invented and perfected the art of stump-speaking, and like the Guillotine of fable, though not of history, he was among the first victims of the instrument his refined ingenuity had invented. Polk realized from the first the qualities of the candidate pitted against him. In making appointments there was evidently a desire if not an intention on his part to avoid joint discussions. But Jones met this by making every necessary sacrifice of pride in order to meet him.

Jones's personal appearance gave him an advantage on the stump. He was ungainly and very slender. He was six feet, two inches tall, and weighed only one hundred and twenty-five pounds. He walked with a precise military step, not unlike a soldier on parade. His complexion was swarthy, his nose was large, and his expression was grave and solemn. In more respects than one he bore a remarkable resemblance to Ned Brace in the "Georgia Scenes." His hair was thin and curly. His mouth was extraordinarily large. His eyes were small and gray, and were shaded by heavy eyebrows. But his address, which was cordial and kind, more than redeemed his personal appearance. He had a touch of pleasant deference which rendered him extremely popular with his female constituents. He lacked the personal dignity which made it difficult for Polk to unbend in the light badinage of flippant conversation. His popularity was very great. On the stump in 1841, he knew it would be impossible to attempt to answer Polk's speeches. He had a wide and fragmentary knowledge of men and measures, but nothing more. The Democrats said he had learned all he knew from "The Spirit of '76," a campaign paper published during the Harrison-Van Buren contest. He avoided all serious argument. But he had a genius for perverting and confounding words and terms, and would frequently harp on what he called a strange inconsistency of his worthy opponent, which resulted alone from his using the same word used by Polk and giving it a different significance. Polk had great powers of mimicry which he had used with unsparing pitilessness against Cannon. His imitations of Balie Peyton were especially effective. But against Jones his powers seemed to fail him. Jones was a master of all the arts of caricature and simulation. His impressive gravity, his powers of ridicule and travesty, his anecdotes told with irresistible humor, joined to his queer figure, his capacious mouth, and his large nose kept his audience in a state of perpetual uproar. People began to laugh the moment he arose. On one occasion, after Polk had made a long and elaborate argument upon the Whigs and Federalists, Jones arose and running one hand gently over a coon-skin which he held in the other, remarked, "Did you ever see such fine fur?" The effect of Polk's speech went up like chaff in a wind before the mocking laughter which recognized the reference to the Harrison campaign and the implied taunt. Occasionally after Polk's Federalist speech, Jones would assert that Ezekiel Polk, the grandfather of his competitor, was a Tory, and would then denounce the Tories in the bitterest terms, leaving his audience to imply that it came with a bad grace from a man with such antecedents to accuse other people of being Federalists. Polk would deny the truth of this assertion and would prove its falsity conclusively, but Jones, at the next appointment, would probably make the same statement and indulge in the same invectives. He was, on the stump, thoroughly unscrupulous. The most glaring falsehoods, when corrected at one place, would be reiterated at another. In this way Polk could never corner him. Polk at first tried his powers of ridicule upon Jones, but the latter never failed to turn the laugh on him. He did this, not by his wit, for in this Polk, though not a witty man, far excelled him, but by his comical expression. The most trivial phrases from Jones would call forth shouts of laughter, when remarks of ten times the humor and force from Polk would pass unregarded. One of Polk's anecdotes has been preserved. He said the desire of the Whigs for office reminded him of an incident in the late war. A Virginia regiment had come from a part of the State which raised very fine horses, and not wishing to endanger the lives of those which were valuable, the soldiers mounted themselves on old mares, the majority of which had young colts. Much time was lost through the necessity of having to stop to let the colts suckle. The colonel commandant, in order to save time, finally made it a routine duty to allow them to suckle all at one time. So when the hour came, he would give the command, " At-ten-tion Reg-i-ment! Halt! Pre-pare to suck-le colts!" The application was obvious, and there was much merriment and some blushing among the women, who in those days always attended "speaking." Jones retorted by saying that what the governor said was true — the Whigs were young colts. But that the governor himself was an old sucker who had been at it for fifteen years. The farmers in his section of country generally let a live, healthy colt be weaned by his dam, but that in the case of a scrubby, unpromising fellow, they generally weaned him about the first Thursday in August. (The day of election.)

After Polk had been unmercifully spurred and goaded, he repudiated his own methods and ridiculed Jones and his anecdotes. He himself, he said, tried to discuss great questions of state in a becoming and serious manner. His worthy opponent wisely made a jest of things which indeed were beyond his comprehension. In fact, he was better fitted for the tights and spangles and sawdust of the circus ring than for the gubernatorial office. Jones did not wince. But in replying he said that in fact both he and his opponent were best fitted for the ring. That for himself he could not deny that he was fitted for tights (here he touched his thin legs), but his worthy competitor was fitted for the little fellow that is dressed up in a red cap and jacket and who rides around on a pony. Polk's smile, which his scoffing contemporaries often called " a horrible grin," was one of the standing jests of his enemies. Jones's reference to the monkey was greeted with vociferous and long-continuing laughter and Polk was long known as "the little fellow on the pony."

Polk made several attempts to break loose from Jones, as Cannon had attempted to break loose from him, but Jones was as eager in 1841 as he had been in 1839. As the canvass progressed, Polk began to lose his temper, and to assail Jones both in the newspapers and on the stump, without, however, in any measure destroying the latter's equanimity. The boisterous cheers, the loud laughter, the huzzas with which the Democrats had followed the canvass of 1839 were now, such was Brownlow's boast, hushed into religious silence when their leader came to face the young farmer from Wilson County. Not only did Polk lose his temper. The Democrats generally became irritated and sore. When the meeting took place in Somerville, there were two partners in business, one a Democrat and one a Whig. They agreed that the Whig should stay at the store, and the Democrat should attend " speaking." He was to listen faithfully, and report impartially what he heard. He was naturally a man of good temper, and not easily angered. When he returned his partner noticed that he appeared flushed and angry. Being asked what Polk said, he answered fiercely, "Mr. Polk made an ass of himself, talking sense to a lot of d—d fools." And Jones? "Jones—Jones! I don't know what Jones said! No more does anybody else. I know this much. If I were Mr. Polk I would n't allow any one to make a laughing-stock of me. He ought to get a stick and crack Jones's skull, and end this tomfoolery!"[1]

As a matter of fact, all the enthusiasm, the dashing impetuosity, the fire, the shouting, and the cheering were with Jones. He had the "Hurrah boys" — the bonfire and the dress-parade element — the young men. The contestants spoke to the largest crowds that had ever assembled in Tennessee. In some counties the roads leading to the county seat where the candidates were to speak were so crowded with people on foot, in buggies, on horseback, and in wagons, that they resembled caravans of emigrants. It was noticed that Polk, before the speaking began, generally stood at some point near the speaker's stand with a few friends, speaking to such as came up to be introduced to him, while Jones was stalking through the crowd, poking fun at the boys, chucking the girls under the chin, flattering the women, and bantering the men.

Nashville was the centre of the political life of the State. Indeed, it was said that there was a Whig junto or clique in Nashville who controlled the party throughout the entire State. Bell and Foster and A. A. Hall were among the leaders of this junto, and the Democrats asserted that Jones owed his nomination to the subserviency with which he had bowed his neck to this yoke when a member of the General Assembly, and voted to retain the seat of government at Nashville. In spite of the jealousy of other parts of the State, it was, as a mat-

[1] Related by Colonel Sam Tate, who was the Whig in this anecdote.

ter of course, from Nashville that the strongest influences radiated, and it was before a Nashville audience that speakers most desired to shine. Polk and Jones met for the first time on the 30th of March at Big Spring, in Wilson County. They reached Nashville on the 19th of May. The partisan complexion of reports sent to partisan newspapers in those times was a subject of amazement to men of liberal minds and unprejudiced understandings. According to the "Union," Jones was a poor creature whose ignorance and coarse buffoonery were rendered more glaring by the brilliancy and statesmanlike profundity of Polk's classical orations. According to the "Whig," Polk's strength of mind and character had departed from him, as completely as if some Delilah-like influence had shorn him of his talents. It was an assured fact that the people of Tennessee would never let a man, such as Polk, be elected over the head of one who towered so high above him. It was significant, however, that the Whig papers occasionally went so far as to admit, in the high-flown style of the day, that it was a "battle of giants." From all of this, it was difficult for the Nashville people to form a moderately accurate estimate of the two champions, as they were often called. Party feeling ran high, and there was a feverish impatience to hear them.

When the time came, there was present an audience larger than that which had collected to ratify the nomination of Harrison. According to the terms of the discussion, each speaker had two and a half hours. The speaking began at 2.30 and continued until 7.30. It was a repetition of what had taken place before. Polk made a speech that would have swept from the stump any man who had ever been governor of Tennessee before him, and any man who was governor after Jones until Andrew Johnson came forward. It was forcible, comprehensive, powerful, vehement, almost eloquent. Bell, with his graceful purity of speech, his thorough political equipment, his rhetorical finish, his incisive analysis and philosophic amplification, might have answered it. Foster, the impassioned, the turgid, the alert, the lofty, might have answered it. The warm imagination and impetuous and dazzling rhetoric of Gus Henry might have sustained the contest on terms not altogether unequal. But James C. Jones, who scarcely possessed a single quality here attributed to these three, did what not one of the three could have done — he completely demolished the speaker. He had no wit, he had no fancy, he had no oratorical powers, he had no knowledge, he had no great qualities of mind, he lacked everything that the others had, but he had what the others lacked, a power of ridicule and mimicry never equaled in this State. It is said that the Greeks, fearing alone the attack of the elephants which accompanied the army of Darius, put them to flight by loud alarums and great tumult. Jones met Polk and routed him by the same tactics. He made the crowd laugh until it became frantic. He twisted and distorted everything that Polk had said until he, whose thoughts and words were so perverted, could not, for his life, have unraveled the maze of sophistry and nonsense. He turned serious arguments into jests, jests again into serious arguments. He discussed the spirit of an assertion or the actual letter of it, or he jumbled both together as suited his purpose. He held out hopes of Polk becoming a Whig. And why? Because he grinned like the little fur-covered animal that had been one of the emblems in the Harrison campaign. He told the most grotesque, the most ludicrous anecdotes with a mien of funereal gravity. When at a loss for something to say, he looked solemnly towards the audience, and then turned slowly and reproachfully towards his competitor, while the crowd burst into roars of laughter at the sight. The Democrats and Polk were mortified but not surprised, when the same party which had elected Harrison president, with cabins, coons, and cider, elected Jones governor with anecdotes, laughter, and waggery.

CHAPTER XXXVII.

POLK AND JONES IN 1843.

WHEN the General Assembly met in October, the two parties were very nearly evenly balanced. In the House, the Whigs had a majority of one, and there was one member who was not strictly a member of either party. In the Senate, the Whigs had twelve and the Democrats twelve. Samuel Turney was again a member, and held the balance of power. In 1839 he had been elected in a Whig community on purely non-partisan grounds. He was elected a member of the Senate on a compromise. At this session was enacted an episode which makes a curious chapter in the history of partisan politics. As a result of the instructions of 1839, White and Foster had resigned. In the encouraging eloquence of the "Whig," "Our noble Foster refused to drag the manacles at the wheels of a chance majority, while he knows his own beloved Tennessee has power to bid him mount on a triumphal chariot, and lead her people rejoicing with him up the steeps of honor and prosperity."

As the right of the General Assembly to instruct the Senators whom it elects has often been a subject of partisan disputation, it may be of interest to know that it was a right never seriously denied before the war. During this session of the legislature, the right of instruction was discussed, and both parties were agreed upon it. In a report made by the majority of the committee to whom were referred the resolutions of 1839, and who recommended their rescission, it was said that as to the right of the constituent to instruct the representative there was very little difference of opinion. "This power is essential to the very existence and perpetuity of a representative government." The minority report took the same position. White and Foster both resigned in 1839, being unable to vote for measures for which they had been instructed to vote. In 1838 Grundy voted against the Sub-Treasury system, although he favored it, in obedience to legislative instructions. In 1846 Spencer Jarnagin voted for the Walker tariff against his convictions but in obedience to instructions. In 1842 Foster refused to vote for the annexation of Texas, contrary to instructions, but defended his vote on the ground that whilst he favored annexation, he regarded the instructions as general, not requiring him to vote for any particular measure. He admitted the right of instruction.

There were two vacancies in the Senate, that of Alexander Anderson, elected to fill out White's term, and Grundy's unexpired term, to which A. O. P. Nicholson had been appointed. The prominent Whig candidates for the Senate were Spencer Jarnagin and E. H. Foster, who had been the Harrison electors for the State at large the year before. Then, as now, this was considered an onerous task worthy of substantial partisan recognition, when adequately performed. Foster was peculiarly objectionable to the Democrats because of his effective party work the year before, and because his general identification with White and his resignation rendered it especially galling to have him now returned to the Senate. It was charged that Jones had suggested the plan afterwards pursued by the Democrats for the guidance of the Whigs, in case they failed to elect a working majority. This was earnestly denied by Jones. The fact that Turney held the balance of power in the Senate suggested an obvious method of defeating Foster which was at once adopted. The Whig caucus nominated Foster and Jarnagin, and the Senate, with Samuel Turney's vote, elected his brother Hopkins L. Turney, at that time a member of Congress. The House refused to concur. The Senate refused to meet the House in joint convention until Turney received instructions from his constituency to vote to bring on an election of United States senators. The day appointed by joint resolution was December 2. On that day, Turney and the twelve Whigs repaired to the house, but the twelve Democrats remained in the senate chamber. Among the number was Andrew Johnson, who was apparently with Laughlin, the leader in this queer filibustering. When the roll of the Senate was called, the clerk reported "no quorum." The speaker sent the doorkeeper to request the absent members to attend the meeting of the joint convention. The House then proceeded to organize, in order, with the majority of the Senate, to proceed to business. About twenty Democratic members of the House at once left the hall. This scene was reënacted for four days, when Turney refused any longer to attend the meetings of the joint convention. On the eleventh of December the Democrats entered a protest against the methods pursued to elect a United States senator, as unconstitutional. Under the law, the election must be made by the legislature and not by convention, that is, it must be made by each body in its undivided capacity and in its own hall, not in joint meeting. Another ground of protest was the refusal of the two candidates elected in caucus to answer certain questions regarding their positions on certain public questions. More even than this, the Democrats had offered to compromise the matter by electing one Democrat and one Whig, each party to elect its own candidate but both to be from different geographical divisions. This proposition was "defeated by the votes of the exclusive Whigs, who have thus refused a measure calculated to produce reconciliation between the two great parties." The Democrat selected was of course H. L. Turney. This puerile proposition and others equally trivial were rejected by the Whigs. The Democrats who signed this protest fully realized the folly of it. There was no record of a United States senator ever having been elected by any other method than by the one proposed. Indeed, Johnson himself had been a member of the General Assembly in 1839 and 1840, and had concurred in previous proceedings of this nature. The other offer to compromise by electing one Whig and one Democrat (like various other propositions to resign and hold forthwith another election in order to get the opinion of the people) was not only imbecile and contemptible. It was a direct sacrifice of principle. Exactly the thing irrational in politics and impossible in a representative form of government is the reconciliation of opposing parties. The stability of republican institutions, as the purity of water, depends not upon stillness and quietude, but upon struggle and commotion. Other conditions are unnatural and of short duration as was the "Era of Good Feeling." The bulk of the people have little time for looking after their collective interests. The exercise of power without supervision leads to depravity and roguery. The organization of parties furnishes the people not only officers to perform necessary functions but also a large body of alert, vigilant, and self-interested inspectors and supervisors, who watch closely public affairs and promptly report any dereliction and delinquency. Andrew Johnson and his associates, who figure in state history as the "Immortal Thirteen," knew the extravagance and inanity of their propositions, but they expected to defeat the election of a Whig senator for the present, hoping to achieve a different result at the next election.

Nor did this stop here. Governor Jones, in accordance with the law, sent in a list of twelve directors of the State Bank early in the session. Two days before the adjournment, the Senate called up the nominations and rejected them. Jones sent in a new list the day of adjournment which met a similar fate. In this way, the Democrats then forming the board held over for two years more. A recommendation to investigate the condition of the bank was also voted down. An extra session was called in 1842, but without effecting any change of affairs.

These things Polk was compelled to face. In answer to what is known as the Memphis Interrogatories, he was forced to defend the "Immortal Thirteen." When in 1843 the second struggle between Polk and Jones came on, the Democrats entered it in the face of a whirlwind. It had often been charged that the old Bank of Tennessee was used to advance the interests of the Jackson party. The defalcation of Joel Parrish was pointed to as the result of this course, and Parrish himself was quoted as saying he would suffer his right arm to come off before he would divulge the secret workings of the bank. These charges had been repudiated by the people and proven false by actual occurrences. But they were now again revived with greater plausibility than before. "The address to the Republican party of Tennessee" of the 4th of July, 1840, had been signed by four directors of the new Bank of Tennessee, one of whom, Dr. Felix Robertson, was chairman of the Republican committee. The Whigs in 1843 bitterly denounced the management of the bank, and pointed significantly to the resolution passed at the extra session declaring an investigation inexpedient and useless. Brownlow, of the "Jonesboro Whig," poured forth a steady stream of vituperation, of terrible invective, of coarse ribaldry, and of sharp, biting sarcasm. The Whigs waged the war with more than wonted enthusiasm. Jones had not failed to profit by his previous campaign, by intermingling with the world, by contact with the leaders of the party. He had developed a talent for political management in recognition of which the Democratic papers had promoted him to the leadership of the Nashville Junto. His knowledge of public questions had broadened, his mind had become more liberalized, the tone of his discussion less flippant. But his unscrupulous ingenuity, his hardened equanimity, his powers of mimicry, of burlesque, of mockery, of farcical exaggeration, the grotesque solemnity of his features, the heavy eyebrows, the small eyes twinkling over the large nose, and the broad mouth still remained with him.

In addition to the issues which had arisen within the State, the two candidates fell to upon the same questions which had occupied them in 1841. The bankrupt law, however, which held then a secondary position, now came in for more extended discussion. The Whigs generally favored it, and the Democrats opposed it. It had been passed in 1841 and repealed in 1842. Polk in 1843, after its repeal, was very severe in his denunciation, and Jones ridiculed this by his celebrated " Lay on, Nancy " anecdote. It reminded him of a fellow — this was then, as now, the anecdote-teller's conventional form of introduction — whose cabin was attacked by a bear, there being no one there but a small child, his wife, and himself. The man ran up into the loft, and left his wife to contest the matter with the bear, which she did most gallantly. The fight took place in the yard close to the door. The husband in the loft watched the fight with intense interest, yelling, " Lay on, Nancy ! *Lay on*, Nancy ! Lay on, Nancy ! " After the bear was laid out, as dead as the bankrupt law, the fellow crawled down puffing and blowing, and going up to his wife said, " W-e-ll, Nancy, ain't we brave ? "

The canvass of 1843 was watched with deep and widespread interest throughout the United States, and in Tennessee bets as high as $3,000 were made between Whigs and Democrats. The " Frankfort Commonwealth " said that " should the Whigs, as we confidently anticipate, carry the election in Tennessee, we believe the result will be considered as decisive of the presidential election of 1844." The " National Forum " thought the contest in Tennessee would decide the complexion of the United States Senate, also "it is the first regularly contested battle of the campaign which is to decide who is to be the next president." Governor Jones in a letter to Prentiss said: "This is the battle-ground of the nation." The election of Jones was greeted by the Whigs throughout the Union with boundless enthusiasm. The Whigs of Philadelphia passed a vote of thanks to him, and the "Boston Atlas" suggested that a suitable gift as a memorial be presented to him by the Whigs of the United States. Various suggestions were made that he should be put on the ticket the year following for the vice-presidency. Another substantial result for the Whigs was the election of Jarnagin and Foster to the Senate.

CHAPTER XXXVIII.

THE GREAT WHIG CONVENTION OF 1844.

THE contest in 1844 was the first political struggle in Tennessee into which slavery entered as an issue, and it was the last in which the Whigs manifested that martial ardor which recalled the tempestuous shouts, the terrific charges, the bursting of shells, the flash of musketry, and the bristling of bayonets in actual warfare. The national Whigs entered the contest of 1844 inflamed with resentment against what they termed the treachery of Tyler, united, enthusiastic, and with a leader whose personal popularity, if we except Jackson and the elder Pitt, surpasses anything recorded in the history of constitutional governments. From the first his nomination was demanded so imperatively that he was nominated by acclamation when the Whig Convention met at Baltimore on May 1. The Whigs of Tennessee so far overcame the prejudices which the White campaign of 1836 had left behind, as to send delegates to join in the nomination. Theodore Frelinghuysen of New Jersey was put forward for vice-president and the country rang with the refrain: —

"Hurrah, hurrah, the country's risen,
For Henry Clay and Frelinghuysen."

The defeat of Van Buren in 1840 had exasperated the Democrats, and acting upon a suggestion originating with Benton, they determinated to nominate him in 1844. Buchanan and Calhoun withdrew, and when the year of conflict opened, it seemed apparent that Van Buren would have no serious opposition. In fact a majority of the delegates were instructed to vote for him. Negotiations had been in progress for some time looking to the annexation of Texas to the United States, and in April, 1844, President Tyler submitted a treaty for that purpose to the Senate. In a letter written from Raleigh, North Carolina, shortly before he was nominated, Clay took conservative grounds against annexation. This was followed shortly by a letter from Van Buren of similar significance. Andrew Jackson and the Tennessee Democrats were thunderstruck, and the former at once declared that Van Buren must "explain," which meant retract this. Delegates had already been appointed and instructed to vote for Van Buren. When this letter was made public, those from the Southern States refused to obey these instructions. Some resigned. In Tennessee the droll and whimsical Joseph C. Guild openly announced his determination under no circumstances to vote for Van Buren. The adoption of the two-thirds rule made it impossible for "the Sage of Kinderhook" to be nominated. On the eighth ballot James K. Polk of Tennessee received forty-four votes, and on the ninth he was nominated. George M. Dallas of Pennsylvania was nominated for the vice-presidency. Polk was known to be a pronounced advocate of annexation and a follower of Jackson. He was called "Young Hickory." The Whigs declared he had been nominated " to gild the evening of the days of the hero of the Hermitage." One of the Whig papers said gravely that the coons in the forest all grinned when they heard of Polk's nomination. Another quoted them as running through the woods singing, —

"Ha, ha, ha, what a nominee
Is Jimmy Polk of Tennessee."

In Tennessee his nomination was received with deep satisfaction by the Democrats, and by the Whigs with a desperate determination to pay off at last the score of the part taken by Polk in the defeat of White. When the Democratic orators pleaded for Polk on the score of state pride, the Whigs with telling effect asked where had been Polk's state pride in 1836? The "Union" at Nashville, with Jeremiah George Harris at its head, and the "Whig" at Jonesboro, with Brownlow at its head, were the most active, the most vituperative, the most impetuous papers in the State. The Democratic papers overflowed with ridicule of the campaign emblems of 1840, and attempted to turn them against their opponents by caricatures representing a coon in the act of being skinned by a Loco Foco, or on the ground being torn and rent asunder by Democratic dogs. They composed a campaign song, "The Coon is Dead," to which the Whigs responded by another, of which the refrain was,—

> "The Coon is dead. Ah, how mistaken!
> For you there's no such luck.
> You wish him dead, I doubt it not,
> But he lives in 'Old Kaintuck.'"

Brownlow sneered at the ridicule of the "Union." "When a Loco Foco, by the remission or apathy of the Whigs, slips into office, Democracy calls it 'the sober second thought of the people'; but when freemen, aroused as in 1840, assert their rights and turn 'rogues and royalists' out of office, they are said to be 'drunk on hard cider.'" The Democrats twitted the Whigs upon being divided among themselves, and renewed the old charges of bargain, intrigue, and corruption. It having been rumored that Jackson had finally conceded the falsity of this, he published a letter in May denying any recantation. The Whigs, in June, were absolutely confident of victory. They far surpassed the Democrats in talent and in oratory. Governor Jones, like Polk in 1840, without actually taking the stump, lost no opportunity of cheering on his political friends and exerting his influence for Clay. John Bell, whose enmity against Polk was fierce and unremitting, attacked him with unsparing denunciations, and with a closely woven tissue of argument, invective, and inference which no man but Polk himself could have answered. Gus Henry, whose name is one of the brightest of those who, in the Southwest, established a school of remarkably brilliant political oratory, and who was fresh from his remarkable struggle against Cave Johnson, won his first laurels on the broader field of state politics in this campaign. Tall, erect, and of a striking beauty of features, his personal appearance rendered him peculiarly adapted to the style of rhetorical brilliancy of speaking which dazzled the imagination of his audience and charmed them into forgetfulness of argument, research, and reason. In this year he gained the sobriquet of "Eagle Orator," a phrase not then worn threadbare. Neil S. Brown took the stump, and displayed those genial qualities of character and intellect which subsequently made him governor of the State. In West Tennessee the enthusiasm of the Whigs was aroused to the highest pitch by the wit and sarcasm and fiery invective and flowery perorations of William T. Haskell, the splendor of whose intellect had not yet been dimmed by disease. Such enthusiastic efforts had but once before been made in the political arena of Tennessee. From Memphis where, as a local Whig organ said, the Clay Club was glorious to look upon, to East Tennessee, where, as Foster said, "the mountains were on fire," it was a stirring time, in which parts were played by many men of brilliant talents. In the midst of the canvass an election for town magistrate was held in Columbia, Polk's home, and the Clay candidate was elected by a vote of 68 to 34, a fact which was not suffered to go unnoted by the Whigs. Each party organized clubs, renewed the organizations of previous elections, canvassed each district closely, and disseminated political literature with ceaseless energy.

In the discussion of public questions, the Democrats

again had decidedly the advantage. The rallying cry was Polk, Dallas, and Texas. The old issues were again prominent, the old charges were again ventilated, again hotly discussed, again stoutly maintained, and again fiercely controverted. The Whigs were thrown upon the defensive by Clay's position on the annexation of Texas. Over and above the question of slavery, Tennesseans were bound by too many ties to Texas to suffer them to be indifferent. Polk's position was pronounced and unequivocal. Clay had on one side the South, and on the other a small body of Abolitionists in the North. His first letters were designed to placate the latter. The Democrats in Tennessee and the South generally denounced him for courting the Abolitionists. The South was not in a mood to suffer any hesitation on this question, and on the 27th of July, 1844, he wrote from Ashland the celebrated letter which was published in a North Alabama paper. In this, without changing his position, he changes front. In the previous letter he had emphasized the imperative nature of certain antecedent conditions before annexation should take place. "I should be glad to see it, without dishonor, without war, with the common consent of the Union, and upon just and fair terms. I do not think that the subject of slavery ought to affect the question one way or the other." The Pythoness could not have uttered an oracle better adapted to the purpose for which it was designed. It succeeded in Tennessee, but the Abolitionists manifested their disapproval by nominating national candidates the following month. Clay's letter failed of its effect, in so far as the Abolitionists were concerned, but Polk's Kane letter, written on the 15th of June, was more successful and saved Pennsylvania to the Democracy.

In August both parties held at Nashville what were called in those days conventions or popular assemblies, designed to elicit expressions of party fervor. The Democrats held one on the 17th of August, called at the time the Polk, Dallas, and Texas Convention, the motive of which was to protest against the "Disunion of Texas" movement. The proceedings were deliberative and dignified. The Whig Convention had been called to meet on the 21st of August, or less than a week after the date appointed for the Democrats. This convention was the most elaborate in detail which had ever been held in the State of Tennessee. That of 1840 had been full of bright fantastical effects, queer sights, grotesque mixtures, gaudy colors, and beautiful images. But even then a large part of its success was due to the presence of Henry Clay. Then he was merely an illustrious Whig. Now he was again a candidate for the high office for which his long experience, his ripe statesmanship, his lofty intellect, and exalted character peculiarly fitted him in the eyes of the Whigs. This was to be held in the native State of his opponent. As Governor Jones said, "All eyes are now turned towards Tennessee." It was among the possibilities that the election might be decided in Tennessee. The Democrats appreciated the gravity of the situation, and in default of local talent, Lewis Cass, who had been defeated by Polk for the nomination, and who was a prospective candidate for the succession, gave both time and talents to the Democracy of the State. Thomas F. Marshall, the undisciplined and recalcitrant Kentuckian, threw the weight of his bright, wayward, and wasted genius in the scales for Polk.

The Whig Convention met on the 21st of August. Minute details of this picturesque pageant have been preserved in contemporary newspapers. The political processions of the present day, such as those which marched through the streets of New York in 1884 in honor of Mr. Cleveland and Mr. Blaine, are intended to impress the imagination of the beholders rather by the spectacle of a vast multitude aided at most by a few banners, and a transparency or two, than to tickle the fancy and dazzle the eye by bright colors and sumptuous display. But there was more abandonment, more enthusiasm, less self-consciousness in those days. "The Great Whig Convention of 1844," as it was long called, was the finest of the kind ever held in the Southwest. It was a tournament from the pages of Froissart, adapted to modern times and republican conditions. The romances of the Middle Ages spread before us tourney-fields upon which were assembled stately knights clad in glittering armor and mounted upon horses nobly caparisoned; heralds resplendent with coats upon which were embroidered in rich colors the arms of distinguished warriors; bevies of beautiful ladies in green silks and purple velvets, gayly decked with garlands of mingled roses and lilies; laughing pages, jovial friars, rubicund burgesses with pretty daughters in modest smocks, jesters in motley wear — in short, a throng of checkered hues, quaint costumes, unbridled merriment, dramatic pomp, glittering pageantry, fanciful ceremonies, and gaudy spangles, surpassing the tulip, the peacock, and the butterfly. The Great Whig Convention of 1844 had in some shape or distortion all of these things. They appeared in the guise of mounted guardsmen, immense bodies of men in costumes, the reds and whites and blues of the "Stars and Stripes," beautiful silken banners with curiously wrought devices, liberty-poles, coons, open carriages filled with the fresh-hued beauties who were the boast of Tennessee, troops of symmetrical and spirited horses, bands of music, speeches sparkling with rhetorical tinsel, lace work, and pearl brocade.

The procession formed on the Public Square, and moved out to Walnut Grove in a vast cavalcade of about six thousand people. The entire number of those present was estimated at between thirty and forty thousand. There were twenty-six open carriages in which were ladies who wore sashes of white and blue. Nearly every State in the Southwest was represented by a delegation. A prize banner had been offered to the county (outside of Davidson) which should send the largest delegation. It was made of rich, pink satin with a fawn-colored fringe, and upon it was painted a full-length portrait of Henry Clay, over whose head was suspended the American eagle, the stars and stripes falling in graceful folds on either side. This was awarded to Wilson County, the native county of the governor, whose life was spent in doing noble homage to the great Whig, and who, by a strange but fitting fatality, was the only friend not of his household that stood by his bedside as his restless spirit sank into eternal rest. The county seat of Wilson County is Lebanon, so named because of the cedars in its neighborhood, and the Wilson County delegation bore cedar boughs covered with checked cloth, and branches of cedar with the green upon them. A local chronicler comparing Polk to Macbeth, said he must have thought that "Birnam Wood had come to Dunsinane." Some of the banners had such devices as "Our Battle-Cry is Harry of the West." The banner of the "Coon-Rangers of Nubbin Ridge" displayed on one side Clay, on the other the "Same old Coon" tearing down a polkberry stock, saying, "Polkberries can't hurt this Coon." Henry County showed "Old Hal" mounted on a race-horse, just reaching the presidential goal, pursued at a long distance by "Little Jimmy" on a donkey. Among the Rutherford County delegation was a troop of little Whigs with a banner on which was the motto, "Oh how we do wish we could vote for Clay and Frelinghuysen." There was in another part, a body of pioneers weighing about two hundred pounds each, with battle-axes and large bear-skin caps. A cotton loom formed a part of the procession. This was mounted on a car drawn by six horses, each bearing a small postilion clothed in variegated colors. One banner displayed a significant motto: "Hemp Cravats for all Disunionists." All the emblems of 1840 were revived. There were great numbers of military companies as in the Harrison campaign — Clay Guards, Harrison Guards, Straightouts, Slashers. The coon, the barrel, the ball, the liberty-pole, the cabin, the grotesque caricatures, the derisive rhymes and mottoes, all were there.

Among the orators, in addition to those from Tennessee and those who have been entirely forgotten, were two figures whose names to this day have a legendary sound. One of these was Albert Pike, whose career had touched all the elements of romance and adventure that existed in the Southwest from the wild Indian tribes, into which he had been adopted and of which he was probably a chief, to the composition of verses which had found recognition and appreciation even so far away and from such high authority as "Blackwood's Magazine." As a lawyer he was one of the most brilliant of his day. Even in these times of advanced scholarship his learning is remarkable and admirable. In those days it was wonderful. Other American linguists may be more thorough, none are more versatile and comprehensive. Genial, warm-hearted, and refined, he has touched the lyre in every strain and has made it sound harmoniously in all. He has written one bit of fugitive lyricism which deserves to find a place in every anthology of English verse.[1] He is still living at Washington, one of the first officers in the masonic order in America, and if we except Joseph Holt, the keen-tongued and incisive lawyer who was in Buchanan's cabinet, Governor "Charlie" Anderson of Ohio, who is spending the sunset of a bright career in the beautiful and picturesque little village of Kutawa in Kentucky, and Harvey M. Watterson, the reminiscent Nestor, whose charming pen has restored the faded glories of the great epic period of Southwestern oratory and statesmanship, Albert Pike is the last survivor of that group of orators

[1] "After the midnight cometh morn."

and lawyers who gave a distinct character to both political and legal life in the Southwest before the war.

S. S. Prentiss was the other, a Mississippian, born and reared in New England, who possessed in an eminent degree all the characteristics which are popularly supposed to be peculiarly Southern. His character was high-minded, his pride was strong and disdainful, his courage was undoubted. Quick and impulsive, he resented an insult fiercely and at times with bloodshed. But his natural disposition was generous and tender, his affections were warm, his devotion was unfaltering. His temper, sometimes unruly, ran riot with wit, but never with malice. If contemporary judgment may be accepted, he was a profound lawyer. But his greatest renown was as an orator. In the estimation of Daniel Webster the most brilliant of American orators, in the estimation of Clay who stood next to Webster, he was an orator of the first magnitude, and by the united voices of his contemporaries he was adjudged to possess in a higher degree even than these two, that quality of oratory which manifests itself in gorgeous and resplendent imagery and dazzling metaphor. So great was his reputation that his presence at the convention was greeted with enthusiasm similar to that which had made the earth tremble for Clay in 1840. His court-house speech at the convention of 1844 was long regarded as the most wonderful ever heard in the Southwest. Being overcome by an indisposition to which he was subject, he sank back into the arms of Governor Jones, who, overcome with emotion, exclaimed, "Die, Prentiss, die. You will never have a more glorious opportunity."

But the struggle was vain. The Whigs of Tennessee had the supreme gratification of seeing the electoral vote of the State given to Clay. This is the only time in American history that a successful candidate for the presidency lost his own State. Clay's majority was very small.[1]

[1] One hundred and thirteen votes.

It has been said and so often repeated, that Clay lost the election by his Alabama letter, that it seems to have been accepted as a historical fact, but it is not true. He lost New York by it, and New York's thirty-six votes taken from Polk's one hundred and seventy electoral votes and added to Clay's one hundred and five, would have given Clay a majority of seven. But the demonstration should go beyond this. He carried Tennessee by a popular majority of only one hundred and thirteen votes. If the letter which lost New York had not been written, he would have lost Tennessee, which had thirteen votes. Give him, therefore, New York, and give Tennessee to Polk, and Clay would have been beaten by nineteen votes.

CHAPTER XXXIX.

THE DOWNFALL OF THE WHIGS.

The gubernatorial contest of 1845 manifested a reaction against the intense partisan zeal of previous years. A Democratic paper said: "It is observable by all that the great mass of the people are less excited than they have been in any canvass for many years." The only local question of sufficient importance to elicit discussion was the Tippling Act, and upon this there was no partisan division. An act had been passed in 1838, prohibiting the sale of spirituous liquors in less quantity than one quart under any circumstances, and likewise in quantities larger than a quart if to be drunk at the place where sold. The intent of this law was to abolish tippling houses as far as possible. Its operation, however, had effected the opposite result. In some places it was partially enforced, in others not at all, and on the whole it increased the number of houses where a single drink of ardent spirits could be purchased. This law was repealed by the Act of 1846, and the license system introduced under strong penalties for the prevention of immoral excesses. The questions of national policy were again the issues upon which the battle was fought. In addition to the tariff, the distribution of the sales of public lands, the veto power, and the bank, the annexation of Texas, and the Oregon question were added to the topics of discussion. The Whigs nominated Ephraim H. Foster, who, with characteristic fire, accepted the nomination after nearly every Whig in the State had positively and in advance declined the dubious struggle. The election of Polk to the presidency, and the death of Jackson in January, 1845, with the incident revival of that feeling of personal regard and devotion which had been weakened during the years following the defeat of Hugh L. White, added to the generally undecided attitude of the Whig party towards Texas, made the prospects more than doubtful. The nomination of Foster at this particular crisis made this more doubtful still. His inconsistency on the tariff was glaring and self-confessed. In 1839 he had opposed a protective tariff, and denounced it as a system that "steals from unconscious purses." He frankly admitted the change — a change which Brown ridiculed as taking place in one who had been a United States senator. On the Texas question, his course was apparently more inconsistent than it was in fact. While a member of the national Senate he had been instructed to vote for the annexation of Texas. He voted against the Tyler Treaty, and after the election of 1844 himself introduced a bill for annexation. Robert J. Walker offered as an amendment that Texas should be one State, and admitted on an equal footing with the existing States. Foster voted against Walker's amendment, and then against his own bill on the ground that the amendment contained a concession to the abolitionists of the North. Brown attributed this vote to the opposition of Henry, Jones, Neil S. Brown, Haskell, and other Whig leaders in the State. He defended his vote on the ground that it left the question of slavery open for future intrigue, and because it contained no provision against the assumption of the public debt of Texas.

Foster was born on the 17th of September, 1794, in Nelson County, Kentucky, and was the son of Robert C. Foster. In 1797 he removed with his family to Nashville, where Ephraim graduated in 1813 at Cumberland College. He studied law, and was admitted to the bar.

He was Jackson's private secretary during the Creek War, and at the close of this resumed the practice of his profession, in which he was successful, even at a bar of which Felix Grundy, Francis B. Fogg, Henry A. Wise, and Balie Peyton were members. He had been at different times elected to the House of Representatives, of which he was speaker. He was twice a member of the state Senate. He was tall, and had a commanding appearance. His disposition was warm-hearted and generous, his bearing was affable, courteous, and gracious. He possessed great personal popularity, and was popularly called "Old Eph." During the campaign with Brown, the Whig papers frequently boasted "Eph's got him." His temper was violent and inflammable. When a young man of twenty-seven, he threw a book at a judge on the bench who had let fall a sneering remark. He was proud and high-spirited, and quick to resentment. He had a ready wit, and was noted for his repartee and raillery. His eloquence was hurried and impetuous, if not brilliant, and his diction was fluent. His enemies sometimes called him Bombastes Furioso.

His opponent, Aaron V. Brown, was born in Brunswick County, Virginia, August 15, 1795, and was educated in North Carolina. He studied law under Judge Trimble at Nashville, and began the practice of his profession at that point. He removed to Giles County, and afterwards formed a partnership with James K. Polk of Maury County. He was frequently sent to the General Assembly as senator or legislator, — and from 1839 to 1845 was a member of Congress. He was, after his gubernatorial term of service, a member of Buchanan's cabinet. As a public speaker, he possessed talents of a higher order than his competitor. He showed the training of the Polk school, and had a trick of entangling his opponent that was worthy of Jones. Referring to Foster's vote against the annexation of Texas, he described the latter standing with blood-stained garments at the door of the Senate leaning upon her sword, and begging permission to deposit her glorious banner of San Jacinto beside those won at Brandywine, Princeton, and Yorktown, and all the great battles of the Revolution, while the senator from Tennessee rushes forward, rudely slams the door in her face and cries: "Begone, begone! Your sword is a traitor's sword, and the blood on your garments is the blood of rebels." The manner and the gesticulation were such that it was long thought he was quoting Foster's exact words.

At times Brown's oratory broke out in passages of lurid eloquence that were remarkably fine and effective before an audience. In one of these flights he describes the magnitude of the American continent. "When did mental vision ever rest upon such a scene? Moses, when standing on the top of Mount Pisgah, looking over on the Promised Land, gazed not on a scene half so lovely. Oh! let us this day vow that whatever else we may do, by whatever name we may be called, we will never surrender one square acre of this goodly heritage to the dictation of any king or potentate on earth. Swear it, swear it, my countrymen, and let heaven record the vow forever." The Oregon question was rather diplomatic and historical than political, and came in for a less share of attention. The Democratic position on the annexation of Texas was more acceptable than that of the Whigs, and the popular sentiment on this question was still more influenced by a visit of Sam Houston to Tennessee during the pendency of the contest. Brown was elected by a majority of 1470 votes.

The strength of political feeling in the ensuing General Assembly was made manifest in the contest for the speakership of the Senate, of which Harvey M. Watterson was elected speaker on the 138th ballot. The Democrats had elected a majority of the members of the General Assembly. There was a vacancy in the United States Senate, which it was supposed, as a matter of course, the Democrats could fill. But by some legislative legerdemain a man was elected who failed to receive even so much as a large minority of Democratic votes. The exact details of this intrigue have not been preserved. Enough remains, however, to furnish us an instructive chapter in the history of state politics. It may also supply additional insight into the tortuous methods to which unscrupulous politicians with small talents resorted in those days, in the hopes of defeating the will of a majority whose assent and approval they could never hope to achieve by the strength of their character, the force of their intellect, or the importance of their public services. A. O. P. Nicholson, who had edited with signal force the "Democratic Statesman," a campaign paper set on foot to offset A. A. Hall's "Politician," was nominated by a conference or caucus of Democrats.

Immediately after the August elections, the Whig papers began to stir up strife by a kind of political barratry, and threw out hints of the possibility of electing a Democrat by the aid of Whig votes. Among the names mentioned was that of H. L. Turney. The leverage for this purpose existed in the feeling of local pride which the "Whig" assiduously cultivated. Two communications appeared in the "Nashville Whig" organ, signed "Shelby," which imperiously demanded as a right that a senator from the Western District should be elected. The "Memphis Appeal," the "Somerville Spy," the "Jackson Republican," and the "Trenton True American," all joined in the demand. The "M'Minnville Gazette" suggested a Democratic caucus under the two thirds rule. When the legislature met, the Democrats had fifty-two members and the Whigs forty-eight. Turney refused to submit his claims to a caucus on the score that he "believed the system to be radically wrong, especially where the opposing party had offered no candidate. It is anti-republican in its tendencies, and virtually destroys the rights of suffrage of those of the party who may prefer another political friend to the caucus nominee." He accused Nicholson of being Polk's candidate. He refused to answer a list of questions tendered him by the Democrats, which he afterwards said he intended to answer before he was denounced by Democratic members of the General Assembly. After the legislature proceeded to a ballot for senator, on the earlier ballots, A. O. P. Nicholson received forty votes, all Democrats; H. L. Turney received eleven, John Bell thirty-five, Gustavus A. Henry two, W. T. Haskell one, and W. C. Dunlap seven. During the balloting, Turney was bitterly denounced by the Democrats for "having betrayed his party," and even by some of the Whigs who despised his treason. He was charged with having written a letter to the Whigs, meeting their views on the tariff, and the distribution of the sales of public lands, and pledging himself to denounce Polk and his administration.[1] Before the election, Joseph C. Guild withdrew General Trousdale, who had been put in nomination, stating that General Trousdale, if elected, desired to be elected by his own party and would not receive the office unless elected by his own party. Turney was finally elected by a vote of fifty-three; of these, forty-seven were Whigs, and six were Democrats.

Immediately after his election, Turney tried to defend his course, and pointedly denied the coalition in a letter to the "Shelbyville Free Press." He said: "I am proud to know that by the use of my name, the system (*i. e.* caucus) has been prostrated in the Tennessee legislature, I trust, forever." He would have answered the interrogatories submitted to him, but before he could do so, the violent assaults of the Democrats, especially H. M. Watterson, forced him to refuse. In this letter he gives his views on the public questions at issue, and deviates from

[1] I have been assured by Mr. Harvey M. Watterson that he saw this letter.

the Democratic position exactly on the two points upon which it was charged he had made concessions to the Whigs. In December thirty-one Democrats published an address formally reading Turney out of the party. Following the election of Turney, Felix K. Zollicoffer, a Whig, was elected comptroller of the State. If any one has a taste for personal journalism in its most vigorous development, let him read the "Union," of which Nicholson was now editor, for the few months succeeding Turney's election to the Senate.

The contest of 1847 came on during the Mexican War. The Democrats had been outspoken in their declarations that there would be no war as a result of the annexation of Texas. In 1845 A. V. Brown had asked Foster, "Where is your war?" In 1847 Neil S. Brown retorted by pointing his long index finger toward the Southwest and exclaiming, "Here is your war." Aaron V. Brown was renominated by the Democrats. This was to be again the opening skirmish of a presidential election in 1848. M. P. Gentry said, referring to this, "the political position which Tennessee may then take will be a powerful, perhaps a controlling influence upon the great contest of 1848." The whole weight of executive patronage and influence will be thrown into the conflict," said "The Spirit of '76," "and Tennessee will become a battleground." The Whigs were anxious not to repeat the mistake of 1845. Foster was solicited to make the race, but his refusal was accepted with unfeigned satisfaction. The names most prominently brought forward were those of G. A Henry, M. P. Gentry, and Neil S. Brown. Gentry made no effort and cut no figure in the struggle for the nomination. It appeared probable at one time that Henry would be selected by acclamation, and meeting after meeting put him in nomination. His strongest opponent was Neil S. Brown, one of the most amiable characters and one of the brightest minds in Tennessee history. Born in Giles County, Tennessee, in 1810, of Scotch-Irish blood, he had fought his way up from poverty and was in the noblest sense of the phrase a self-made man. In 1834 he had gone to Texas, but returned and entered the army destined for Florida, and was at the battle of Mud Creek. In 1836 he was a White elector. In 1837 he was sent to the legislature. He had taken a prominent part in all the contests of the day. In 1843 he was nominated to contest his congressional district with Aaron V. Brown and reduced his majority from 1,600 to 460. In this year he was made adjutant-general. The brilliancy of the reputation made in the Brown contest and as elector in 1844, his war record, his lack of political record, for he had never been to Congress, his popular disposition, the keenness of his wit, the effectiveness of his oratory, for he was a stump speaker of the first magnitude, all pointed to him as the available candidate. He had not been involved in any of the wrangles which had engendered bitterness among the Whig leaders, and he was perhaps more acceptable to the various factions than either Henry or Gentry. The scales were eventually turned in his favor by the absence of the East Tennessee delegations, who were detained by impassable roads, and who would have given their votes to Henry.

The only great issue between the two candidates was President Polk and General Zach Taylor. Neil S. Brown attacked the general prosecution of the war on the part of the administration and eulogized General Taylor, whom he advocated for the presidency in 1848. Aaron V. Brown having accused him of trying to ride on Taylor's back, he turned and pointing his long finger squarely at his opponent, exclaimed, "Who was it for twenty long years without intermission rode upon the back of General Jackson, even to the making spots upon his sides? Aaron V. Brown, the governor of Tennessee, and James K. Polk, the president of the United States."

Neil S. Brown accused Polk of making the Mexican War a partisan war by appointing only Democrats to generalships. Brown retorted by claiming for the Democratic party the credit for the results of the war, for no one doubted the result, and denounced the Whigs for originally opposing it. But the heartiness with which the Whigs supported the military measures of the administration weakened the force of this blow. In June, 1846, the Oregon question had been settled by a treaty in which the line of forty-nine degrees was decided upon, after all the turmoil of "Fifty-four-forty-or-fight," and Neil S. Brown turned the Mount Pisgah comparison on his opponent with effective sarcasm. The popularity of Polk's administration had in truth begun to wane and Neil S. Brown ridiculed his opponent's attempt to stir up the old time enthusiasm in his behalf by quoting a popular song,

> "There was a piper had a cow,
> He had no hay to give her ;
> He took his pipes, began to play,
> Consider, cow, consider."

Neil S. Brown was elected by a majority of 1,015 votes.

The contest between Taylor and Cass in Tennessee in 1848 was a faint echo of 1840. The Whigs literally vociferated everything before them. There was an attempt to make Taylor a people's non-partisan candidate, but without success. The division between the pro-slavery and free-soil Democrats destroyed the harmony and unity of that party, and they entered the struggle with but little enthusiasm. Taylor carried Tennessee by a majority of 6,286. In this election the slavery question played an important part. Cass was with the South — a Northern man with Southern principles. Van Buren, who was the Abolition candidate, received 291,263 votes; in New York alone, 120,510. It now became apparent that there was a tendency within the ranks of the Democratic party to divide upon the slavery question. The free-soil element was gradually forced out. The issue was rather sectional than political. The Whigs had no political status in the presence of a controversy which recognized no political division. The Whigs of East Tennessee managed to survive the deluge of the Democratic victory and in 1851 turned the tide and elected the last Whig governor. They had no slaves — they were for the most part Unionists during the war and have been Republicans since. But over the rest of the State the Democrats gained a supreme ascendency. The reaction from the Taylor movement swept Governor Brown, the genial, the amiable, the pure-hearted before it, and W. G. Brownlow, the caustic Whig, the militant preacher, the Ishmael of Tennessee politics, sharpened his wit and envenomed his pen to no purpose. The Democrats had nominated against Brown, General William Trousdale, whose popular sobriquet was the "War Horse of Sumner County." He was born September 23, 1790, in Orange County, North Carolina, and was of Scotch-Irish descent. In 1796 his father removed with him to Davidson County, Tennessee. When a boy at school he had joined the expedition against the Creek Indians and was at Tallahatchie and Talladega. During the Creek War, in pursuance of some duty, he swam the Tennessee River near the Muscle Shoals, being on horseback, although unable to swim himself. He was also at Pensacola and New Orleans during the War of 1812. In 1835 he was in the state Senate, and in 1836 major-general of militia. He fought through the Seminole War of 1836. In 1837 he was an unsuccessful candidate for Congress. In 1840 he was a Van Buren elector. He fought through the Mexican War with great bravery and was twice wounded at Chepultepec. He was made brigadier-general by brevet in the United States army for gallant and meritorious conduct in that engagement. Trousdale was a man of sound understanding and pure character and intellectually not inferior to his competitor. He was elected by a majority of 1,390. In Knox County, however, the future course of East Tennessee was foreshadowed by a majority for Brown of 1,616 in that county.

In 1851 William B. Campbell defeated Trousdale, who was a candidate for reëlection. G. A. Henry, who had been brought forward again by his friends, wrote on the 7th of February, 1851, a letter which emphasizes the position of the Whigs and which sounds strangely as coming from a subsequent Confederate senator. He withdraws from the race for governor and announces his candidacy for the House of Representatives at Nashville. "I need not inform you that I am a Whig — that I have so lived and that I shall die in the faith. Above all, however, I am for the Union of these States, under our present glorious constitution, with all the guaranties which were thrown around it by the foresight and wisdom of our fathers. For its preservation I am now and at any time prepared to pledge my life, my fortune, and my sacred honor."

Campbell was elected by a conjunction of circumstances which forced the Democrats into the position of favoring disunion. The Southern Convention had met at Nashville in May, 1850, as the Whigs said, "to inaugurate a Southern Confederacy." This convention was originally called at the suggestion of A. J. Donelson, who repudiated its action as soon as its anti-union tendencies became apparent. W. L. Sharkey, the ablest judicial mind which the Southwest has ever produced, presided over its deliberations, but his known union sentiments were more than counterbalanced in the public mind by the presence and active participation of R. Barnwell Rhett of South Carolina, the impetuous Cassius who was ever ready to sacrifice the common cause rather than yield individual preferences. He introduced an address, a long-drawn document condemnatory of the compromise measures then before Congress, bristling with threats of an intangible catastrophe and which contained this significant utterance: "Until Congress adjourns, we cannot know what it will do or fail to do. We must therefore meet again after its adjournment to consider the final condition in which it will leave us." The resolutions which were adopted were such as could have been formally promulgated in America, alone of all the nations of the world, without some arrests for treason. The fifth resolution was very bold. "The slave-holding States cannot and will not submit to the enactment by Congress of any law imposing onerous conditions or restraints upon the rights of masters to remove with their property into the Territories of the United States, or to any law making discriminations in favor of the proprietors of other property and against them. In the seventh resolution is this passage: "The performance of this duty . . . is required by the fundamental law of the Union . . . the warfare against this right is a war upon the constitution. The defenders of this right are defenders of the constitution. Those who deny or impair its exercise are unfaithful to the constitution, and if disunion follows the destruction of this right they are disunionists." The twelfth resolution declares that "it is the opinion of this convention that this controversy should be ended, either by a recognition of the constitutional rights of the Southern people or by an equitable partition of the Territories." The thirteenth contains a covert threat against Congress and denounces the compromise measures "as a plain violation of the Constitution of the United States."

As soon as the Southern Convention adjourned, the Democratic leaders were called on to face a storm in Tennessee. During its sessions, meetings had been held from one end of the State to the other indorsing the compromise measures then pending in Congress. A. O. P. Nicholson and Aaron V. Brown, who had been prominent members of the convention, repudiated its action. Nicholson attacked the address, Brown attacked the resolutions. Both were frightened. Both attacked the doctrines of nullification and secession with intense violence and fierce vituperation. The passage of the compromise measures was a merit of the Whigs; and though many Democrats had voted for them, the Democrats of Tennessee were in no condition to avail themselves of this fact. Trousdale was compelled to bear the odium which gathered against his party because of the Southern Convention, and this was increased by a vote of sympathy for the South Carolina agitators in the convention that nominated him.

William B. Campbell was put forward as the man to redeem the banner from the hands of a candidate "whose culminating feat was swimming the Muscle Shoals." He was descended from a line of distinguished Revolutionary heroes. He finished his education, which was solid and liberal, under his uncle, Governor David Campbell of Virginia, and under whose supervision he studied law. He returned to Tennessee, and in 1829 was elected attorney-general. In 1836 he resigned his seat as a member of the legislature, and as captain entered the Florida War, through which he fought with honor. In 1833 he defeated General Trousdale for Congress, and again in 1839. In 1841 he was elected without opposition. He fought gallantly through the Mexican War as colonel of the First Regiment, whose desperate bravery won for it the sobriquet of "The Bloody First." Campbell himself led the charge at Monterey, and his troops hoisted the first flag on the walls of the Mexican city. This was perhaps the most brilliant feat of arms accomplished during the war. The form of Campbell's command to charge — "Boys, follow me" — became historic and was also the favorite battle-cry of the Whigs during the campaign that elected him governor. In 1848 he was elected circuit judge by the legislature, and in 1851 he was nominated by acclamation for governor by the Whigs.

Trousdale and Campbell were cast in the same mould. Both were men of pure character, of high purpose, of stern integrity, possessing sound practical sense, without brilliancy of parts or fluency of tongue, and both were conservative and courageous. "Two gamer cocks," says one writer, "were never pitted against each other." The joint debates were not full of the stirring blows which drew crowds to hear the two Browns, and there was none of the sparkle, the skill in fence, the broad caricature, and the resounding laughter that distinguished the Polk-Jones canvasses. The two military candidates argued like martinets, and they who were the most headlong and stormy in battle were the most formal and punctilious in debate. Trousdale, who had defeated Neil S. Brown in 1849 by 1,390 votes, was now defeated by Campbell by 1,660 votes.

In 1852 the National Democratic party was again thoroughly united and carried every State in the Union except four — Tennessee was one of the four. Scott, who was objectionable to many of the Whigs, carried the State by a majority of 1,880 votes, in spite of the fact that M. P. Gentry, a Whig member of Congress, made a speech against him in the House of Representatives which was declared to have been one of the ablest ever delivered there. The Democrats had it printed in pamphlet form and used it as a campaign document This embittered the Tennessee Whigs. J. C. Jones, then in the Senate, supported Scott earnestly. The year following, the Jones faction nominated Gustavus A. Henry as their candidate for the governorship. Henry was popularly called "The Eagle Orator" and was noted for the fluency of his speech, the brilliancy of his fancy, and the dignity of his declamation. The Democrats nominated Andrew Johnson, an East Tennessean who had served several terms in Congress, and who, beginning as a mechanic, had slowly risen to power and eminence by the strength of his character, the force of his intellect, and the aggressiveness of his political methods. Nearly every prominent Democrat in the State was opposed to him, but he was nominated almost without opposition. He accepted the nomination with almost cavalier-like indifference and practically repudiated the platform which had been adopted. Johnson had certain theories upon national questions which, if not original, were certainly startling. This canvass and all subsequent ones were fought out upon questions of national policy. Johnson was elected. In 1855 the Whigs brought forward M. P. Gentry, but his part against Scott in 1852 had not been forgiven. More than this, the slavery question was becoming daily less political and more sectional, and Tennessee was a Southern State. In East Tennessee, where there were no slaves, sectionalism was less developed. Johnson was an earnest Democrat, and stood with the Southern Democrats upon the questions of constitutional authority growing out of the Kansas-Nebraska embroglio and the compromise measures. His popularity was overwhelming and his abilities as a stump-speaker were supereminent even in a school of which Jones, Henry, and Gentry were leading members. The last Whig victory in Tennessee was in 1852. The alliance with the Know-Nothing movement, its sympathies with many of the measures of the new but rapidly growing Republican party in the North, the sectional phase of the slavery question, were all instruments in the hands of Andrew Johnson through which he cemented the power of the Democratic party and utterly annihilated the Whigs in Tennessee. In 1856 Buchanan carried the State of Tennessee — the first time the National Democrats had been successful since Jackson's second election.

One of the electors for the State at large upon the Buchanan ticket was Isham G. Harris. By the universal concurrence of the Democratic papers he contributed more than any other individual to the success of the Democratic ticket. The year following, in 1857, he was nominated by the Democrats as their candidate for governor — the first who had ever been taken from West Tennessee. Against him the Whigs, or as it had now become, the opposition party, nominated Robert Hatton, a young politician who had made some reputation as a Fillmore elector the year before. His nomination was a cause of surprise to many, and of indignation to the friends of the wayward and brilliant Haskell, who addressed the nominating convention in a speech full of eloquence and bitterness. Hatton possessed more than ordinary ability, was methodical and exact in his methods, and singularly high-minded and noble. But in Harris, who was put forward by the Democrats as a "matured statesman," he met more than his match. History as a science can deal worthily only with that which has been removed by the lapse of time and the onward sweep of the current of events from the influence of personal prejudice, partisan considerations, and the biased judgment which comes from the wrangling and jarring conflicts of political life. Those who have figured in scenes which are passed upon by the historian, and who still live in the activity of the present, are like those spirits of whom Virgil tells that they wander restlessly upon the banks of the river Styx, unable to pass over until their bodies in the earth above have received the last rites of sepulture. Isham G. Harris still lives, the senior senator from Tennessee. A man of strong feeling, the time has not come when his enemies can do full justice to his virtues or his friends view his faults with critical impartiality. In 1857 he aroused a degree of enthusiasm which could only have been aroused by a man strong of intellect and powerful in debate. He swept like a whirlwind from one end of the State to the other, and literally buried his opponent beneath the weight of a majority greater than had been given any candidate in Tennessee since the Harrison campaign in 1840. He was renominated in 1859 and made the canvass with John Netherland, a bright, witty, and genial speaker, but who, like Hatton, was unable to bear up against the ponderous blows of his opponent. The questions which were debated were each leading in a direct line to the irrepressible conflict.

In 1860 a sectional candidate, as the Southern leaders termed Abraham Lincoln, was elected. The Southern States began to withdraw from the Union, and all the senators and representatives from seceding States left the capitol. Andrew Johnson, who was in the Senate and who from the first had repudiated the doctrine of secession, remained at Washington, and many leading Tennesseans, such as Emerson Etheridge and W. G. Brownlow, gave him a hearty support. Governor Harris called an extra session of the legislature to meet at Nashville on the 7th of January, 1861. The question of calling a state convention to meet at Nashville to take into consideration the secession of Tennessee from the Union was voted upon by the people on the 9th of February, 1861, and defeated. On the 12th of April, Fort Sumter was fired upon. A great number of Tennesseans whose traditions reached back to the time of Andrew Jackson were violently opposed to the disruption of the Union. These had hoped for a peaceful settlement of the question. The firing upon Fort Sumter was at once followed by a proclamation from President Lincoln calling for 75,000 volunteers. The legislature of Tennessee was again called together in extra session, and the question of secession was submitted to a popular vote on the 8th of June. John Bell and other leading Constitutional Unionists declared for secession and it was overwhelmingly carried. On the 18th of June the legislature met, and on the 24th of June Governor Harris issued a proclamation dissolving the ties which bound Tennessee to the United States of America. The period of the war was practically a blank, in so far as the history of Tennessee is concerned. With the close of the war an entirely new era began — the era in which we live, varied of late by the spirit of industrial, commercial, social, and political change which is emphasized by the establishment of manufacturing enterprises, the growth of towns and cities, the building of railroads, the improvement in public schools, and the election of new men to office, men whose memories do not reach back to the bitterness of the ante-bellum period.

If we review the history of Tennessee from this point, we shall be struck by several facts, curious in themselves and flattering to state pride. The history of Tennessee is an epitome of the history of the United States. Its financial history is the financial history of the general government, even to an embryonic system such as we now have in the national banks. The general avidity with which internal improvements were pushed forward after the completion of the Erie Canal found its reflex in Tennessee. The slow and logical development of population under the influence of governmental ideas, already fully matured and expanded, is made more clearly comprehensible than upon the broader field of the continent. The history of parties in Tennessee is the history of parties in the United States; and in spite of the fact that the results achieved were the same, the causes which produced the Whig party in Tennessee were parallel but not the same causes which produced the Whig party in American politics. We find, after the formation of parties, the same partisan rancor, the same sudden changes of popular sentiment, the same alternations in party supremacy which we find, not in other Southern or Southwestern States, and indeed in very few of the Eastern States, but in the country at large. We find here all the paraphernalia and insignia which distinguish great political battles, — the ardent eloquence, the personal courage, the thorough knowledge of political literature, the arts, the tricks, the surprises of forensic display, the enthusiasm and vehemence of desperate determination, the remorseless trampling down of the weak, the exalting of the steadfast and the strong, the glittering pageants and ostentatious exultations of victory, and the stout-hearted acceptance of defeat. Even the secession of the Southern States had already been foreshadowed in this State. In one of the debates which took place in the United States Senate on the eve of the war, when a great Tennessean was making a profound and eloquent argument against the doctrine of secession, he was taunted with having come from a State which was "born in secession and rocked in the cradle of revolution."

It is no wonder that men trained in such a school should have risen to places of great distinction on a field which gave them merely an enlarged scope for the exercise of their talents. Virginia and Massachusetts are the only States which have furnished more names that stand higher on the National Roll of Honor than Tennessee. Not to mention Tennesseans who, like Tipton of Indiana, Houston of Texas, Benton of Missouri, Garland and Sevier and Hindman of Arkansas, Claiborne of Louisiana, Henry Watterson of Kentucky, Sharkey and Yerger of Mississippi, Gwin of California, and Admiral Farragut, attained influence and celebrity either local or national in other States, Tennessee has given the national government a number of presidents and cabinet officers entirely out of proportion to its wealth and population. George W. Campbell was secretary of the treasury under Madison. Andrew Jackson was president from 1829 to 1837. John H. Eaton was secretary of war under Jackson. Felix Grundy was attorney-general under Van Buren. John Bell was secretary of war under Harrison and Tyler. Cave Johnson was postmaster-general under Polk, and Polk himself was president from 1845 to 1849. Aaron V. Brown was postmaster-general under Buchanan. Tennessee has furnished the House of Representatives two speakers, — Bell and Polk, and the Senate one presiding officer in the person of H. L. White in 1832. Andrew Johnson was vice-president from the 4th of March, 1865, to the 15th of April the same year, when he became president and served until 1869. In addition to this, Tennessee has had two unsuccessful candidates for the vice-presidency, James K. Polk in 1840, and A. J. Donelson, on the ticket with Fillmore in 1856, and two unsuccessful candidates for the presidency, H. L. White in 1836, and John Bell in 1860. John Catron was on the supreme bench of the United States from 1837 to 1865. Joseph Anderson was the first comptroller of the United States from 1815 to 1836. William B. Lewis was second auditor from 1829 to 1845. Daniel Graham was register of the treasury from 1847 to 1849, and A. A. Hall from 1849 to 1850. S. D. Jacobs was first assistant postmaster-general from 1851 to 1853. In addition to this Tennessee has furnished innumerable representatives to the diplomatic service abroad — two of them, George W. Campbell and Neil S. Brown, to the same court, Russia. Most of these, however, played their part upon the broader field of national politics, and though their fame was sufficiently splendid to emerge above the limits of a merely local and temporary distinction, they are of importance in a history such as this only in so far as they influence the current of politics within the bounds of the State. Another curious feature in Tennessee history is the number of strongly stamped and even bizarre individualities which have either lived here or been produced within its limits. Henry S. Foote, the wonderful Tamerlane of Southwestern politics, who ran a muck at all the world, lived part of his life in Tennessee and represented one of its districts in the Confederate Congress. Jere Clemens, the Alabama senator, the Texas warrior, the author of several delightful books and novels of adventure, and whom W. L. Yancey dubbed a "political Hessian," lived for a time in Tennessee. After the war Albert Pike, the record of whose life faithfully told would make a charming addition to "The Tales of the Alhambra," removed to Memphis. John Mitchel, the stormy Irish patriot, once lived in this State.

The quaintest, the most striking, the most original figure in Southwestern history was David Crockett. Brownlow, the fighting parson, the caustic writer, the politician, was a Tennessean — governor and senator. The fillibustering expeditions just preceding the war were full of romantic episodes. The leading figure in them was William Walker, the "Grey-eyed man of Destiny," whose exploits in Nicaragua for a time attracted the gaze of Europe and America, and whose sad and tragic fate has been described in the glowing and sensuous verse of Joaquin Miller. Walker was a Tennessean. The war between the States brought to the surface many men of strong character and pronounced individuality. But the most brilliant, the most original, the most attractive, the most dashing of all was N. B. Forrest, a Tennessean. Joe C. Guild, the odd wag and the quaint humorist, whose memory still lives in the traditions of the story-teller and the anecdote-monger, was a Tennessean. Balie Peyton, the peripatetic politician and brilliant orator, was a Tennessean. The period from 1836 to 1860 was an era of great men and great orators. The style of oratory was characteristic and nearly always brilliant, — full of fire and gorgeous flights of fancy and rhetorical adornment. Gus Henry was "The Eagle Orator." James C. Jones was a figure of national prominence, and was frequently suggested as a candidate for the presidency by leading papers outside of the State. George W. Jones was often suggested as a fit candidate for speaker. M. P. Gentry was a leader in Congress and an orator of the first magnitude. After his first speech in Congress, John Quincy Adams, who took pleasure in observing new members of Congress, declared that he was "the greatest natural orator in Congress." Landon C. Haynes, the Confederate senator, was also noted for the dazzling brilliancy of his rhetoric. At the Baltimore Convention of 1852, Gideon J. Pillow of Tennessee received twenty-five votes for the vice-presidency; and at the Cincinnati Convention of 1856, A. V. Brown received twenty-nine votes for the same nomination.

Tennessee had a commanding influence in the Southwest by virtue of its intellectual supremacy. But this was increased and strengthened by the success which attended Tennesseans who removed to other States. From this came the sobriquet of "Mother of Southwestern Statesmen." Another title often quoted was, "Volunteer State." Tennessee carried on almost single-handed the Creek War. It won the battle of New Orleans. It contributed more than its share to the success of the Mexican War. In 1846 there was a requisition for 2,400 volunteers. Thirty thousand offered their services. From the time when Crockett and Autry upheld the honor of the State at the Alamo, to the end of the Civil War, Tennesseans have been noted for the promptness with which they are ready to face the dangers and hardships of war. They are also noted for their intense love for their native State which they carry to the end. Perhaps the glorious position which the State has held in both military and civil life since the time of Sevier may have had some influence upon this natural and noble feeling.

LIST OF AUTHORITIES.

In the following list of authorities, works of a general nature, such as Bancroft, books of reference, and the general histories of banks and the churches are not included. In addition to those here given, all the Journals of the Territorial Legislative Council, of the various Constitutional Conventions, and of the House and Senate from Sevier to Harris, as also the various Codes and Digests and Reports, the Messages of the Governors, the reports of the State Officers, and the records of Shelby County and DeBow's Review have been carefully examined, and much more material collected than is here used. Manuscript material bearing upon the history of some counties, collected during the Centennial year and preserved in the Tennessee Historical Library, has been sparingly utilized, as of doubtful authority. The entire absence of all historical treatment of the period following that covered by Haywood, Ramsey, and Putnam, in fact the entire nineteenth century, has forced the author to make original investigations. This fact renders it necessary to give a detailed list of the authorities consulted.

I have included in the list of authorities J. M. Keating's History of Memphis, now in press. These pages had already gone through the press before I saw that book. But by the kindness of the author I was recently permitted to examine the advance sheets. It is a scholarly and thorough treatment of the subject.

The author's grateful acknowledgments for various acts of kindness are due to Mr. J. S. Carels, librarian of the Watkins Institute in Nashville, Ex-Governor James D. Porter, Mr. H. M. Doak, Mrs. Felicia Grundy Porter, Senator W. B. Bate, Mr. J. M. Dickinson, Mr. John M. Lea, Mr. Lemuel R. Campbell and Mr. Thomas B. Craighead of Nashville, Miss Elizabeth Garland of Clarksville, Mr. J. H. McDavitt, Judge Eli Shelby Hammond, Mr. J. P. Young, and Mr. Hugh L. Brinkley of Memphis.

Correspondence of General James Robertson in two volumes, extending from 4th of November, 1784 to July 30, 1814. (Vol. i. from November 4, 1784 to January, 1795. Vol. ii. probably lost.) This contains also manuscripts and letters of William Blount, Carondelet, Mero, James Winchester, and others.

De Soto's March through Georgia. By Charles C. Jones, Jr. Savannah, 1880.

The Annals of Tennessee to the End of the Eighteenth Century. By J. G. M. Ramsey. Philadelphia, 1853.

The Civil and Political History of the State of Tennessee from its Earliest Settlements up to the Year 1796. By John Haywood. Knoxville, 1823.

History of Tennessee, Western Monthly Review, vol. ii. p. 226.

The Siege of Fort Loudon and Massacre of its Garrison by the Cherokee Indians in 1760. Copied from "The Whig," by "The Politician," September 15, 1847.

Magazine of American History, vol. iii. p. 45.

Life and Times of Colonel Daniel Boone. By Cecil B. Hartley. (This contains Boone's Autobiography as dictated to John Filson.) New York, 1860.

Daniel Boone and the Hunters of Kentucky. By W. H. Bogart. Boston, 1869.

Indian Battles, Murders, Sieges, and Forays in the Southwest. Nashville. (Reprinted from Southwestern Magazine.)

Essay by Thomas Washington to prove that Tecumseh was not at the attack on Buchanan's Station. (Manuscript in Tennessee Historical Society's Library.)

The Rear-Guard of the Revolution. By Edmund Kirke. New York, 1886.

The Pioneers of the Southwest. Two papers by Edmund Kirke in Lippincott's Magazine, July and August, 1885.

The Pioneer Mothers of the West; Catharine Sevier. By A. W. Putnam. Godey's Lady's Book, vol. xliv. p. 71.

John Sevier as a Commonwealth Builder; a Sequel to the Rear-Guard of the Revolution. By Edmund Kirke. New York, 1887.

Sketches of Western Adventure. By John A. McClung. Maysville, Ky., 1837.

Annals of the West, embracing a Concise Account of the Principal Events which have occurred in the Western States and Territories, from the Discovery of the Mississippi Valley to the Year 1850, compiled from the most Authentic Sources. By James H. Perkins, revised and enlarged by J. M. Peck. St. Louis, 1850.

Pioneers of Nashville and of Tennessee. By Charles May. Nashville, 1880.

History of Greene County, Tennessee. By William Doak, D. D., of Tusculum, Tennessee. (MSS.)

The Dunham Pioneers of Middle Tennessee. By A. W. Putnam. (MSS. in Hist. So. Lib.)

The Life of Joseph Bishop, the Celebrated Old Pioneer in the First Settlement in Middle Tennessee. By John W. Gray. Nashville, 1856.

Donelson and the Pioneers of Middle Tennessee. By Hon. John M. Bright. Washington, 1880.

Thrilling Narrative, How the Judgment of Heaven fell on the Indians who wounded the Rev. Joseph Brown in 1794. (MSS. in Hist. So. Lib.)

History of Lexington, Kentucky. By George W. Rauch. Cincinnati, 1872.

Early Times in Middle Tennessee. By John Carr, a Pioneer of the West. Nashville, 1857.

A Summary Notice of the First Settlements made by White People within the Limits which bound Tennessee. July, 1816. Massachusetts Historical Collection, vol. vii. p. 59.

History of Middle Tennessee, or Life and Times of General James Robertson. By A. W. Putnam, Esq. Nashville, 1859.

The Government of the Notables in Middle Tennessee, May, 1780. The Historical Magazine, vol. iii. p. 35.

History of Alabama. By A. J. Pickett. 2 vols. Charleston, 1851.

Life of Tecumseh and his Brother the Prophet. By Benjamin Drake. Cincinnati, 1841.

Indian Wars of the West. By Timothy Flint. Cincinnati, 1833.

Red Eagle and the Wars with the Creek Indians. By H. C. Eggleston.

Life and Times of General Sam Dale, the Mississippi Partisan. By J. F. H. Claiborne. New York, 1860.

Old Times or Tennessee History for Tennessee Girls and Boys. By Edwin Paschall. Nashville, 1869.

The Admission of Tennessee into the Union. By Professor Nathaniel Cross. (MSS. in Hist. So. Lib.)

Short Description of the State of Tennessee, with the Constitution. Philadelphia, 1796.

Kentucky, Tennessee, Ohio ; their Admission into the Union. Article by Professor J. W. Andrews in Magazine of American History, October, 1887.

Journal of a Tour in Unsettled Parts of North America in 1796 and 1797. By the late Francis Baily. London, 1856.

Travels in the Interior of America in the years 1809, 1810, and 1811. By John Bradbury. Liverpool, 1817.

The Journal of the Rev. Francis Asbury. 3 vols. New York, 1821.

Notes on the Settlements and Indian Wars of the Western Parts of Virginia and Pennsylvania from 1763 to 1783 inclusive, together with a view of society and manners of the settlers of the western country. By Joseph Doddridge. Albany, New York, 1876. (Reprint.)

Old Settlers of Tennessee, Household Words, vol. viii. p. 188.

The Survival of English Institutions, illustrated in the Legal and Political History of North Carolina. (MSS.) By Professor Henry S. Shepherd.

A Journal of the Proceedings of William Blount, Esq., Governor, etc. (MSS.)

The laws of North Carolina and Tennessee respecting vacant lands and deeds, which are no longer in force, but necessary to the investigation of land titles in Tennessee. Printed by T. G. Bradford.

Revolutionary History of North Carolina in Three Lectures. By Rev. Francis L. Hawks, Hon. David L. Swain, and Hon. William A. Graham. Raleigh and New York, 1853.

The History of South Carolina. By William Gilmore Simms. New York, 1860.

History of North Carolina, with Maps and Illustrations. By Francis L. Hawks. 2 vols. Fayetteville, 1859.

Sketches of North Carolina, Historical and Biographical. By Rev. William Henry Foote. New York, 1846.

History of North Carolina from the Earliest Discoveries to the Present Time. By John W. Moore. 2 vols. Raleigh, 1880.

Sketches of Western North Carolina, Historical and Biographical. By C. L. Hunter. Raleigh, 1877.

Historical Sketches of North Carolina. From 1584 to 1851. By John H. Wheeler. 2 vols. in one. Philadelphia, 1851.

The History of North Carolina. By Hugh Williamson. 2 vols. Philadelphia, 1812.

Mecklenburgh Declaration of 1775. Summary of Historical Evidence. By A. R. Spofford. New York Herald, May 14, 1875, p. 4. See also authorities there cited by Governor Graham and Mr. Spofford.[1]

Memoir of James Harvey Otey, D. D., LL. D., the First Bishop of Tennessee. By William Mercer Green, D. D., Bishop of Mississippi. New York, 1884.

The Constitution of the Cumberland Presbyterian Church in the United States of America. Russellville, 1821.

---

[1] In the text (*vide* p. 39) I have followed the usual account, in referring to the Mecklenburgh Declaration of Independence. But the case made out by Mr. Spofford against the Resolutions of May 20th, in his admirable paper cited above, seems almost conclusive.

LIST OF AUTHORITIES.

Origin and Doctrines of the Cumberland Presbyterian Church. In Two Parts. By E. B. Crisman. St. Louis, 1877.

Life and Times of Rev. Finis Ewing, one of the Fathers and Founders of the Cumberland Presbyterian Church. By Rev. J. K. Cossitt. Louisville.

Thoughts on Various Subjects. By Rev. Robert Donnell of the Cumberland Presbyterian Church. Louisville, 1854.

Brief Biographical Sketches of Some of the Early Ministers of the Cumberland Presbyterian Church. By Richard Beard, D. D. Nashville, 1867.

Life of Rev. George Donnell, First Pastor of the Church in Lebanon, with a Sketch of the Scotch-Irish Race. By Rev. T. C. Anderson. Nashville, 1859.

Methodist Pulpit South. Compiled by William T. Smithson. Third Edition. Washington, D. C., 1859.

History of Methodism in Tennessee. By John B. McFerrin, D. D. 3 vols. Nashville, 1875.

History of the Organization of the Methodist Episcopal Church South. Nashville, 1845.

Biographical Sketches of Eminent Itinerant Ministers, distinguished for the most part as Pioneers of Methodism. Edited by Thomas O. Summers, D. D. Nashville, 1858.

The Life of Henry Biddleman Bascom. By Rev. M. M. Henkles. Louisville, 1854.

Autobiography of Rev. James B. Finley, or Pioneer Life in the West. Edited by W. P. Strickland. Cincinnati, 1859.

Autobiography of Peter Cartwright, the Backwoods Preacher. Edited by W. P. Strickland. Cincinnati, 1859.

Ten Years of Preacher Life. Chapters from an Autobiography. By William Henry Milburn. New York, 1859.

The Rifle, Axe, and Saddle-Bags, and Other Lectures. By William Henry Milburn. New York, 1857.

The Pioneers, Preachers, and People of the Mississippi Valley. By William Henry Milburn. New York, 1860.

The Craighead Family. A Genealogical Memoir of the Descendants of Rev. Thomas and Margaret Craighead; 1658–1876. By Rev. James Geddes Craighead, D. D. Philadelphia, 1876.

The Works of Philip Lindsley, D. D. Edited by Leroy J. Halsey, D. D., with Introductory Notices of his Life and Labors. By the editor. 3 vols. Philadelphia, 1866.

A Sketch of the Life and Educational Labors of Philip Lindsley. By Leroy J. Halsey. Hartford, 1859.

Address delivered before the Alumni Society of the University of

Nashville. By Judge John D. Phelan, June 13, 1872. Nashville, 1872.

An Address delivered at Nashville, Tennessee, October 5, 1830. Being the First Anniversary of the Alumni Society of the University of Nashville. By John Bell, Esq. Nashville, 1830.

An Address by Hon. Edwin H. Ewing at the Celebration of the Centennial Anniversary of the University of Nashville. Nashville, 1885.

Catalogue of the Officers and Graduates of the University of Nashville, with an Appendix containing sundry historical notices, etc. Nashville, 1850.

American Journal of Education, vol. vii. 1859.

Laws of the State of Tennessee, including those of North Carolina now in force in this State from the year 1715 to 1820 inclusive. By Edward Scott. 2 vols. Knoxville, 1821.

Laws of the United States, Resolutions of Congress under the Confederation, Treaties, Proclamations, and other documents having operation and respect to the public lands, collected, digested, and arranged pursuant to two acts of Congress. Passed April 2, 1810, and January 20, 1817. Washington, 1817.

Report of Committee on Education to the General Assembly of Tennessee, 1 November, 1821. (Very important on the subject of lands and public education. Copied in Niles' Register, vol. xxi. p. 299.)

An Address prepared by Rev. Joseph I. Foot, D. D., for his inauguration as President of Washington College, East Tennessee. Knoxville, 1840.

The History of Banks. Boston, 1837. (A manuscript note in the copy in the Harvard College Library gives as the name of the author Richard Hildreth.)

An Address on Banks and Banking. By W. N. Bilbo. Nashville, 1857.

Remarks of Hon. W. W. Guy, Representative of Hardeman County in the Tennessee Legislature, Thursday, February 24, 1860, on the amendment offered by himself to the Senate Bill to re-charter the Union and Planters' Banks.

Some Suggestions on the Subject of Monopolies and Special Charters. By W. H. Humphreys. Nashville, 1859.

Memorial of the Depositors in the Bank of Tennessee to the Forty-fifth General Assembly of Tennessee. 1887.

Considerations on the Currency and Banking System of the United States. By Albert Gallatin. Philadelphia, 1831.

A Short History of Paper-Money in the United States. By William M. Gouge. 2d edition. New York, 1835.

Answers to the Questions; what constitutes Currency, etc. By Henry C. Carey. Philadelphia, 1840.

Credit of the West. Nashville, 1833.

Proceedings of the General Internal Improvement Meeting, held at Knoxville, 1847.

Internal Improvements (a review of Calhoun's Memphis Speech). Southern Quarterly Review, vol. ix. p. 243.

Transcript of Record; Supreme Court of the United States; No. 781. Calvin Armory Stevens, Appellant, vs. The Chicago, St. Louis, and New Orleans Railroad Co. Appeal from the Circuit Court of the United States for the Western District of Tennessee, filed November 10, 1881.

Letters of Sam Tate to Jere Baxter, President, on the condition of the Memphis and Charleston Railroad, its finances and management for twenty-four years. First letter dated November 30, 1881.

The State Debt. Report of the Committee appointed to investigate it. Nashville, 1879.

A History of the State Debt. Nashville, 1880.

Tennessee and her Bondage. A vindication and a warning. Speech of Hon. John L. T. Sneed of Shelby County on the State Debt Question. Delivered at Lagrange, Tennessee, November 26, 1881. Memphis, 1881.

The State Debt. Duty and Responsibility of the Tennessee Democracy. William J. Sykes. Columbia, 1880.

History of Davidson County, Tennessee, with illustrations and biographical sketches of its prominent men and pioneers. By Professor W. W. Clayton. Philadelphia, 1880.

A History of Hardin County, Tennessee. By B. G. Brazelton. Nashville, 1885.

A Historical Sketch of Maury County. Columbia, 1876. (By W. S. Fleming.)

Reminiscences of the Early Settlements and Early Settlers of McNairy County, Tennessee. By General Marcus J. Wright. Washington, 1882.

Historical Address, delivered by Colonel John A. Gardner, on the Early Times in Weakley County. (MSS. in Hist. So. Lib.)

A Brief Sketch of the Settlement and Early History of Giles County. By James McCallum. (MSS.)

Manuscript Memoranda in reference to Fayette, Robertson, Obion, Lawrence, Montgomery, Dyer, Crockett, Lauderdale, Gibson, Hickman, Sevier, Humphreys, Henry, and Gibson counties are in the Historical Society's Library.

Historical Sketch of Tipton County, Tennessee, prepared by R.

H. Munford for the Centennial Celebration, July 4, 1876, at Covington, Tennessee. (MSS. in Hist. So. Lib.)

The Industries and Resources of Tennessee, historical, descriptive, and biographical. Commercial advantages of the City of Nashville. 1882.

Nashville Illustrated. 1872.

Nashville Directors. 1855, 1856, 1857, 1859.

Recollections of Nashville in Early Days. By Anson Nelson, John M. Lea, and A. S. Colyar. (MSS. in Hist. So. Lib.)

Reminiscences, a Brief History of Davidson County, Tennessee, mostly collected from the records of the county. Prepared for and read before the Historical Society, June, 1849, by A. W. Putnam. (MSS. in Hist. So. Lib.)

Sketch of the Life of Major Daniel Graham, late of Tennessee. (MSS. in Hist. So. Lib.)

Rev. Thomas B. Craighead. By A. W. Putnam. (MSS. in Hist. So. Lib.)

Recollections of Tennessee. By M. H. Howard. (MSS. in Hist. So. Lib.)

Zion Church and Frierson Settlement in Maury County, Tennessee, prepared for Historical Society. By A. W. Putnam. (MSS. in Hist. So. Lib.)

King's Mountain and Its Heroes: History of the Battle of King's Mountain, October 7, 1780, and the events which led to it. By Lyman C. Draper, LL. D. Cincinnati, 1881.

Celebration of the Battle of King's Mountain, October, 1855.

Memoirs of the Services of General John Sevier, written by Major James Sevier, 1839. (MSS. in Hist. So. Lib.)

Manuscript Letters of John Sevier, James Robertson, Evan Shelby, Isaac Shelby, Willie Blount, Archibald Roane, David Crockett, Andrew Jackson, and of many of the governors of Tennessee are in the Historical Society Library.

Clark's Miscellany in Prose and Verse. By Isaac Clark of Sumner County, Tennessee. Nashville, 1812.

The South-Western Monthly. A Journal devoted to the Early History of the South-West. 3 vols.

The Tennessee Gazetteer, or Topographical Dictionary. By Eastin Morris. Nashville, 1838.

The Resources of Tennessee. By J. B. Killebrew, assisted by J. M. Safford. Nashville, 1874.

The Tennessee Hand-Book and Immigrants' Guide, giving a description of the State of Tennessee. By Herman N. Bokum. Philadelphia, 1868.

Report of the Committee of the House of Representatives of the United States, appointed to prepare and report Articles of Impeachment against William Blount, a Senator of the United States. Printed by order of the House of Representatives.

Some Account of the Life and Public Services of William Blount. By General Marcus J. Wright. Washington.

The Biography of the Principal American Military and Naval Heroes, comprehending details of their achievements during the Revolutionary and the late wars. By Thomas Wilson. 2 vols. New York, 1819. (Contains biography of William Carroll.)

Address of the Hon. Abraham P. Maury on the Life and Character of Hugh Lawson White. Delivered at Franklin, May 9, 1840. Franklin, 1840.

A Memoir of Hugh Lawson White, with Selections from his Speeches and Correspondence. Edited by Nancy N. Scott, one of his descendants. Philadelphia, 1856.

Reminiscences of the Clarksville Bar. An Address by Hon. Gustavus A. Henry. Nashville, 1877.

The Self-Vindication of Colonel William Martin against certain charges and aspersions made against him by General Andrew Jackson and others in relation to sundry transactions in the campaigns against the Creek Indians in the year 1813. Nashville, 1829.

Address of General R. G. Dunlap to the East Tennessee Volunteers. 1836.

The Life of Sam Houston. The only authoritative memoir of him ever published. Illustrated. New York, 1855.

Life and Select Literary Remains of Sam Houston of Texas. 2 vols. in one. By William Carey Crane, D. D., LL. D. Philadelphia, 1885.

Sam Houston. The Pioneer, vol. iv. p. 162.

Review of the Life of General Sam Houston as recently published in Washington City by J. T. Towers. By D. G. Burnet, First President of Texas. Galveston, 1852.

Sam Houston and his Republic. American (Whig) Review, vol. v. p. 566.

General Sam Houston. By Alexander Hynds. Century Magazine, vol. xxviii. No. 4, p. 506.

Sketch of the Life of William B. Campbell, compiled and arranged by Lemuel R. Campbell. (MSS.)

Ben Hardin, His Times and Contemporaries, with Selections from his Speeches. By Lucius B. Little. Louisville, 1887.

Anecdotes of Public Men. By John W. Forney. 2 vols. New York.

Reminiscences of Public Men. By Ex-Governor B. F. Perry. Philadelphia, 1883.

The Memories of Fifty Years, containing Brief Biographical Notices of Distinguished Americans and Anecdotes of Remarkable Men, interspersed with Scenes and Incidents occurring during a long life of observation, chiefly spent in the Southwest. By W. H. Sparks. 4th edition. Philadelphia, 1882.

Casket of Reminiscences. By Henry Stuart Foote. Washington, 1874.

Bench and Bar of the Southwest. By H. S. Foote. St. Louis, 1876.

Mississippi as a Province, Territory and State, with Biographical Notices of Eminent Citizens. By J. F. H. Claiborne. 1 vol. Jackson, Mississippi, 1880.

Random Recollections of Early Days in Mississippi. By H. S. Fulkerson. Vicksburg, Miss., 1885.

The Flush Times of Alabama and Mississippi. By Joseph G. Baldwin. San Francisco, 1883. (Reprint.)

The Bench and Bar of Mississippi. By James D. Lynch. New York, 1881.

The Life and Times of Sergeant Smith Prentiss. Edited by his Brother. 2 vols. New York, 1855.

Romantic Passages in South-Western History, including Orations, Sketches, and Essays. By A. B. Meek. 2d edition. Mobile, 1857.

Report of the Commissioners appointed to mark the Boundary Line between the States of Kentucky and Tennessee to the Governor of Kentucky. Frankfort, 1860.

Report of the Select Committee of the House of Representatives in relation to the Southern Boundary Line of the State of Tennessee. Nashville.

History of the South Carolina Cession and the Northern Boundary of Tennessee. By W. R. Garrett, A. M. Nashville, 1884.

The Life of Andrew Jackson. By Alexander Walker. New York, 1859.

The Life of Major-General Andrew Jackson. By John Henry Eaton. Philadelphia, 1828.

Life of Andrew Jackson in 3 vols. By James Parton. New York, 1860.

Andrew Jackson as a Public Man. By William Graham Sumner. Houghton, Mifflin & Co. Boston, 1883. (American Statesmen.)

Life of Thomas Hart Benton. By Theodore Roosevelt. Houghton, Mifflin & Co., Boston, 1887. (American Statesmen.)

Colonel Crockett. Fraser's Magazine, xvi. p. 610.

Pictorial Life and Adventures of Davy Crockett, written by himself. Philadelphia.

David Crockett. His Life and Adventures. By John S. C. Abbott. New York.

An Account of Colonel Crockett's Tour to the North and Down East, written by himself. Philadelphia, 1835.

Colonel Crockett's Exploits and Adventures in Texas, written by himself. London, 1837.

Review of this in (London) Monthly Magazine, New Series, vol. ii. p. 215.

Sketches and Eccentricities of Colonel David Crockett of West Tennessee. 11th edition. New York.

Life of Martin Van Buren, Heir Apparent to the Government and the Appointed Successor of General Andrew Jackson. By David Crockett. Philadelphia, 1837.

Colonel David Crockett of Tennessee. By Marcus J. Wright. Magazine of American History, vol. x. p. 489.

Old Times in Tennessee, with historical, personal, and political scraps and sketches. By Jo. C. Guild. Nashville, 1878.

Political Circulars of John L. Allen, G. W. L. Marr, Cave Johnson, M. Lea, A. O. P. Nicholson, and others.

Senator Grundy's Political Conduct, reviewed by Charles Biddle. Nashville, 1832.

Biography of Felix Grundy in the United States Magazine and Democratic Review, vol. iii. p. 161. Washington, 1838.

An Oration on the Life, Character, and Public Services of the Hon. Felix Grundy. By Hon. John M. Bright. 1859.

The National Portrait Gallery of Distinguished Americans, vol. iii. 1836.

Speech of William Humphreys of Fayette County on the Preamble and Resolutions of William McLain of Smith, nominating Judge White as a candidate for the Presidency, Thursday, October 15, 1835.

Preamble and Resolutions adopted by the Legislature of the State of Tennessee, November 14, 1839, and the Reply and Resignations of Ephraim H. Foster, a Senator of said State in the Congress of the United States, delivered November 15, 1839. Nashville, 1839.

The same of H. L. White, delivered January 13, 1840.

Speech of Mr. Wheeler of the Senate upon the Instruction Resolutions. Nashville, 1839.

Address of James K. Polk to the People of Tennessee, April, 1839. Columbia, 1839.

James K. Polk, and a History of his Administration. By John S. Jenkins. Auburn, 1851.

James K. Polk. Democratic Review, vol. ii. p. 197.

Life and Public Services of James K. Polk. By G. H. Hickman. Baltimore, 1844.

A Political Register. By W. G. Brownlow, Editor of the Jonesboro Whig. Jonesboro, 1844.

Speech of Mr. Turney on the Bill to suppress Indian Hostilities, in the House of Representatives, 1838.

An Address of the Democratic Members of Congress for the State of Tennessee to their Constituents, March, 1841.

Circular from Washington City, June 25, 1841, signed by A. O. P. Nicholson, Cave Johnson, Hopkins L. Turney, A. McClellan, A. V. Brown, and H. M. Watterson.

Cave Johnson. Democratic Review, vol. xvii. p. 241.

Sketch of the Life and Public Services of James C. Jones. By W. G. Brownlow in his "Political Register."

The Life, Speeches, and Public Services of John Bell, together with a Life of Edward Everett, Union Candidates for the Offices of President and Vice-President of the United States. New York, 1860.

Speech of John Bell of Tennessee on the Tariff. Delivered in the House of Representatives, June 15, 1832. Washington, 1832.

John Bell. His Past History connected with the Public Service. (Published in 1860. Author unknown.)

Speech of Mr. Bell of Tennessee on the Bill to secure the Freedom of Elections. Delivered in the House of Representatives, January, 1837. Washington, 1837.

Proceedings of the Democratic State Convention, held in Nashville on the 23d of November, 1834, for the purpose of electing Delegates to represent the State of Tennessee in the National Convention for the nomination of Candidates for President and Vice-President. Nashville, 1843.

Speeches Congressional and Political, and other Writings of Ex-Governor Aaron V. Brown of Tennessee. Nashville, 1854.

Aaron V. Brown. United States Democratic Review, N. S., vol. xli. p. 140.

Speech of John M. Bright, Esq., against Know-Nothingism, at Flat Creek, Bedford County, September 11, 1855. Nashville, 1855.

Speech of Ex-Governor Aaron V. Brown on Know-Nothingism, at Gallatin, July 4, 1855. Nashville, 1855.

Reflections and Suggestion on the Present State of Parties. By an Old Clay Whig. Nashville, 1856.

Address of the Democratic State Central Committee to the Voters of Tennessee. Nashville, 1856.

Letter of Hon. James C. Jones of Tennessee to his Constituents on Political Parties; His Past Course and Future Intentions. Washington, 1856.

A Political Romance. Putman's Magazine, N. S., vol. iii. p. 428.

The Life and Public Services of Andrew Johnson, Seventeenth President of the United States, including his State Papers, Speeches, and Addresses. By John Savage. New York, 1866.

Three Presidents of the United States. Blackwood's Magazine, vol. c. p. 623.

Life and Times of Andrew Johnson, Seventeenth President of the United States, written from a National Standpoint by a National Man. New York, 1866.

Andrew Johnson. By Isaac Smucker, in Potter's American Monthly, vols. iv. and v. p. 733.

Life, Speeches, and Services of Andrew Johnson, Seventeenth President of the United States. Philadelphia.

Andrew Johnson, his Life and Speeches. By L. Foster. New York, 1866.

Speeches of Andrew Johnson, President of the United States, with a Biographical Introduction, by Frank Moore. Boston, 1865.

Memorial Addresses on the Life and Character of Andrew Johnson (a Senator from Tennessee). Delivered in the Senate and House of Representatives, January 12, 1876.

The President on the Stump (Andrew Johnson). North American Review, vol. cii. p. 530. [J. R. Lowell.]

Life of General Robert Hatton. By James Vaulx Drake. Nashville, 1867.

To Active Working Friends of the Opposition in Tennessee. Executive Committee Rooms. Nashville, July 23, 1859.

Sketches of the Rise, Progress, and Decline of Secession, with a Narrative of Personal Adventure among the Rebels. By W. G. Brownlow, Editor of the Knoxville Whig. Philadelphia, 1862. (This is commonly called "Parson Brownlow's Book.")

The Annals of the Army of Tennessee and Early Western History. Edited by Dr. Edwin L. Drake, vol. i., April to December, 1878. Nashville, 1878.

Old Times in West Tennessee. By a Descendant of one of the First Settlers. Memphis, 1873.

History of the Discovery and Settlement of the Valley of the Mississippi by the three Great European Powers, Spain, France, and Great Britain, and the Subsequent Occupation, Settlement, and Extension of Civil Government by the United States until the Year 1846. By John W. Monette, M. D. 2 vols. New York, 1846.

The History and Geography of the Mississippi Valley. By Timothy Flint. 2 vols. in one. Cincinnati and Boston, 1833.

The Mississippi Question Fairly Stated and the Views of those who clamor for War examined. In Seven Letters. By Camillus. Philadelphia, 1803.

Elmwood: Charter, Rules, Regulations, and By-Laws of Elmwood Cemetery Association of Memphis. History of the Cemetery. Biographical Sketches. Attractive Monuments. Names of Proprietors. Memphis, 1874.

De Soto and the Early Settlement of Memphis. By J. M. Keating, in the Southern Monthly Magazine for January, 1881.

Old Folks' Historical Record, from October, 1874, to September, 1875. Memphis, 1875.

Grant from the Original Proprietors to the Citizens of Memphis (Broadside issued in 1828), signed by John Overton, John C. McLemore, George Winchester, and William Winchester.

The History of the City of Memphis, being a compilation of the most important documents and historical events connected with the purchase of its territory, laying off of the city and early settlement. Also "Old Times Papers." By James D. Davis. Memphis, 1873.

History of the City of Memphis, Tennessee. By J. M. Keating. Syracuse, N. Y. 1888 (October).[1]

A History of the Detection, Conviction, Life, and Designs of John A. Murrell, the Great Western Land Pirate, together with his system of villainy and plan for exciting a Negro Rebellion, with a catalogue of the names of 445 of his Mystic Clan, fellows and followers, and their efforts for the destruction of Mr. Virgil A. Stewart, a young man who detected him. To which is added a biographical sketch of Mr. V. A. Stewart. By Augustus Q. Walton, Esq. 1835.

The History of Virgil A. Stewart and his Adventures in capturing and exposing the great "Western Land Pirate" and his Gang, etc., compiled by H. R. Howard. New York, 1836.

A Refutation of the Charges against Mathew Clanton, together with an Exposition of the Character of Virgil A. Stewart, its Author. By Mathew Clanton. Pittsburgh, Miss. Printed by John J. Hamilton. 1835.

Nashville Orthopolitan. October to January, 1845, July to October, 1846.

Speech delivered by James C. Jones at the Clay Whig Meeting at Nashville on the 8th of April, 1848. Lebanon, 1848.

Address of Ex-Governor Aaron V. Brown before the Democratic Association of Nashville, 24th of June, 1856. Nashville, 1856.

[1] See p. 446.

A History of the Life of General William Trousdale (MS.). By J. A. Trousdale.

William Blount. By M. J. Lamb. Magazine of American History, vol. xiii. p. 313.

The Narrative of Colonel David Fanning (A Tory in the Revolutionary War with Great Britain), giving an account of his Adventures in North Carolina, from 1775 to 1783, as written by himself, with an Introduction and Explanatory Notes. (Reprint.) New York, 1865.

A Topographical Description of the Western Territory of North America. By Gilbert Imlay, a Captain in the American Army during the war and Commissioner for laying out lands in the back settlements. 3d edition. London, 1797.

NEWSPAPERS.

The Knoxville Register, 5 November, 1791, to 31 July, 1795 ; 10 March, 1830, to 19 February, 1834 ; 8 May, 1849, to 9 July, 1850.

Impartial Review and Cumberland Repository (Nashville), February, 1805, to December, 1808.

Nashville Whig, 1 November, 1814, to 20 November, 1815 ; 21 November, 1815, to 15 August, 1818 ; 1 January, 1823, to 29 December, 1824; 9 January to 31 December, 1838 ; 2 October to 31 December, 1839 ; 6 January to 30 December, 1840 ; 1 January to 31 December, 1841 ; 3 January to 31 December, 1842 ; 3 January to 30 December, 1843 ; 2 January to 28 December, 1844 ; 1 January to 31 December, 1846.

The Clarion and Tennessee Gazette (Nashville), 19 September, 1820, to 29 August, 1821. (On 20 February, sub-title was discontinued.)

Nashville Gazette, 26 May, 1819, to 2 July, 1821.

Jackson Gazette (Jackson, Tennessee), May, 1824, to June, 1826 ; June, 1828, to September, 1830.

National Banner and Nashville Whig, 3 January to 28 December, 1827 ; 1 January, 1828, to 29 December, 1829 ; 1 January to 31 December, 1830 ; 2 January to 30 December, 1835 ; 4 January to 22 August, 1837, when it was united with the Republican and continued under the title of Republican Banner to 30 December, 1837.

Nashville Republican and State Gazette, 8 January to 30 December, 1828 ; 1 December, 1831, to 31 December, 1832 ; 2 January to 13 November, 1834, and Nashville Republican to 30 December, 1834.

Southern Statesman (Jackson, Tennessee), 5 February, 1831, to 22 September, 1833.

LIST OF AUTHORITIES.

National Banner and Nashville Daily Advertiser, January to 21 October, 1833.

The Kaleidoscope (Nashville), 18 July, 1888, to 24 July, 1834.

Nashville Republican, 1 January to 31 December, 1835; 2 January to 16 December, 1836.

Commercial Transcript, vol. i. from January 2 to December 31, 1836.

Daily Republican Banner (Nashville), 1 January to 31 December, 1839.

Nashville Union, 2 January to 30 December, 1839; January to 28 December, 1840.

The Whig Banner (Nashville, a campaign publication). 13 May to 29 July, 1843; 11 May to 26 October, 1846.

The Spirit of '76 (Nashville, a campaign publication). 25 April to 26 October, 1844; 6 April to 26 August, 1847.

Democratic Statesman, (Nashville, a campaign publication). 12 April to 6 September, 1845.

The Politician (Nashville, a campaign publication). 18 April to 10 October, 1845; 17 October, 1845, to 10 April, 1846.

The Politician and Weekly Nashville Whig (a campaign publication). 2 April to 17 October, 1846; 9 October, 1846, to 9 April, 1847; 16 April to 6 October, 1847; 8 October, 1847, to 31 March, 1848.

Rough and Ready (Nashville, a campaign publication). 8 April to 3 September, 1847; 1 July to 14 October, 1848.

Nashville True Whig and Weekly Commercial Register, 5 April to 27 September, 1850; 4 October, 1850, to 28 March, 1851.

Memphis Daily Appeal, 4 July to 24 December, 1854; 1 July to 19 December, 1855; 1 January to 9 June, 1856; 23 August, 1856, to 16 June, 1857; 18 June, 1857, to 24 March, 1858; 1 January to 20 December, 1859; 1 January to 27 June, 1861.

Weekly Appeal, (Memphis). 21 May, 1851, to 11 January, 1854; 21 December, 1859, to 25 December, 1860.

Memphis Daily Eagle and Enquirer, 3 January to 12 August, 1855.

Nashville Daily Gazette, January, 1858, to December, 1861 (inclusive).

The Opposition. (A campaign document designed to support John Netherland for the governorship.) First number appeared 3 May, and last 29 July, 1859.

INDEX.

ABINGDON or Wolfs Hill, 30; church at, 218.
Academies established, 235; prejudice against, 236.
Act of Congress of 1806, beginning of schools, 235.
Act of Oblivion, 91, 98.
Adams, Prof. Herbert B., 191 (note).
Admission, cause of opposition to, 187, 188.
Adventure, The, 111.
Advocate. *See* Phœbus.
Ætna, first steamboat at Memphis, 311.
Alamance, Battle of, 31, 216.
Alexander, Adam R., 309.
Alien Law of 1798, 341.
Ambrister, 9.
American System, 278.
Amusements, 181.
Anderson, Alexander, 224.
Anderson, Governor Charlie, of Ohio, 421.
Anderson, Joseph, 186, 443.
Anderson, Patton, 359.
Arbuthnot, 9.
Armstrong, Robert, 374.
Asbury, Bishop, quoted, 88, 172, 173, 175, 183, 187; his diary, 111, 182; at Ramsey's house, 182.
Asher's Station, 118; location, 120.
Ashley, Lord, 8.
Association. *See* Watauga.
Assumption, Fort, Bienville at, 11; built, 313.
Asylums, building of, 300.
Athens, 270.
Attorney-general, 194.
Authorities, list of, 446–461.
Autry at the Alamo, 445.

Baily, Sylvester, 340.
Balch, Hezekiah, 88, 218; scandalizes the church, 220; removed, 221; president of Greene College, 234.
Balch, James, 220.
Bank of Tennessee, 258; H. L. White, president, 258; does not suspend specie payment, 260.
Bank of the State of Tennessee (1820), Loan Office changed to, 263; White's charge, 262; Jackson's protest, 263; opposed by Carroll, 263; a failure, 265; Carroll suggests winding it up, 266; irregularities in, 266; wound up, 266.
Bank of the State of Tennessee (1831), 267.
Bank of the State of Tennessee (1838), objects of, 237, 268; opposed by Neil S. Brown, 237; chartered, 268; directors nominated by governor, 269; branches located, 270; sale of state bonds, 271; dissatisfaction, 271; Cannon on, 271; used to further secession, 273; wound up, 273; issues receivable for taxes, 274; depositors of, unjustly treated, 274; "sterling bonds," 397; directors rejected by the Senate in 1841, 410.
Bank at Gallatin and other places, 259.
Bankrupt Law, 411.
Barge, 352.
Barret, Peter, 140.
Barring teacher out, 181.
Barrow, Washington, 375.
Barton, Samuel, 132, 133, 134.
Batture at Memphis. *See* Mud-bar.
Bean, Russell, 21.
Bean, William, 21, 29, 34, 321.
Bean's cabin, 5, 20; location of, 21; built, 21.
Beard, John, kills Indian chiefs, 157.
Beatty's settlement in McNairy County, 305.
Bedford County, salt in, 279.
Begelow, E., 309.
Bell, John, 357, 404; attacks American system, 351; opposes Grundy in 1827, 362; sketch of, 363; elected to the U. S. Senate, 363; opposed by Jackson, 364; Globe's attack on, 367; rivalry with Polk, 367; driven into opposition, 367; his design, 368; his political record, 368, 395; his speech of May, 1835, 368; returned to Congress without opposition, 370; defeated for speaker, 371; Cassidy letter, 372; enmity against Polk, 377; prominent Democrat, 378; sustains White, 366; New Whig, 379; on Polk's address, 381; builds Whig cabin at Nashville, 385; speeches in 1840, 387; leader of Whig Junto, 403; attacks Polk in 1844, 415; vote for U. S. senator, 429; declares for secession, 440; secretary of war, 442; candidate for presidency, 364, 443.
Benton County, 311.
Benton, Jesse, duel with Carroll, 255; settles Tipton County, 306; testimony as to mouth of Wolf River, 319, 334; commissioner to lay off road, 322; his hatred of Jackson, 361; his pamphlet, 361; fight with Jackson in Memphis, 361.
Benton, Thomas H., 322, 442.
Bettis, William, 311.

Bickford, W. A., 335.
Bienville attacks Chickasaws, 11.
Bird, Colonel, builds fort on Holston, 11.
Black Bob, 182.
Blackburn, Gideon, 220.
Blair, John, 98.
Blair, John, 366.
Bledsoe, Anthony, runs boundary line in East Tennessee, 32; resists departure from Cumberland, 130; builds fort, 134; opposes Hopewell Treaty, 140; letter to Sevier, 144; killed, 151; two sons killed, 158.
Bledsoe, Isaac, 108; justice of the peace, 133; fort at Bledsoe's Lick, 134.
Bledsoe's Lick, 108.
Bledsoe's Station, 118; location of, 120.
Block-house, 119.
Blount College, 234.
Blount, Willie, Judge, 200; elected governor, 250; urges Sevier to appoint Jackson, 250; sketch of, 250; services during the Creek War, 250; on canal in New York, 276; candidate for governor in 1827, 296.
Blount, William, disapproves Hopewell Treaty, 139, 140; territorial governor, 148; his character, 148; his administration, 149; deceived by the Indians, 152, 155; reprimands Robertson, 162; member of Constitutional Convention, 186; U. S. senator, 187.
Bluffs, Battle of, 126; decides fate of Cumberland settlement, 127.
Bolivar, 306; canal to, 387.
Bolivar, Simon, 306.
Boone, Daniel, identified with Southwest, 14; explorations of, 14; at Sycamore Shoals, 18, 29, 35, 112; cuts words on a tree, 29; at Bean's cabin, 29; passes through East Tennessee to Kentucky, 29; why he entered the wilderness, 111; Byron's lines on, 112.
Boone's Creek, 5.
Boone, John, 35.
Boundary lines, ignorance of, in North Carolina, 50; in act of 1777, 50; confusion of, 49, 140; between Tennessee and Mississippi, 315.
Bowman, Thomas, 221.
Boyd's Creek, Battle of, 63.
Bradbury, John, 309.
Branding, abolition of, urged by Carroll, 302.
Broadhead, Daniel, store at Ohio Falls, 177.
Broadhorn. *See* Kentucky Flat.
Brinkley, R. C., 287.
Brown, Aaron V., nominated for governor, 426, 430; partner of Polk, 426; member of Buchanan's cabinet, 442; as a stump speaker, 427; trick of debate, 427; style of oratory, 427; Mount Pisgah metaphor, 427, 432; elected, 428; riding on Jackson's back, 431; at Southern Convention, 436; candidate for vice-president, 445.
Brown, Jacob, settles on Nollichucky, 31; member of Committee of Thirteen, 34; increases his purchase of lands, 36.
Brown, James, 308, 315; his stage line, 323.

Brown, Joseph, released by Sevier, 150, 160; captured by Indians, 160; leads expedition against Nickojack, 158.
Brown, Neil S., 416, 425; opposes bank of 1838, 237; suggests county taxation for schools, 237; nominated for governor in 1847, 430; sketch of, 431; turns Mount Pisgah metaphor on A. V. Brown, 432; his ridicule of Polk, 432; elected, 432; defeated by Trousdale, 433; minister to Russia, 441.
Brown, Samuel R., 310.
Brown's settlement. *See* Nollichucky settlement.
Brownlow régime, 291.
Brownlow, W. G., suggests investigation of old bank, 273; of 1843, 410; in 1844, 415; in 1851, 433; supports Johnson, 440; Fighting Parson, 442.
Brownsville, 270, 308.
Buchanan's station attacked, 156; marvelous escape, 157.
Bushy Head, 18.
Butler, or Untoola, or Gun Rod, killed by Hubbard, 81-83.
Burr, Aaron, dreams of a Southwestern empire, 103, 164.
Byron, lines on Daniel Boone, 112.

Cabin, how built, 24.
Cage, William, 78.
Caldwell, John, 216.
Calhoun, John C., at Memphis, 285.
Callaway, Caleb, 209.
Callaway, Samuel, 14.
Calvin, John, 216.
Cambreling, A. M., 308.
Cameron, Alexander, 41.
Campbell, Arthur, 104.
Campbell, David, judge of the superior court of Franklin, 78; commissioner to North Carolina, 89; letter to Caswell, 92; accepts North Carolina judgeship, 97; refuses to arrest Sevier, 99; territorial judge, 148.
Campbell, David, member of North Carolina assembly, 98; impeached for bribery, 245; defeated in 1809, 245 (note).
Campbell, George W., secretary of the treasury, 251, 442; minister to Russia, 443.
Campbell, Col. William, joins Sevier and Shelby, 59; made commander, 59.
Campbell, Wm. B., 434; candidate for governor, 436; sketch of, 436; defeats Trousdale, 437.
Campbell's Station, 173.
Camp-meeting, origin of, 223; the first, 223.
Canal between Hiwassee and Coosa River, 284; between Tennessee and Big Hatchie Rivers, 284, 307. *See* New York Canal.
Caney Fork, lottery to remove obstructions from, 279.
Cannon, Newton, candidate for governor in 1827, 296; defeated in 1821 by Houston, 297; lukewarm towards Jackson, 358; sketch of, 358; attracts Jackson's attention, 359; denies statement in Life of Jackson, 359; candidate in 1835, 370; supports White, 370; elected, 370; re-elected, 374; candidate against Polk, 379, 384; first Whig candidate, 379; abandons

INDEX. 465

stump in 1839, 381; defeated, 381; vote in 1837 and 1839 compared, 384.
Canoe, 352.
Capitol built, 300 (note).
Carondelet, 106, 166.
Carlisle, John G., 376.
Carr, Anderson B., 310.
Carr, Gideon, 311.
Carr, Thomas D., 310.
Carrick, Samuel, 88, 218, 220; president Blount College, 234.
Carroll County, 304.
Carroll, William, 201, 357; contest with Ward, 252; significance of, 252, 253; sketch of, 254; duel with Jesse Benton, 255; incurs Jackson's contempt, 255; his desperate bravery, 255; his character, 256; compared with M'Minn, 257; his brilliant administration, 257; influence over the legislature, 257; protest against law against United States Bank in Tennessee, 262; opposes Bank in 1820, 263; rejects property laws, 263, 302; effects of Carroll's message, 264; friend of internal improvements, 279; compared with Sevier, Polk, and Johnson, 301; urges reform in courts, building of penitentiary and abolition of barbarous methods of punishment, 302; a friend of education, 302; the Reform Governor, 302; opposed by Jackson, 357; candidate for governor in 1835, 370; chairman Baltimore Convention in 1840, 385; attacks Harrison, 385.
Carter, Landon, secretary Jonesboro Convention of 1784, 71; speaker first Senate, 78; land speculations with Sevier, 242, 246.
Carter, John, member of Committee of Thirteen, 34; delegate to North Carolina Congress, 46; land office, 245.
Carter's Valley, 14, 30; fort in, 31; in North Carolina, 32.
Carter and Parker's store, 32, 36.
Cass, Lewis, 418.
Cassidy letter, 372.
Castleman, Abraham, 128, 129; reports danger, not believed, 156; "The Fool Warrior," 157.
Caswell County, 79.
Caswell, Governor, 84, 86, 95.
Catron, John, prominent Democrat, 378; in White contest, 378; opposes White, 378; his career and character, 378; letters against United States Bank, 379; earnest friend of Jackson, 379; associate supreme judge, 379, 443.
Caucus for election of U. S. senator, 428; Turney declares it anti-Republican, 429; and prostrated in Tennessee, 429.
Cavet's Station, 150.
Centreville, 304.
Cession of 1784, 60; causes of objection, 70; repealed, 77.
Cession of 1789, 146.
Chancery Courts in North Carolina, 194.
Chancery Courts in Tennessee, 202.
Chapman, Thomas, 78.
Charles II., grant of, 8.
Cherokee Trace, 316.
Cherokees, war with Virginia, 12; defeated at Etchoe, 12; ratify cession of Six Nations to England, 17; their country invaded, 45.
Chester, Robert I., 310.
Chickamaugas, their character, 54.
Chickamauga towns destroyed by Sevier, 63.
Chickasaw Bluffs (Fourth), mentioned in Marquette's Journal, 6; described, 312; Spanish seize, 313; Washington's protest, 313; thought to be in Mississippi, 315.
Chickasaws, 5, 10.
Chisca, 7.
Church of England, 40.
Circuit Courts in North Carolina, 195.
Circuit Courts in Tennessee, 201.
Circuit rider, sketch of, 226–232.
Civil Jack, 122.
Claiborne, W. C. C., 186, 442.
Clan. See Murrell.
Clapboards, 24, 175.
Clarendon, grant of Charles II. to, 8.
Clark, Lardner, store at Nashville, 177.
Clark, Benjamin, 56.
Clark, Col. George Rogers, 55; supposed to hold cabin rights, 114.
Clarke, Col. Elijah, 57.
Clarksville, 115, 270.
Clay, Henry, on internal improvements, 278; his speeches on, 278; not a stump speaker, 377; at Whig Convention in 1840, 390; his speech, 391; his Raleigh letter, 414; position on annexation, 417; Alabama letter, 417; carries Tennessee, 422; not defeated by Alabama letter, 423.
Clearing the land, 24, 27.
Clemens, Jere, 443.
Cleveland, Col. Ben, 60.
Clique. See Whig.
Cocke, William, at Fort Heaton, 43; member of Jonesboro Convention, 76; applies for the admission of Franklin to Union, 85; commissioner to North Carolina, 89; his speech, 50; member of Constitutional Convention of 1796, 186; U. S. senator, 187; candidate for governorship, 247; letter of explanation, 247.
Coffee, John, 255.
Colbert's Gang, 178.
Coldwater Expedition, 142, 143.
Colleges, prejudices against, 236.
Colonies, relations between and Indians, 8; combine with Cherokees, 9; trouble with Cherokees and cause, 12.
Columbia, 270.
Commercial Convention. See Memphis.
Committee of Thirteen. See Watauga Association.
Committee of Notables, 132; records of, preserved by Putnam, 132; jurisdiction of, 132.
Common-fame letter against Cumberland Presbyterians, 224.
Common law in North Carolina and Tennessee, 192.
Common schools. See Schools, 233.
Compact of government, 118; details of, 120; revived, 131.
Compromise between two factions in State of Franklin, 94; defeated by North Carolina, party, 95.
Confederacy, 78.

INDEX.

Confession of Westminster, 216.
Constable, 210, 212. *See* County Officers.
Constitution of 1796, 192, 200, 253.
Constitution of 1834, 201; on school fund, 237; anticipated by Carroll's election, 252; on internal improvements, 281; marks an era, 300.
Constitution of Franklin debated, 84; of Frankland, 85; of North Carolina adopted, 85.
Constitutional Convention of 1796, 186.
Continental confederacy, its weakness, 134.
Convention (*See* Whig party, also Democrats).
Convention of 1784 at Jonesboro, 71.
Convention, second at Jonesboro, 77; action of, 78.
Convention at Greeneville in 1785, 85.
Corn-mill, 137.
Coroner, 212. *See* County Officers.
Corn-stalk at Point Pleasant, 55.
Cossan, John, 220.
Cotton, first, in West Tennessee, 310.
Cotton gin, patent right purchased for Tennessee, 279.
Cotton Grove, 309.
Council in North Carolina, 193; becomes Upper House of General Assembly, 194.
Council of State, 198, 200.
Counties, established in North Carolina, 195; divided in 1833 into districts in Tennessee, 210.
County courts in North Carolina and Tennessee, 207; in 1360, 208; growth of jurisdiction, 208; jurisdiction of, 209–212; at the present time, 212; to organize schools, 236; to tax county for schools, 237; ordered to lay off roads, etc., 211, 276.
County officers, 212; elected by county courts, 200, 253.
Court-house for Watauga Association, 56.
Court leet, 207, 209.
Courts of oyer and terminer and general gaol delivery, 194; at Jonesboro, 67.
Courts of pleas and quarter sessions. *See* County courts.
Courts of Tennessee, Carroll urges a reform of, 302.
Covington, 306.
Cozby, James, helps Sevier escape, 99.
Craighead, Alexander, 217; paves the way for the Mecklenburgh Resolutions, 217; favors revival, 217.
Craighead, Thomas B., 137; comes to Tennessee, 218; sketch of, 219; tried for heterodox sentiments, 219; opposes revival, 220, 222; president Davidson College, 234.
Crawford, Edward, 220.
Crittenden, J. J., 391.
Crockett County, 311.
Crockett, David, 366; people of Memphis support, 330; on Jackson, 358; father of Tennessee Whiggery, 360; sketch of, 360; votes for John Williams, 360; candidate for Congress, 360; on Van Buren, 373; his motto, 389; his position in Southwestern history, 444; at the Alamo, 445.
Croghan, George, deposition of, upon Iroquois title to Southwestern region of country, 16.

Crozat Grant, 314.
Cumberland College, 235, 239; lottery for benefit of, 279.
Cumberland Gap, 14, 107.
Cumberland Mountains, 14.
Cumberland Presbytery, 224; dissolved, 225.
Cumberland Presbyterianism, compared to other religious movements, 221; origin in revival of 1800, 223; Cumberland Presbytery established, 224; divided after appointment of laymen, 224; doctrinal dissensions, 224; Craighead and others write common-fame letter, 224; young men refuse to submit to examination, 224; Independent Presbytery formed, 225; first General Assembly, 225; strong leaning towards Methodism, 225.
Cumberland River, 14.
Cumberland Settlement (*see* James Robertson), compared with Watauga, 105; attitude of Spanish towards, 106; takes no part in Franklin movement, 107, 132; first settler, 108; included in Transylvania purchase, 113; compact of government, 120; names of stations, 118; Henderson's policy towards, 119; severe winter, 121; first man killed, 121; scarcity of corn, 122; Robertson prevents abandonment of, 122; Indians prepare for general invasion of, 126; Battle of the Bluffs decides its fate, 127; dangers surrounding the settlers, 127; departure again discussed, 130; government revived, 131; forts rebuilt, 132; dangers still great, 133; expenditures for, to be paid by, 141; cane cut down, 153, 173; pursuit of Indians forbidden, 154; invaded by 600 Indians, 156; McGillivray tries for ten years to destroy, 167; effect of Nickojack expedition, 162.
Cummins, Charles, 218, 220.
Currency in State of Franklin, 79, 88; cowbells, etc., used as, 180.
Currin, R. P., 237.

Davidson Academy, 137, 234; united with College in West Tennessee, 235.
Davidson County organized, 133.
Davis, James D., historian, 325; discovers mud-bar, 334; quoted, 361.
Davis, William A., 311.
Deaderick, J. W., shingles his cabin, 175.
Dean, William, 311.
Decatur County, 311.
Democratic Convention of 1844, 418.
Democrats, prominent Democrats in 1832, 378; elect Polk, 381; Union their organ, 380; nominate Van Buren in 1840, 385; confident of victory, 385; lose heart, 391; their trick, 392; lose Tennessee in 1840, 392; their stoutness of heart, 393; prepare for 1841, 393; follow Polk-Jones contest with eagerness, 394; record on National Bank, 394; diversity of opinion on, 395; Bank Democrats read out of the party, 395; enthusiasm in the Polk-Cannon contest, 399; anecdote of party feeling in 1841, 403; in the General Assembly of 1841, 406; contest over senatorial election in 1841, 408; protest, 409; reject bank directors, 410; enter contest of

1843 under disadvantages, 410; effect of 1843 on 1844, 411; receive Polk's nomination with enthusiasm, 414; brilliancy of 1844, 416; have the advantage in 1844, 417; convention at Nashville, 418; denounce H. L. Turney, 429; nominate A. V. Brown in 1847, 426.
De Mumbreun, 108.
De Peyster, 61.
De Soto in Tennessee, 6, 7.
Dirt and stick chimney, 25.
Divisions. *See* Grand Divisions.
Doak, Samuel, 76, 88; protest, 71; sketch of, 218; first teacher and first preacher, 218; member Abingdon Presbytery, 220; forms Independent Presbytery, 220; erects first school, 233.
Doak, William, 309.
Dobbs, Fort, 11.
Donelson, A. J., calls Southern Convention at Nashville, 434; candidate for vice-president, 443.
Donelson, John, makes Indian treaty in 1769, 32; his Journal, 111, 115; agreement with Robertson, 113; father of Andrew Jackson's wife, 117; builds cabin on Clover Bottom, 118; narrow escape, 122; plants corn, 136.
Donelson, Stockley, 149.
Douglass, Edward, 136.
Dragging Canoe, his expedition, 42; killed, 43.
Drake, Joseph, 108.
Dresden, 311.
Dug-out, 352.
Dunlap, E., 54.
Dunlap, R. C., 370.
Dunlap, W. C., 429.
Dunmore, Lord, 31.
Du Quesne built, 164; captured, 12.
Durant, George, 209.
Dyer County, 306.
Dyer, Col. Henry, 306.
Dyer, Robert H., 278.
Dyersburg, 306.

Eaton, Fort, 108; built, 115; location, 120.
Eaton, John H., life of Jackson, 359; defection in 1840, 387; minister to Spain, 387; his speech and mention of Jackson, 387; secretary of war, 442.
East Tennessee and Georgia Railroad, sale of state stock in, 293.
Edmiston, John, 154.
Education. *See* Schools.
Elholm, Major, negotiates treaty between Georgia and State of Franklin, 96.
Embargo Act, effect of, 259.
Emigrant (*see* also Pioneer) described, 21; his outfit, 22; method of clearing the ground, 24; imagines himself on Virginia soil, 23; builds the cabin, 24; furniture, 25; fare, 25, 26; clears the ground, 26; sowing seed, 27.
Emigration, after Battle of Etchoe, 13; pours over the mountains in 1769, 20, 29; produced by resistance to Stamp Act, 30; by Battle of Alamance, 31; to Cumberland settlement, 114, 115, 122, 131, 133.
English, struggle with the French, 9; erect forts among the Indians, 11.
Enoree, Battle of, 58.

Equity jurisprudence, 201.
Erie Canal. *See* New York.
Etheridge, Emerson, 440.
Evans, Nathaniel, helps Sevier escape, 99.
Ewin. *See* Ewing, 224.
Ewing, Andrew, member of Committee of Notables, 132; clerk, 132, 133.
Ewing, Finis, 224; his circuit, 224.
Ewing, Henry, 269.
Excise law of 1792, 241.
Exploring expeditions, 30.

Farmers' and Merchants' Bank, 268.
Fayette County, 305.
Fayetteville Tennessee Bank, 259.
Fearne, Robert, hostility to proprietors, 322, 329; originates South Memphis scheme, 340; leaves the State, 340.
Federalists in Tennessee, 241.
Female Academy, 235 (note).
Fentress, James, 322.
Ferguson, Alexander, 310.
Ferguson, Patrick, attacked by Clark and Sevier, 58; threatens the mountaineers, 59; refuses to surrender at King's Mountain, 61; is killed, 61.
Ferry over the Cumberland, 138; ferry rights in Memphis, 321.
Fite, Thomas, 395.
Flat. *See* Kentucky Flat.
Fletcher, Joshua, 321.
Fletcher, Ralph, 209.
Fogg, Francis B., 426.
Foote, Henry S., 443.
Fooy, Benjamin, 311, 319, 333.
Forked Deer River, lottery to improve navigation of, 279.
Forest, Gen. N. B., 444.
Fort Assumption. *See* Assumption.
Fort Freeland. *See* Freeland Station.
Fort Gillespie. *See* Gillespie.
Fort Lee. *See* Lee.
Fort Pickering, built, 314; struggle with Memphis, 342; Winchester fears its rivalry, 342; Overton does not, 342; McLemore's scheme, 343; crushed by Overton's ownership of half the landing, 334; sale of lots, 345.
Fort San Ferdinando de Barancas, 314.
Fort Union, location of, 120.
Forts, French, 10.
Foster, E. H., 404; speaker of House of Representatives in 1835, 371; New Whig, 379; forced to resign U. S senatorship, 382, 406; speeches in 1840, 387; chairman of Whig Convention of 1840, 390; denounces protection, 395; leader of Whig clique, 403; admits right of instruction, 407; candidate for U. S. Senator, 407; elected, 412; candidate for governorship, 424; his inconsistent record, 425; sketch of, 425.
Foster, Robert C., candidate for governorship, 251, 252; sketch of, 252; supports Hall for speaker, 299.
Frankland, name proposed for new State, 85; constitution of, 85.
Franklin, Benjamin, 85.
Franklin, State of, 76; plan of association, 71; act of cession repealed, 77; first Jonesboro Convention, 71; legislature, 78; organized, 78, 79; currency, 79;

named in honor of Dr. Franklin, 85; contest between two parties, 87, 88; no deaths, 88; marriages under, legalized by Tennessee, 88; confusion of jurisdiction, 89; Franklin party weaken, 93; compromise, 94; defeated by North Carolina party, 94; memorial of Tipton and others, 95; rebuked by Governor Caswell, 95; Governor Caswell's address, 96; end of State of Franklin, 96–98.
Franklin Tennessee Bank, 259.
Free Banking Act, 272; contains germ of present National Bank system, 272; repealed in 1858, 272; in 1866, 274.
Freeland, Capt. George, member of the Committee of Notables, 132.
Freeland Station, 120; saved by Robertson, 125.
French in Mississippi Valley, 9; upon the Lakes, 9; their plan of conquest, 10; their power broken, 12.
French Lick, 108, 114, 134.
French traders captured, 177. *See* Spanish Traders.
Fundamental constitution. *See* Grand Model.
Furniture, primitive, 25.

Gaines, James L., 295.
Gallatin, Albert, 188.
Gamblers hung at Vicksburg, 346, 354; effects of this in the Southwest, 355.
Garland, A. H., 442.
Gasper's Station, 118; location of, 120.
Gates, General, defeated at Camden, 59.
Gazette of Knoxville, 149.
General Assembly of Tennessee, 187; origin of, 187; qualifications of members, 188; powers, 188.
General Banking Act of 1860, 273.
Gentry, M. P., 430; votes for tariff of 1842, 395; candidate for governorship, 438; speech against Scott, 437; John Quincy Adams's estimate of, 444.
George III., proclamation of, 15; establishes rule for purchase of Indian titles, 15.
Gibson County, 305.
Gibson, Samuel, 305.
Gibson, Col. Thomas, 305.
Gibsonport, 305.
Gilkey, Robert, dies natural death, 127.
Gillespie, Fort, 31, 42, 150.
Gillespies settle McNairy County, 305.
Glasgow, James, 246.
Globe, supported by Overton, 329; attacks Bell, 367; predicts Jackson will crush White, 369; extra edition in 1835, 371.
Gomley, Thomas, 34.
Goodrich, Chauncey, 188.
Goosherd, 205.
Governor-general in Carolina, 193; appointment of, 193.
Governors. *See* John Sevier, Archibald Roane, Willie Blount, Joseph M'Minn, William Carroll, Sam Houston, Newton Cannon, James K. Polk, James C. Jones, Aaron V. Brown, Neil S. Brown, William Trousdale, William B. Campbell, Andrew Johnson, and Isham G. Harris.
Grice, Peggy, 320.
Granville, Lord, 49.
Graham, Daniel, 443.

Grand divisions of Tennessee, 201.
Grand model, devised by Locke, 8; fails, 8, 209.
Grant, Colonel, defeats Cherokees, 12.
Great Bend of the Tennessee River, 96.
Great Natchez Trace, 171, 179, 277, 316.
Great National Road, 279, 280.
Great Whig Convention. *See* Whig.
Greene County formed, 56; divided, 79.
Greene College, 234.
Greeneville, 56, 78.
Grundy, Felix, 357, 366; favors United States Bank at Nashville, 262, 394; private letter to president suggesting officers for United States Bank, 262; prepares bill for Loan Office, 263, 301; contest with Bell, 364; sketch of, 361; supported by Jackson, 364; in White canvass, 366, 369, 378; prominent Democrat, 378; pillar of Jacksonism, 379; his reward, 379; anecdote of Harris, 381; obeys instructions, 407; attorney-general, 442.
Guard certificates used as currency, 136.
Guild, Joe C., barring out escapade, 181; quoted, 381; refuses to vote for Martin Van Buren for president, 414; as a wag, 444.
Gwin letters, 369.

Hadden, D. P., 326.
Hagler, Joel, 304.
Haile, John, 46.
Hall, A. A., leader of Whig clique, 403; edits Politician, 428; register of United States treasury, 443.
Hall, William, succeeds Houston as governor, 299; sketch of, 299; supported by Carroll and Foster for speaker of Senate, 299; Houston's compliment to, 299.
Hamilton, Alexander, 241; plan for paying state debts, 147.
Hamilton District, 200.
Hamilton, Thomas, 304.
Hammond, Eli, crosses Tennessee River and raids Indian country, 157.
Hanover Presbytery, 217.
Hardeman, Col. Thomas J., 306.
Hardeman County, 306.
Hardin County, 305.
Hardin, James, 305.
Hard Labor, treaty of, 17.
Hargrave, John, 309.
Harris, Isham G., 269; recommends winding up of State Bank of 1838, 272; elector for Buchanan, 438; his powers on the stump, 439; senior senator in Tennessee, 439; arouses enthusiasm, 439; reëlected, 440; calls extra session, 440; issues proclamation declaring Tennessee out of the Union, 440.
Harris, J. George, 380; in 1840, 386; Harrison's letter, 392; acknowledges the corn, 392; in 1844, 415.
Harrison, W. H., nominated by Whigs, 384; accused of being an Abolitionist, 392; carries Tennessee in 1840, 392.
Hart, Nathaniel, 36.
Hartsfield, Nathan, 306.
Harvey, Governor, appoints justices of the peace, 209.
Haskell, Joshua, impeached, 301.
Haskell, W. T., 425; candidate for U. S.

INDEX. 469

senator, 429; in 1844, 416; defeated by Hatton in 1857, 439.
Hatchie, county seat of Hardeman County, 306.
Hatton, Robert, 439; Fillmore elector, 439; candidate for governorship, 439; defeated by Isham G. Harris, 439.
Hawkins, Benjamin, 147.
Hawkins County, 93.
Hay, David, takes part in Coldwater Expedition, 142.
Hay, Joseph, killed, 121.
Haynes, Landon C., 444.
Haywood County, 308.
Haywood, John, Federalist, 241; county named for him, 308.
Hearsay letter. *See* Common-fame.
Heaton, Fort, attacked by Indians, 42.
Heath, Sir Robert, grant to, 7.
Henderson County, 365.
Henderson, Nathaniel, 98.
Henderson, Col. Richard, 18; at Sycamore Shoals, 35, 112; Transylvania Purchase, 112; suggests compact of government, 119.
Henderson, Major Samuel, sent to Franklin, 81.
Henry County, 304.
Henry, Patrick, stops attempt in Virginia to join Franks, 84, 104; opinion of the mountaineers, 90; suggests Mason of Virginia as territorial governor, 148.
Henry, Gustavus A., 404, 438; in 1844, 416; "Eagle Orator," 416, 437; vote for U. S. senator, 429; refuses to be a candidate, 434; Confederate senator, 434; nominated for governor, 437.
Henry's Station, 157.
Hickman County, 304.
Hickman, Edwin, 354.
Hindman, T. C., 442.
Hogs, 179.
Holman, Charles, 321.
Holmes, James. *See* Mountain Academy.
Holston Circuit, 225; divided, 226.
Holston Tennessee Bank, becomes Eastern Bank of Tennessee, 259.
Holt, Joe, 421.
Hominy pounder, 137.
Hooper, William, declares for total separation, 38.
Household, founding of, 20.
House of Burgesses in North Carolina, 193; qualification of voters, 193; of members, 197.
Houston, John, 310.
Houston, Rev. Samuel, 88, 218; member of Abingdon Presbytery, 220; dismissed from same, 220.
Houston, Sam, 442; elected governor in 1827, 296; sketch of, 296; devoted to Jackson, 297; his character, 297; marries and his wife leaves him, 297; he resigns and leaves Tennessee, 298; cause of separation, 298; visits Nashville, 427.
Hubbard, James, kills Butler, 81–83.
Humphreys County, 304.
Humphreys, W. H., 370.
Hundred reeve, 208.
Hunt, Memucan, 304.
Huntingdon, 304.
Huntsman, Adam, 386.

Impeachment. *See* David Campbell, N. W. Williams, and Joshua Haskell.
"Immortal Thirteen," 409.
Independent Presbytery of Abingdon. *See* Presbytery.
Indian titles, 14–17.
Indians, spoliation of, 17; removal from Tennessee, 149.
Indorsement laws, 261.
Ingraham, J. H., establishes schools in Nashville, 238.
Institutes of Tennessee, 190; nothing new, 192.
Instructions to senators, 406, 407; right of, not denied before the war, 406.
Internal improvements (*see* also State debt), 268; friends of, unite with friends of common schools, 269; beginnings of, 276; canal in New York, 277; M'Minn's message, 277; committee on, in 1823, 279; hampered by local jealousies, 280; Carroll's message, 280; first systematic plan (of 1829), 281; its details, 281; Constitution of 1834, 281; plan of 1829 not succeded, 282; plan of 1835 (Pensylvania Plan), 282; also Partnership Plan, 283; amount of state bonds issued for, 283; repealed, 283; crash of 1837, 284; plan of 1848, 290; amended, 291; Act of 1852, 292; amended, 292; Constitution of 1870 puts an end to, in Tennessee, 295.
Iroquois cede Southwestern region, 15; their title, 16.
Irwine, William, 310, 321.
Isbell, Zach, member of Committee of Thirteen, 34; in both Watauga and Cumberland Settlements, 105.
Island Flats, Battle of, 44.
Itinerant. *See* Circuit rider.

Jack, Jeremiah, 66.
Jackson, Andrew, 442; compared with Sevier, 74; wife of, 117; superior judge, 135; the owl story 136; pursues Indians, 151; not on Nickojack Expedition, 158; vote against Washington, 178; member of Constitutional Convention of 1796, 186; did not name Tennessee, 186; member of Congress, 189; trustee of Davidson College, 234; takes sides against Sevier, 243; quarrel with Sevier, 244; goes to Southwest Point, 245; friend of Carroll in Benton duel, 255; recommends United States Bank officers, 262; protest against Loan Office, 263; Overton gives him half of Rice Grant, 327; disposes of his interest, 327; criticised for Treaty of 1818, 327; Overton's dying message to, 355; opposes Carroll, 357; controls politics of Tennessee, 358; intolerance of his friends, 358; Crockett on, 358; marks Cannon, 359; fight with Jesse Benton in Memphis, 361; opposes Bell, 364; wants Van Buren to succeed him, 364; estrangement from White, 365; his threat against White, 366; inaugurates campaign, 368; Gwin letters, 369; letters to Blount and Grundy, 369; denounces "White Whigs," 369; franks Globe to Tennessee legislators, 371; wants to redeem Tennessee, 375; relations with Polk, 378; four pillars in Ten-

nessee, 379; their reward, 379; dragged into contest of 1840, 386; his popularity, 413; Jackson on Van Buren in 1844, 414; denies recantation of bargain intrigue and corruption charge, 415.
Jackson, town of, 270, 309, 310; first town in West Tennessee, 309; the Pioneer, the Gazette, the Southern Statesman, 310; centre of political activity, 310; court-house, 310; first house, 311; its present importance, 311.
Jacobs, S. D., 443.
James, Joseph, 321.
Jarnagin, Spencer, obeys instructions, 307; candidate for United States Senate, 407; is elected, 412.
Jay's Treaty, 178.
Jennings, Edmond, 128; swims Tennessee River, 142.
Jennings, Jonathan, 122.
Jerks, 223.
Jetton, Robert, 322.
Johnny cake, 26.
Johns Hopkins University, 191.
Johnson, Andrew, 364, 404, 443; compared with Sevier, Polk, and Carroll, 301; refuses to allow election of Whig senator, 408; signs protest, 408; one of the "Immortal Thirteen," 409; nominated for governor, 437; opposed by all prominent Democrats, 438; elected, 438; his position on secession, 440; refuses to secede, 440.
Johnson, Cave, president State Bank, 269, 272; member of Congress, 375; postmaster-general, 375, 442; prominent Democrat, 378; in White canvass, 378; pillar of Jacksonism, 379.
Johnson, Daniel, 305.
Johnson, John, 227.
Johnson, Thomas, 251.
Johnston, Samuel, 147.
Joiner, Zaccheus, 311.
Jones, Calvin, 303.
Jones, George W., his prominence, 444.
Jones, James C., 338, 438; advocates Memphis and Charleston Railroad, 286; president of it, 287; elected U. S. senator, 287; Whig candidate for governor in 1841, 394; his views on national questions, 394; sterling bonds charge against Polk, 397; his origin and character, 398; ardent Clay man, 398; nominated "to go for Polk," 399; "Lean Jimmy," 399; convass of 1841, 401; "What fine fur!" 400; Polk's suckle-colt anecdote, 401; with Polk at Nashville, 404; demolishes Polk, 405; elected, 405; talent for political management, 410; bankrupt law of 1843, 411; "Lay on, Nancy," 411; Jones elected, 412; attracts national attention, 412; speaks for Clay, 415; supports Scott, 437; suggested as a candidate for the presidency, 444.
Jones, John, 34.
Jones, Lewis, 309.
Jones, William, 56.
Jonesboro laid off, 56; court of oyer and Terminer and general gaol delivery, 67; court-house, 175.
Judiciary of Carolina, 194; courts and their jurisdiction, 194-196; officers and mode of election, 194.

Judges, elected by General Assembly, 200; number increased, 201; elected by the people, 201; life tenure a failure in Tennessee, 201.
Junto. See Whig.
Jurisprudence in Tennessee, 195.
Justice of the peace, in 1360, 208; in 1530, 208; in North Carolina, appointed by the governor, 209; in Tennessee, until 1834, by General Assembly, 209; appointed according to captain's companies, 209; elected, 210; jurisdiction, 208-211.

Kanawha, Battle of, 31.
Kaskaskia, 9, 114, 177.
Keel, 177, 352.
Kennedy, Daniel, 98.
Kentucky Flat, 177, 352.
Key Corner, 311.
Kilgores abandon their fort, 131.
Kimberlin, Jacob, finds lead, 181.
King, Samuel, 224.
King's Mountain, Battle of, 57; the fight, 60-62.
Kirbys, settle McNairy County, 305.
Kirk, Henry, 305.
Knox County, 149.
Knox, James, 30. See Long Hunters.
Knoxville, 149; branch bank at, 270; seat of government, 149, 300; masonic hall in, 279.

La Grange, 270, 305.
La Grange and Memphis Railroad, 282, 824-286, 342.
Lake County, 311.
Lake, Joseph, 220.
Lambert, Jeremiah, first Methodist preacher in Tennessee, 225.
Lance de Grace. See New Madrid.
Land communities, 205.
Land office, in Watauga, 36; in Washington County, 47, 49, 52; reopened in Washington and Sullivan counties, 67; Cumberland land office, 133.
Land speculations, 247.
Land system of Tennessee, 233, 246; compared with North Carolina, 47.
La Salle, 5, 10, 164, 313.
Latham, F. S., 307.
Lauderdale County, 306, 311.
Lauderdale, Col. James, 311.
Lawrence, William, 310, 328.
Lee, Fort, dismantled, 42, 44.
Legislative council, 199.
Lewis, Andrew, 11.
Lewis County, 304.
Lewis, Major W. B., 361; second auditor, 443.
Lewis, William, 305.
Lillington, Alexander, 209.
Lincoln, Abraham, elected president, 440.
Lindsley, Dr. Philip, 238, 239.
Linsey, Isaac, 132, 133.
Loan Office, 261, 301; issues based on, 262; bill for, prepared by Felix Grundy, 263; title changed to Bank of Tennessee, 263.
Local self-government, 204; two systems, 204; compared, 204-207.
Locke, John, 8; fundamental constitutions, 8, 209.
Locke, G. B., 354.
Louisville and Nashville Railroad, 293.

INDEX. 471

Long Hunters, expeditions of, 30.
Long Island, 11.
Lookout towns destroyed by Sevier, 63.
Lotteries in Tennessee, 279.
Loudon, Fort, built, 11; garrisoned, 11; cannon there, 12; captured, 12.
Lover, Samuel, ridicules Memphis, 318.
Lower Cherokee towns. *See* Nickojack.
Lucas, Robert, 34, 36, 105.
Luxembourg, 9.

Maclin, William, 200.
Macon, Nathaniel, 188.
McAdow, Samuel, 225.
McAlpin, R. C., 335.
McAlpins settle McNairy County, 305.
McClung, Charles, 186.
McDowell, Col. Charles, 57, 58, 59.
McEwen, Robert H., superintendent public instruction, 236; plunderer of school funds, 237, 307.
McGee, John, 223.
McGee, William, 223.
M'Greandy, James, re-awakens the Christian spirit, 222; sketch of, 222; excludes doctrine of fatality, 224; does not become a Cumberland Presbyterian, 225.
McGillivray, Alexander, dupes Washington, 152; his character and intrigues, 166; Robertson tries to placate, 167.
McIvers settle Madison County, 309.
McKenzie, 304.
McLean, Charles D., 309.
McLemore, John C., 306, 321, 343, 344, 395.
McMillin, Andrew, 267 (note).
M'Minn, Joseph, candidate for governor, 251; sketch of, 251; vote for, 252; compared with Carroll, 302; on financial stringency in 1820, 261; recommends property laws, 261; Loan Office, 262, 263; message of, 277; on navigation, 278.
McNairy County, 305.
McNairy, John, 186; judge, 200; county named for, 305.
M'Neal, Thomas, 306.
McNutt, of Mississippi, as a stump speaker, 377.
Madison County, 309.
Madison, James, 112, 188; on internal improvements, 278; county named for, 309.
Manifesto of Governor Martin of North Carolina, 81; strengthens the cause of North Carolina, 83; Sevier's reply, 84; Caswell's reply to Sevier, 84.
Mansker, Casper, trip to Natchez, 108; goes to Cumberland settlement, 114; adventure with an Indian, 129.
Marquette, 6.
Marshall, Thomas F., 418.
Marshall, William, 98.
Martin Academy becomes Washington Academy, 233.
Martin, Alexander, governor of North Carolina, 81.
Martin, Francis Xavier, 191.
Martin, John D., 336.
Martin, Joseph, 98; leads expedition against Cherokees, fails, 150.
Martin, William, 245.
Martin and Donelson treaty, 139.
Mauldin, James, 132.
Mauldins abandon their fort, 131.

Maxwell, George, 98.
Meagher, Pat, 320, 321.
Mecklenburgh Resolutions, 39, 217.
Memphis (*see* Chickasaw Bluffs and South Memphis), 7, 171, 270, 312; meetings to abolish charter, 213; struggle with Randolph, 327; geographical position, 315; thought to be in Mississippi, 315; appearance when settled, 316; Rice and Ramsey grants, 316; proprietors agree to lay off town, 317; origin of name, 318; contest between owners of Rice and Ramsey grants, 318; first sale of lots, 318; mistake in laying off, 320; public squares, 320; southern limits, 319; change of county seat, 322; incorporated, 325; indignation meeting, 325; Winchester first mayor, 326; Rawlings mayor, 326; from 1821 to 1833 an experiment, 327; Overton decides contest for supremacy, 327; mail stages, 330; distributing point for mail, 330; hostility towards proprietor, *see* Proprietors; letter in Portfolio, 331; typical lease, 331; Memphis Advocate, 331; cutting of timber, 332; Promenade dispute, 332; mud-bar, 333, 334; landing, 335; navy-yard, 337; Compromise Addition, 338; struggle between North and South Memphis, 339; contest about landing, 340; united with South Memphis, 341; McLemore, a disadvantage to Memphis, 344; flat-boat war in 1842, 354.
Memphis and Charleston Railroad, 285, 286; J. C. Jones, president, 287; succeeded by A. E. Mills, 287; Sam Tate president, 288; completion, 290; its effect on the Southwest, 290.
Memphis Commercial Convention, 285.
Memphis Interrogatories, 410.
Menees, James, 234 (note).
Menifee, John, 245.
Merchandise, 176, 177.
Meridith, Frederick, 304.
Mero, Governor, 106; his policy, 166.
Mero District, 105, 200.
Methodists in Tennessee, ascendency of, 215; relation to Cumberland Presbyterianism, 225; vitalizing influence, 225; sketch of, 225; first Methodist preacher in Tennessee, 225; circuit rider, 226; growth of, 226.
Mexican War, 430.
Middle Tennessee (*see* also Cumberland settlements), a part of Charles II. grant, 106; Robertson saves, 106.
Militia company, unit of local self-government, 71; elect two representatives in each county, 71; in Washington District, formed into a brigade, 77; organized to protect Cumberland settlement, 135; inadequate, 143; nucleus of local self-government, 209.
Miller, Austin, 315.
Miller, Joaquin, 444.
Miller, Phineas. *See* Cotton gin.
Millikin, John, killed, 121.
Mills, A. E., 287.
Mills, first in Middle Tennessee, 179.
Mississippi River, navigation of, 141, 178; Spaniards claim exclusive navigation, 154, 165; made free, 168.

472　　　　　　　　　　　　INDEX.

Mitchel, John, Irish patriot lives in Tennessee, 444.
Molloy, Thomas, 132, 134, 136, 178.
Monk, General, 8.
Monroe's veto message, 278.
Montcalm, 10.
Montgomery, 160.
Moore, Captain, hand to hand fight with Indian, 43.
Moore, Mark, 226.
Moore, Patrick, at Pacolet, 58.
Mountain Academy, 308.
Mount Florence, 138.
Morgan District organized, 67.
Morgan, Charles, erects fort on Bledsoe's Creek, 134.
Mud-bar, 319, 333; discovered by Davis, 334; dispute as to ownership, 335; becomes navy-yard, 337; Compromise Addition, 338; donated back to Memphis, 339.
Murfreesboro, seat of government, 300.
Murrell, John A., 346; sketch of, 347; methods, 347; example of, 348; organizes a clan, 348; his strikers, 348; marries, 349; his character, 349; his ambition, 350; his vanity, 350; plans a negro insurrection, 351; convicted, 351.
Murray, Abel V., 305.
Murrays settle McNairy County, 305.
Muscle Shoals, efforts to improve, 277, 280.

Nachitoches on Red River, 164.
Nashborough, built, 118, 120; court-house built, 133; becomes Nashville, 134.
Nashville succeeds Nashborough, 134; laid off, 134; its prosperity, 179; common schools, 238; first steamboat, 255; seat of government, 300.
Nashville and Chattanooga Railroad, first built in Tennessee, 284 (note).
Nashville Bank, 258; during war of 1812, 259; does not resume, 265; crippled, 265; fails, 265.
Nashville Convention. See Southern and Whig Conventions.
Nashville University. See University.
Natchez, 106, 164, 177.
Natchez Trace. See Great Natchez Trace.
National questions in local contests, 381.
Navigation, inland, 276; appointment of a board of managers, 277; M'Minn's message, 277.
Navy-yard, 337.
Negro-running, 350.
Netherland, John, 438; candidate for governor in 1859, 439.
Newbern (now New Berne), 38.
New Brunswick Presbytery, 217.
New Light, 219.
New Madrid, 164.
New Orleans, 106, 177.
New Side, 217.
New York Canal, 276, 277.
Newspapers, take part in Ward-Carroll contest, 256; vituperation of, 380; the Union, 380; their partisanship, 404.
Nicaragua. See Walker.
Nichol, William, 269, 272.
Nicholson, A. O. P., supports Van Buren, 387; U. S. senator, 307; candidate for U. S. Senate, 427; vote for, 429; editor of Union after his defeat by Turney, 430; at Southern Convention, 435.
Nickojack, origin of name 122; expedition against and end of Indian hostilities in the West, 149; preparation for expedition 158; Ore takes command, 158; plan of attack, 159.
Nixon, Col. Richard, 308.
Nollichucky circuit, 226.
Nollichucky settlement, compelled to take the oath, 34.
North Carolina, indifferent to its western settlements, 33, 35, 69, 144; part in Revolution, 38; Provincial Congress meets, 38; elects members of Congress, 38; votes Sevier and Shelby sword and pistols, 62; cedes its western territory to United States, 69, 146; enters Union, 146.

Obion County, 311.
Oconostota, foresees fate of Indian tribes, 18; his character, 18; his speech, 19; signs treaty, 19.
Ogden, Benjamin, takes charge of Nashville circuit, 226; sketch of, 226.
Old Abraham, 44.
Old Side, 219.
Ore, Major, ordered to destroy lower Cherokee towns, 160; report to Governor Blount, 163.
Ore's Expedition, See Nickojack Expedition.
Overseers of Roads, 213.
Overton, John, Federalist, 241; buys Rice grant, 328; transfers half to Andrew Jackson, 318; decides contest between Memphis and its rivals, 328; his oversight over Memphis, 329; his character, 329; has mail routes established in interest of Memphis, 329; his treatment of visitors, 330; his letters, 330; friend of Jackson, 330; his idea of city building, 339; does not fear Fort Pickering as a rival, 342; his estimate of McLemore, 343; crushes Fort Pickering, 344; his death, 345 (note).
Owen, William, 305.

Paris, 304.
Paris, Treaty of, 14.
Parish, 194, 210, 211.
Parrish, Joel, 266, 410.
Parsons, Enoch, candidate for governorship, 252.
Parsons, Thomas H., 321.
Partnership plan of internal improvements, 283.
Patrick Henry, Fort, 113, 115.
Patterson, J. T., 305.
Patdton's Still House, 182.
Peddler, 176.
Penitentiary, built, 300 (note); building of urged by Carroll, 302.
Pennsylvania Plan of internal improvements, 282.
Perkins, J. P., 311.
Perkins, W. O. N., 294.
Perry County, 304.
Peyton, Balie, at Whig Convention of 1840, 391; Polk's imitations of, 400; peripatetic politician, 444.
Phrases, political, 367; from Carter to Shel-

by, 387; "hurrah-boys," 379; "Keep the ball rolling," 388; "Crow, Chapman, crow," 388.
Phœbus, Thomas, 331; Memphis Advocate, 331.
Pike, Albert, at Whig Convention of 1844, 421; his romantic career, 421; his poetry, 421; "After the midnight, cometh morn," 421; lives in Tennessee, 443.
Pillory, abolition of urged by Carroll, 302.
Pillow, Gideon J., candidate for vice-president, 445.
Pinch, origin of name, 340.
Pioneer (*see* Emigrant) learns Indian methods, 28.
Pirate, 177.
Pirogue, 177, 352.
Planters' Bank, 268.
Polk, Ezekiel, 306.
Polk, James K., 366, 442, 443; report on school lands in Tennessee, 235 (note); message on internal improvements, 283; compared with Sevier, Carroll, and Johnson, 301; rivalry with Bell, 367; elected speaker, 371, 376; fails of nomination for vice-president, 375, 385; not an unknown man, 376; sketch of character, 376; brilliancy of his administration, 377; first stump-speaker, 377; his relations with Jackson, 378; prominent Democrat in 1832, 378; pillar of Jacksonism, 378; candidate against Cannon, 379, 381; ridicule of Cannon, 381; canvass with, 381; address of 1839, 381; vote in 1839 compared with vote of 1837, 384; speaks for Van Buren and is presented as a nuisance, 387; contest with Jones followed by Democrats, 394; his views on national questions, 394; Polk's record, 394, 395, 396; Kane letter, 395; on internal improvements, 396; speech on origin of Whigs, 396; sterling bonds, 397; Jones turns tables on, 400; one of Polk's anecdotes, 401; repudiates his own methods, 402; his smile, 402; with Jones at Nashville, 403; Polk's speech, 404; has to defend "Immortal Thirteen," in 1843, 410; Bankrupt Law in 1843, 410; nominated for president, 414; Young Hickory, 414; Clay magistrate elected at Columbia, 416; position on annexation, 417; not elected by Clay's Alabama letter, 423; partner of A. V. Brown, 426; riding on Jackson's back, 431.
Polk, Thomas, signs Mechlenburgh Resolutions, 39.
Polk, William, 306.
Population, growth of Watauga settlement, 35; in 1776, 40; effect of better roads, 52; in 1790 and 1795, 170.
Porter, Benjamin, 311.
Porter, Benjamin T., 311.
Pound-master, 213.
Powell's Valley, 183.
Precinct courts, 194, 210; become county courts, 195.
Prentice, George D., 380.
Prentiss, S. S., refuses to vote thanks to Polk, 379; letter of Jones to, 412; at Whig Convention of 1844, 421; sketch of, 422; court-house speech, 422; "Die, Prentiss, die!" 422.

Presbyterianism (*see* Cumberland), ascendency in Tennessee, 215; from Scotch-Irish, 216; line of emigration, 216; seeds of discord, 220; doctrinal illiberality, 221.
Presbytery of Abingdon, 217; members of, 220; trouble in, 220; divided, 220; independent formed, 220; secession of, 220.
President's Island, 6.
Priestly, James, president Cumberland College, 337.
Prince Francis, 133.
Prince George, Fort, built, 11; besieged, 12; settlers around, 13; emigrants pass, 21, 39.
Proclamation of George III., 15; no effect on traders, 15.
Property laws, 261, 302.
Proportionate representation, 197 (note), 200.
Proprietors of Memphis, hostility towards, 323, 331; their names, 328.
Protestants of Ireland, 216.
Prud'homme, Fort of, 5; built, 313.
Public lands and schools, 234; confusion in laws relating to, 235.
Public schools. *See* Schools.
Public warehouse at Memphis, 316.
Puncheon floor described, 25.
Purdy, 305.
Putnam, A. W., rescues Compact of Government, 120 (note), 132.

Quakers oppose Church of England, 211.
Quarter sessions courts, 211, 214; origin of county courts, 212.
Quilting, 181.

Railroads, attention turned to, 284; first chartered, 284; first built, 284 (note); projected, 285; ideas of the results they accomplish, 286; State aid to, plan of 1848, 290; Act of 1852, 292; amount issued to before war, 293; bonds issued to after war, 293; take advantage of Acts of 1869, 1870, 294; bonds issued to, 295.
Rains, John, comes to Cumberland, 114, 118; drives cattle across Cumberland on ice, 120; mentioned, 143; on Coldwater Expedition, 142; on other expeditions, 143.
Raleigh, Sir Walter, grant to, 6, 7.
Raleigh becomes county seat of Shelby County, 322.
Ramsey, F. A., 78, 175.
Ramsey grant, 316; Ramsey's will not recorded in Shelby County, 317; South Memphis, part of, 339.
Randolph, 270; struggle with Memphis, 307; canal to connect Tennessee and Hatchie rivers, 307; Recorder, 307; bank, 307; Cambreling suit, 308; attempt to become county seat of Tipton County, 308; mail route, 307.
Ranger, 213.
Rankin, William, 66.
Rattle and Snap, 182.
Rawlings, Isaac, 311, 325; sketch of, 323; compared with Winchester, 324; mayor, 324; his last vote, 325; defeated for mayor, 338; enforces law against lawbreakers, 351.

Reconstruction, State saved from, 294.
Red Heifer, 137, 182.
Red River Meeting House, great revival there in 1800, 223.
Reed, Joseph, 305.
Regulators, 31.
Religion in Tennessee, 215.
Renfroe, Moses, settles on Red River, 115.
Renfroe settlement massacre, 122.
Replevin laws, 263, 302.
Reporter, Somerville, 305.
Republicans. *See* Democrats.
Revival of seventeenth century, 221; great revival of 1800, 223; its growth and effects, 224.
Reynolds, Benjamin, 322.
Reynoldsburgh, 304.
Rhett, R. Barnwell, 434.
Rhodes, Tyree, 306.
Rice grant, 316; its boundaries, 318; trouble as to starting point, 318; shifting of Wolf River, 319; in mud-bar dispute, 319; processioned in 1820, 320.
Rice, David, 224.
Rice, Elisha, 316.
Rice, John, 316; his death, 316.
Ripley, 311.
River life. *See* River towns.
River towns, exposed to evil influences, 352; life on the river, 353; flat-boat men refuse to pay wharfage to Memphis, 354.
Roads (*see* Great National Road), from Wolfs Hill, 39; by Fort Prince George 39; into Washington County from North Carolina, 52, 170; allows passage of vehicles, 52; from Nashville to Clinch Mountain, 136, 171, 173; condition of roads in early times, 172.
Roane, Archibald, member Constitutional Convention of 1796, 186; judge, 200; governor in 1801, 242; opposes Sevier, 243; teaches H. L. White, 243; sketch of, 243; delivers papers about Sevier, 246.
Robertson, Charles, member of Committee of Thirteen, 34; trustee for Watauga Association, 36; delegate to North Carolina Congress, 46; allowed to coin money for State of Franklin, 89.
Robertson, Felix, 393, 410.
Robertson, James, comes from North Carolina, 30; trip to Indian village, 35; defends fort, 44; in both Watauga and Cumberland settlements, 105; why he migrated to Cumberland, 110, 113; sets out, 113; trip to Kaskaskia, 114; suggests compact of government, 119; son of, killed, 123; Robertson's character, 123; compared with Sevier, 123; is made colonel, 124; chairman of Committee of Arbitrators, 124; North Carolina Indian Commissioner, 124; saves Freeland Station, 125; powder runs short, 124; member of Committee of Notables, 132; chairman of Committee of Notables, 132; member of North Carolina General Assembly, 133; opposes Hopewell Treaty, 140; goes on Coldwater Expedition, 141; organizes battalion, 143; prepares for expedition against Indians, 144; brigadier-general of Mero District, 149; wounded, 151; visits Indian nation, 152; organizes militia to resist Indians, 153; makes preparations for Nickojack Expedition, 158; is reprimanded by Governor Blount, 162; offers his resignation, 162; intrigues with Spain, 165; loses his way returning to North Carolina, 172; member of Constitutional Convention of 1796, 186; trustee of Davidson College, 234.
Robertson, Mark, killed, 141.
Rogersville, 149, 270.
Rounsevall, David, 132.
Rucker, E., 367.
Running Water, 159, 161.
Russell, George, 34, 56.
Rutherford, Griffith, 149, 311.
Rutherford, Henry, 303, 311.

Salem Academy, 218.
Salisbury, District of, divided, 67.
Salt, manufacture of, 138.
Salt licks of the West, 108.
Salt springs, reserved by the State, 133; sold, 138.
Sanderlin's Bluffs. *See* Raleigh.
School funds plundered, 236.
Schools, 233; first in Tennessee, 218, 233; set on foot, 234; condition of, in 1801, 235; school lands entered, 235; importance appreciated, 235; first definite plan for public, 235; condition in 1837, 236; self-taxation advocated, 236; introduced, 237; fund plundered, 237; Act of 1845, 237; Governor Brown on, 237; in Nashville, 238; condition of educational questions in Tennessee, 239; to receive funds of Bank of 1820, 267; State Bank of 1838, 268, 272.
Scotch-Irish, 216, 234.
Scott, A. M., 307.
Scott, James, 245.
Scott, John, 98.
S ott, John, plunders school-fund, 266.
Scouts, compared with regular troops, 143; sent out by Robertson, 156, 162.
Secession, call of State Convention to consider, 440; defeat of, 440; carried, 440; Governor Harris's proclamation, 440; foreshadowed in Tennessee, 442.
Sedition Laws of 1798, 241.
Self-taxation for support of schools advocated, 236.
Settlements in the East, trouble about boundary line, 31; found to be in North Carolina, 32; Donelson's Treaty, 32; made in violation of treaties, 33; obtain ten years' lease from Cherokees, 35; population in 1776, 40; growth of, in 1780, 65.
Settlers. *See* Emigrants.
Sevier County formed, 79; left without any government, 101; organizes one itself, 101.
Sevier, John, member of Committee of Thirteen, 34; clerk of Watauga Association, 34; delegate to North Carolina Congress, 46; forces annexation to North Carolina, 50; alone had correct idea of limits of State, 50; colonel of Washington County, 57; with Clark attacks Ferguson, 58; attacks Moore at Pacolet, 58; prepares for attack on Ferguson, 59; at King's Mountain, 60; voted sword

INDEX. 475

and pistols by North Carolina, 62; requested to take up arms again, 62; General Greene writes to Sevier, 62; joins Marion with two hundred men, 62; meets Indians at Boyd's Creek, 63; invades and destroys Indian country, 64; his mode of warfare, 64; Tuckasejah Expedition, 65; "is a good man," 66; clerk of court, 67; president of Jonesboro Convention of 1784, 71; sketch of, 71-75; Nollichucky Jack, 72; foresaw future greatness of Tennessee, 73; "treaty maker," 74; compared with Jackson, 74; leader of movement to form a new State, 75; is reluctant to proceed to extremes, 75; made general of brigade, 77; thinks this the end of Franklin, 77; reply to Martin's manifesto, 84; term as governor of Franklin expires, 96; negotiates with Georgia, 96; meditates Indian expedition, 97; asks Shelby to accept governorship of Franklin, 97; meditates expedition against Spaniards, 98; besieges Tipton's house, 99; makes expedition against Cherokees, 99; arrested on charge of high treason, 99; sent to North Carolina, 99; escapes, 100; elected member of North Carolina Senate and takes his seat, 100; brigadier-general, 100; goes to Congress, 100; letter from Bledsoe, 144; member of Legislative Council, 149; brigadier-general of Washington District, 149; expedition against the Indians, 150; the last expedition, 151; intrigues with Spain, 165; governor of Tennessee, 187, 241; his administration, 242; style of living, 242; land speculations with Carter, 242, 246; accused of fraud by Jackson, 243; encounter between Sevier and Jackson, 244; report of committee on, 246; the evidence, 246; state senator, 247; member of Congress, 247; his popularity, 247; his generosity, 248; his death, 249; no monument to, 250; compared with Carroll, Polk, and Johnson, 301.

Sevier, Valentine, three sons killed, 153.
Shannon, Thomas, 310.
Sharkey, W. L., 434, 442.
Sharpe, major of territorial militia, 153.
Shaw, James, 134.
Shelby County, 310, 316; change of county seat, 322.
Shelby, Evan, at Kanawha, 31; at Point Pleasant and Fort Du Quesne, 55; Chickamauga Expedition, 55.
Shelby, Evan, arbitrator between two parties in Franklin, 94; memorial to Governor Caswell, 95; rebuked by Caswell, 95; requested by Sevier to accept governorship of Franklin, 97.
Shelby, Isaac, at Battle of Island Flats, 44; furnishes supplies for Chickamauga Expedition, 55; justice of the peace of Sullivan County, 56; also colonel, 56; prepares for attack on Ferguson, 59; at King's Mountain, 60; voted sword and pistols by North Carolina, 61; requested to take up arms again, 62; joins Marion, 62; leaves before end of war, 62.
Shelbyville, 270.
Sheriff (see County officers), succeeds marshal in North Carolina, 195; serves writs for precinct and county courts, 210.
Shingles, 175.
Sinking Fund created, 272; under act of 1852, 292.
Six Nations claim southwestern region, 13; cede this to England, 16.
Skiff, 177, 352.
Smith, Daniel, secretary of territory, 149; allows invasion of Indian country, 150; member of Constitutional Convention of 1796, 186; trustee of Davidson College, 234.
Smith, George W., 287;
Smith, James, 34, 36, 107.
Smith, Col. James, explorations of, 14.
Sodom, 340.
Solemn League and Covenant, 216.
Somerville, 270, 305.
South Memphis, 339; mania for city building, 339; Fearne originates, 340; plan of operation, 340; incorporated, 340; includes Fort Pickering, 340; united with Memphis, 341.
Southern Convention, 434; its action and resolutions, 435; compromise measures condemned, 435.
Southwestern Empire, Sevier dreams of, 98; also Aaron Burr, 103, 164; feared by Continental Confederacy, 165; Spanish designs, 165, 166.
Southwestern Railroad Bank, 271; does not suspend 272.
Southwest Point, fort at, built, 157, 172.
Spaniards, in Florida, 9; and State of Franklin, 102; their intrigues, 103, 163-168; their dream of empire, 103, 164; their intercourse with the Indians, 164; part of Tennessee claimed by, 165; their policy, 165.
Spanish or French traders, 142, 144, 152, 166, 176; offer rewards for American scalps, 166.
Sparta, 270.
Specie payment, suspended, 260; Carroll recommends return to, 264; day set, 264; resumption, 265; suspension of, forbidden, 273; resumption in 1839, 270.
Spencer County, formed, 79; changed to Hawkins, 93.
Spencer, James, 305.
Spencer, Thomas Sharpe, first settler of Middle Tennessee, 108; mentioned, 133.
Spickernagle, William, 354.
Spies, 162.
Spinoza, 8.
Spottswood, Governor, crosses Appalachian mountains, 14.
St. Augustine, 9, 13, 106.
Ste. Genevieve, 164.
St. Louis, 164.
Standifer, James, 367.
State Debt, causes disquietude, 272; bonds issued to turnpikes, 282; contracted under Act of 1852, 290; at beginning of war, 291; war interest, 292; act to liquidate, 293; Act of 1870, 294; repudiation of fraudulent bonds prevented, 294; railroads take advantage of Acts of 1869-70, 294; a political issue, 295; settled, 296.
Station, how built, 31, 119.
Statutes of Westminster, 208.

476 INDEX.

Stay Laws, 261, 302.
Steamboats, on Mississippi River, 177; first at Memphis, 311.
Steep Rock, 32.
Sterling Bonds, 397.
Stewart (or Stuart), James, 56, 86, 98, 200.
Stewart, Virgil A., 350; his account, 350; arrests and convicts Murrell, 351.
Stocks, abolition of, urged by Carroll, 302.
Stoddard, John, 304.
Stone River named, 107.
Stuart, Henry, 42.
Stuart, James. *See* Stewart.
Stuart, John, 41.
Sullivan County, formed, 56; part of Morgan District, 67.
Sumner County, 135.
Superintendent of Public Schools, office created, 236, 237.
Superior Courts in North Carolina, 196.
Superior Courts in Tennessee, 200, 201.
Supervisor of Banks, 273.
Supreme Court established, 201.
Surplus revenue deposit, 271.
Sweats settle McNairy County, 305.
Sycamore Shoals (*see* Treaty of), 18.
Synod of Lexington, 219.
Synod of the Carolinas, 217.

Talbot, Thomas, 78.
Talon, 10.
Tappan, Arthur, 392.
Tate, Col. Sam, 393; his executive ability, 287; president of Memphis and Charleston Railroad, 288; anecdote related by, 403.
Tatham, William, 34, 105.
Tatum. *See* Tatham.
Taverns, 174; rates in Greene County, 174.
Taylor, Parmenas, 149.
Taylor, Thomas, 310.
Taylor, Zach, 431.
Taxes, remission of, 92.
Taxation, self, for schools, 236.
Tennessee County, 149.
Territory south of the Ohio River, 47; Legislative Council, 149; seat of government removed to Knoxville, 149; its organization, officers, etc., 149, 198, 199.
Terry, Scott, 237.
Thomas, D. B., 294.
Thomas, Joshua, swims Tennessee River, 142.
Thornton, Hamilton, 305.
Thornton, R. G., 305.
Tippling Act, 424.
Titus Ebenezer, 132.
Tipton County, 306.
Tipton, Capt. Jacob, 306.
Tipton, Gen. Jacob, 306, 310.
Tipton, John, lukewarm in Franklin movement, 77; North Carolina senator, 86; his character, 86; envy of Sevier, 86; attacks Sevier's honesty, 86; delegate from Washington County to North Carolina, 98; arrests Sevier, 99; fight with Roddy, 100; member of Convention of 1796, 186; Tipton party, 241; wants to investigate Sevier's land speculations, 245; address of confidence in Jackson, 245.
Tipton, John, of Indiana, 442.
Tipton, Sam, 245.

Tithingman, 205.
Tobacco inspection, 136.
Toka, 142,
Toka Expedition. *See* Coldwater.
Torbett, G. C., 273.
Tories in Tennessee, 34, 41, 52.
Township system of local self-government, in New England, 204, 206; in the West, 207.
Trace. *See* Great Natchez.
Trade, 177; Spanish intrigues, 177.
Traders, Indian, must have license, 15, 178.
Transportation, 177.
Transylvania, purchase of, 36, 112, 119; purchase declared void by Gov. Martin, 39; ignored by North Carolina, 133.
Transylvania Presbytery divided, 224.
Traveling, 174.
Treaty of Dumplin Creek, 79, 101.
Treaty of Fort Stanwix, 139.
Treaty of Hard Labor, 139.
Treaty of Hopewell, 139.
Treaty of Lochaber, East Tennessee settlements made in violation of, 33.
Treaty of Martin and Donelson, 139.
Treaty of New York, 152.
Treaty of Pioningo, 140.
Treaty of Sycamore Shoals, 18, 36, 112, 139.
Trenton, 270, 305.
Trester, flat-boat man, 354; killed, 355.
Trimble, James, 245 (*note*).
Trousdale, William, 436; candidate for U. S. senatorship, 429; for governorship, 433; sketch of 433; defeats Neil S. Brown, 433; defeated by Campbell, 437.
Truck Patch, 27.
Trustees, county. *See* County officers.
Tyron, governor of North Carolina, tries to repress regulators, 31.
Tuckasejah, destroyed by Sevier, 65.
Turenne, 10.
Turnidge, Henry, 306.
Turney, Hopkins L., 408; scheme to elect him to U. S. Senate, 408; refuses to answer questions, 428; vote for, 429; denounced by Democrats, 429; his pledges to Whigs, 429; his letter of defense, 429; read out of the party, 430.
Turney, Samuel, 406.
Tuscarora Indians, migration of, 9.
Tyger's Valley, 173.

Uchees, destroyed by Cherokees, 15.
Union Bank chartered, 267.
Union, Fort. *See* Fort Union.
Union Presbytery, taken from Abingdon, 221.
United States Bank in Tennessee, 258, 260; law to prevent, 262; protest against, 262; branch at Nashville, 265.
University of Nashville, 137; Philip Lindsley becomes president, 239; his plan and his influence, 239; influence on Southwest, 239.
Untoola. *See* Butler.

Van Buren, 364, 367.
Vernon, 304.
Vestries in North Carolina, 211.
Vestrymen levy taxes, 210; how appointed, 210.
Veto, 193, 197.

INDEX.   477

Vicksburg, gamblers hanged, 346, 354.
Vigilance Committee in 1778. *See* Washington County.
Village communities, survival of, 205.
Vincennes, 164.
Virginia, attempt in, to join Franklin movement, 84, 103.

Waddell, Seth O., 309.
Walker, Felix, 34.
Walker, Dr. Thomas, expedition in 1748, 13, 107.
Walker, William, or "Nicaragua," 444.
Wallen party of explorers, 14.
Wallen's Creek, 14.
Wallen's Ridge, 14.
Walton, Jesse, 56.
Ward, Edward, candidate for governorship, 252; Federalist, 254; sketch of, 254; supported by Nashville Whig, 256; and Jackson, 255.
Ward, Nancy, warns settlements of Indian invasion, 42; saves Jack and Rankin, 66.
Wardens in North Carolina, 211.
Washington County, 47; part of Salisbury Judicial District, 47; restores order by organizing companies, 52; part of Morgan District, 67.
Washingto. Judicial District, 77.
Washington District of Tennessee, 200.
Washington District of North Carolina, named for George Washington, 40; declares for the Colonial cause, 40; overrun by the lawless, 40; threatened by Indians, 41; ceded by Indians to North Carolina, 45; courts of pleas and quarter sessions established in, 47; sheriffs and justices of the peace, 47; becomes Washington County, 47.
Washington, George, 38, 112.
Watauga Association, beginning of, 33; articles of, lost, 33; details of organization, 33; Committee of Thirteen, 33; five commissioners, 33; chairman, 34; nonsubscribers, 34; no provision for, 40; petition for annexation, 46; court-house, 56.
Watauga Fort, one of the earliest, 31; protects Watauga settlement, 31; attacked by Indians, 42; defended by Robertson, 44.
Watauga River, 5.
Watauga settlement, resting-place for emigrants and surveyors, 30; an independant colony, 33; secure ten years' lease, 35; buy the reversion, 36.
Watson, Samuel, trustee of State Bank, 274.
Watterson, Henry, 442.
Watterson, H. M., 421; elected speaker of state Senate, 427; tees Turney's letter, 429; denounces Turney, 429.
Waverly, 304.
Wayne County, 304.
Weakley County, 79, 311.
Weakley, Robert, candidate for governorship, 251.
Webster, Daniel, estimate of Prentiss, 422.
Wells, Heydon, 132, 179.
Western District. *See* West Tennessee.
West Tennessee, its history not yet written, 302; account of in 1819, 303; priority of locations in, 303.

Wharton, Jesse, on committee to investigate Sevier's land speculations, 245; U. S. senator, 251; candidate for governorship, 251.
Wheatley, Seth, 338.
Whig clique or junto at Nashville, 403, 410.
Whig Convention of 1840, 387; Henry Clay present, 390; details of, 387-391.
Whig Convention of 1844, 418; called the the Great Whig Convention, 419; its brilliancy of colors, 420, 421.
Whigs, cut off from Federalists, 242; rise of in Tennessee, 357; White Whigs, 369; New-born Whigs, 369; date from White's candidacy, 371; Anderson accepts title of Whig, 375; effect of Polk-Cannon contest, 375; first contest of parties, 379; New Whigs, 379; first Whig candidate, 379; Polk's address of 1839, 381; organized for 1840, 383; the Union denounces their organization, 384; Harrison nominated, 384; the plan of campaign, 385; festivals, processions, and emblems, 385; Harris's doggerel, 386; Convention of 1840, 387; carry Tennessee in 1840, 392; record of, on National Bank, 394; on tariff, 395; Polk's speech on origin of, 396; in the General Assembly of 1841, 406; contest over senatorial election in 1841, 408; canvass of 1843 and its effects on 1844, 411; last great struggle, 413; send delegates to Baltimore in 1844, 413; determine to defeat Polk in Tennessee, 444; brilliancy of 1844, 416; carry Tennessee in 1844, 421; nominate Foster in 1845, 424; nominate N. S. Brown in 1847, 420; carry Tennessee in 1852, 438; alliance with Know-Nothings, 438; become opposition, 439.
Whiskey, 137, 174, 182.
White County, cotton manufactures in, 279.
White, Hugh Lawson, 258, 443; on Loan Office of 1820, 262; offered seat in Jackson's cabinet, 365; his friendship for Jackson, 365; estrangement from and causes, 365; Jackson's threat, 366; becomes candidate for presidency, 366; letter from Tennessee members of Congress, 365; Van Buren and Jackson, 367; Jackson denounces him as a Federalist, 368; White Whigs and New-born Whigs, 369; Tennessee press for White, 369; issue between, and Jackson not made, 369; his course on Expunging Resolutions, 371, 374; carries Tennessee legislature, 371; is defeated, 374; his political principles, 372; carries Hermitage District, 374; opposes Van Buren's administration, 374; forced to resign, 382; supports Harrison, 387; death of, 387; president of United States Senate, 443.
White, James, lays off Knoxville, 149; member of Constitutional Convention of 1796, 186.
White, Richard, 76, 86.
Whitney, Eli. *See* Cotton gin.
Whittaker, Mark, 225.
Wilkinson, James, has store at Lexington, 177.
Williams, Col. James, 60.
Williams, John, 361.

INDEX.

Williams, N. W., impeached, 301.
Williamson, Jones, 304.
Willis, Benjamin, Jr., 310.
Willis, Henry, 225.
Wilson, Adam, 304.
Wilson, W. M., 311.
Winchester, James, member of Legislative Council, 149; speaker first state Senate, 200; runs southern boundary line, 315; interest in Memphis, 327.
Winchester, M. B., 310, 321; on railroads, 286; sketch of, 324; compared with Rawlings, 324; postmaster and mayor, 324; agent for proprietors of Memphis, 324; suspected of being a Whig, 330; on La Grange and Memphis Railroad, 342; vilified by Murrell's clan, 351.
Winchester, William, 328.
Winchester and Carr, 323.

Winterbotham's History of America, 187.
Wise, Henry A., 426.
Wolcott, Oliver, Sr., 188.
Wolf River, shiftings of its mouth, 319; Jesse Benton's testimony, 319, 334.
Wolf tax, 316.
Wolfs Hill. *See* Abingdon.
Womack, Jacob, 34.
Wood, John, 56.
Wood's party of explorers, 56.
Woods, John, 304.

Yancey, W. L., 443.
Yarbrough, H., 306.
Young's Warehouse. *See* Public Warehouse.

Zigler's Station, destroyed, 153.
Zollicoffer, Felix K., elected comptroller, 430.

www.ingramcontent.com/pod-product-compliance
Lightning Source LLC
Chambersburg PA
CBHW051846300426
44117CB00006B/278